WIN SOME
LOSE SOME

*G. Mennen Williams, Nancy Williams, and Helen
Berthelot in Williams's supreme court office
in Lansing, June 1986.
(Helen Berthelot's personal collection)*

Win Some
Lose Some

G. Mennen Williams

and the

New Democrats

Helen Washburn Berthelot

Foreword by
Tom Downs

 Wayne State University Press   Detroit

GREAT LAKES BOOKS

*A complete listing of the books in this series
can be found at the back of this volume.*

Philip P. Mason, Editor
Department of History, Wayne State University
Dr. Charles K. Hyde, Associate Editor
Department of History, Wayne State University

Copyright © 1995 by Wayne State University Press,
Detroit, Michigan 48201. All rights are reserved.
No part of this book may be reproduced without formal permission.
Manufactured in the United States of America.
99 98 97 96 95   5 4 3 2 1

Library of Congress Cataloging-in-Publication Data

Berthelot, Helen W.
Win some, lose some : G. Mennen Williams and the New Democrats /
Helen Washburn Berthelot ; foreword by Tom Downs.
p. cm.
Includes bibliographical references and index.
ISBN 0-8143-2476-2 (pbk. : alk. paper)
1. Williams, G. Mennen, 1911– . 2. Michigan—Politics and
government—1951– 3. Governors—Michigan—Biography.
4. Berthelot, Helen W.   I. Title.
F570.25.W55B47   1995
977.4′043′092—dc20

[B]   94-21329

Designer: Joanne E. Kinney

To
G. MENNEN WILLIAMS
WHO WAS THE INSPIRATION TO US ALL
AND TO
NANCY Q. WILLIAMS
MENNEN'S LOVING WIFE
WHO STOOD BESIDE HIM
IN EVERY ENDEAVOR

CONTENTS

FOREWORD
Tom Downs

WHEN G. MENNEN WILLIAMS first ran for governor of Michigan in 1948, there weren't many who thought he could win—or if he did, that he could get reelected. At that time the state was firmly controlled by the Republicans, who held runaway majorities in the legislature—but not necessarily because the voters preferred Republican rule. Democrats were underrepresented in the legislature and in Congress in part because of malapportioned districts.

"One person, one vote" has been the law now for about thirty years. Before that became reality, however, districts didn't have to have a uniform number of people—and they usually didn't. Representatives from sparsely populated areas almost always had a much smaller number of constituents than those from the big population centers. As a result, people in rural areas had more clout in Congress and the statehouse, and that watered down the voice of people in the big cities.

In the late 1950s, August Scholle, then president of the Michigan Congress of Industrial Organizations, initiated an analysis of voting patterns which showed that even though more people voted for Democratic senate candidates than for Republican ones, Republicans held a two-to-one majority in the Michigan Senate and a three- or four-to-one majority in senate committee assignments. This imbalance occurred because senatorial districts varied in size from 60,000 to 400,000 people. Democrats, African Americans, ethnic groups, and union members were all underrepresented.

Attorney Theodore Sachs was the legal hero in the apportionment fight. He carried our battle to the Michigan Supreme Court in 1960 and from there to the U. S. Supreme Court. However, it was a Tennessee case, the historic Baker versus Carr decision, which in 1962 opened the door to a series of rulings affirming the principle of "one person, one vote"—or "one man, one vote," as it was described at the time. In its rulings, the U.S. Supreme Court adopted much of the reasoning in our Michigan case. And the decision in the Tennessee case, of course, meant that we were victorious when ours was sent back to Michigan later that year. After a time, the result was that both the Democratic and the Republican parties better represented the people. The advantage for the Republican party was that moderates such as George Romney and William Milliken had a stronger voice in the political arena and were able to become governor. The lopsided strength of the old-line Republicans was weakened.

All of that came much later. When Mennen Williams arrived on the scene, the Democratic party was a shambles. As a 1979 tribute to Williams declared: "It is hard for many younger members of the party to realize that 'before Soapy,' Democrats in Michigan were as rare as whooping cranes."[1] People whose vision was limited to benefits for themselves and their cronies manipulated and controlled the party organization. But Neil Staebler, Adelaide Hart, Helen Berthelot, Sidney Woolner, Martha and Hicks Griffiths, Margaret Price, and many others joined Mennen and, through monumental effort, built the modern Michigan Democratic party.

Mennen Williams's success was due to a political strategy that had been unheard of in Michigan but which came from a deeply rooted belief held by the man himself—that the people are best represented by the building of coalitions. He brought women and minorities into the party, into the state government, and into politics. He had an innate understanding of people and politics and knew that the building process must never stop. He paid attention to party affairs and organization, working with a dedicated group of supporters who helped him beat the odds, first in 1948 and then in subsequent campaigns. The role of Hicks and Martha Griffiths in the 1948 election cannot be overstated. The law firm was Griffiths, Williams & Griffiths, and Hicks and Martha spent untold hours that year building the Democratic party and campaigning for Williams in both the primary and general elections. Helen Berthelot was also one of the people who made things happen. She was a heroine in Mennen Williams's toughest fight—the 1948 primary in which he and two others ran for the Democratic nomination.

That year, Helen Berthelot and other liberals urged people who embraced the Williams program to run for precinct delegate to party conventions. For the first time in Michigan history, people ran at the precinct level on a printed slate, and they contributed directly to Williams's victory. Reform members of the party distributed slates which identified candidates, from precinct delegate on up, with specific positions on the issues—Mennen's program. At the precinct level, voters were urged to choose the candidates as a team. Such methods were popularly known many years later as the basis for "grass-roots politics."

"Old guard" Democrats struggled to maintain the status quo and vigorously opposed opening up the party structure. The most cynical analysis held that some, though not all, of the old guard wanted a Democratic president but a Republican governor and U. S. senators. That way, in collusion with state Republican leaders, entrenched Democrats could retain control of all patronage, out of Lansing as well as Washington. This little playhouse was broken up by the vigorous injection of liberal, socially conscious candidates for precinct delegate in 1948.

Mennen's biggest fight involved fraudulent petitions for precinct delegates two years later. On some of those petitions, every name was fraudulent—the names of the circulators, the petition signers, even the candidate. These "candidates" would appear on the ballot and be elected. The chair of one of the old-line districts would pick up the certificates of election from the county clerk under the guise of delivering them to the newly elected precinct delegates. Instead, he amassed the votes he needed to maintain control of his district. He would have them, literally, in his hip pocket. He had no trouble hanging onto his district chairmanship with the support of all those "delegates" who never talked back and whose votes he completely controlled.

During the entire revitalization of the Michigan Democratic party, Helen Berthelot was a key volunteer with a strong sense of organization. She wanted the involvement of people from all segments of the electorate, and she had a knack for bringing them in. Along with Mary Gilmore, Alice Downs, and Adelaide Hart, Helen developed a technique that lifted the party out of the male-dominated "smoke-filled rooms" and into the public light. They planned teas, fashion shows, and other activities specifically designed for women. While social events were the initial strategy for bringing women into the party, the goal was to include them in policy-making decisions—long before "women's liberation" became a popular phrase or a movement.

Make no mistake about it: the old-guard Democratic party of the 1940s was a far cry from the party of fifty years later. Back then it was assumed that men were running the show, and the party could be intimidating to women. Helen Berthelot, Adelaide Hart, and Sid Woolner— the reader will get to know all of them in this book—were among the people who took the meeting place of Wayne County's 17th District Democratic party from the macho bar into the very clean and neat, newly constructed Carpenters Union Hall at Grand River and Lahser. They did, at the end of the meetings, permit us to have beer, but the meetings themselves were conducted in a manner that encouraged men and women to participate. What happened in the 17th District spilled over into other Wayne County congressional districts and gave courage to out-state districts to organize in the same way.

From 1948 on, Helen Berthelot was a major figure as the Democratic party gained strength, although she preferred to work behind the scenes. Along with others, she believed that Mennen Williams offered what Michigan needed at the time. A *Detroit Times* reporter referred to Helen as "the Democratic Party's 'hidden punch.'" A *Detroit News* article said she was the party's "secret weapon." She was proud of the fact that she managed to avoid public recognition for more than twelve years.[2]

Few people outside the party leadership were aware of Helen Berthelot's crucial role during the Democratic resurgence, although she remained active well into the 1970s in Michigan campaigns and national politics. She was a valued colleague of Lawrence O'Brien, the former national party chair. She helped Hubert Humphrey and Sargent Shriver. And although she wasn't involved in the Jimmy Carter campaign, she helped the Carters organize some important events in honor of their volunteers after the 1976 election.

What follows is Helen Berthelot's personal story of the Mennen Williams years and beyond. It also is a revelation of the ways in which campaigning has changed—and the ways in which it has not. Those of us who remember Mennen Williams's shoestring campaigns are in awe of today's multi-million-dollar media exercises, with their image makers, political consultants, and market researchers. In the Williams days, we had only our wits and our energy. Mennen's success was largely due to his personal, contact-with-the-people campaign style—a marked contrast to the detached electronic image we see today. Mennen Williams was a scholar with a vision of a state enriched by the contributions of all its people. His heart was with the working people, and he allied himself with them. From this combination of insight and dedication grew the broad coalition of people who worked for a common cause.

Helen Berthelot—or Buffy, as she became known—was one of those people. She was a telephone operator who became active in the Communications Workers of America when her union needed her. When Mennen Williams needed help to make a run for the governor's office, she responded. In campaigns from 1948 on, Helen Berthelot solved problems, dealt with crises, and was alert to the candidate's best interests. Mennen trusted her completely. Those who worked closely with her always realized that her behind-the-scenes efficiency was a key element in

12

Michigan Democratic party successes. She saw to it that campaign activity moved ahead according to schedule. And when the unexpected occurred, she was the one who knew what to do. Helen had empathy for the people she worked with, outstanding patience, and an ability to hear out and handle the inevitable number of disgruntled volunteers and office seekers. When victories were achieved by narrow margins, many people could claim that but for their help, G. Mennen Williams would not have been nominated or elected. Helen Berthelot is one of the most important of those people. Her organizational efforts, stamina, and broad understanding of social and political concepts were essential to his triumphs.

As the first woman to run a statewide political campaign for either party, Helen Berthelot made Michigan political history. The CWA appointed her the first full-time woman labor lobbyist in Washington. She insists her accomplishments were due to hard work. That's true. They also were the result of extraordinary political acumen combined with commitment to a vision for Michigan that was of, by, and for *all* of the people—the vision of Mennen Williams.

This is a story both to inspire young people to be active in government and to warn them of the cruelty and likelihood of defeat. Victory is not the result of one individual any more than defeat is the result of any one individual's errors. Mathematically, there are more losers than winners after the votes are counted. What is important—and what Buffy can teach us all—is that there is something worth working for, that it is worthwhile to jump in and do it, and that those who do are winners no matter what the outcome.

NOTES

1. This is part of a tribute from the United Auto Workers Southeastern Michigan Community Action Program (UAW SEMCAP), printed in a commemorative booklet in 1979, when the Michigan Democratic party's annual fund-raiser, the Jefferson-Jackson Day dinner, was dedicated to Mennen and Nancy Williams. The booklet is among Helen Berthelot's papers in the Michigan Historical Collections, Bentley Historical Library, University of Michigan, Ann Arbor.

2. Elizabeth Conway, "State Dems' 'Hidden Punch': She's Co-ordinator of Candidates' Activities," *Detroit Times* (September 14, 1960), p. 17. George L. Walker, "Key Staebler Aide Likes Winning—Behind Scenes," *Detroit News* (August 29, 1962), p. 10-A. See Appendix for the text of both articles.

PREFACE

URING THE COURSE of an informal meeting more than twenty years ago, Mennen Williams, Neil Staebler, and I were bemoaning the fact that no one was writing anything about all Mennen had accomplished in his twelve years as governor. Mennen doubled up one fist and hit it hard into his other hand. "I'm going to write a book on how we tried to build a better Michigan," he said vehemently. Neil thought a minute and then added earnestly, "Then I'll write the story of how we rebuilt the Democratic party." Giggling, I remarked, "And I'll write a book and tell what really happened." With one voice, the two of them stoutly declared, "We don't want to read it!"

Over the years, a number of my friends had urged me to at least put on tape some of my experiences in the labor movement and in politics. "You were really a pioneer in so many different things," they would insist. "No one else remembers those incidents. They will be lost forever if you don't write them down. All you have to do is write how often you were the first woman to ever do all sorts of things." My response would be to laugh and say, "I'll write some stories about my activities one of these days." That day was a long time coming; I always seemed to be too busy on the next project.

Meanwhile, Mennen was thinking about writing his book. In February of 1981, answering a letter I had written, he said: "Right now, whenever I have a chance, I try to put together a couple of thoughts on how we turned back the Republican tide in 1948. I'm convinced it was a genuine popular movement and I'm trying to put the evidence together."

I had started to write down a few of the stories myself, after I retired.

15

But it wasn't until the celebration of Mennen's fiftieth anniversary in government in June of 1986 that I began to write in earnest. In September of 1987, he wrote to tell me he was pleased that I had started on this book and said that he was anxious to get going on his. He said he thoroughly enjoyed teaching at Oakland University and at the University of Detroit Law School, and that he would like to have students help with research for the book. He died less than five months later, in February of 1988.

It was most devastating to come home from his funeral and find a letter he had dictated the day he died. In the letter, he told me how much he was looking forward to reading my book. He said he was going to start immediately to write his book. Typically, he asked several questions about the 1948 campaign. Then he stopped and said he'd need my help.

He never got to sign it. His wife Nancy, knowing how much it would mean to me, had signed it "Soapy—by Nancy Williams." It's the only letter I ever remember getting from him that was signed "Soapy." Nancy always teased me because I would never use that nickname—even though nearly everyone else, including Nancy, did.

And so, tragically, Mennen's book was never written. Neil Staebler's chronicle, *Out of the Smoke Filled Room: A Story of Michigan Politics*, was published in 1991.[1]

Many friends have helped me through all the problems of putting my book together. There are too many to list, but I want them all to know how much I appreciate their help.

There are a few people without whom I probably never would have started to write. They kept telling me I should and I could do it. Among them are Sidney Woolner, Judah Drob, Victor Reuther, Eleanor Coakley, Joyce Curtis, and Bill Welsh. Then there was the Reverend Paul Shaw, who asked me every time he saw me if I had started to write yet.

So many contributed along the way.

Pat and Kent Gagnon supplied me with a quiet place to write and kept up my spirits when the words wouldn't flow.

Brenda and Roger Hamilton graciously allowed me to use their copy machine and always had encouraging words.

Dr. Frank Fedor and Dr. Prabha Mohta helped keep me healthy.

David Broder suggested I contact some universities to see if they would be interested in publishing this book.

Dr. Robert Warner helped inspire me years ago by asking me to tape interviews for the University of Michigan's Michigan Historical Collections at the Bentley Historical Library and then gave me advice on how to contact the universities for help.

Bill Welsh paved the way for me to approach Dr. Philip Mason at

Wayne State University. Dr. Mason did so much to keep me hopeful during the process of getting this book published, and he helped make it happen. Arthur Evans and the staff at the Wayne State University Press persevered valiantly throughout. Alice Nigoghosian at the Press and Alberta Asmar at the Wayne State University Archives of Labor and Urban Affairs helped keep me going. Kathryn Wildfong expertly guided this book into print.

Phil Power helped make it possible for me to get the manuscript in final form, and his enthusiasm greatly encouraged me.

Mary Margetts struggled for hours listening to my many tapes and transcribing them all, and then she cheerfully helped with typing, final editing, indexing, and countless other tasks.

Judah Drob and Sid Woolner read first copies of this book, corrected them, and made many important suggestions. David Bellile, Tom Downs, Louis Dunn, Dr. Mason, Marilyn Stoutenburg, Dr. JoEllen Vinyard, and Sandra Williamson were among those who read the final copy and made it better.

The fine work of many photographers appears in this book. Their pictures help tell the story with warmth and realism. Many of their names are missing, but those whose identities are known have my deep thanks: Dale Atkins, Mickey Duggan, Ray Glonka, Hugh Grannum, Jerry Heiman, Alan R. Kamuda, Michael Kitchen, Leo Knight, Snuffy McGill, Pat Mitchell, Marston A. Pierce, Fred A. Plofchan, John Pratt, Tony Spina, Walter Steiger, Jimmy Tafoya, George Waldman, Vincent Witek, and Taro Yamasaki.

News organizations, individuals, photography studios, and historical collections also deserve thanks for their role in supplying many of the pictures. They include the Archives of Labor and Urban Affairs, Wayne State University; the *Associated Press*; the *Detroit Free Press*; Michigan State University School of Journalism; the John Murray family; and the United Auto Workers public relations department. Tom Farrell, Marilyn Hall, and Michigan Supreme Court Chief Justice Michael Cavanagh graciously helped supply photographs and helpful background material.

Neal Shine, publisher of the *Detroit Free Press*, graciously helped me gain access to many of the photographs in this book. Tony Spina, chief photographer emeritus of the *Free Press*, generously loaned pictures from his personal collection. One of his photographs, showing Mennen at the 1960 Democratic National Convention, is on the front cover. Alan R. Kamuda captured the historic celebration of Mennen's fiftieth year in politics (shown on the back cover), on assignment as a staff photographer for the *Free Press*. Six years later, he photographed the author in front of Mennen's portrait in the supreme court chambers in Lansing. My special thanks go to him, to Tony Spina, and to Neal Shine for their wonderful

17

sense of history and their interest in helping future generations appreciate the past. Jon Buechel, the artist whose delightful work has graced the pages of the *Free Press* for many years, created the bow-tie design used on the title page of this book. My heartfelt thanks and good wishes go to him in his retirement.

The many people who over the years have had a hand in compiling the Michigan Manuals have my thanks and deserve special appreciation. Their work has created an invaluable historical record of Michigan's political life. The details they so painstakingly gathered helped refresh my memory on names and dates and vote totals.

Without my daughter and her husband, Peg and Bill Beagle, this book never would have been finished. Their struggles with defective word processors and mastering a new one, after many problems with illness, would fill another book. The care they took of my copy and the suggestions they made were of inestimable value. They never complained when I upset a whole chapter by adding bits and pieces. They added, revised, and corrected. Nancy E. Dunn, who edited this book with me, helped make it possible for me to tell the story I wanted to tell, in words and pictures. Once again, she and I added, revised, and corrected, until finally, it was done.

NOTES

1. Neil Staebler, *Out of the Smoke Filled Room: A Story of Michigan Politics* (Ann Arbor: George Wahr Publishing Co., 1991).

INTRODUCTION

M Y STORY is essentially one of being at the right place at the right time and always being ready to help. The more difficult the project, the better I liked it. No matter how tedious the job, I wouldn't refuse.

I vividly recall one lovely, warm spring afternoon in 1914. I was ten years old and in the fifth grade, attending a two-room country school about fifty miles south of Boston, Massachusetts. The year before, gypsy moths had destroyed many of our trees. Their eggs were plastered all over the surviving branches, ready to hatch into hundreds of greedy caterpillars.

Our teacher decided the children could help destroy at least some of the eggs. She divided her half of the school, grades one through five, into teams and chose a leader for each team. She promised a special treat for the team that collected the most egg clusters in burlap bags she'd gotten from the grocer.

She named me one of the leaders. We were allowed to choose five people for each team. I picked five of the dirtiest, most raggle-taggle boys in the class. Although I hardly knew these fellows, they were strong and could climb trees, so I wanted them on my team.

Armed with knives and hatchets, we set out. With me in the lead, our crew headed to a field in back of my house where there was a grove of wild cherry trees. Working through the afternoon, we filled our bags to overflowing. We would have carried bundles of egg-infested twigs in our arms, too, except that my grandmother caught sight of me climbing trees with that grimy bunch of boys. She sent me back to school, dire threats ringing in my ears for being such a bold tomboy.

My grandmother was too gentle to carry out most of her threats, but when I got home from school, she did express her dismay that I wasn't content to sit and sew doll clothes like other little girls. And she didn't allow me to go with the boys and the teacher on the outing that was our reward.

My team had, after all, won by a huge margin.

Many decades passed before I was involved in another campaign. Despite the early signs of my ability to get the job done, it took many years for me to grow into a responsible citizen. During my school years, I didn't have a serious thought in my head. In high school I was never a good scholar. Athletics and other school activities interested me more than studies. When summertime came, I camped, fished, and swam. My grandmother and grandfather, who raised me, were continually flabbergasted at the little rebel they had on their hands.

Until I came along, the Washburns were Republicans. There was even a governor or two, and an ambassador, in the family. Politics held no interest for me, however, and I knew nothing about unions. When I got thrown into both, there was nothing to do but sink or swim. So I learned to swim. It didn't frighten me to be the first woman to take on a task. Slowly, it seemed, I would get involved in what turned out to be big projects.

Against my will, I came to Detroit in the fall of 1923 at the age of eighteen. My uncle had persuaded my grandparents to move to Detroit because of the work that was available there. They moved reluctantly, and so did I. Bridgewater State College in Bridgewater, Massachusetts, was near our home, and I had finished a year of college there.

In Detroit, my aunt offered to pay my way to whatever college I chose. Instead, I decided to earn my own way. Michigan Bell would pay me while I learned to be a telephone operator, so I accepted the job. We lived in the Brightmoor neighborhood, on Detroit's west side, and I enrolled in an evening college program at Northwestern High School. Somewhere along the way, my desire to finish school got lost, but I liked it in Michigan.

At the age of nineteen, I got married. Within a few years, I became the mother of two children, a daughter, Margarette (Peg), and a son, Douglas. When the children were a little older but no longer babies, the phone company asked me to come back to help out. It was a good thing I had done so; before long I became a widow, raising and supporting my children alone during the Great Depression. They survived, and so did I. It gives me pleasure to say that we had fun along the way, and they never seemed to know we were poor. In many ways, mine is the story of the evolution of a lighthearted girl who, because of her own experiences, began to take life seriously.

At the phone company in the 1930s, we never had a chance to make suggestions or have a voice in our working conditions. In 1938, after the Wagner Act opened the door to union organizing, I started asking the women who worked with me to sign up for the telephone workers' "federation" (nice girls didn't join "unions"). By 1942, the organization had grown to the point that the membership records needed to be put in order, so I volunteered. After that, I was elected to several positions in the organization, and when the federation became the Communications Workers of America (CWA), I served in various offices. Eventually I became the labor movement's first full-time woman lobbyist in Washington, D. C. Except for time out for campaigns, I held that position with the CWA from 1953 until 1969.

By 1946, my kids were grown and on their own. The union was coming along well. Although I would continue to help, I wanted to work in a wider field. Almost before I realized it, I was involved with a group of people who were trying to make sure that the Democratic party truly reflected its principles.

It was about this time that I met Mennen Williams; I can't remember exactly when it was. Early in my acquaintance with him, I felt he was going to accomplish a great deal for the people of Michigan and the country as well. He was an idealist, but he had the determination, knowledge, and intelligence to formulate and carry through programs that would make a better life for the people. Although I wasn't able to do what he could do, helping him was a way for me to be a part of building a better life for many people. The state desperately needed a leader who had the people's interests at heart. So I volunteered in every one of his campaigns for governor, including the primaries.

When Mennen was elected governor the first time, in 1948, that was hard enough to believe. Then we survived recounts in two subsequent elections, and, in 1954, took over the other executive positions of state government by winning all the offices on the Administrative Board. We even came close to winning a majority in the state House of Representatives, although the district boundary lines were drawn in such a way that the Republicans had an advantage. So many people contributed to that wonderful victory in 1954. One of Mennen's favorite sayings was that the Democratic umbrella was big enough to cover everyone. Because it was a team effort, and because of Mennen's leadership, it did cover everyone who wanted to be a part of it.

My most valuable contribution was telling him what I saw going on, whether it was good or bad. More than once, I disagreed with him. "I don't always agree with Helen," he used to say, "but at least she speaks up and tells me the truth as she sees it." Getting things done—as in the gypsy moth egg expedition—was another way I helped Mennen over the years. He never asked me if I *could* do a project. He always said, "Will you handle this?" or "I'd like you to do this," or "Have this done."

After I had worked in the first two campaigns as a volunteer, the CWA gave me a leave of absence for the 1952 elections. That meant I could take on a larger role. My task was to manage a party office that coordinated Democratic campaigns in Michigan, the first such combined office in the country. After the fall election, before I went back to work in Lansing, I managed the office that oversaw the recount. A few months later, in 1953, I became the first woman to chair the party's annual fundraising affair, the Jefferson-Jackson Day dinner, and handled the party's spring election campaigns. That 1953 spring campaign was a sad and lonely time for Democrats. Democratic winners were few and far between. "I like Ike" had washed over the country like a tidal wave.

In the campaigns of 1954, 1956, and 1958, I was Governor Williams's campaign manager. He didn't run in 1960, but I was state coordinator for Democratic campaigns. I managed Neil Staebler's successful election as congressman-at-large in 1962 and, in 1964, his campaign for governor. In 1966, I managed Mennen's fall campaign for the U.S. Senate. For years after that, I was asked to work for one candidate or another. I'm deeply grateful to the CWA and its president during those years, Joseph Beirne. For now it can be told: I was the CWA's contribution to Mennen Williams and Michigan in all those campaigns, from 1952 through 1966.

Except for some involvement in national campaigns and conventions, I stayed away from a major role until Tom Kavanagh's campaign in 1974. Michigan Supreme Court Chief Justice Kavanagh—Thomas M.—was a good friend, so at almost seventy years of age, I came back to Michigan to run his campaign office and handle his schedule. We won, but it was a bittersweet victory. Shortly after the election, he learned he had cancer, and he died in the spring of 1975.

In 1969, I retired from the Communications Workers—but never really from politics. The year before, I had worked on Hubert Humphrey's campaign for president. In 1972, I accepted the job of office manager for the Democratic National Convention in Miami Beach. Four years later, I worked on Sargent Shriver's presidential campaign. After Jimmy Carter won, Carolyn Burns and I helped Rosalynn Carter's staff set up a system to handle the onslaught of mail the First Lady receives, and then we helped organize several receptions the Carters had at the White House for their volunteers.

Mennen Williams is the main reason I actually sat down and started to write this book. My purpose is to let people know that there is no limit to what a small group of people can accomplish if they put their hearts and minds to it. Mennen Williams was the inspiration for us. He really believed in what he said and did. Faced with opposition in the legislature and resistance from the newspapers, Mennen took his program to the people. With their support, he literally built a state government that met the needs of the time. He left a legacy of elementary and secondary schools, college and university buildings, mental hospitals, roads, and bridges—especially his beloved Mackinac Bridge.

Mennen Williams loved that bridge. To him, it stood for the unity of the state and the strength of the people. He wrote the following passage as part of the foreword to *Miracle Bridge at Mackinac*, a book by Dr. David B. Steinman, the architect of the bridge, with John T. Nevill.[1] To me, these words show the optimism and faith in the people that Mennen always had:

> In every true Michigander breathes the great and indomitable spirit of that heroic folk figure Paul Bunyan. For this giant woodsman, no challenge was too big, no obstacle insurmountable.
>
> The people of Michigan built the world's greatest bridge in the face of discouragement, of faintheartedness on the part of many of their leaders, of warnings that the rocks in the straits were too soft, the ice too thick, the winds too strong, the rates of interest on the bonds too high, and the whole concept too big. The Mackinac Bridge is really a testimonial to the determination, the courage, the vision of the people of this state. It was truly a people's dream and a people's victory.

And now, with great pride and a certain amount of sadness, I invite you to read the stories in this book and see that the one and only Governor Williams had a twinkle in his eye as well as a vision for the state.

NOTES

1. David B. Steinman, with John T. Nevill, *Miracle Bridge at Mackinac* (Grand Rapids: William B. Eerdmans Publishing Co., 1957).

1

How It All Began

G. Mennen Williams might have found it harder to get elected governor of Michigan if Cy Bevan had done his homework in 1946. Cy was a prominent Wayne County lawyer and the Democratic party's national committeeman for Michigan. Cy was friendly to the labor movement and handled a number of cases for the unions.

A few weeks before the Wayne County congressional district conventions, Cy Bevan woke up to the fact that he did not have enough delegates pledged to re-elect him. Though the national committeeman is elected by party members from around the state, Cy needed the backing of Democrats in his home county and congressional district organization. If he didn't have the delegates lined up there, he wouldn't have them in other places, at least not enough of them.

As soon as he realized he needed help, Cy scurried around and got a number of his friends to recruit people to go into the Detroit area congressional district conventions and ask to be seated as delegates. Of course, he and his friends only wanted people who would support him as national committeeman later on at the state convention. (It was unusual for people to just show up at a party convention and try to be seated as delegates. But if there weren't enough precinct delegates chosen at the previous election, people who cared enough to show up and express an interest could become voting delegates if the seated delegates approved.)

Gus Scholle, president of the Michigan Congress of Industrial Organizations (CIO), and Hicks Griffiths, Mennen Williams's partner in their Detroit law firm, were among the people who agreed to line up delegates for Cy in the congressional districts in Wayne County. They knew Cy, and they didn't want to see him lose to some dark-horse candidate. There were rumors that the Teamsters Union was trying to take over the party organization, and many people, especially Gus, didn't want that.

Many of the 17th Congressional District recruits were active in civic and community activities, but this was the first political meeting of any sort that most had ever attended. We were all in our thirties or early forties—I was forty-one—and lived in one of the northwest Detroit neighborhoods that made up the 17th District. Most of us were there because we knew either Gus Scholle or Tom Downs. My involvement with the telephone workers had taken me to CIO meetings, where I became acquainted with Gus. He had persuaded me to come to this 17th District convention. Hicks Griffiths and his wife, Martha, a law partner with Hicks and Mennen Williams, lived in the 17th. Mennen himself lived in Grosse Pointe Farms, across town in the 14th Congressional District, so he wasn't involved with the 17th District.

Among the group of political neophytes who gathered for the 17th District meeting on that cold fall night were Sidney Woolner, assistant to the slidefilm production manager at the Detroit audio-visual company known as Jam Handy; Adelaide Hart, who was a teacher and also the school music director at Jefferson Junior High in Detroit; Tom Downs, a lawyer and Gus Scholle's assistant; and myself. At the time, my labor organization was known as the Michigan Telephone Traffic Federation. It was an independent union of telephone operators, and I was secretary-treasurer.

A nasty wind blew in great gusts as we entered the west side Detroit public school for the convention. The chill didn't leave us once we got inside. The room was dimly lit and dingy. We sat uncomfortably on folding chairs at the back of the room. Although I had been active in my union for about four years, I was a little out of my element. It was even necessary for me to nudge Sid and whisper, "What exactly does a precinct delegate do?" He didn't have time to answer then, but I soon found out from personal experience.

The convention got under way about 7:00 P.M. When I looked around, I was shocked to see that there were only thirty-seven people besides ourselves in the room. We had been told that the district party organization was entitled to send more than two hundred delegates to the state convention. I recognized two people. One was a woman known for opposing anything progressive in the American Federation of Labor (AFL), which at the time consisted largely of skilled trades and building trades. The other, if not an out-and-out "Commie," was at least a fellow traveler and member of a dissident group of the CIO. At

26

that time, Communism was a red scourge on any political organization or labor group.

The convention was chaired by Charlie Nugent, who taught at the University of Detroit. He called on a Mr. Hughes, who made a motion that contained the entire agenda. The motion seated those present—but not us—as official delegates of the 17th Congressional District. That entitled them to attend the state convention, where some of them would be elected to go to the national convention. The motion was passed by a voice vote, and it was over within ten minutes. Except for the chairman and Mr. Hughes, the delegates sat quietly, saying nothing but "yes" on the motion. This seemed more like an exclusive club than what it was supposed to be—the party of the people. Later, I was to learn that, by not fully rounding out the roster of precinct delegates, these Democrats kept the party small and exclusive. In return, they received a goodly number of political favors from the Republicans who controlled state politics at the time.

Quickly, before a motion could be made to adjourn, Gus Scholle stood up and said he had a group of people with him and they all desired to be seated as official delegates from the 17th District. In terms that were far from polite, he was told to sit down and shut up. Gus persisted, and the language from the other side became abusive.

Gus tried three times to get us seated. Finally, Charlie Nugent told us in no uncertain terms to get the h—— out. They didn't want any "ADA do-gooders" in their congressional district organization, Charlie Nugent said. (The term referred to the Americans for Democratic Action, a group whose common bond is believing in and working for a government that helps people.) The delegates turned to stare at us and murmured their assent.

It was as if we had a disease. We were being told—rudely—that we were not welcome in the party of the people. Our greatest "crime" was being idealistic. At the very least, our accusers had questionable motives for their involvement in the Democratic party. And they were attacking us as undesirables!

We filed out angrily and stormed across the street to a small restaurant. Highly indignant, we vowed this would never happen to us again. Someone said something that hit me like a thunderbolt and made me an active Democrat for the rest of my life: "Those are the people who are going to nominate the President of the United States." For a first lesson in politics, we certainly had been given an incentive to become involved.

We later learned that all the Wayne County districts met with similar problems. None of the people who had been recruited by Cy Bevan were allowed to become delegates to the state and national conventions. There must have been some truth to the rumor that the Teamsters were trying to take control of the Democratic organization in Michigan. The next national committeeman from Michigan was George Fitzgerald, a lawyer who was closely associated with Jimmy Hoffa and the Teamsters.

It didn't matter. Big changes were in store for the Michigan Democratic party, partly because of what went on at that 17th Congressional District convention. Although most of us knew either Gus Scholle or Tom Downs, we didn't know each other. Gus had been helpful to the telephone workers when we were forming our first federation. Adelaide Hart and I had met at a labor meeting; she was active in her teachers' federation. Sid Woolner was a fellow officer with me in the ADA. Gus and Tom had met Hicks and Martha Griffiths.

That night, our mutual indignation quickly drew us together. Eventually, we became the team behind G. Mennen Williams and his administration. Two years later, in 1948, Hicks Griffiths was Mennen Williams's first campaign manager. Mennen won, and Hicks was elected chairman of the Michigan Democratic party. Martha Griffiths was elected to the state House of Representatives in 1948, campaigning for and with Mennen Williams along the way. Sidney Woolner worked in each of Mennen's campaigns for governor and coordinated all Democratic candidates' campaigns from 1950 through 1958. Adelaide Hart was vice chairman—"chair*man*" was the term we used then—of the state party for five of Mennen's six terms as governor. Gus Scholle and Tom Downs helped with the entire labor movement. As for me, I started filling in wherever I was needed, recruiting delegates for the 17th Congressional District, circulating nominating petitions, stopping in the offices to see what needed to be done.

After Martha Griffiths filed as a candidate in the Democratic primary for the Michigan House of Representatives in 1948, the ADA talked me into running too. We ran in a large field for twenty-one seats, with Detroit as a single district. She won in the primary and went on to win a seat in the legislature. I lost, but I had been campaigning more for Mennen than for myself anyway.

In 1950, when Sid Woolner was coordinating the campaigns for Democratic candidates, Sid's mother Olive and I were his "second shift." That meant twelve hours a day and sometimes more. We shared the work with the "day shift," which also consisted of two people, Pat Taylor and Peg Edwards. Two years later, we actually opened an office to coordinate Democratic campaigns. My title was director of organization, and I later appointed myself office manager. In 1954, 1956, and 1958, I became Governor Williams's campaign manager and helped Sid handle all the campaigns.

Cy Bevan had no way of knowing it in 1946, but he helped change Michigan history.

2

Full Citizens
of the 17th District

I n 1947, Hicks and Martha Griffiths invited about fifteen people
from all over the state to their home to discuss the possibility of
Mennen Williams running for governor. At the time, those of us political neophytes who had attended that fateful 17th District convention
weren't active in the party, so we weren't invited to the meeting. Many
years later, at a reunion dinner for the group that met at the Griffiths's
home, Mennen joked about the fact that I wasn't there. "Helen Berthelot
was not at that first meeting, but no doubt she was holed up somewhere
addressing envelopes for a mailing," he said. The truth is, I wasn't involved at that point—but it wasn't long before I was.

After that unforgettable 17th District convention, Sid Woolner and
I kept running into Hicks and Martha Griffiths. Sid and I knew each
other from ADA meetings—nothing Charlie Nugent or anybody else
said could keep us from those—and we often ended up attending some
of the same community functions as Hicks and Martha. The four of us
would often talk about our treatment at that convention. We agreed that
something should be done. We had been shut out of the party organization in an election year.

Murray D. "Pat" Van Wagoner was the Democratic candidate for
governor in 1946. He had had a difficult time as governor in 1941 and
1942. Van Wagoner had been a highway commissioner for a number of
years in the 1930s—it was he who pushed the development of roadside
parks—but he was hampered by a divided cabinet and a Republican legislature while he was the state's chief executive. This time he was run-

ning against Kim Sigler, a Republican who had made a name for himself over scandals in the statehouse. In 1943 and 1944, dozens of legislators and business people were accused of wrongdoing. With Sigler as special prosecutor, forty-six people were convicted. Sigler was a colorful character who played his role well. Although he had been a Democrat, he ran for governor in 1946 as a Republican. Pat Van Wagoner turned out to be no match for the flamboyant Kim Sigler.[1]

But Mennen Williams was looking ahead to the day when *he* would run for governor. Even before the 1946 election was over, he was starting to lay the groundwork for a campaign. Mennen already had considerable experience in politics. He had held a number of jobs in state and federal government and had a wide range of administrative and legal experience. He had interrupted his career to serve in the Navy during World War II and returned with ten battle stars. After the war, he became deputy director for Michigan in the federal Office of Price Administration (OPA). From his Detroit base, he was able to make contacts throughout the state. When the OPA office was shut down, he became a law partner with Hicks and Martha in Detroit. He was so well known and respected that early in 1947, Governor Sigler appointed him to fill a Democratic post on the Liquor Control Commission.

Mennen had confided his plans for the governorship to Martha and Hicks, and they responded with enthusiasm. Through their law practice, the Griffithses had been meeting people who were just as frustrated as they were about what was going on in Michigan. The state seemed paralyzed. With World War II only recently ended, there was a great need for housing, jobs, and public services.

The ADA was committed to solving those postwar problems, so I became involved in that organization. Of course, we were called liberals and sometimes worse, but I was used to that from my activities with the telephone workers.

What happened at that 17th District convention made us want to get involved in the Democratic party. We wanted things to change for the better. To us, that meant a Democratic party and state government that were free of scandal and that took care of the people, not somebody's cronies. It wasn't too surprising that the group who had been thrown out of the party convention eventually should get invited to Hicks and Martha's house to plan the takeover of the 17th Congressional District party organization. After all, first things first.

That meeting at the Griffiths's house was in early 1948, down in the basement recreation room. Gus Scholle and Adelaide Hart were invited but couldn't attend. Sid Woolner brought his wife, Doris; Tom Downs brought his wife, Alice. That night, over coffee and a delicious dish prepared by Martha—she always was a great cook—we formed ourselves into a committee to begin seriously recruiting precinct delegates in the 17th District. Hicks Griffiths told us our objective was to recruit enough new delegates to take over the organization of the Wayne County half of the 17th District. (The other half was in Oakland County and had its own officers and organization. We only met and combined our votes at state and national conventions.)

Hicks was prepared. He had a map of the district blown up and divided into precincts. We realized it would be a formidable task to get people to run as precinct delegates in more than two hundred precincts. Our portion of the 17th covered the far northwest area of Detroit. (Although the boundaries changed over the years, much of our old area remained in the 17th District until the 1990 census reduced the number of districts to sixteen. The 17th was absorbed into other districts starting with the 1992 elections.) At the time, many of the neighborhoods were new. There were a lot of young families and couples starting their lives together in the postwar years.

There were seven of us who worked on the recruiting drive. We started with our friends and put a yellow pin in every precinct where we knew someone. From there, we combed every list of names we could lay our hands on—union members, teachers, you name it—to find people in our district who might be sympathetic to the cause.

One by one, the people were contacted. In each instance, we tried to sell them on the idea that it was their civic duty to become a precinct delegate. Although Wayne County was heavily Democratic, it wasn't easy to convince people to become active in politics. Very few people wanted to take the time to circulate nominating petitions and get the twenty signatures needed to file for precinct delegate in the primary election. We readily agreed to circulate petitions for them, but only if they agreed to become delegates and attend the 17th Congressional District convention. We didn't want a repeat of 1946.

Of course, we all had to circulate petitions for ourselves, too. In checking my precinct, I found I would have to run against a man who had been a delegate for a long time, so I circulated my petition first. Luckily for me, my son Doug was the paper boy for that area. Also luckily for me, he was doing a good job. Time after time, when I said, "I am Helen Berthelot and I'm running for precinct delegate," I was greeted with a warm smile. "Are you Doug Berthelot's mother?" they would ask. "Do come in." It took me longer to circulate my petition than I had anticipated because the neighbors wanted to get acquainted with Doug's mother. Thanks to my son, I won my precinct with little competition that first time. The next time I had to campaign harder. It was tempting to enlist the support of precinct members whose addresses were in Grand Lawn Cemetery, but I resisted.

Night after night, three teams of us would circulate petitions throughout the district. The Woolners and Downses had small children, so Doris Woolner and Alice Downs took turns minding the four children while I made up the other partner in that team. It was like taking turns sitting out of a game of bridge or canasta.

After our precinct committee had worked together for several weeks, Hicks and Martha introduced me to Mennen Williams. That meeting changed my life, but I don't remember much about the circumstances. I recall that it was at the law office that Mennen shared with the Griffithses in downtown Detroit. Shortly afterward, Hicks told me about Mennen's ideas for the state and said he was going to run for governor. The next time I ran into Mennen, I looked at him with a new awareness. What I saw and heard appealed to me as well as to the others in our little 17th District group. The idea that he would run for governor gave us new impetus to get delegates to support him.

Things began to take shape. Whenever a delegate petition was circulated, a red pin replaced the yellow one on our district map. The red pins began to outnumber the yellow ones, and the whole map became nearly blanketed with pins. After the primary, when the district conventions were nearly upon us, Hicks suggested that I contact all the friendly delegates we had recruited in the 17th District and ask them to come to a briefing meeting.

Among ourselves, we had agreed that Hicks Griffiths should be elected as the new 17th Congressional District chairman. It was easy for me, while I was asking the delegates to come to the briefing, to put in a plug for Mennen Williams's program and to delicately suggest that a number of us thought Hicks Griffiths, who by then was Mennen's campaign manager, would make a good congressional district chairman. Because I had not only called the delegates about the briefing meeting but welcomed them at the door, thanking them for coming, I was suggested as the vice chairman. It was cinched after I called them all again, urging them not to forget to come to the congressional district convention.

The night finally arrived. In contrast to the confrontation two years earlier, it was a starlit and balmy evening—in many ways. It would be hard to imagine a more diverse group at a political convention. At least ninety percent of our people had never attended any political gathering, let alone an official congressional district party convention.

Charlie Nugent, the district party chairman, called the convention to order, and immediately recognized Mr. Hughes, the same man who had made the long motion at the 1946 convention. He made exactly the same motion, this time naming their new list of delegates to be seated. The chairman then called for passage of the motion. Our people were not as forceful in their negative voting as the opposition was in favor. The chairman ruled that the motion had passed.

Then this conglomerate group of amateurs made political history. Acting as floor leaders, Tom Downs and Alfred Meyers, a school principal, called for a show of hands. It took quite a little persuading before Charlie Nugent agreed. He appointed a nondescript little man, one of his henchmen, to be the teller, the one who decided how the vote went. I never did know his name, but he later became a bugbear to me. The show of hands was called for and the "no" vote was overwhelming. But the teller, with a cursory look around, announced that the motion had passed.

For the next thirty minutes, pandemonium reigned. Tom Downs and Al Meyers called for a roll-call vote. They were completely ignored, and the chair was about to adjourn the convention when that orderly group of neophytes began to yell, holler, and stamp their feet, demanding a roll-call vote. Before the convention, no one would have believed it possible to so arouse this group.

Finally, Charlie Nugent agreed to a roll call. The first four precincts were represented by men who had supported him previously, but who had been persuaded to join us. At first their "no's" were spoken very softly. Shocked at what he had heard, Charlie Nugent stopped. "I don't believe you understand the motion. We are voting on Mr. Hughes's motion—Mr. Hughes right over there," he said, pointing to the maker of the motion. Then he proceeded to start the roll call again. By this time, the first delegates had more courage, and their "no's" could be clearly heard. Before the roll call was completed, it was evident that the motion was soundly defeated.

The chairman and his group, with nasty side remarks, all got up and left the convention, giving us complete control of the Wayne County 17th District organization. They never knew how foolish they were. We had agreed among ourselves to give them at least one officer and half the executive board. By leaving, they gave up their only chance of having any say in district affairs.

Tom Downs presided over the convention temporarily until Hicks was elected chairman and I was elected vice chairman, both of us by acclamation. Hicks took the chair, and we then held an informal meeting to elect the remaining officers and the executive board of the Wayne County 17th. The whole group was greatly pleased with themselves, and most of them became active precinct delegates.

Don't ever believe that a few active people cannot change the complexion of a congressional district party. We did it.

NOTES

1. For more about this period, see Willis F. Dunbar, *Michigan: A History of the Wolverine State* (Grand Rapids: William B. Eerdmans Publishing Co., 1965). See also

F. Clever Bald, *Michigan in Four Centuries* (New York: Harper and Row, 1954, rev. 1961); and Bruce A. Rubenstein and Lawrence E. Ziewacz, *Three Bullets Sealed His Lips* (East Lansing: Michigan State University Press, 1987).

3

WE MAKE OUR MOVES

W E HAD WON a sweet victory, but we were a long way from taking over the state Democratic party—or even the 17th District Democratic party organization. When our Wayne County group got together with the Oakland County half of the district party, we were frequently outvoted. We were able to get our proper share of delegates to the state convention, however. Our group joined other delegates in electing Hicks Griffiths as the next state party chairman.

Hicks's hard work for Mennen had impressed Democrats across the state and helped him win the chairmanship. But the old guard wasn't ready to give up control: none of the other officers who were elected wanted any part of Hicks Griffiths or that upstart G. Mennen Williams. During Mennen's early days as governor, Hicks was the only state party officer Mennen could really trust.

Even among Mennen's supporters, some had wanted him to wait until the party was solidly under his control—up to ten years, if necessary —before running for governor. By early 1948, however, the campaign was well under way. Mennen wanted to move immediately; so did Hicks and Martha. And because I liked Mennen's ideas for the state, I was ready, too.

So were the new precinct delegates who were being recruited in the Wayne County congressional districts. In late May, Mennen sent each of them a letter announcing his candidacy. On law office stationery imprinted with "Griffiths, Williams & Griffiths," Mennen aimed straight for the new and enthusiastic Democrat who was frustrated by the status quo:

Because you are a leader in the Democratic Party, I am writing you to announce my candidacy for governor and to ask your support. From this moment on, I shall devote my every effort to become the Democratic nominee and the next governor of Michigan.

The situation in Michigan is ripe for change. Our people are tired of "bossism." We are sick and tired of a Republican governor wrangling with his own Republican officials and with his Republican Legislature. We are fed up with Republican fiddling while the state goes to pot.

We Democrats can and will do something about problems which the Republicans have criminally neglected: housing, labor relations, care of the sick, schools, roads, etc. Our "team" will act, not wrangle.

He described his work in state and federal government and said it had given him "government 'know-how'" and taught him "how to work with public officials—administrative and legislative, state, local and federal—and with private citizens all over our state." And he appealed to those who wanted to reform the party: "I honestly believe we Democrats can organize a 'team' that will fill our state and local offices with Democrats who will unselfishly work for the good of the people of Michigan. Your support would strengthen this 'team.'" He signed it "Cordially, G. Mennen Williams."

Because I was a candidate for precinct delegate, I got one of those letters. He had added a handwritten note: "Glad you're on the team." And he had crossed out the formal greeting, so it read "Dear Helen." It was one of several letters that I received from him with my last name misspelled as "Berthelott" instead of "Berthelot." For years, I teased him about that.

The first project we gave our delegate recruits was to ask them to get signatures on Mennen's nominating petitions for governor so he could run in the primary. It was a tremendous task to collect one hundred valid signatures in each of twenty counties, as the law required, in order to qualify for the ballot. Mennen sent a thank-you letter to each person who circulated a petition for him. By that time he was using "Williams for Governor—Democrat" campaign stationery. In the letter, he wrote that the campaign had gone beyond the minimum, and had the required number of signatures in thirty-two counties. "We qualified in some dozen rock-ribbed Republican counties and made a nice showing in others. . . . With this fine start, we are well on our way, but the big job lies ahead," he wrote. He was referring to the fact that he would have several opponents in the fall primary. For the Democratic party was anything but united. Mennen knew he had a tremendous task on his hands. Hicks knew it, too. He was working hard to get the word out to Democrats that Mennen was the one who could rebuild the party and the state—for the people.

36

Meanwhile, Martha Griffiths had filed as a candidate for the state legislature. How I came to run in a crowded field with her—and lose—helps explain much about the Democratic party and Michigan politics at that time.

For a number of years after I became active in civic affairs in Detroit, it had become a tradition that either Sid Woolner or Jim Hare, a Detroit teacher and truant officer who later served sixteen years as secretary of state, would be chairman of whatever group or committee we were involved in, while the other would be vice chairman. My role was to be the secretary. Our friends, and maybe other people too, called us "The Unholy Three." We worked well together, and I'm proud of the many projects we undertook. We were involved in the Michigan Committee for Fair Labor Standards, which was trying to help workers get a bigger piece of the pie, and the Michigan Committee for Civil Rights, among others.

The ADA had a fine, progressive membership in Detroit. That year—1948—Sid Woolner was the chairman, Jim was vice chairman, and I was the secretary. Sid always said my tales of how we were thrown out of our congressional district convention, along with our struggles to get precinct delegates, generated a lot of interest in politics when we went to ADA meetings. Then, too,—thanks to Cy Bevan two years earlier—people in other Wayne County districts were working hard in 1948 to get precinct delegates elected in the primary to support Mennen Williams.

The more ADA heard about Mennen's people-oriented campaign pledges, the more its members became interested in doing something constructive in state government. After Martha Griffiths announced she was running for state representative, my fellow members of ADA pressured me strongly to run, too. There was so much division among progressives that the ADA wanted to have somebody from its own ranks in the campaign for the legislature.

At that time, Detroit was one big legislative district with twenty-one seats. Often, there were three times that number of Democratic candidates. And given the heavy Democratic vote, the primary was the real election.

Despite the odds, the idea of running for office on the same platform as Mennen Williams intrigued me. An informal endorsement from ADA gave me the encouragement I needed, and I filed for the state legislature by depositing $100 with the county clerk. I then wrote a letter to each of the heads of the labor organizations in Detroit. Just because I had been an early organizer of telephone workers was no guarantee that labor organizations would be behind me—even my own.

Using Mennen's campaign pledges as a guide, I outlined my support of programs of particular interest to the labor movement, including:

37

- an immediate state program for financing low-cost housing because of the shortage of affordable housing after the war;
- state funding to help relieve understaffing and overcrowding in public schools;
- a fair labor standards law in Michigan, and a minimum wage of at least seventy-five cents an hour;
- improvements in workers' compensation and unemployment compensation, which at that time were pitifully low;
- fair employment and civil rights guarantees;
- reapportionment to give individual voters in the cities as much influence as those in rural areas (this was long before the "one man, one vote" decision guaranteed equal representation);
- an end to the sales tax on food.

In addition, I wrote: "I feel that women should take a more active interest and part in civic and legislative affairs."

Not one labor organization, including my own, endorsed me. They didn't think I could win. Foolishly, I did not solicit any contributions so, naturally, I was not taken seriously. Frances Smith, the president of my labor group, which by then was known as the Michigan Telephone Workers Federation, laughingly gave me a check for $15. Our telephone workers' attorney, Leon Cousins, gave me $25. That was the sum total of my contributions.

But I had fun, and I learned a lot that helped me later on. Campaigning with Mennen when he came into Wayne County got me into a number of places that would not have been open to me otherwise. Each time I was out among the people with him, my enthusiasm mounted. Johnny Penczak, an auto worker active in his United Auto Workers Union local and also a candidate for state representative, took me on a couple of tours of downtown and west side bars. Even though many of the people I met were somewhat inebriated, my vote in those areas was quite heavy.

My only campaign material was a card with my picture on it, announcing I was running for the state legislature and giving my number on the ballot, so the voter would know how to plunk for me. Johnny left my card in all the bars he visited, too. Instead of carrying my campaign cards in a briefcase and handing them out from there, I stapled campaign cards for Mennen, Martha, Johnny, and me on both sides of a file folder. Then I stapled the sides together and used it to carry my campaign cards. Every time I hauled out one of my cards, my "fancy" card holder showed off the names of my friends who were running for office.

Early in the campaign, I realized how seriously Detroit's many ethnic groups took their privilege to vote. Stella Lecznar, the leader in the West Side Polish Assembly, was a mentor for both Mennen and me. Without her teaching, Mennen and I both might have made a great many mistakes. From the start, she was impressed by Mennen's people-oriented program and his earnestness. She told him, "Never mention the name of your opponent. The people you are talking to may not know who he is." She gave him good lessons in shaking hands, making sure he remembered to always look directly at the person. (In those days, the handshake was the main means of reaching out to touch the public. People would remember a candidate's handshake and, sad to say, sometimes would use it as the only basis for judging the candidate.)

Probably because of her interest in seeing Mennen elected, Stella Lecznar adopted me, too. She saw that I was invited to appear before the West Side Polish Assembly. Every candidate had to stand up before that group, make a presentation, answer questions, and ask for its endorsement. Stella coached me well. After my speech, I was told to go outside the room and wait. After the assembly members had voted, Stella came out and told me I had received their endorsement. That really gave me a big lift. My name appeared on the printed slates which all the Polish people in that area took into the voting booths.

On election night, I was pleasantly surprised to see that I had come in twenty-first—last in the winner range, but a winner nonetheless. I went home happy and fell asleep, only to wake up and find that the vote in Ted Wilk's neighborhood on the east side had come in after I had gone to bed. With help from his fellow Polish-Americans, Ted Wilk had taken over twenty-first place and won the last spot with 37,974 votes. Johnny Penczak was twentieth. Out of thirty-nine candidates, I was twenty-third, with 35,362 votes to my name. That wasn't bad, considering I had had no support from my own labor movement. The West Side Polish Assembly and two other small Polish clubs, along with the ADA, were the only groups to endorse my candidacy. Martha Griffiths got 41,156 votes and was seventeenth among the twenty-one who won the Democratic primary. Her election that year was the beginning of a long and distinguished political career for Martha.

That night certainly taught me a valuable lesson. In all the elections I participated in later, I never again went to bed before the last vote was counted. After the first shock of losing, when I thought I had won, I really didn't feel too bad. After all, I got my $100 deposit back from the county. It didn't take me long to realize I would much rather work behind the scenes, helping someone else get elected, than sit for hours in a legislative body.

From the primary on, Sid Woolner, Jim Hare, and I devoted our energies to helping elect Mennen Williams and the rest of the Democratic ticket. When it came time to elect the new officers of the ADA, we all three ran for reelection. To my amazement, I found there was an active telephone campaign being waged to defeat all three of us. I was the particular butt of their criticism. As I heard it, I had lost all my principles when I ran for office on the Democratic ticket. That my ADA group had been the prime mover to get me to run and had endorsed me made no difference. A new group of officer candidates had arisen in the ADA. Rather than start a feud, I withdrew my name as a candidate for office. Later, I resigned from the Detroit chapter. Sid and Jim left soon after I did.

4

MENNEN
WINS HIS FIRST ELECTION

FROM THE PERSPECTIVE of the 1990s, Mennen's 1948 primary campaign seems like a public relations dream. He and his wife, Nancy Williams, traveled the state, usually by themselves, in their old, beat-up DeSoto convertible. The old car wasn't a gimmick. Although Mennen came from a well-to-do family, he and Nancy were far from rich. In that first campaign, they had to borrow money to pay the bills. They backed the loan with a mortgage on their unpretentious home. The DeSoto was the only transportation they could afford.

The family business—the Mennen line of baby powder and skin products—was controlled by Mennen's mother and uncle. Elma Mennen Williams, Mennen's mother, would pay his way at the Grosse Pointe Country Club, but that was all. She said that if he was old enough to marry, he was old enough to take care of his own family. Mennen's birthplace was the family home on Merrick Avenue in Detroit. (The home no longer stands, and the property is now part of the campus of Wayne State University.) In later years, the Grosse Pointes became their home.

At thirty-seven, Mennen was relatively young to be running for governor. He had only recently returned from service in the Navy during World War II, and he was virtually unknown to Democratic organizations throughout the state. He was not invited to many official meetings of Democrats, so he and Nancy decided to go and meet the people themselves.

No town was too small for them to stop in and no group too few for him to tell his story. Their procedure in many places was for Nancy to stand in front of a market or on a corner where people usually crossed. With her best smile, she would hand out Mennen's card, telling the people that her husband was running for governor and in a few minutes he was going to talk about his program. She then asked them to wait to hear him. Curiosity got the best of most of them, and they stayed. After listening to that earnest young man relate his people-oriented program, many were impressed with the couple's youth and enthusiasm—even if they didn't take too much stock in his actual program at the time.

One of the reasons he was so believable was that he really was convinced about what he was saying. When he talked about something, it was an idea that he had thought through and genuinely believed Michigan needed. He didn't have a staff of people writing position statements with one eye on the latest polls. Before deciding to run for governor, Mennen Williams had given a great deal of thought to what the people of Michigan needed. In developing his program, he drew on his education from Princeton and the University of Michigan Law School, his knowledge of the state, and the experience he had gained while working for the state and federal governments. He figured out the specific needs of each group—farmers, factory workers, business people, teachers, students, the mentally ill, the elderly, veterans.

The Democratic party was also beginning to address the needs of specific groups of people. After the party's national convention that summer, Mennen composed a two-page letter and mailed it to other Democratic candidates in Michigan, making it clear that he was tying his program to the national party. Mennen came from a family of Republicans, but he wasn't shy about saying he was a Democrat. Nor was he reluctant to criticize the Republicans, who at that time controlled the Michigan legislature as well as the governor's office. Kim Sigler, the Republican elected in 1946, had become unpopular even in his own party.

In early August 1948, Mennen wrote to his fellow Democratic candidates:

> Let us take to the people of Michigan our answers to the problems of the high cost of living, housing, social security and all those "hot potatoes" untouched by Republican hands. We must go beyond our national program. We must spell out the state, county and local aspects of these issues and what they mean to the people of our state.

His letter outlined a program that called for establishing a state housing commission to allow cities to use bonds to finance affordable housing; increasing the amount and length of unemployment compensation to come closer to meeting the cost of living; improving education by upgrading decrepit facilities and finding a way to raise teachers' salaries above the meager levels of the time; enacting legislation for fair employment practices and creating a state agency to advance the cause of civil rights in Michigan; developing a road system that would help industry, agriculture, and tourism; doing more for veterans; raising government benefits for the elderly and needy families; and ending scandalous overcrowding of prisons, hospitals, and state mental institutions. He also declared that his goal was

> a coordinated state administration, free from favoritism, free from scandal, devoted to efficient, conscientious service to *all* the people of the state. . . . With the issues clearly drawn and with a united effort to bring the voters to the polls, we shall succeed in bringing our government out of the special interest cloakrooms and in restoring it to the open assembly rooms of the public interest.[1]

Mennen was disgusted with what was going on in Lansing. Governor Sigler had been elected after pledging to clean things up and turn state government back to the people, but it seemed that nothing was getting done. Even the Republicans were getting fed up.

Mennen's main competition in the primary was Victor E. Bucknell, a lawyer from the Kalamazoo area who was favored by the up-and-coming Teamsters Union leader Jimmy Hoffa. Mennen sensed that there were many Democrats who did not want the Teamsters Union running the party. He banked on the fact that the people, Democrats as well as Republicans, wanted to get back in control of state government and politics.

In that 1948 election, Nancy and Mennen nearly wore out their car, driving around the state to deliver their message in person. It was a strange sight—a tall, handsome young couple getting out of an old convertible and approaching total strangers on the street. But their manner was such that people would stop to listen. Mennen was 6-feet-4, with a friendly smile and a polite, earnest way about him. Nancy wasn't the least bit shy about approaching people, because she really believed in Mennen and in what he was trying to do. She was attractive, she was smart, and she was very determined.

Mennen and Nancy were a perfect political team. They had met at the University of Michigan, while Mennen was in law school and Nancy was studying for her bachelor's degree. Nancy Quirk was from Ypsilanti, where her father was a banker. Like Mennen, Nancy was from a family with a strong Episcopalian background and Republican loyalties. It wasn't long before the young couple discovered that they shared the same ideas about the world. Nancy studied social services and shared Mennen's outlook and interest in public service.

Mennen came from two lines of self-starters. On the Williams side, Mennen's great-grandmother was a resourceful widow who established a produce business with her children in Detroit in the late nineteenth century. It grew into a successful pickle and jam processing operation and remained in the family until shortly before Mennen was born. On the Mennen side, his mother was the daughter of the entrepreneur, Gerhard Mennen, who built a fortune in his adopted homeland by learning the pharmacy business and then formulating useful new toiletries—the Mennen products, from baby powder to shaving preparations.

Gerhard Mennen Williams was born on February 23, 1911, the first of three sons born to Elma and Henry Williams. The boys were raised in a home where discipline, duty, and love of learning were stressed. Mennen acquired the nickname Soapy—for the family business—one summer at a dude ranch with some boyhood pals. Most people, including Nancy, took to the nickname and used it affectionately. He didn't mind, though it seemed a little out of character for him.[2]

Mennen Williams was a deep thinker. His political ideas began to swing toward the Democratic party as he grew up. As a student, he was deeply affected by historical accounts of the suffering of ordinary people, and he saw how working people suffered in the Great Depression. His religious faith was part of what motivated him. From boyhood, the Episcopal church was a part of his life. Although he was very private about his beliefs, his devotion was real and helped him over the rough spots. He honestly believed that if people thought they could do something, and really worked hard at it, they could accomplish it. Nancy shared his faith. They brought their sincerity and optimism to the people they met in that 1948 campaign.

Mennen Williams really had fun campaigning. He especially enjoyed himself at the annual picnic of the Telephone Pioneers at Bob-Lo Island. He'd been invited by Fran Smith, the president of our telephone workers federation, and me. We were being a little mischievous, as this was a company picnic for several hundred longtime workers. When Fran and I got to the wharf, there was Mennen, loudly hawking tickets for the picnic. It turned out he had been mistaken for someone else. With a twinkle in his eye, he explained, "Well, they asked me to."

Fran and I took him around and introduced him to everyone we knew, not as a candidate but as a friend. In typical fashion, Mennen joined in all the events. He probably would have won the bow-tie race—which involved untying, running, and then retying a bow tie—if I hadn't been his partner. The master of ceremonies was a good union friend, so Fran and I cornered him and cooked up a plan. Near the end of the program, the master of ceremonies announced that he had learned who the stranger was, the one who had been selling tickets. It was G. Mennen Williams, one of the Democratic candidates for governor. Would he stand and be recognized, if he is still here? Mennen got a good round of applause from the workers. All through the crowd, we could hear people saying, "Why, I met him with Fran Smith and Helen Berthelot." The company VIPs were there in force. The master of ceremonies never told us what they said to him, but they were more than a little perturbed to have a candidate for governor introduced—and a Democrat at that.

Mennen was new to campaigning, and he learned some valuable lessons. So did I. Through our telephone federation, Fran and I invited Mennen to judge a beauty contest at a party for the telephone workers, both men and women. At that affair we all learned that a candidate can't win by judging a beauty contest—or any other contest, for that matter. No great harm was done, since most of the contestants weren't old enough to vote. Years later, however, one of our telephone workers greeted him with narrowed eyes and said, "You don't like brunettes, do you?" Mennen never judged another contest.

Besides having Mennen out almost daily meeting the people, the campaign relied on something that seems simple by current standards— postcards with Mennen's picture on one side and a brief statement of his proposals on the other. They were mailed out by the thousands to friends and neighbors and people we thought might be interested in Mennen. In those days, when television was still a novelty, it was a very effective way of letting people know about a candidate. The postcards were by far the best campaign tool—economical and effective. Mennen also had a few flyers describing his program and a small number of posters to be put in store windows.

The postcards started going out in June. After Mennen won the primary, they were changed to say that he was the Democratic candidate for governor, and a better picture was used. To save money, they were sent by fourth-class mail. That meant they had to be sorted by town or city and tied in bundles of fifty or one hundred. One of my most vivid recollections of that first campaign was bringing in postcards to be mailed and seeing two young men sprawled on a couple of desks in the small campaign office in downtown Detroit. They were holding a "learned" discussion on the best way to handle a candidate. At the same time, Mennen was in the back room counting posters with his picture on them, tying them in packages of ten so he could take them to campaign meetings. When he finished, he left for the meetings all alone, carrying bundles of posters, while the young men continued their pontification.

Mennen's campaign workers came from every walk of life and background imaginable. What brought them together was their belief in his program. As campaign manager, Hicks Griffiths was faced with melding this diverse group into a campaign team. Hicks was a tough taskmaster. If there was no money, we just didn't carry out a particular project. It wouldn't surprise me if we held some kind of a record for the lowest amount spent on a campaign. Hicks was an extremely able campaign manager, even though he had had no previous political experience. He was just the kind of person who was needed. He took every opportunity that came up to see that his candidate was introduced at meetings, even if in some cases he was not allowed to speak.

Julie Lawler, who became Mennen's personal secretary after he was elected governor, had to sit on two telephone books to reach her typewriter.

Jim Lincoln was a young attorney in the law office shared by Mennen and the Griffithses. Jim, whose work as a judge on juvenile matters later won him national recognition, took on the job of handling the postcards. With the help of whatever volunteers he could recruit, he sorted, tied up, and mailed hundreds of these cards each day.

Jim had recruited me to help with the postcards early in the primary. Knowing that our telephone workers were in hundreds of small towns as well as bigger cities, I tried to get Fran Smith to let us run off postcards on the telephone workers' Addressograph machine and send them to our membership. By this time, Fran had become convinced that Mennen Williams was worth supporting. She and the executive board of the federation began to help in the campaign. On this occasion, however, she said our staff was too busy to run off the cards. When I asked her if I could do it, she laughed and said I couldn't run that old machine. The office staff taught me at night and I ran them off. Then I persuaded Walter Schaar, president of the plant union which represented the linemen and other male employees, to let me do the same with their list. Neither Fran nor Walt would agree to sign the postcards for Mennen, but they didn't object to my signing them. Before I finished I often wished that I had a shorter name.

Jim Hare was a teacher and truant officer in Detroit. It would be years before he would become "Secretary of State James M. Hare," with his name printed on driver's licenses and signs all over Michigan. Sid Woolner, who by then was a stalwart behind-the-scenes campaign worker for Mennen, decided Jim and Anne Hare were better known than Sid and Doris Woolner. So, with Jim and Anne's approval, the Woolners signed "Jim and Anne Hare" to hundreds of postcards. Jim told me later that because I was so sure of Mennen's election, he took a good second look at him.

Mennen began to receive invitations to meet with various ethnic groups. Through the efforts of Stella Lecznar, the west side Polish group started the ball rolling by organizing several small gatherings of newly formed Polish clubs. At each one, Mennen was invited to speak and then ask for their support. He stepped outside while they voted, and in each instance he was endorsed.

46

More than thirty-five years later, Mennen recounted some of the details of the 1948 campaign during a seminar on politics at Princeton University, his alma mater. With the primary and general election campaigns run on a total of about $32,000, personal appearances were crucial, he told the students. He also explained how he learned some valuable lessons:

> Let me close by assuring you that I was anything but a dynamic speaker and by giving you some idea how far I was from any experience in campaigning, so you can see how far you can go on vision and determination.
> . . .
>
> Stella Lecznar, a motherly Polish lady, took me in charge and got me started in Detroit's largest ethnic group. She gave me the classic political advice for the pre-television campaigner. In her motherly way, she said, "Now, when they introduce you, step out into the center of the hall so that everyone can see you, speak up so they can hear you, and say 'My name is G. Mennen Williams and I am running for governor.' Then halfway through your talk, say 'I am G. Mennen Williams and I am running for governor.' Finally, as you finish your talk, say 'I am G. Mennen Williams and I am running for governor.'"

That was as close as my primary campaign ever got to Madison Avenue.

One by one, the ethnic groups began to be aware of his candidacy. The Greek- and Arab-American groups had several gatherings at the Sheik restaurant and invited him. Others followed suit. It was usually the same story—a polite speech, a vote and an endorsement. At each of these meetings, he was always strongly urged to partake of the wonderful delicacies that each group produced. It didn't take its toll on Mennen, but it did on some of us—ten pounds in each campaign for me.

As enthusiasm for Mennen mounted, more and more signed postcards were brought in to be mailed. More than once those of us who were packaging the cards emptied our pocketbooks of spare change to send out a few more. After Mennen won the primary, I ran off both sets of telephone workers' addresses once again on postcards. This time, Fran and Walt signed their names.

Mennen's victory in the primary was a surprise to most people, but not to those of us who had been involved from the beginning. There never had been any doubt in our minds that Mennen Williams would win. It was a good thing we were all political babes in the woods. Surely, most of us never would have begun the campaign if we had realized what the odds were. Luckily for Mennen, a businessman from Albion, Burnett J. Abbott, entered the primary. He and Victor Bucknell split the old-line Democratic vote, allowing Mennen to win. The final primary tally was 109,988 for Mennen, 101,814 for Bucknell, and 93,302 for

Abbott. Mennen truly was the right man in the right place at the right time; the vote totals proved it.

It was no fluke, however. Besides the postcard campaign, another simple strategy turned out to be surprisingly effective. During the campaign, candidates for precinct delegate in Wayne County handed out little cards imprinted with their name and Mennen's, along with a few words about Mennen's program for improving the state and the party. Tom Downs and several others checked and discovered that Mennen won overwhelmingly against the other two Democrats in precincts where the cards had been distributed by the precinct delegate candidates and their supporters. Mennen's belief in a strong, broad party organization was already beginning to show results.

On primary election night, we all acted as challengers in our precincts, watching to make sure things were as they should be, and then went to Mennen and Nancy's home to listen to the radio to get the results of the outstate vote. Jim Hare drove me over. It took us a long time to get there because he stopped at every polling place to check the latest vote.

Nancy Williams learned a hard lesson that evening. The Williamses had a heavy, white string rug in their living room. In preparation for the election night party, she had scrubbed the whole rug on her hands and knees, acquiring several bad rug burns in the process. She looked crushed when, early that night, someone tipped over a full bottle of beer and a golden-brown stain spread over a large section of her clean white rug.

Election returns had hardly started to come in when the house was soon filled with people, many of whom we had never seen before and never would see again. As soon as it was known for sure that Mennen had won the primary, reporters descended upon the house. The momentum was picking up.

For the first time, the Detroit and Wayne County AFL and the CIO publicly joined hands to back the same candidate in the general election —Mennen. His campaign benefited from the unified labor endorsement. Frank Martel, who led the Detroit and Wayne County AFL, and Gus Scholle, president of the Michigan CIO, both furnished manpower and opportunities for Mennen to speak to their members. The outstate AFL supported Abbott.

The speaking opportunities were a mixed blessing. Mennen's voice had rather a harsh tone when he addressed a group. The earnestness with which he spoke, however, won people over. His unique voice turned out to be an advantage, because people instantly recognized it. As time went on, we were told that people actually looked forward to hearing that Williams accent. This was particularly true when he talked over the radio and, later, on telvision.

Kim Sigler campaigned hard on his reputation as a former crime buster in Lansing and promised better conditions of all sorts for working people, something he had said he would do before but had not done. The three major Detroit newspapers were all firmly in Sigler's corner.

On election night in November, an even larger crowd than the primary group congregated in Mennen and Nancy's house in Grosse Pointe Farms. Mennen's mother, Elma Mennen Williams, insisted she was not going to have her picture taken with him. She was still unaccustomed to her son's Democratic politics, much less the fact that he appeared to be winning. He gently took her by the hand and led her up the stairs for a photo session. Later, at the inauguration, it was fun to watch her arranging the receiving line at the capitol. Nancy looked on with disbelief.

Mennen rented several tickertape machines on election night so we could have the latest results as quickly as possible. They used so much electricity that the power kept going off until new fuses could be connected.

The crowd was a little overwhelming, too. Television news was just getting started in those days, and the television crews were in that house, with all their bulky gear, for hours. No one expected such an influx of people—or that they would stay all night. The mountains of food Nancy had prepared were all gone by the early morning hours. As the hours went by, Nancy remembered that someone had brought over a couple of crates of eggs and a huge box of bacon. Mennen's brother Dick Williams and I found ourselves out in the kitchen frying bacon and scrambling eggs, half the time in the dark as the power kept going off.

In the early morning hours, the election returns showed Mennen the winner, but Governor Sigler did not call to capitulate until much later. The reporters and television crews had already left by the time the phone call came. After the tumult and shouting were over, a few of us stayed on for a little while, tired but jubilant, still savoring our accomplishment.

"Before you go," Mennen said, "Let's drink a toast to our victory." He went and got a slightly battered loving cup and filled it with champagne. He passed the cup around, and we each took a sip and raised the cup in triumph. "To victory!" we exclaimed. "This cup has a history," Mennen said. "When Nancy Quirk and I got engaged, I gave her this engraved loving cup. In it I put a few sips of beer, but unknown to Nancy, I slipped her engagement ring into the cup. Because there was so little in the cup, she had to tip it up high and almost swallowed her ring." We all had a good laugh and told them both how delighted we were to be able to share this new celebration in their lives.

Mennen's decision to run for governor had come at just the right time. Not only had two old-line Democrats knocked each other out in the primary, but Governor Sigler really defeated himself. He had become

49

very unpopular, even among Republicans, and was seen as aloof and somewhat arrogant. Even though Mennen had worked hard, the election was more of an anti-Sigler vote. The final count was 1,228,604 for Williams, 964,810 for Sigler.[3]

Mennen had his first victory. From then on, it was up to him. After the election, someone said: "So now you have won. How are you going to get reelected? You will have to campaign in every city and town. You can't do that." Mennen replied, "But I can try." And over the years, he not only tried, but did visit most Michigan communities.

NOTES

1. For correspondence and other materials on the first campaign of G. Mennen Williams, see the collection of his papers as well as those of Helen Berthelot in the Michigan Historical Collections, Bentley Historical Library, University of Michigan, Ann Arbor.

2. For more about the Mennen, Williams, and Quirk families and the early days of G. Mennen Williams, see Frank McNaughton, *Mennen Williams of Michigan: Fighter for Progress* (New York: Oceana Publications, 1960).

3. President Harry S Truman did not carry Michigan in 1948, but he did make a good showing. The presidential vote in Michigan was 1,003,448 for Truman and 1,038,595 for Thomas E. Dewey, who was a native of Owosso. For more background on the 1948 election in Michigan, see McNaughton, *Mennen Williams of Michigan*, and Dunbar, *Michigan*.

5

POLITICAL
RESPONSIBILITY IS A
FULL-TIME JOB

O N THE HEELS of the 1948 victory, Mennen and the Michigan
Democrats received their most important campaign symbol
since the donkey. It was a green-and-white, polka-dot bow tie,
given to Mennen by his brother Dick to mark the beginning of his first
term as governor. In the years that followed, people all over the country
identified that tie with Mennen and the Democrats of Michigan. When
Dick, the youngest of the three Williams brothers, presented that tie,
Mennen took to it right away. He wore the tie all during that first inaugural, even to the inaugural ball. He treasured it and sometimes wore it
for elections and other special occasions. Of course, Mennen bought
many others over the years. They were a little smaller and, especially in
his supreme court years, occasionally were in colors like navy, but he
never wore another kind of tie for any occasion.

Green and white were Mennen Williams's official colors. They even
made their way onto the governor's stationery, with green typewriter ribbons on white paper. He signed his name in green ink.

The Williams campaign had a clip-on, miniature bow tie made as a
campaign button. It became so popular that it was copied by the thousands. In later campaigns, heavier-metal campaign tiepins were sold to
raise money. The polka-dot tie was reproduced in many sizes and materials over the years. As Mennen won election after election, that tie became
a symbol of a strong Michigan Democratic party. If Dick Williams had
been paid as a campaign consultant to come up with a successful symbol,
he couldn't have done any better.

51

In January 1949, when Mennen stepped into the governor's office to face a hostile legislature, he knew he had deep divisions even within his own party. He kept repeating a familiar Williams saying: "You can't solve today's problems with yesterday's answers."

Hicks Griffiths's election as state party chairman gave us a feeling that we had finally arrived, even though the old guard won the other offices. As state party chairman, Hicks gathered together people who could build the active, issues-oriented party that Mennen was dreaming about. Hicks weeded out the hangers-on who had been lining their own pockets at the expense of the integrity of the Democratic party. He was tough when someone tough was needed and took the brunt of the blame for any unhappiness. This left Mennen free to develop his plans for the state.

The truth was that Mennen was all but alone in the capitol in wanting bold new solutions. Just as he had done in the campaign, he knew he would have to take his case to the people. With the election of two more Democrats, however—John W. Connolly as lieutenant governor and Stephen Roth as attorney general—Mennen had two friendly voices on the State Administrative Board. But that was it. (The Ad Board is the governor's cabinet. At the time, its members were all elected by the people. Now, some of them are appointed by the governor.[1])

The legislature was not only Republican, it was downright unfriendly to Mennen. After years of unpleasantness and public scandal, Lansing politicians were wary of a Democrat, especially an outsider who wanted to start fresh. Mennen didn't hold back. In one of his earliest speeches, to a special meeting of Wayne County Democrats, he predicted that Michigan faced a financial disaster if the legislature continued to ignore the state constitutional provision which stated: "The Legislature shall provide by law for an annual tax sufficient with other resources to pay the estimated expenses of the state government . . . the interest on any state debt and such deficiency as may occur in the resources."

Before he left office, Governor Sigler had warned the legislature that cuts would have to be made if new taxes weren't levied soon.[2] The needs were overwhelming. At the time, there was no state income tax. There wasn't even a tax on corporate profits. But to the horror of the Republicans, Mennen proposed a corporate profits tax a few weeks after his inauguration.

He didn't make the recommendation lightly. He had reviewed all possible sources of revenue and concluded there was no other way. In a special tax message to the people and the legislature, Mennen listed all the other available funds and showed that, even taken together, they would not do the job. Mennen's tax message was put out as a press release with copies sent to party leaders around the state. It was described in the *Detroit News*, of all places, as "the ablest paper to come out of Lansing for many years." The Republicans, who held the majorities in both houses of the legislature, fully believed that Mennen Williams would be defeated in 1950. Then they could pass any tax law they so desired. So they ignored the governor's warning and defeated his tax bill.

It was a difficult few months. For a little while after the 1949 inauguration, there was a strained feeling between Mennen and all of us who had worked so hard to elect him. "He's the governor now," we thought, and sort of sat back in awe at what we had accomplished. Mennen must have wondered what had happened to his close associates. They had gone back to their jobs and their normal lives, leaving him all alone to handle the myriad problems that faced a new governor from a different party, a party that had not been in power for years.

The number of appointments to be made by the governor was staggering. Mennen wanted to pick only those people he knew he could trust. He also wanted to use the power of appointment to build a solid base for the Democratic party. Hicks was doing his best to help Mennen choose the right people in the party, but he could not know all the candidates who were shouting and pushing to be appointed. Things were going along all right until Mennen gave a minor appointment to George Fitzgerald, the national committeeman who was backed by the Teamsters Union. We all disagreed with that. We came to and realized that although Mennen Williams was governor, the battle had just begun.

From then on, Mennen's close associates set up an unofficial screening committee for all appointments. Those of us with special knowledge of the positions to be filled took on assignments to thoroughly investigate the people and the positions, and we made strong recommendations to the governor. He was given the background of each person and strong reasons why the person should or should not be appointed. The governor had his own ideas and often disagreed with us, but at least we were able to keep any rascals out.

We used to laugh, but it was no joke when Mennen had to appoint someone to the Apple Commission and the Electrical Administrative Board, for instance, in the same day. Back then, there were several dozen state boards and commissions and many advisory committees overseeing every phase of life and welfare in Michigan. Over the years, hundreds of people gave their time and energy—often forsaking lucrative jobs—to help Mennen reshape state government through these administrative boards.

Even in later years, when Democrats were in the majority on the State Administrative Board, it wasn't easy for Mennen. The state senate controlled the governor's appointments to all the other boards, committees, and commissions that ran state government. At first, Republicans in the state senate turned down Mennen's appointments. After much criticism, they changed their tactics. They just ignored Mennen's lists of names. As a result, Mennen was forced to appoint and reappoint people, time and time again, when the legislature would go in and out of session. The people would serve, but the senate wouldn't even dignify them with a vote.

This was especially insulting because Mennen took his power of appointment very seriously. He won universal praise for the caliber of his appointments during the twelve years he was governor. The people he brought in did much to change state government for the better during that time. When he was traveling throughout the state, he was always listening carefully and looking for people with his kind of leadership and philosophy of government. Certainly Mennen wanted to give loyal Democrats a chance to serve in state government, but he always took great pains to choose only the best people.

In that first year Mennen was governor, we discovered that the previous party leadership had left the Michigan Democratic party in a shambles. To make matters worse, many of them were still holding party office. When Hicks, as party chairman, had to get the lists of Democratic county officials from the Republican secretary of state, we realized that something had to be done, and done quickly. Where to start was the big question.

The consensus was that first we needed to make some rules for the county organizations to follow and have them down in writing so there would be no misunderstanding. With Tom Downs's help, Sid Woolner and I worked on compiling the legal rules for electing party officers and candidates. Judah Drob, one of Mennen's early supporters, was a freelance writer and had an excellent way with words. We prevailed on him to write what had to be the first manual for precinct political organizations ever written in Michigan. Judah wrote in a clear and simple style that everyone could understand. Hicks Griffiths composed a short message to go on the cover and made a number of corrections and revisions. We were all proud of that little booklet when it came out in print. The precinct manual was distributed to all the county chairmen, and Hicks held meetings with them to sell the ideas in the manual wherever he could.

We also produced a handbook to educate party workers on election practices, so that they could become official challengers and watch over the handling of ballots at the precinct level. The booklet was very basic; it contained illustrations of ballots and explained how to look for errors. As the introduction asserted, the aim was ". . . to make sure that all the proper procedures are followed, and that every Democratic vote is counted. This is one of the most important jobs in the entire political process, because democracy is a sham if elections are stolen or errors by election officials change the outcome."[3]

Under Hicks, the party even adopted a slogan in 1949: "A candidate for every office, a challenger in every polling place and a worker in every precinct." In spite of complete opposition from the other officers of the party, Hicks Griffiths got things at least partly organized. For two years, party officials continued to refuse to give up the records and kept control of the funds. It wasn't until 1950 that we were able to set up our own records and take control of the finances.

The former party chairman had set up what was commonly called a bucket shop. This was an unofficial telephone bank, used to raise money in the name of the Democratic party; the money actually went into a clandestine account. The people who came up with this scheme foolishly left their Michigan Bell phone bill unpaid, which drew the company's attention. A friend of mine at the phone company alerted me to what was going on, and we were able to nip that racket in the bud by exposing the imposters.

Hicks didn't stay on long as party chairman. Early in 1950, a vacancy occurred in Wayne County Probate Court, and Hicks asked Mennen to appoint him to the post. When Hicks told our original little group what he planned to do, we all begged him not to ask for the appointment. But Hicks wanted badly to be a judge and seemed to think this was his only chance to become one. Unfortunately, he had to run for election that fall to hold the judgeship to which he'd been appointed. While he was popular among the Democrats, his name was not well-known to the public. He was badly defeated. Hicks was very disappointed and stated publicly he was through with politics. When he was asked what he was going to do now, he said he was going back to his law office and concentrate on making money.

Those of us who had been so close to him were devastated. Not only was the party losing an able leader, but we were losing a beloved friend. Hicks kept his word and devoted his time to his law practice. He was never remotely connected with any other campaigns—except those of his wife, Martha. He strongly supported her through all her many elections.

Martha Griffiths won another term in the legislature but lost in 1952, the year of Dwight Eisenhower's first presidential victory, when she ran for the 17th Congressional District seat. A few months later, she persuaded Mennen to appoint her to a vacancy in Detroit Recorder's Court. She handled some very dangerous cases, including racketeering, while she was in that office.

Martha went on to serve for twenty years as a member of Congress from the 17th District. She had a distinguished career in the U. S. House from 1955 through 1975. She was known especially for the progress she made in women's rights legislation. In her own political life, she achieved a number of firsts. She topped off her political career by being elected to two terms as Michigan's lieutenant governor. In all her reelection campaigns, she concentrated on her own candidacy, but she always put in a word for the rest of the ticket and had their literature available. In 1950, Martha went a little further than that, and so did Nancy Williams and I. In keeping with Mennen's color scheme, we all wore green shoes during the *entire* campaign. They were pretty scruffy at the end, but you could still tell they were green.

After Hicks resigned as state chairman, Neil Staebler took his place. Neil, who was from Ann Arbor, was a born political organizer who believed deeply in the party. For the next several years, Neil, with his wife Burnette always helping him, laid the foundation for building a stronger Democratic party in Michigan. He and Mennen had great respect for each other, and they enjoyed talking politics and issues. Neil had more new ideas in five minutes than the rest of us combined, but it always took Neil a while to explain them. Burnette was the stabilizer—no pun intended—because Neil talked his ideas through with her before presenting them to the rest of us. And then he would change them again. Alice Mott was an ideal secretary for him and a real heroine of the building of the party over the years. She typed page after page—and then turned around and typed rewritten versions. Ever the optimist, Neil never gave up until he was completely outvoted in our sessions. We all moaned and groaned at the length of the meetings and the details we had to debate, but we wouldn't have missed it for the world.

Neil was repeatedly reelected party chairman until 1960. He was elected national committeeman in 1961. He resigned when he was elected congressman-at-large in 1962. In 1964 he ran unsuccessfully for governor, against the popular and colorful incumbent, George Romney, the Republican who had rescued American Motors and then led the effort to rewrite Michigan's constitution. After that, Neil again became national committeeman. He is one of those rare people perfectly suited for party work. Patience and tolerance are a must for the job, and it helps to be interested in ideas. Neil has those qualities. If he couldn't persuade you, he would keep talking until you gave in.

In 1955, Paul Butler, the Democratic national chairman, appointed Neil to chair the National Advisory Committee for Political Organization, a committee to help rebuild the Democratic Party. Neil traveled the country at his own expense, helping Democrats strengthen their party organizations. They kept at it until John F. Kennedy was elected and disbanded the group. In spite of all the party responsibilities Neil assumed, he never missed an election for precinct delegate. He would canvass the area faithfully at election time, asking the people for support and finding out what was on their minds.

NOTES

1. The 1963 constitution changed the terms of office for many state officials, including the governor, from two years to four. It also reduced the number of State Administrative Board members who were to be elected. This effectively put more control in the hands of the governor as chief executive. The board continues to exist and meets regularly, although it has less power than it did before 1963.

2. Governor Sigler's correspondence and other papers relating to his administration may be found in the Michigan Historical Collections, Bentley Historical Library, University of Michigan, Ann Arbor.

3. A copy of *How to Be a Challenger* is among Helen Berthelot's papers in the Michigan Historical Collections, Bentley Historical Library, University of Michigan, Ann Arbor.

6

OUR FIRST
EXPERIENCES WITH
DIRTY TRICKS

BEFORE WE KNEW IT, 1950 had rolled around and it was again time to recruit people to run for precinct delegates if we were to retain control of the 17th District. Adelaide Hart and Horace Gilmore were added to the group we had formed previously to circulate petitions. That brought our little band to about ten. We circulated petitions on behalf of people who were willing to be delegates, but who either had no time to get signatures or were reluctant to ask people to sign their petitions.

It was hard work, and it took up most of our evenings as the filing deadline approached. We had a merry time that year before Hicks Griffiths resigned as state chairman and chairman of our 17th District organization. After the teams had filled their quotas for the evening, we would all get together at the Griffiths home and exchange stories. We were met with all kinds of receptions at the doors, from having them slammed in our faces to being invited in to join a party.

One evening, as we were telling our tales, Tom Downs disappeared for a few moments. When he came back, he announced that he had solved all our problems in collecting petitions. With a flourish, he produced from behind his back a well-decorated denim bag with deep pockets on each side and a long shoulder strap. He began a demonstration that was something like the Fuller Brush man's. "Here," he proclaimed,

you see the first Jim Dandy, lifetime precinct circulator. It is equipped with every resource. You will only have to collect signatures once because here are a dozen petitions complete with carbon paper between each one. Here in the pockets are pencils, pens, erasers, and even a ruler to slap the wrist of the person who does not sign quickly enough. In this other pocket is a thermos bottle to hold your favorite beverage so you never need to be thirsty. Everyone will be glad to refill it for you if you promise never to ask them to sign again.

On and on he went. Tom Downs, now one of the country's experts on recounts and reapportionment, has always had a wonderful sense of dramatic humor. It served us well that night—we laughed until we cried—and kept us from crying many other times when things looked bleak for Mennen and for the party. Looking back, we should have seen what was ahead—and I'm not referring to the 1952 recount, when Tom's leadership helped pull the party together and preserve Mennen's victory. Tom Downs, a wonderful man and a fine lawyer, later became an experienced clown. For years he has made as many clown appearances as his schedule will allow, entertaining children of all ages, including elderly ones.

We did have fun that year, but things soon got serious. After Hicks Griffiths resigned from his party offices, I automatically moved up from vice chairman to acting chairman of the 17th District organization. Shortly after that, Tom Downs decided to take a look at the precinct delegate petitions at the Wayne County clerk's office. They were being filed in such large numbers for the 17th District that he became suspicious.

Petition after petition showed lists of names in identical handwriting —with the same people signing each petition, but using different names. Making it all the more obvious that something was amiss, every seventh signature was signed in green ink. After checking house numbers, Tom found that the persons getting the signatures would have had to zig-zag back and forth across the street to get the names in the order they were recorded on the petitions.

It was our first experience with "round-table" petitions—petitions which are not circulated at all but are forged by a group of people, each signing different names and addresses from the city directory. Large numbers of petitions can be produced in a single sitting, with all the signatures on a petition seeming different—unless you compare petitions.

We alerted our friends in other Wayne County districts. They checked and found they were having similar problems. When Neil Staebler learned of the fraudulent petitions, he filed a complaint with the Wayne County clerk and asked that they be thrown out. His request was denied.

After much consultation, we decided that I, as congressional district chairman, should file a complaint in court and ask to have the bad petitions for our district thrown out—another first for me. No one had ever heard of such a case at that time. Judging from how slick the operation was and how widespread, it seemed obvious that our opponents in the party had done this many times, with no one the wiser. After Tom Downs did some investigating, we were sure the fraudulent petitions were part of a pattern. With George Edwards as our attorney, we went to court. The judges weren't eager to become involved, but a Williams appointee finally took the case. Our opponent from previous district conventions, Charlie Nugent, was still around. Even though Charlie wasn't officially involved in this case, Tom remembers Charlie arguing from the jury box that the court should let the party settle the matter at its next convention. Relying on a technicality, the judge ruled it was an internal affair that should be handled outside the courtroom by the congressional district party.

We prepared to do exactly what the judge suggested. Before the district convention, my executive board and I made elaborate plans for foiling the seating of illegal delegates. The main business of the convention would be the selection of the next district chairman. By now, all my spare time was spent helping Sid Woolner in the governor's campaign office, and I had no desire to remain as chairman.

My union experience had taught me that, if you want something done, you call a caucus of your friends and seek their advice and help. Having no idea of the furor it would cause, I mustered about fifteen of my trusted leaders and workers in our part of the 17th District. Several people had suggested that Alfred Meyers, a high school principal, would make a good chairman. That was fine with me but I wanted to get the advice of my leadership.

Unknown to me, the United Automobile Workers (UAW) union leaders had decided on the man, certainly not a woman, they wanted as chairman. He was Mike Lacey, one of their own directors and one of my trusted advisers. The UAW leaders didn't trust me enough to even mention it to me. With the UAW's candidate sitting right there, I innocently put the question to my advisory group as to who should be the next chairman. Mike Lacey had always been a kind and dear friend of mine, so when he immediately attacked me and my right to call a caucus of my friends to discuss the chairmanship, I was taken aback. As I defended my right, he continued his unreasonable and savage assault. The whole meeting became a very unpleasant affair.

Finally I broached the subject of Al Meyers as chairman and got good support from the others in the group, but not Mike. He continued to challenge my authority to call such a meeting, telling me in harsh language that everything we had discussed at the meeting would have to be settled at the district caucus. Of course I knew that, and had planned on doing so. Refusing to let him deter me, I requested suggestions for other officers and members of the executive board, explaining that we needed people who would carry on the work of the district and work hard in the election. Everyone, including Mike Lacey, agreed that I should continue as vice chairman.

The experience didn't stop me from carefully protecting us from our opponents who had filed those phony petitions. Because of the probability of a battle with the "round-table" delegates, I called a caucus of the entire group of legitimate delegates to figure out who we wanted for district officers and the executive board and to be prepared for whatever happened at the congressional district convention.

Our caucus was in a small upstairs auditorium at one of the schools in the district. It was very confining in more ways than one. The UAW, I discovered, had sent a large delegation of staff members and their wives. Not all of them were even residents of the district. They were all busily buttonholing the delegates and attempting to sell their UAW candidate, Mike Lacey, for chairman. Watching the faces of the delegates, I realized that they resented the strong-arm methods that were being used.

No one knew why I was so slow in starting the meeting. But I had decided the longer I let the UAW staff work, the better chance we had of electing Al Meyers chairman. It got to be pretty exciting, with a number of my leaders worrying why I hadn't yet begun the session. At least twenty minutes went by. When I called for order, nominations for chairman were put on the floor. Al Meyers won handily. The other officers we wanted won, too. But our group was so pleased at winning that we forgot to nominate the people we had agreed upon for the executive board, and there the UAW won a majority. They were all good workers, however, and once they were over their hard feelings at losing their fight for chairman, we all worked in relative harmony.

The actual convention and election was still a few weeks away. The UAW evidently wanted to be sure I wouldn't go off the deep end anywhere during the short time that I had left as chairman. They assigned Tom Downs, my good friend, to follow me around and find out what I was doing. Tom was not the best detective in the world, so it didn't take me very long to catch on to what was happening. One day I cornered him. "Tom," I said: "if the UAW or the labor movement wants me to do something, tell them to ask me. If I can, I will. If I can't, I'll tell them why I can't. But tell them to stop sending you around to watch me. I resent them using my friends this way." Tom was embarrassed, but I am sure he was secretly relieved. He left me hurriedly and I never heard anything more about it.

Another interesting sidelight of my winning that battle with the UAW over the chairmanship was a polite invitation for Mrs. Berthelot to attend a political action meeting in the office of Walter Reuther, the president of the UAW. I went willingly, but I wondered what was coming. There was only one other woman there, a UAW staff member, but I was used to being in meetings with men. There was a vacant seat beside Mike Lacey, their defeated candidate for 17th District chairman, and I deliberately went over and sat on the sofa beside him. The only apology for his attack on me was a whispered remark. He said, "They'll never again use me as the balance of power." Immediately I smiled, and we picked up our friendship where it had left off.

The get-together was a legitimate political action meeting concerning that year's campaign for governor and other state offices. There was something I wanted to suggest, but I didn't speak loudly enough for Walter Reuther to hear me. Half a dozen voices chorused, "Mrs. Berthelot has something she wants to say." Instantly, I was recognized. It was hard not to show my embarrassment. My contribution was useful and the group agreed with me. That was the first and only time I was invited to Walter Reuther's office. But a lot of wounds were healed that day when they saw my attitude toward their ex-candidate.

The meeting hall for the congressional district convention was in tune with our new winning style. It was a fairly modern brick building loaned to us by the carpenters' union. The inside was brightly lighted and very nicely decorated. All of our 17th District conventions were held in that hall for years.

My executive board and I had made plans for keeping illegal delegates out of the convention. Tom Downs got photostatic copies of all the "round-table" petitions, so we had a complete list of names. A credentials committee was appointed to handle the seating of eligible delegates. That committee was composed of Al Meyers, as chairman; Adelaide Hart, one of our group's original members; and Barney Taylor of the UAW publicity staff. They were all slim and short, with a combined weight of not much over 450 pounds. Normally, that wouldn't matter. But their counterparts on the other side, we soon would learn, were a formidable group. Sizing up the situation ahead of time, we appointed several husky sergeants-at-arms. We agreed to keep the door locked and to check each delegate's credentials at the entrance. Those who had legitimate petitions were to be let in, but any from the "round-table" lists were to be refused admission.

Charlie Nugent, the former chairman, had a legitimate petition, so he was allowed to come in, along with a number of his delegates who had won their precincts. Charlie stood right by the door, watching every move. All at once he gave his friends outside a sign and jumped to open the door wide to let them in. Al Meyers never moved so fast in his life. He leaped over the credentials table to get Charlie by the neck and pull him back. The sergeants-at-arms quickly blocked and shut the door. The credentials table was in the hallway, right at the head of a short flight of stairs. When Al jumped, Adelaide Hart fell backwards and landed several steps below, on the first landing. No one was hurt, but there was plenty of excitement for a few minutes.

It wasn't over yet. A rumor had circulated that the opposition was going to take over the chair and the meeting by force. To prevent this, I went onto the platform and sat in the chairman's place. George Bowles, a respected attorney whom Mennen later appointed to the bench, was parliamentarian for the meeting. He came and sat with me. The rumor must have been correct, for I kept getting urgent messages that someone wanted to speak to me at the door. Casually, I said I would see them later and just sat there. Outside, there was a short skirmish, and one of our hot-tempered delegates got a bloody nose.

When all the legitimate delegates were assembled, members of our old-guard opposition all sat on one side of the middle aisle and the delegates we had recruited were on the other—a fortunate arrangement for me, as it turned out. The meeting was called to order, and I requested the report of the credentials committee. Barney Taylor, the committee chairman, gave the report and moved that the delegates named be seated. The motion was duly seconded. Immediately, Charlie Nugent jumped to his feet and asked to speak. With my best smile, I granted his request. He said the names read by the credentials committee were not correct and that he would read the list of delegates. He started to read his list of two hundred names. It seemed best to let him read for a few minutes before I called him out of order and asked him to be seated.

There were cries of "Question" from our delegates, which would force a vote on the motion. More firmly this time, but still politely, I asked Charlie to sit down. He kept on reading, and the delegates kept shouting "Question." Finally, I pounded the gavel and said in my most authoritative voice: "Mr. Nugent, you are out of order. Please sit down." After I did this twice and he still refused to stop reading, I turned to our delegates and asked, "Anything further on the question?" They shouted "Question," so I ignored Charlie, who was still reading, and called for the ayes and nays. The motion passed overwhelmingly. Charlie, who did not have a mike, kept on reading while we went on with our agenda. He finally got tired and sat down. The rest of the meeting was completed with no further problems. All the officers who had been nominated at the earlier caucus were elected. Again, the opposition group stalked out in anger.

Charlie Nugent should have known better. It wasn't the first time that year that I had outmaneuvered him. He had one of his cohorts, that little man who had irked me previously, haunting me at every meeting, knowing that I would find it hard to shut him off without creating a fuss.

This man always showed up with his hat pulled down over his eyes. He had a sinister voice and he scared me.

One night, Charlie's friend was raving on and on, pouring out unkind objections to everything I was saying. It was maddening, but I was at a complete loss as to what to do. Gus Scholle, the president of the Michigan CIO, often helped me handle difficult situations. This time, he was to rescue me without even knowing it. As the little man ranted on that evening, I spotted Gus and a couple of friends walking into the meeting. Very loudly, I said, "Oh, here is our next speaker, Gus Scholle," and I started to clap vigorously. The group followed my lead and applauded also.

Gus had a bewildered look on his face but he caught on that I needed him. He came up to the podium and, shielded by the applause, I told him: "Talk. I don't care what about. Just talk. You are campaigning for Mennen." Gus Scholle loved to talk, and the campaign of 1950 was already upon us, so he made an impassioned plea for Mennen Williams and put in several plugs for the current issues that were part of the Democratic program. When the meeting was over, we both had a hearty laugh. It had been no laughing matter to me while I was being heckled. Gus had a lot of fun later, teasing me about shutting up unwanted speakers.

That district convention became legendary, although the legend was distorted by the Republicans, who used it as the basis for a radio skit called "Blood on the Pavement." The highly exaggerated story of the Wayne County Democratic district conventions was aired as an ad on several radio stations for weeks. My fishwife voice was mimicked, calling "Order, order" throughout the skit. Nick Rothe, the 14th Congressional District chairman and a labor lawyer, also had problems maintaining order at his district convention. He had used his wife's small wooden potato masher as a gavel, but the skit had him presiding with a baseball bat. The radio skit was a ridiculous performance, but it created a lot of talk and helped rather than hurt us.

7

MENNEN
WINS A RECOUNT BY A
SLIGHT MARGARINE

T HE BATTLE FOR THE GOVERNORSHIP in 1950 started almost as soon
as the 1948 election was over. The Republicans wanted to make
sure that Governor Williams's first election was a fluke and that
none of his programs would ever go into effect. They didn't know Mennen Williams very well.

From the day he was sworn in as governor on January 1, 1949, Mennen was determined to find a way to meet the growing needs of the state.
He was equally adamant that working people shouldn't have to shoulder
the burden alone. Every chance he got, he let the legislature and the people know that he would not stand for additional taxes on things that people bought and used. He also said he wouldn't allow the tax burden to be
shifted onto property owners. There had been some talk of holding back
or reducing state funds to schools, cities, or other local units of government, and forcing property owners to pick up the slack.

Mennen never neglected his duties as governor, but he spent evenings and weekends taking his story to the people—in the streets, in the
neighborhoods, in the factories, in the barbershops, in the bakeries, in
small businesses all over Michigan. In those days, that's how a good politician got the message across. Mennen did it better than anyone before
him had done. His efforts increased public awareness and caused people
to start asking questions.

The Republican-controlled legislature refused to consider any significant bills presented by the governor and fought him at every turn. He vetoed any bill that he felt would be detrimental to the people. And there

were enough Democrats in the Michigan House of Representatives to uphold his vetoes. Because of the standoff, little progress was made.

Several Republican candidates announced their intentions to run for governor late in 1949. As each new one emerged, Mennen's chances of being reelected grew stronger. The Republican candidates foolishly started an early fight against each other. By primary time, five of them were competing for their party's nomination.

It was a credit to Mennen's strength and the growing respect he was building among Democrats that no one ran against him in the primary. But it was clear that there was a big fight ahead. Neil Staebler, the new state party chairman, persuaded Sid Woolner to leave his job in audio-visual work at the Jam Handy firm to become coordinator for the Democratic candidates, with heavy emphasis on the governor's campaign. Later on, Mennen appointed Sid as the deputy wherever there was trouble, because Sid could handle it.

Sid was a wise choice. He had studied economics and political science at the University of Michigan. Through his audio-visual production work with Jam Handy, he had good experience in getting things done and in getting a message across. The 1950 campaign was the first of five which he coordinated for the party. He knew how to keep us all together and going in one direction. He had solid ideas and the gentle firmness to carry them out. If he said, "This is it," it was. He never argued or lost his temper.

Sid's only fault, if he had one, was not having the heart to maintain discipline in later campaigns when we had a larger staff. The mechanics of running the office and the day-to-day problems of the campaign just were not his thing. Planning strategy and matching wits with our opponents were his great strengths to the party. We made a great team. Running the office was fun. When things seemed overwhelming, Sid's wonderful sense of humor always saved me.

Sid and I had great respect for Mennen, and he trusted us both implicitly. Sid and I knew Mennen well enough to expect the unexpected from him. When Mennen wanted to talk, we knew we had better be ready. Mennen wasn't one for small talk, and he didn't like to waste time.

About noon one day, Mennen called and asked Sid and me to meet him at Sanders downtown. The place was packed. And, standing up in the middle of the restaurant, eating the gooiest of hot fudge sundaes, was the governor. Sam McIntire, Mennen's first state police aide, was with him. We had our meeting standing right there. The customers, who had to walk around our little group, probably wondered what was going on. When we were finished, Mennen waved and smiled at the crowd and left for his next meeting, leaving Sid and me standing alone. We hadn't had time to catch our breath, let alone eat a sundae or a sandwich. We got a bite to eat somewhere else.

Sid made practical use of every advantage available to the Democrats that year. Wayne County districts now had friendly chairmen, and Sid inspired them to make every effort to spread the governor's story, to put on a heavy registration drive and, later, to get out the vote. Neil Staebler devoted his time to traveling outstate unearthing Democrats in every county, and he found some who had been inactive for years. He persuaded them, too, to have a registration drive and concentrate on getting out the vote.

It was slow going. In many areas of Michigan, especially away from the bigger cities, it was still not socially acceptable to admit being a Democrat, but Mennen was having an effect. People began to speak out more in favor of him and his ideas, and the party began to grow.

Even though Mennen was governor, the campaign was still a sparse affair. There was little money in the Democratic party till and an even smaller campaign staff than in 1948. During the day I kept up my work as secretary-treasurer of the telephone workers' federation, but evenings and weekends found me in Mennen's campaign headquarters. My most vivid recollection of the 1950 campaign was standing on the corner by the old National Bank of Detroit on Woodward Avenue in Detroit at ten o'clock at night, my arms full to overflowing with packages of campaign material to mail. Sid was to join me, but a last-minute telephone call had held him up. It had started to snow, and the wind almost swept me off my feet. For a few minutes I doubted my sanity.

No one on the campaign staff except Sid was on salary. The only evening staff he had was his mother, Olive Woolner, and myself. If we did anything but run the mimeograph, stuff envelopes, lick stamps, count material, and package it, I don't remember it. Learning the hard way stood me in good stead when I had to put volunteers to work in later campaigns. Peg Edwards and Pat Taylor were the mainstays of the volunteer daytime staff. The campaign office was so small, Peg and Pat were almost sitting in each other's laps. There was little room for other volunteers.

Besides giving us all practical experience, the 1950 campaign showed us how Mennen Williams campaigned. The first time I was given the responsibility to see that he got from one meeting to another on time gave me new insight into his character. He was missing when it was time for him to leave one gathering and head for the next one. Hearing excited voices in the kitchen, I investigated. There he was, congratulating the cook and greeting all the help. The times that I found him in similar places are too many to recall. It didn't matter whether we were late leaving to go to the next meeting, this was always a stop he made whenever he could.

That day taught me something else. Mennen took me aside just before he went up to the speaker's table. "Be sure Sam McIntire gets lunch, too," he said, referring to his state police aide. All the years I worked with Mennen Williams it was understood I would make sure his trooper aides were fed. It was no chore because the state police aides were like family. Their faces became familiar to everyone, and their pleasant dispositions won them many friends. Many years later, at the wedding of Wendy Williams, Mennen and Nancy's daughter, Bill Carter rushed up and hugged me and Adelaide Hart and her sister, Helen. Bill's wife looked on in amazement, wondering why her husband, who had been one of Mennen's state police aides, was so glad to see three elderly ladies.

The 1950 campaign saw the first glimmer of what later would be an important part of Michigan politics—the involvement of religious leaders in campaigns and issues. Sid and I learned that a number of Protestant ministers and Catholic priests were interested in forming a committee to sponsor a nonpartisan "Meet Your Candidate" night. As the secretary-treasurer of my union, I received an invitation to become a sponsoring member. After several talks with Sid and the governor, I contacted the Reverend Thomas Murphy, of the Roman Catholic Archdiocese of Detroit, on Mennen's behalf. Two meetings were held, although it would be another two years before much activity began.

We concentrated on registration and getting out the vote for Mennen and the other Democratic candidates. There was very little money for campaign literature or anything else. We relied on the congressional district party organizations, which by now had friendly chairmen, to do the work the 1948 staff had done.

Mennen's influence on the party was beginning to take hold. Neil Staebler, who had been appointed to succeed Hicks Griffiths as state party chairman, was elected to that office at the state convention. This time, we won other party offices as well. Adelaide Hart, who was working very hard for Mennen, was the convention's choice for vice chairman.

That year, the state Democratic party had a big conference on Mackinac Island. Vice President Alben Barkley, who had helped enact New Deal legislation during his many years in Congress, was the speaker. He was a Kentuckian and quite popular among Democrats. It was my responsibility to see that everyone had rooms. Of course, they all wanted to stay at the conference headquarters, the Grand Hotel—the one with the sweeping white veranda a full block long, with planters full of red geraniums every few feet. Reservations were supposed to have been received at least a week before. Working with the hotel management, I had felt we were in good shape and most of my work had been done before the conference started.

At the last minute, a large number of people decided to come to the conference, without reservations. The only thing I could do was have the hotel set up a desk and a telephone for me in the lobby. Armed with a list of the phone numbers of the smaller hotels, one by one I found places for the often irate people who didn't see any reason why they couldn't stay right there in the Grand Hotel. Thankfully, I had a good supply of patience and quietly convinced the people there just was not another room left and that they were very fortunate the other hotels were making rooms available for them. I didn't know it at the time, but all afternoon Earl Reynolds, vice president of the Congress Hotel in Chicago, had been sitting near me in the lobby, taking in the scene. When it all quieted down, he came over, introduced himself, gave me his card, and said: "If you ever decide you want a job in Chicago, come and see me. I would like to have someone like you working for me at convention time."

(Two years later, at the 1952 Democratic National Convention in Chicago, I stayed at the Congress Hotel. One day I found a note in my mailbox inviting me to have lunch with the man I had met at the Grand Hotel. As usual, I was tied up in a committee meeting and couldn't get away for lunch, but I went to see him and thanked him. Obviously, I was hopelessly, and happily, tied up in politics.)

In the 1950 election for governor, the five Republicans brought out a big primary vote, but it was well split among them. Former Governor Harry F. Kelly, who had been Michigan's chief executive from 1943 to 1946, won easily. Mennen was unopposed in the primary, so there was no contest for us. The general election was another story.

Unless you have worked closely in a political campaign, you can't possibly imagine the lengths your opponent will go to defeat you. The weekend before an election always had us all a bundle of nerves, watching for what trick might be played on us, although in the fall of 1950 we were caught by surprise.

I had asked for space on the back page of that month's issue of our telephone federation paper, knowing that it would be read by anyone who handled it as well as by our members across the state. I had Mennen Williams's picture and a story of his accomplishments displayed prominently on that back page. According to our usual schedule, the papers would be delivered to our members a few days before the election, but somewhere between the printer and the post office they all disappeared. They weren't delivered until two days after the election. Neither the union nor the party ever found out exactly how the papers were diverted.

Rain and snow on an election day always meant trouble for us. On that Tuesday, November 7, our hearts were as heavy as the rainclouds that gathered just as the factory workers were walking out the gates. The rain soon turned to a light snow and the streets were quickly covered by slush. We knew it would take real dedication for working people to stop on the way home, or to forsake a warm and dry home later on, just to vote. We were right. Later, more than one told us sadly, "I didn't think you really needed my vote."

The 1950 election had been a hard-fought campaign, and the vote was extremely close. Not long after the polls closed, Harry Kelly took a look at the first returns and concluded he had beaten Mennen. He headed for Florida and a much-needed vacation. Neil called Sid early the next morning to tell him there was evidence that some mistakes had been made. Neil was sure that enough errors would turn up to change the outcome. Over the next few days, as local election officials checked the results, additional mistakes were discovered. The outcome kept changing back and forth as the official count continued. When it was complete, Mennen had a narrow victory. Harry Kelly had to turn around and come back from his trip. All the rest of us had to go back to work.

The Republicans still controlled the local election boards outstate as well as the state Board of Canvassers. They were sure they could easily win a recount over the poverty-stricken Democratic party. But in demanding a recount, the Republicans didn't reckon on the determination of the new Democratic party or the quick thinking of the governor. The Republicans had asked that ballots be protected in Detroit and other areas where Democratic votes were heavy. Governor Williams sent the Michigan State Police all over the state to impound the ballots so they couldn't be tampered with. A written accounting was made, showing where the ballots were found. Some had been hidden under beds and mattresses in the homes of precinct captains in Republican areas. One box had been stashed in an empty tomb in a village cemetery. Without the power of the governor to impound the ballots, many of the votes for him would surely have been lost.[1] (There was another recount in 1952. The vote wasn't close in 1954, but Jim Hare, who was elected secretary of state that year, immediately took steps to reform the election procedure.)

The Democratic party had no money to hire personnel for that first recount in 1950, although the Republicans seemed to have unlimited funds to retain high-priced lawyers. Each party had its own team watching over the process. Sid Woolner was asked to oversee the recount for us. George Edwards, a lawyer who had been a popular member of the Detroit Common Council, immediately offered to help. (George later became a state supreme court justice and a federal appeals court judge.) He brought a sharp legal mind and shrewd understanding of politics to the effort. He was joined by other able attorneys, including John Brennan and Sam Ostrow.

To get ready for this fight, George and Sid made an intense study of election laws relating to counting and recording ballots. Sid always said that a strategy devised by George was the key to winning the recount. The Republicans tended to handle the recount in each county independently. All our people, however, were alerted to watch for several specific errors, such as pencil marks that would invalidate the paper ballots. Many times the same problems would be found from county to county.

George and Sid had two full-time volunteers who helped train other volunteers to supervise the ballot counting. My union office released me, so I ran the Democratic office overseeing the recount for us. Neil Staebler, meanwhile, had put out an urgent call for volunteers and was successful beyond his dreams. They turned up in great numbers and worked long hours. Every afternoon, after teaching all day, Adelaide Hart supervised the vote counting in the Wayne County office. Others pitched in and did the same thing in other places. Despite the seriousness of the matter at stake, we had some chuckles.

We hit the jackpot the day our volunteers found that in Macomb County the yes votes for yellow margarine had been included in the tally for the Republican candidate for governor. The yellow margarine vote was a statewide ballot question on whether yellow coloring should be allowed in oleomargarine. It was a big issue. The people wanted it, but for years the dairy industry had opposed it out of fear it would hurt the butter business. After we uncovered the error in Macomb County tabulations, when anyone asked us how the recount was going, we'd reply that we were ahead "by a slight margarine."

Winning the recount was a great victory for the governor and his loyal staff and volunteers. The Republicans had sent in secretaries and hired help to do the counting for them. One of their workers asked one of ours why the Democratic side fought so hard for every vote, remarking, "You'll get paid anyway." The Democratic worker drew himself to his full height and said proudly: "We don't work for pay. We are volunteers."

There was great jubilation among Mennen's supporters when the recount was finally halted. As the recount continued, Mennen's unofficial vote total had been growing. The recount wasn't completely finished, but it was obvious Kelly couldn't win, and he gave up. The official tally then went back to the original totals—935,152 for Mennen Williams and 933,998 for Harry Kelly, a scant difference of 1,154 votes. Mennen's official victory margin would have been even greater if the recount had continued, because most of the early counting mistakes had erroneously given votes to Kelly.

Mennen was the only Democrat elected to the State Administrative Board that year. Attorney General Stephen Roth, who later became a federal judge, was defeated. So was Lieutenant Governor John Connolly.

71

Phil Hart, who later became a much-loved U. S. senator, didn't get elected as secretary of state. Mennen couldn't even get a second to a motion in the Ad Board meetings. And Republicans still had a majority in both the Michigan House and Senate.

The problems in tallying the 1950 election totals led to the creation of a state Bureau of Elections to help the secretary of state oversee the voting process. The recount that year, and the one in 1952, also served another important function for Democrats. Appeals for help in the 1950 and 1952 recounts brought out ever-increasing numbers of men and women who were no longer afraid. Working together and winning gave them courage. In fact, Sid Woolner said that it was the recounts of 1950 and 1952 that laid the foundation for the huge victory we were to enjoy in 1954 and for a strong Democratic party. Wisely, the governor was meticulous in thanking everyone for all the help he got in the recounts, no matter how small the contribution of time and energy. People began to realize that giving money was not the key to being recognized as an active Democrat.

The fact that Governor Williams won in 1950 was an unpleasant surprise for the Republicans. Two years earlier, there was speculation that Mennen pulled votes from Republicans who saw him as a way to get rid of Kim Sigler. The Republicans hadn't expected Mennen to win again. The legislature had been so sure he would lose in 1950 that they continued to play games with the state financial deficit. They pretended to make cutbacks and passed a few bills, but they knew more funds would have to be found later on, just to keep things going. Mennen continued to use his veto power to prevent the Republican majority from getting too far afield or saddling working people with the problem.

Here's how the Democratic State Central Committee sized up the situation in a party issues paper written in 1958:

> In January 1951, to their surprise, Williams was back and he again recommended the corporation profits tax. This time the Republican leaders admitted that new revenues would have to be found. Republicans joined with Democrats in the House to pass a bill for a corporation profits tax. But the bill went to the Senate Taxation Committee which was headed by Republican Senator George Higgins, one of the world's largest General Motors dealers. He killed it by the simple process of refusing to call a committee meeting, posting a sign on his committee room door saying "Closed till 1952."

> This performance caused the Republican Speaker of the House, Rep. [Victor] Knox, to issue his famous statement that the "baleful influence" of lobbyists representing the Michigan Manufacturers Association had prevented a solution of the state's financial problem.

In spite of what seemed a losing battle, Mennen continued to take his story directly to the people. The Democrats even put on a fund drive so that he could present a special television program to make his case that a corporate profits tax was needed to balance the budget. But Republicans in the legislature wouldn't hear of it. Instead, they kept increasing taxes and fees of all sorts, many of them especially hurtful to working people. That was no solution; it barely kept things afloat from year to year. Eventually, in 1967, under a *Republican* administration, the state adopted a tax on corporate and business income along with a personal income tax. In 1975, the state switched to a business tax that would bring in steady revenue even when profits were down—and that change, too, was made under a Republican administration.

NOTES

1. More on this recount may be found in the Bureau of Elections of the Michigan Department of State in Lansing and among the papers of G. Mennen Williams in the Michigan Historical Collections, Bentley Historical Library, University of Michigan, Ann Arbor.

8

STATE FAIR APPOINTMENT
COWS, HORSES, AND BOB HOPE

M ENNEN HAD GREAT STRENGTH of character and a strong sense of
honor and duty, in his personal as well as his public life. He
demanded similar conduct from his staff. Frank Blackford,
Mennen's legislative secretary from 1951–54, was impressed by the responsibility Mennen placed upon himself—and his staff—to remain
above reproach in public and personal matters.

Frank understood the pressures of political life. He gave many years
of distinguished service in some of the most difficult positions in state
government while Mennen was governor. While serving on the Liquor
Control Commission, Frank continued to advise the governor on several
of the touchiest issues, such as taxes. Later, he became insurance commissioner under Mennen.

"Wives loved him," Frank recalled. "If he found one of his appointees was cheating on his wife, that was it. I know of many resignations
that resulted from this. We were all aware of this side of him. We were
privileged to serve with him. In twelve years there wasn't even a hint of a
scandal in his administration. Not that there weren't those who looked
for it."

The closest Mennen Williams came to having a scandal was when he
was slow in firing the State Fair manager. Admittedly, no elected official
who has to make a large number of appointments can possibly know all
the people personally. Even now, there are at least three major appointments where the wrong choice can spell disaster for a Michigan governor:
the Liquor Control Commission, the Office of the Racing Commissioner,

and the State Fair. It's easy for people in these places to take money under the table.

For example, around 1950, it would have been possible to shake down State Fair concessionaires for a favorable location—one easily accessible to fairgoers—and for other concessions (no pun intended). The biggest source of under-the-table money to be made was from the huge carnival, which had fifty or sixty rides and exhibits, to say nothing of the shill games and girlie shows. Operators of dozens of food stands could be made to purchase all their supplies through an agent appointed by the management, with prices double what they would have been from a wholesale dealer. Obviously, when this goes on, all kinds of people get something out of it.

There were persistent rumors that all was not well at the State Fair. The governor had taken to calling me his catalyst, so in the middle of August 1950 he appointed me to a vacancy on the State Fair Board. As I think of it now, I am sure he wouldn't have appointed me if he could have known what I would go through my first two years on the board. Everyone knew that I was there as the governor's eyes and ears and certainly did not welcome me with open arms. No one spoke to me unless it couldn't be avoided. At fair time Jimmy Friel, the manager, completely ignored me. None of the perks that came with appointment to the board were offered to me, and I had to learn my way around.

Later, I learned that each Fair Board member was allocated a large number of free tickets, for entrance to the Fair itself and to the entertainment in both the coliseum and the grandstand. Each member was also given round-the-clock, personal use of a well-equipped house trailer on the grounds during the entire ten days of the fair, as well as several parking spaces. Fair Board members had their pictures taken with every celebrity who showed up to entertain. These are only a few of the niceties that came with being a member of the State Fair Board—none of which I received.

The only friendly face for me was the Republican member in charge of the grandstand. He and I became good friends, and he gave me a lot of tips. One day, he asked for my help. He was having problems with a couple of top people on the governor's staff who were demanding special treatment for themselves and their guests. He said it wouldn't be so bad if they had not made their demands in front of anyone who happened to be around, and it had gotten to be embarrassing for him. A quiet word in the right ear on the governor's staff, and I was able to take care of that problem quickly. Mennen never knew I had intervened.

During fair time, I walked around the grounds at all hours of the day and night, ostensibly to take down any political signs posted on poles, garbage containers, and so forth. What I was looking for was proof that there were payoffs. Since no one would talk to me, I decided to find the evidence myself. By sheer perseverance, I picked up a little information here and a little there. Often, I was followed. It never bothered me until a private plane carrying one of the alleged principals in the collection of the payoffs was blown up and he was killed. His office was rifled and all his records stolen that same night. After that, I was more careful.

Repeatedly, I urged Mennen to fire Jimmy Friel, because I feared the goings-on at the State Fair were going to cause Mennen trouble. Mennen would answer by telling me to give him proof. It frustrated me that I never could tell him that, at midnight, Party A put $10,000 in the hands of Party B and told Party B it was a bribe. One night, I came very close to seeing that, but the principals caught a glimpse of me and quickly went in opposite directions.

Partly at my urging, Mennen asked Attorney General Stephen Roth to make an investigation of the entire operation. Steve worked with Irving Feldman, assistant attorney general, and Lieutenant Joseph Sheridan of the Michigan State Police. In December 1950, Steve Roth submitted a report to the governor with a number of good suggestions, among them that the Fair Board set up formal procedures for conducting business and spell out the limits of power exercised by the fair management. The report especially mentioned the need to control the handling of concessions and other fair contracts. It questioned whether "so-called 'games of skill'" should be permitted at a state fair. If they are, Roth said, police should perform background checks to keep out "undesirable" operators and "fronts." He also urged the board to prevent fair employees from benefiting, directly or indirectly, from any business or concession at the fair.[1]

Between the lines, the report said a great deal, but there were no outright accusations of wrongdoing. It bothered me that not even the state police and the attorney general could unearth any proof. All I could think was that either the board members condoned what was going on or didn't know about it. It certainly seemed to be common knowledge among a great number of other people, however.

Billie Farnum, a close friend of the governor's who gave many years of service to Michigan both inside and outside of government, helped resolve the issue. A discreet man as well as a keen observer, he convinced Mennen to replace the manager after the fair in 1951. Later, we learned that Frank Millard, the Republican who defeated Steve Roth for attorney general in 1950, was planning an exposé of State Fair operations. Mennen's move made that unnecessary.

When Jimmy Friel was fired, so was his assistant, an ambitious young fellow by the name of Jerome P. "Jerry" Cavanagh. This is the same Jerry Cavanagh who later would become mayor of Detroit and somewhat of a national urban figure in the 1960s. He ran against Mennen in the Democratic primary for the U. S. Senate in 1966 and was defeated.

Enough vacancies had occurred on the Fair Board by 1951 to yield a healthy majority of Democrats, most of them farmers and experts in all the areas represented by the fair—cattle, horses, sheep, pigs, poultry, you name it. Two other women besides me were appointed. One was a schoolteacher; the other was the mayor of East Detroit. The men on the Fair Board acted like a bunch of schoolkids, behaving only when the teacher was around and getting into mischief when she wasn't. In this case, I was the teacher. Their mischief mainly consisted of drinking too much beer and making the rounds of the girlie shows. None of it was very bad or malicious. They were sure I would tell Mennen if they misbehaved. Once or twice I was tempted to tell him, but I never did.

The Fair Board formed a committee to find a new manager, and I was appointed chairman. At the time, the Fair Board voted to select the manager but it was always the governor's choice. To my mind, Jim Hare would be perfect for the job. He was an excellent organizer, had been very active in teachers' affairs, and had worked several summers as personnel director at the Fair. When I suggested him to Mennen, he told me to convince Ed Meade, his assistant for agriculture, who already had proposed a candidate.

It seemed to me that the man Ed had in mind could be susceptible to temptation. Not only that, but he lacked the qualifications of Jimmy Friel, who, to his credit, had brilliant ideas. Ed Meade, who was from Newaygo County and owned a farm, was suspicious of anyone from the city, such as Jim Hare and me, and fought hard for his candidate. We met often in the office of Frank Blackford to discuss the appointment. With great relish, Frank would say to the other staff members, "Pull up a chair. Here we go again." They all thought our heated discussions were great fun, but I didn't. It was serious business, and I worried about what would happen if Ed won. Several times I thought I had him convinced, only to get home and have Mennen call to tell me that Ed still wanted his candidate. Ed was well-known and well-liked in the outstate area where Mennen wanted to become better known, so he listened carefully to him. Mennen Williams disliked this sort of controversy between valued friends, and he kept putting off a decision until the very last moment. It's hard for me to remember ever being more upset with him.

The evening before the meeting at which the Fair Board was to choose a new manager, the whole clique of outstate farmers on the board, buoyed by "light" refreshments, stayed up most of the night deciding how they were going to get the best of Berthelot this time.

Again, Billie Farnum, who served on the board with me, came to the rescue. He reached Mennen that night and convinced him I was right on the choice of Jim Hare for manager. Imagine the connivers' reactions to the governor's last-minute phone calls telling them "Hare for manager."

Jim Hare was chosen, brought in, and congratulated, and then the whole rest of the board disappeared, leaving Jim and me to go to lunch alone—Jim with a congratulatory carnation from the board in his lapel. Some kind soul called the newspapers, and there was a nasty story about Berthelot's railroading Jim Hare in as manager of the State Fair.

Jim had a tough job, but he was extremely capable and was able to recruit an excellent staff. Many were teachers. By sheer good nature and perseverance, he won over the whole board, and by State Fair time in 1952, everyone was working in harmony. They even allowed me use of a trailer on the grounds at fair time.

The State Fair is another world. One of the best illustrations is what happened when we were interviewing companies who were bidding to put on the carnival. Glenn Wade had a good operation, and I convinced the board this was the show we should have. Later, the man who made the presentation for Glenn got me in a corner and asked, "What is this going to cost us?" Confused, I asked him what he meant. He said, "The contract, of course." With real pride I was able to say: "Not one red cent. You've gotten the contract fair and square and there are no strings attached." He couldn't believe it. It was very hard to convince concessionaires and others doing business with the State Fair that they didn't have to pay under the table for anything. This was the clearest evidence I ever got about what I had suspected.

Little by little, we were able to get rid of the worst of the girlie shows —Sally Rand, the fan dancer, had been there one year—and all of the crooked game shows. It was a proud time for all of us when the State Fair started to show a profit. The fair made money, and the people had a good time and were not cheated by the games. Some critics began to refer to it as the "Sunday School Fair," but we didn't mind.

During the eleven years I served on the Fair Board, the Republican-controlled Senate would not confirm me. They never turned me down, they just wouldn't confirm me. Every time the legislature convened, Mennen reappointed me; when they went home, he went through the same procedure—for ten years. But in the last year of my service, I was finally confirmed, largely because of the brother of my old Republican friend who had managed the grandstand.

One of the improvements we were able to get from the legislature was a new Women's Building. The old one was jammed full of everything produced for the fair by women, from apple jelly to yarn dolls. The structure was so old and cramped that I feared a tragedy might happen. The building was unsafe, and a number of people could have been badly hurt if the top floor had given way. We finally convinced the powers that be to raze it.

Another way I helped was to mediate when a strike threatened. One was a silly battle between two labor unions over the employees of the ginger ale concessions. In settling that argument, I suffered as much as they did. The only meeting place I could find, or so I said, was a Quonset hut with windows facing west. It was a hot day, and the sun really glared through the closed windows. That didn't stop me from running a businesslike meeting and keeping them there until they came to a sensible compromise. The sun helped me settle that dispute, I am sure.

There were some moments straight out of vaudeville, but they weren't part of a show. The year we had a big Army exhibit, an ex-GI, fueled by some liquid encouragement, started one of the tanks in the middle of the night and headed straight for the row of house trailers where the Fair Board members stayed during the fair. Someone stopped him before he rolled over the trailers, board members and all.

Every year we had big-name celebrities in the grandstand and the coliseum. Some just went through the motions. Others, like Bob Hope and Louie Armstrong, gave their all. Armstrong came off the stage the year he was there, smiled and said, "Don't get near me. I'm soaking wet." It was true. He looked as if he didn't have a dry stitch on him.

Bob Hope not only performed but wanted to ride in the State Fair parade. Along the parade route, he hopped out of his car and did a few dance steps. When we got to the fairgrounds, the waitresses from the coliseum restaurant had gone out on strike. Bob told us very nicely that he could not perform while the strike was on. He asked if he could just sit quietly in the grandstand. While he sat there, I made sure no one bothered him. Carolyn Burns, the official hostess for the State Fair, quickly rescued Bob and took him to meet her staff, who shared their lunch with him. What started as a potential calamity turned into an enjoyable time for all, and Bob Hope scored some points with working people.

Meanwhile, Billie Farnum was trying to settle the strike. His negotiations succeeded, but not before it was too late for both the afternoon and evening shows. True to his word, Bob Hope did not perform that day. But Bob and a new young singer gave an excellent performance the next day. She was scheduled to perform alone on the following day, since he had been booked for only two days. She was scared—I heard her telling him she couldn't carry the show by herself. He stayed and performed free for another day, just to help a young entertainer.

We had top celebrities at the State Fair the eleven years I was on the board, and I never bothered to have my picture taken with them. My children and grandchildren could shoot me for it now, but I was too busy at the time.

The year we had Ricky Nelson (that's what they called him when he was a teenage heartthrob) we had all sorts of problems keeping him safe. Jerry Lacey, one of our staff members with a faint resemblance to young Nelson, nearly had his back broken when a wild teenage girl climbed up on a temporary partition in one of the offices and jumped down on him. Snuffy McGill, a photographer who worked with Mennen and his staff on many projects, was our State Fair photographer that year. His office was broken into and all the boxes of undeveloped film were stolen. Whoever took them was expecting to see Ricky Nelson. Instead they got pictures of my grandchildren and other board members' families.

The fact that Mennen Williams lived in a more serious world than the entertainment sphere was brought sharply to my attention the year Tennessee Ernie Ford was a featured singer. Since it was an election year, we decided we could get a little free publicity if Mennen had his picture taken with Ford, who was a Democrat. It was easy for Dick Frederick, the Fair's public relations man, to arrange, and I accompanied Mennen to Ford's hotel. We were to meet the photographer and the press there. All the way in the car, Mennen was in a deep study, surely involving legislative matters. When we were almost there, he suddenly looked up at me and said, plaintively, "Who is Tennessee Ernie Ford?" The meeting between the two was cordial, and Ford helped make news by telling Mennen he brought best wishes from the governor of Tennessee, also a Democrat. The picture was good, and the papers made quite a story of it on the entertainment pages.

Despite Mennen's lack of interest in the operations of the State Fair, he looked forward to the fair itself and always wanted to cut the ribbon on opening day. As often as possible, Mennen attended the dinners honoring the many fair winners and civic groups that helped with the fair.

Each year a State Fair queen was chosen by a group of civic organizations. The crowning was always a gala and well-attended affair. For several years Mennen did the honors and was planning to do so this particular year. We had told the papers that the governor would crown the queen, and the event was planned around that. To our dismay we belatedly learned Ed Carey was being honored at a dinner the same night. Ed, who later became a member of the Detroit Common Council, was at the time a leader of the beleagured Democratic minority in the state House of Representatives. He and Mennen had become great friends.

Mennen was adamant that he had to go to Ed Carey's dinner. We had already announced that he was to crown the queen at the State Fair, I pointed out, and he just couldn't let down all the people who were expecting him. We went round and round, with Mennen insisting he had to at least drop in at Ed's dinner. We finally compromised. He agreed he would stay at the dinner just long enough to make a laudatory speech in Ed's behalf, and then would leave to crown the queen. To make sure he didn't get waylaid, I went with him to Ed's dinner. Luckily the dinner was held at a hall not far from the fairgrounds.

Pete Buback, the Wayne County clerk, was toastmaster of the dinner. I got him aside and asked him to please put Mennen on the program early so he could keep his obligation to crown the queen. Pete also was a member of the State Fair Board, so he understood perfectly and agreed to let Mennen go as quickly as possible. However, the desire to keep Mennen there got the best of Pete, and he allowed two other people to make long-winded speeches before he called on the governor. Mennen had had no time to prepare a speech but he was very fond of Ed Carey, so his tribute went on and on. Just when I thought he was going to wind up his speech, he'd think of something else he wanted to say.

Time was short, and I was getting desperate. It was a good thing I had alerted the people handling the Fair ceremony that we might be late and asked them to stall as long as they could. There was only one way I could think of to get him to stop talking and excuse himself. Remembering that Nancy Williams used the tactic of "I'm coming" footsteps when the kids were acting up, I paced loudly up and down the back of the hall. Clump, clump, clump, I went, back and forth, until everyone began to turn around to see who was being so rude.

It worked. Mennen reluctantly wound up his speech and excused himself by telling them he wanted to stay but couldn't because he was expected to crown the queen at the State Fair. His state police aide and I rushed him out of the room. Without a doubt, we broke the speed limit getting back to the Fair. There were loud sighs of relief from Don Swanson, the State Fair manager, and the committee members when we burst into the room. Mennen apologized to the group for keeping them waiting and bestowed all the proper pleasantries on the queen, who beamed happily at being crowned by the governor.

All the way out to the fairgrounds neither one of us spoke. He never mentioned the episode again, but I know he wasn't very happy with me. No matter how much I provoked him at times, he was always a gentleman. Much to my delight, he usually delivered his apologies to me in public, in such a way that no one except the two of us would recognize them as such.

It took two successful State Fairs with Jim Hare as manager for Mennen to concede that I had been right to insist on Jim. As usual, Mennen made his admission in public. He was speaking at the State Fair annual dinner and said how much the fair had improved and what a great job the manager had done. Then he looked over at me and grinned. That was worth all the sleep I had lost over the whole deal.

81

Mennen Williams had so many things to watch, the State Fair was quite far down his list of problems. For me it seemed a never-ending battle to make him understand how important it was that he make good appointments. At the time, the Department of Agriculture wanted complete control of the Fair. It was a continual battle between the department and the Fair Board.

In my two-fingered typing style, I tapped out a two-page, single-spaced letter to Mennen, hoping to convince him it would be a mistake to appoint a certain member of the Agriculture Board to the Fair Board. (He followed my advice.) The letter, written in late May of 1955, was typical of my struggle over the years to make him realize what was at stake with the Fair. Complete with my typos and misspellings, here is what it said in part:

Dear Mennen:

. . . The Agricultural Board is *not* your friend except possibly for a few exceptions. As long as I can remember there has been a running battle between the State Fair Bd. and the Bd. of Agriculture. They have many devious methods for getting their own way. . . . The State Fair would be a much better Fair if we did not have to fight them at every step.

Typical of the stalling tactics they practice is the battle we have every year to get repairs done by the time the Fair opens. . . .

Mennen, I hope I don't have to remind you that the Fair Bd. is one place where you can't be too careful who you put on the Bd. and be too suspicious of their actions. Personally, I don't believe I could stand it to go through what we did a few years ago.

The painful truth is that you do not have any strong people on that Bd. now who will look after your interests in the way it is necessary to do in order to make sure there is no scandal. It worries me greatly that I can't be around there more to just remind them that they'll get stepped on quickly if they get out of line. You probably have several Bd. members that are more popular than I am but they do respect me and recognize that I am going to look after your interests, no matter who gets hurt.

This seems to be such an easy Bd. to fill with members but it is so large as well as touchy that I would use the utmost care in filling the vacancies. . . . You need two or three people on the Bd. that will be interested in getting at the bottom of the business end of the Fair and strong enough to take on the rest of the Bd. in such a nice way that they don't realize what is happening to them. They are good people, most of them but they would be sure we were crazy if we tried to tell them what is going on all the time. . . .

Please trust me in my suspicions of what is going on even if I am not able to give you legal proof. That darn Fair can make your halo slip in the eyes of the people faster than any place I know.

Don't forget either that while both Irv Feldman and Joe Sheridan

[Feldman was the assistant attorney general and Sheridan the state police officer who worked on the attorney general's investigation and report to the governor] are not the easiest people to get along with, you owe both of them a lot in keeping that fair on an even keel and some day I'll tell you some of the peoples lives they saved from scandal by catching them before they got too far off base and letting them off with a good scare. There are a lot of people in this world that spend a great deal of their time protecting you from scandal. Just thank God they believe in you and help yourself by really looking below the surface when you make your appointments. You will keep a lot of us from getting gray hair if you find some top notch people for that Fair soon. . . .

One thing I can tell you emphatically is that we don't need any more "nice People," that have no idea how the other half lives. We need someone who will be pleasant enough but who will be suspicious of even apparently innocent things and dig until they get the right answers.

You don't have to worry about your enemys. You know what they are going to do but in this case your fair weather friends are your worry.

Best regards from your chief worry wart,

Helen Berthelot[2]

It's funny how someone you thought was your enemy can turn out to be your friend, or at least not as much of an enemy as you thought. That came home to me one day in Washington at a social-business function I attended in my role as lobbyist for the Communications Workers of America. One of the other guests was a former state senator who, while in office, had tried to remove me from the Fair Board. He had even checked my attendance record at board meetings, in hopes of building a case against me (my record was fine). He greeted me warmly, turned to his wife, and told her I had been the hardest-working member of the board and that it was because of me that the women had a beautiful new building. He stunned me so that I could scarcely say anything.

When I left the board in 1961, the board passed a warm resolution of tribute, acknowledging rather bluntly that the governor had appointed me specifically to make changes. The resolution credited me with helping to build one of the best "family fairs" in the nation and called me "a beloved woman who has humbly concerned herself only with the tasks of helping others." Walter Goodman, who became manager of the fair shortly after I left the board, wrote me a personal note saying I exerted "a constant effort for good." It almost made it all worthwhile.

NOTES

1. For more on this subject, see the papers of G. Mennen Williams and Helen Berthelot in the Michigan Historical Collections, Bentley Historical Library, University of Michigan, Ann Arbor.

2. For the full text of this May 24, 1955, letter and other correspondence between

Helen Berthelot and G. Mennen Williams, see the papers of Helen Berthelot in the Michigan Historical Collections, Bentley Historical Library, University of Michigan, Ann Arbor.

9

NEVER A DULL MOMENT
GEORGE EDWARDS, BLAIR MOODY, MENNEN WILLIAMS

A FTER THE 1948 CAMPAIGN, politics was in my blood. It took me on
adventures I had never dreamed of as a girl back in Massachusetts—and brought me friendships with more than a few remarkable people.

Peg and George Edwards had become good friends of mine. Because
of our various political activities, we were always running into each other
at meetings, and we had many of the same interests. When they asked
me to help with George's campaign for mayor of Detroit in 1949, I
didn't even think of refusing.

George was a very popular member of Detroit's Common Council.
He was first elected in 1941 while only in his twenties. Two years later,
shortly after he won another term, George entered military service. He
was given a leave of absence from the council but attended the sessions as
often as he could while on furlough. He sent dispatches back home
through the newspapers to let the people know about his program for the
city. In his third campaign for reelection, George won more votes than
any other member of the council, which gave him the honor of becoming
the council president. At the time, he was still overseas, waiting to be
mustered out of the Army. George was reelected two years later and had
been council president four years when he decided to run for mayor in
1949. Before he had enlisted in the service, George had worked for the
UAW. He had been arrested during one of the fierce battles between the
union and the auto companies. The Republican party and all the conservatives shuddered at the thought of a union man as mayor.

From the start there were no holds barred. Mock-up pictures of George Edwards behind bars were tacked up on street corners. Vicious cartoons were everywhere. George was originally from Texas, so the cartoons distributed in black neighborhoods showed him in cowboy hat and boots, swinging a lariat that took the form of a noose. In the heavily white, Archie Bunker-type neighborhoods of Detroit, pictures were distributed showing George meeting with black ministers—a blatant attempt to stir up racial hatred and make enemies for him among white voters as well.

We clearly had our work cut out for us. My CWA duties took up all my time during the day, but I volunteered almost every evening and all the weekends. One Saturday night toward the end of the campaign, Peg and I were frantically trying to get out a mailing, with the help of Pat Taylor, another close friend I had made in politics. In those days you sealed the envelopes by hand and licked the postage stamps yourself. When it came time to put on the stamps, we found a note in the stamp drawer: "Did not have time to get stamps. Will get them first thing on Monday." Time was of prime importance, and we were devastated at the thought of not being able to get those letters in the mail before midnight.

We were in the Lafayette Building in downtown Detroit, just across the street from our CWA office, so I went over and borrowed our entire stock of stamps. The union had just put out a mailing, so there were not as many there as usual. We were still far short.

"Let's take them over to the main post office. Maybe we can find a window open," Peg said. By the time we got there, however, the last window had closed. We checked the vending machines that dispensed stamps, but they only took quarters. Checking CWA petty cash, the Edwards's campaign petty cash, and our pocketbooks, we still came up with only $5 worth of quarters. Not nearly enough.

"Give me what bills you have," I said. "I'll get some quarters." It was after ten o'clock on a Saturday night, but I walked down Michigan Avenue and went into bar after bar, begging quarters from the bartenders. When I told them why I needed the coins, almost all of them were most cooperative. It didn't take me long to get enough quarters to complete our mailing. Peg, Pat, and I took turns, one of us feeding quarters into the stamp machine while the other two stood there and licked the stamps. Looking back, I can't believe that I went bar-hopping so blithely in a rough area of a tough town on a Saturday night. My long-suffering grandmother would have thrown up her hands in frustration.

All our hard work was in vain, however, and George was badly defeated—although the outcome was probably a good thing in the long run. George's career as a jurist started in 1951 when Governor Williams appointed him to the Wayne County Probate Court bench and, shortly after that, to the Wayne County Circuit Court. In 1956, Mennen elevated him to the Michigan Supreme Court. Later, George served as police commissioner in Detroit and helped the city and the police department through some difficult times. President John F. Kennedy appointed him to the federal judiciary in 1963, and George spent the rest of his career as a respected and distinguished member of the U. S. Sixth Circuit Court of Appeals in Cincinnati.

After 1951, George could no longer be involved in party politics because of his judicial position. Nonetheless, he left his mark in a playful way. Starting in the 1952 campaign and in every one I worked in thereafter, I could depend on George Edwards to drop into my office, usually when I wasn't there. On my return I would find a bottle of aspirin, an empty coffee cup, and an Ogden Nash poem along with a note. "You weren't here, so I drank the coffee," he invariably wrote. Seldom did I have to use the aspirins myself, but it wasn't for a lack of adventure or, at times, great difficulty.

In 1952, not only was Mennen in a tough campaign for reelection—Blair Moody faced a difficult fight to retain his U. S. Senate seat. Mennen had appointed him in April 1951, shortly after the death of Senator Arthur Vandenberg, a popular Republican whose leadership during the war had earned him the respect of President Franklin Roosevelt. Afterward, Vandenberg's backing of programs such as the Marshall Plan and a strong international defense system further endeared him even to some Democrats. Vandenberg had been a newspaperman in Grand Rapids before being appointed to the U.S. Senate in 1928.

In some respects Vandenberg was a difficult act to follow, but Blair was more than up to it. He had worked for the *Detroit News* in Washington, D. C., and had a reputation as a solid reporter of national news. Hardworking and eager, he was in his element as a senator. Unfortunately, the Republican who had his eye on the seat, Charles Potter, was a war veteran who had lost part of one leg. Blair had served as a war correspondent, but was not in the service, and sympathy was with the veteran.

Blair had to begin campaigning almost immediately after his appointment. By 1952, Mennen and Blair were out as often as possible, all over the state. While the campaign was in full swing, Mennen and Blair planned to cover the entire Upper Peninsula in one week, going from town to town by private plane. Everyone thought this would be an excellent time for three other people to go too—Nancy Williams, Mennen's wife; Adelaide Hart, the state party vice chairman; and me, the director of organization for the state campaigns. Mennen and Blair told me, repeatedly, that they wanted me to see firsthand all the problems they ran up against, while Nancy and Adelaide could campaign with the women's groups. We were to go by car. By getting up early, and with Nancy driving late, we could keep up with most of the schedule.

It was not what I would call a normal campaign trip. There were times when our adventures seemed like plots for "I Love Lucy," which was just becoming popular. Between catastrophes, we had a lot of fun. Nancy and Adelaide insisted for years that I ate whitefish at every meal, but I only had it for lunch and dinner.

One of our first stops was at Sault Ste. Marie. Our meetings in the Soo were great, thanks to the advance work by Paul Adams and Ray Clevenger, two prominent Democrats from the region. We were all elated. That night, Nancy, Adelaide, and I shared a big room on the second floor of the Ojibwa Hotel. The hotel was not very high up, and our room looked right out on the sidewalk. When I went to pull down the shade on the big picture window, the shade came down all right—right off the roller. It was late, and calls to the desk brought no response. After several attempts, the three of us, laughing so hard that we could hardly manage it, hung a blanket over the curtain rod. We didn't know it until morning but, sometime in the night, the blanket came down, too. It was a good thing we had been too tired to turn on the lights.

This was a sign of what was to come. The morning we started out from Manistique, it was freezing, so we put on long-sleeved blouses and wool suits. How we were to regret it before the day was over and, later in the same day, how we would rejoice in their warmth. We grabbed a quick cup of coffee, orange juice, and toast and rushed off. We had to be in Iron River for a luncheon at noon, and we had a good 150 miles to cover on two-lane roads.

When we arrived, the people of Iron River were celebrating their centennial, and everyone was in period costume. Nancy looked for Mennen. Blair Moody took her aside and told her that he had flown to Mackinac Island because their daughter Wendy had been run over by a horse-drawn carriage. Nancy nearly fell over, but Blair assured her that Mennen had talked to the doctor who had examined her and was told she was only slightly bruised. If everything was all right, Mennen would be back after lunch. By this time, the local committee had taken Nancy Williams's car with all our luggage, including our makeup. Little did we know then that we would not see the car, the luggage, or our makeup again until the committee people met us in Wisconsin at midnight.

The crowd had expected speeches by both Mennen and Blair. Blair handled it with ease. He explained what had happened and gave a good outline of what Mennen had planned to say. Then he changed hats and gave an informative talk on foreign policy and other national issues.

By now it was lunchtime, and lunch was in a town fifteen miles away. A parade of old cars was formed, with drivers and passengers in vintage costumes. They made room for us in various cars. Nancy Williams was to lead the parade with the centennial chairman, Burr Sherwood, the local superintendent of schools. He drove an early Ford coupe. Because he was juggling the details of so many events, a little thing like gasoline for the car slipped his mind. About halfway to lunch, Burr and Nancy's car stopped short, completely out of gas. There was a screeching of brakes all down the parade route. The parade was held up fifteen minutes until someone got a can of gas for the lead car.

By the time we arrived, the luncheon hosts were a little nervous, but the program went as planned. As soon as the welcoming speeches and Blair Moody's response were over, we were rushed back into town to the high school football stadium for the next event. Mennen met us there with the good news that Wendy was fine.

There was a reservation of American Indians in the area, and local leaders had decided that Blair and Mennen should be inducted as members of the tribe. We weren't too close to the ceremony, but we could see them in the distance, wearing long feather headdresses, doing a traditional Indian dance. Mennen Williams, who enjoyed calling square dances, could always learn any ethnic dance easily, and was doing fine. Blair Moody was trying mightily, but he was looking at his feet and the feet of the man ahead of him most of the time. From there, the two candidates were carried off for a tour of the local iron mine. Women were not allowed to go down into the mine. The committee had other plans for Nancy Williams.

Since nearly every male in the city had grown a beard, one of the big events of the day was a beard-judging contest. Nancy was to award the prizes. Luckily, she didn't have to be a judge: that would have been as much of a mistake as judging a beauty contest. The spectators were all seated in the bleachers. The three of us were given places of honor, several yards away from anyone else or any shade and fully exposed to the elements. By now, the sun had come out, and it was blistering hot. There we were, in the full rays of the sun, still in our wool suits. Finally, we gave up our pride, took off our jackets, and rolled up our sleeves. By late afternoon, our noses were red from sunburn.

We saw hundreds—perhaps thousands—of beards. Red ones, black ones, brown, white, striped ones, full beards, goatees, handlebar mustaches—you name it, it was there. Because Nancy had to award the prizes, we sat there for hours and tried to look interested. Every once in a while, a particularly odd one would make everybody laugh. At last the contest was ended and the judges were toting up the results. But what was this? Two big cars full of angry men with beards had arrived for the contest. They had been given wrong information about the location. They insisted on being included.

At last it was over, and Nancy made a gracious presentation of the awards. She even put on her jacket to do it. "Hurry," we were told. "We are going to be late for the dinner and the pageant starts promptly at eight P.M."

All three of us were put in one big room to get ready. There were fresh flowers, baskets of fruit, and an orchid for each of us. However, there was little time and still no car, which meant no makeup and no fresh clothes. We did our best to freshen up, and I managed to grab one grape. We had barely washed our hands when a delegation of local ladies arrived with three huge picture hats, decorated with big roses. Each hat had wide ribbons to be tied under the chin in a giant bow. Nancy Williams was to pick the one she'd like to wear. She protested briefly, but knew she couldn't avoid it. Thank goodness, Adelaide and I were excused. Nancy was quite a picture: a big centennial hat with a bow under her chin, still wearing that hot and, I am afraid, sweaty, wool suit.

She was a good sport. On the tall and stately Nancy Williams, the hat was actually becoming. So down we went, with our orchids and our sweaty wool suits, and Nancy with her big hat. They were all waiting for us. The governor promptly jumped up, kissed Nancy, and asked the crowd if they didn't think she looked adorable. There was a loud burst of applause, and we all sat down. We were seated on benches, and if there was another square inch in the room, I don't know where it was. There was a delicious fried chicken dinner. The only thing that saved me was that I sat beside Jim Lincoln. Jim weighed well over two hundred pounds, but he was on a strict diet. He drank a glass of water and then watched us devour mounds of food. Because he didn't eat anything and leaned back a little, I had room to eat in comfort.

Soon, we were rushed back to the stadium where we were joined by Mennen, Blair, and members of the centennial committee for a local history pageant. It was now dark, and a cold wind had arisen. The show, a story of the city over the years, was very well done and helped a lot to keep our minds off of how cold we were. We were grateful for those wool suits, but they weren't enough.

All day, no one had told us what was coming next. We were just sent from one place to another. Now, we were informed, the owner of the biggest restaurant in town had offered her home to us for the night. Her house was quite a little ride, across the state line into Wisconsin. We were assured our luggage would be waiting for us. How wonderful bed was going to feel. When we arrived, we were ushered into our hostess's parlor. The governor promptly stretched out on the floor, half turned over, and found himself staring at two huge white ceramic elephants. We all laughed. There weren't any donkey statues in sight.

We were wondering how we could politely excuse ourselves and go to bed. At midnight, the doorbell rang and in trooped twenty of our hostess's neighbors and friends. She had invited them over to meet the candidates and have a midnight snack with us. We followed her downstairs and into a recreation room, complete with a bar, comfortable stools, a number of small tables, and one long table for the food. Waitresses from our hostess's restaurant went to work immediately. At one side of the room were three huge, walk-in refrigerators. Out came whole hams, whole turkeys, roasts of beef, salads of all descriptions, and every kind of sweet imaginable. There was enough to feed an army.

We all tried to eat something and make polite conversation. Finally, Adelaide and I could stand it no longer. We were dead on our feet. Finding our hostess, I asked her if she would mind very much if we could be excused to go to bed. She was very gracious and said: "Of course, but please just wait a minute. I'll have to go up with you and undress the beds." She meant the phrase literally: there must have been at least fifty stuffed animals, dolls, and pillows on each of those beds. On the way down the hall, we saw that Jim Lincoln had found his room. He was lying face down, sound asleep, amid a collection of dolls and animal pillows.

We had barely closed our eyes when we were called for breakfast, where there was food in the same quantity as our midnight snack. Luckily, we served ourselves, so except for urgings to take more, we got away with fairly small portions.

It was Sunday. Adelaide wanted to go to Mass, and Nancy and I went with her. We found a tiny church just outside of town and got there just in time for the ten o'clock Mass. In the middle of the most sacred part of the ritual, a door behind the altar slammed like a clap of thunder. Everyone turned and looked at us as if, somehow, we were responsible. Holding back a giggle, I managed to keep a straight face. Nancy said later she was glad I had not looked at her. Everyone greeted us kindly after the Mass in spite of the slammed door, which apparently was the result of a wind gust.

This was our last day. In one small town we were invited to a luncheon where we sat on a veranda looking out onto a beautiful little lake. It was lovely and tranquil, and we wished heartily we could stay there instead of driving to a meeting in Ironwood.

It had been my custom on the trip to go into hotels or motels, tell the desk clerk that the governor's wife was outside, and ask for help with our luggage. Because she had so many different appearances to make, Nancy had packed a large wardrobe suitcase that weighed a ton. Until then, the system had worked beautifully, and we had been taken care of in high style. Not at this hotel. It was here, on a CWA trip, that I had found peepholes in the bathroom, so I should have known.

At the desk, I found the clerk three sheets to the wind. He couldn't care less who was outside. Mustering my sternest voice, I insisted he send

someone out. He swore he didn't have any porters. It was no use. Together, Nancy, Adelaide, and I had just managed to get the bags out of
the trunk when a man came staggering out and stammered drunkenly
that he had come out to carry the "shootcases." He tried to take Nancy's
bag, but Nancy took one look at him and said: "No, thanks. I'll carry it
myself." He tried to take it from her again, but she just pushed past him
and carried that huge bag in herself.

The clerk had pulled himself together enough to give us the key to
our room. It was on the second floor, and there was no elevator. The beds
were clean, but the floor looked so dirty that Adelaide put her shoes up
on the dresser. When I called the county Democratic chairman to find
out where we should go for our meeting, the chairman's wife remarked
nonchalantly: "Oh, the meeting's been cancelled, and the chairman isn't
here. He's gone to a Moose picnic." How we wished we were back by
that beautiful lake.

My next move was to call Eloise Andrews, the CWA representative
for that area, and ask her where we could go out to eat. She promptly replied that she and her boyfriend, Johnny Basto, would be right over.
They took us to an Italian restaurant with excellent food. Halfway
through our meal, they told us we were just across the state line in Hur-
ley, Wisconsin, which had the reputation of being one of the toughest
towns in the Midwest. There was only one main street, with bar after bar,
a few restaurants, and one grocery store. They told us that the restaurant
where we were eating was owned by a cousin of a notorious gangster
from Chicago. Johnny assured us that there was no danger of a police
raid while we were there because they had made their ritual periodic raid
the week before. Later that night, the three of us were in hysterics, imag-
ining the pictures and headlines if the governor's wife and her cohorts
had been caught in a raid in a Wisconsin bar owned by someone related
to a gangster.

On the way back, Nancy insisted we all go to the state-owned summer residence for the governor on Mackinac Island for a day's rest before
Adelaide and I started home. Altogether, our campaign tour across the
Upper Peninsula had provided us with a new respect for the rigors of political campaigns—and heightened the affection that Nancy, Adelaide,
and I had for each other.

Adelaide Hart was one of the most important people in the state
party while Mennen was governor, and she remained active long afterward. She and I became good friends through many years of working
and traveling for politics. Adelaide was a music teacher for many years at
Jefferson Junior High School in Detroit. She was also the school music
director. At the time, teachers in Michigan were very poorly paid, and
the schools were badly crowded and inadequate. Adelaide became active

in the Detroit Federation of Teachers and was an early supporter of Mennen. Undoubtedly one of the things that appealed to her was his conviction that money had to be found to build an adequate school system.

From the start, she was always out there, making the rounds in her neighborhood as a precinct delegate and giving up evenings and weekends to perform countless chores for Mennen's campaign. Soon after Neil became state party chairman, Adelaide was elected to her first term as vice chairman. She was a hardworking and able partner to Neil. What with party meetings and speaking engagements all over the state, Adelaide went for weeks during the school year with a minimum of sleep. During the holidays, she always had to put on special musical programs at school. Through it all, she never let down her end of the political work.

Adelaide's older sister, Helen Hart, was a big help to Adelaide and the party. Without Helen Adelaide would never have been able to follow the pace she kept for the ten years she was vice chairman. Helen not only took care of Adelaide but all of us. After Helen was free from the care of their mother, she would go with Adelaide to the innumerable state meetings where Adelaide was invited to speak. Helen would sit in the back of the room so she could get the feel of the audience from listening and talking to the people around her. She became our eyes and ears.

Adelaide took on the responsibility of organizing the women in the state and often had to suffer the hardly concealed objections of the men. She called her group the Federation of Democratic Women. There were no top officers. Women in each community formed their own group but were direct members of the state organization. No one will ever know the hours Adelaide—and Helen, too—put in with those groups, particularly outstate. Their work paid off in consistent growth in the party organization, and in larger margins of victory for Mennen and other Democrats even before reapportionment made it easier for Democrats to win Michigan elections.

Adelaide was recognized, by all who knew her well, as the conscience of the party organization. She remained a volunteer who paid all of her expenses herself. She was so conscientious that she never missed one of the numerous campaign and planning meetings, even on school days. Often the party meetings were in Lansing, a two-hour drive from her home. Those meetings seemed interminable, but none of us could complain that any phase of the campaign strategy was not discussed. Driving home alone, Adelaide often pulled off beside the road and slept for an hour if she got too sleepy. More than once, she was startled at the sight of a state trooper rapping at her window to make sure she was all right.

10

THE 1952
DEMOCRATIC NATIONAL
CONVENTION

THE MICHIGAN DEMOCRATIC PARTY was blessed with many talented and conscientious people, like Adelaide Hart, who helped restore the party's vigor and integrity. Margaret Price, for example, was a brilliant and tireless campaigner. She was a homemaker, working hard for the party and for Mennen in 1948, when the state convention suddenly nominated her for auditor general. Running for that office was probably the last thing she had thought of doing. She and her husband, Hickman, a well-to-do businessman, lived in Ann Arbor and were raising two sons. The Michigan Democratic party, however, was ahead of the times and had decided it would be helpful to have a woman on the ticket.

There was considerable debate on the issue. Neil Staebler had been the other candidate considered, but those who wanted a woman prevailed. Margaret was taken by surprise. Because the nomination would bring publicity and require a lot of time away from home, Margaret didn't feel she could accept the nomination until she consulted her husband, who was away on a business trip. The convention recessed until Margaret was able to reach Hickman and discuss it with him. Along with most of the Democratic candidates for the State Administrative Board, Margaret lost. She was nominated again in 1950 and, again, she and the others were defeated.

As she campaigned with the other Ad Board candidates, Margaret endeared herself to party people across the state. She was intelligent, beautiful, smartly dressed, and knew how to meet and talk with people.

She not only carried herself well—she insisted on carrying her own suit-cases. As she laughingly said later, she took care of herself so well that, on one trip, her running mates drove off and left her behind. Instead of making a fuss, she took it as a good joke, gaining the respect and admiration of her fellow candidates.

It was no surprise when, in 1952, the Michigan Democratic party elected Margaret Price as national committeewoman. She kept that post for the rest of the decade. She also managed Adlai Stevenson's presidential campaign in Michigan that year. By this time, her ability was widely known throughout the state. Indeed, Margaret became so well-respected around the country that she was Scoop Jackson's choice as vice chairman of the Democratic National Committee after John Kennedy won the presidential nomination in 1960.

Her first election as national committeewoman was proposed and agreed upon informally at the midnight caucus of the state party convention in the spring of 1952. By this time, I was deeply involved in the campaigns and had earned the privilege of attending the midnight caucus. It was a coveted honor.

The midnight caucus was a far cry from the politics of smoke-filled rooms; in fact, it opened up the political process. Before the introduction of the midnight caucus, there was no open discussion about Democratic party policies or which candidates to support at state party conventions. As a result, the convention floor was chaotic. Delegates and district chairmen responded to arm-twisting by powerful people without regard for the overall good of the party.

Mennen and Neil believed strongly that as many people as possible should have a say in what went on in the party and that things should be done in the open. So, not long after Neil became party chairman in 1950, they established the tradition of a caucus the night before the opening of the state conventions. All the district groups would meet to discuss their positions on the issues of the day. If there were candidates to be nominated, the district meetings heard all the presentations. By midnight, the district leaders, state party officers, and several other key people were invited to gather for the caucus. There was considerable discussion—Mennen and Neil encouraged everyone to speak up—and several times the caucus was recessed to allow the district chairmen to consult with their delegates.

Choosing candidates for the State Administrative Board and for national committeeman provoked much debate at the 1952 midnight caucus, but there was no question about Margaret Price. The most dissension arose over the selection of at-large delegates to the Democratic National Convention. The main reason was that a fight was brewing over civil rights. Southern Democrats were resisting a strong party stand on the issue.

95

Mennen had taken a firm position for civil rights. For years he had been doing what no other Michigan governor before him had dared to do: appointing blacks and ethnic minorities to judicial positions and other important jobs. Although at this time in history, it could be politically dangerous to be strongly in favor of civil rights, Mennen never thought about anything other than what was right. He really believed in equal opportunity. He insisted that great care be taken at the state convention to have an even selection of women, blacks, and ethnics in the delegation going to the national convention. Mennen was named chairman of the delegation. There was no question where he stood. It was morning before the midnight caucus was over, but nobody could complain of being slighted. For once, I observed without voicing my opinions because I wanted to just absorb how the caucus worked. Knowing that silence was unusual for me, the governor became curious and checked with me a couple of times. He grinned to himself when I said I didn't have anything to say. As vice chairman of the 17th District, I was to go to the national convention from my district and therefore was not part of the conflict over the at-large delegates. When it was all over, I not only had learned a great deal from watching; I was a full-fledged delegate headed for my first Democratic National Convention.

The convention was exciting and filled with controversy. The pro-civil rights liberals, headed by Senator Estes Kefauver of Tennessee, were determined that the Southern delegates who had deserted the party in 1948 should sign some statement of party loyalty and support for the candidates and platform from the 1952 convention. Adelaide Hart and Blair Moody had been named to the Platform and Resolutions Committee, which elected Blair to chair the Rules Committee. With the strong support of Estes Kefauver and Franklin Roosevelt, Jr., Blair took on the thankless task of negotiating the wording of a statement that would be acceptable to the conservative Southern group and still satisfy the liberal delegates.

The resolution was presented to the convention at the second session of the first day, before any other business was conducted. A furious debate filled the rest of the day. Several amendments and substitute resolutions were offered, but the majority of the delegates remained firm, and substantive changes were defeated. At 2:00 A.M. the resolution was adopted after a move for a roll-call vote was rejected.[1] Neither the Southern delegates nor the liberals were really pleased, but everybody agreed it was better than nothing.

Senator Kefauver was a candidate for the nomination for president. Mennen had allied himself with Kefauver and the other liberals. Of all the people who were under consideration for the Democratic presidential nomination—including Adlai Stevenson—Kefauver took the strongest position on civil rights. He had stood up to the conservative Southern delegates because he wanted to keep the party together and true to its principles. Mennen stood fast with Kefauver. The party remained united, and a strong civil rights plank was included in the platform.

Mennen faced some opposition within our state delegation, but there was enough support for his point of view to give him a majority. Since the group had voted to follow a unit rule—meaning that all the delegation's votes would be cast with the majority position—Michigan was with the liberals on the crucial votes of the convention.[2]

Politics wasn't the only reason things were heating up in that convention hall, the old Amphitheater down by the stockyards in Chicago. The cleanup crews had been on strike the whole week of the convention. Newspapers and piles of trash were ankle-deep all over the place. Not far from where the Michigan delegation was seated, someone carelessly dropped a hot match. A huge pile of papers immediately caught fire. If it had not been quickly smothered, there could have been a tragic fire.

The Michigan delegates had other things on our minds. We had unanimously decided to nominate Mennen Williams for president as a favorite son. We knew it wouldn't go far—although Mennen was becoming better-known, he was not yet a strong national candidate—but we wanted the rest of the country to know how proud we were of our governor. Blair Moody made an eloquent speech nominating Mennen Williams of Michigan. His nomination was seconded by Margaret Price, our newly elected national committeewoman, and by John Goldmark, of the state of Washington, president of the Young Democrats.[3]

Then, we had fun. Carrying our Michigan sign, we staged a demonstration, marching around the hall and waving Williams placards. We made a lot of noise and attracted considerable notice. We had had a huge bow-tie sign made and attached to the Michigan delegation sign. It stayed there throughout the convention. On the first roll call for the nominees, Michigan cast its forty votes for Mennen Williams. After that ceremonial stand, Michigan went for Kefauver on the second roll call.

It wasn't easy for Mennen. He and his associates in the delegation were for Kefauver, while labor delegates were split between Stevenson and Kefauver. In a poll of the Michigan delegation, Kefauver received twice as many votes as Stevenson, so under the unit rule, Michigan's forty votes went to Kefauver. No candidate received a majority of the votes on the second tally, and a third roll call of the states was held. Michigan delegates finally conceded that Kefauver could not win, and they switched to Stevenson.

Adlai Stevenson was a fine man, brilliant and principled, who had distinguished himself as the popular and able governor of Illinois. He also had served the public well in various positions during President

Franklin D. Roosevelt's New Deal and was involved in the early days of the United Nations. Stevenson had not originally been a candidate for president. Nor had he become embroiled in the party fight between the conservative Southerners and the pro-civil rights liberals. Some people saw him as the one man who could unite the party and make peace, so he was drafted as a consensus candidate. Eventually, he was nominated by acclamation.

India Edwards, vice chairman of the national party, was nominated for vice president. She expressed appreciation but asked that her name be withdrawn. Judge Sarah Hughes of Texas was also nominated. She followed suit. Senator John Sparkman of Alabama, Governor Stevenson's choice as his running mate, was nominated by acclamation.

Kefauver really appreciated our support of him and the firm message he sent to the Southern rebels. Shortly after the convention, he sent me a short note that said in part: "I cannot tell you how much it meant to me to have your support. Nancy [his wife] and I have no regrets. . . . We fought a hard, clean fight without deals. We shall continue to work for the ideals and principles in which we believe."

No damage was done to the Michigan Democratic party despite the convention turmoil. That was largely because of Mennen and Neil, who insisted that the delegation be consulted and kept informed. That meant that we spent a great part of our time in caucus and didn't see much of the social side of the convention—although we were deluged with invitations to attend receptions and cocktail parties every day. Blair Moody even got me a coveted invitation to Perle Mesta's spectacular affair, but we were in caucus and I missed it. At the time, Perle Mesta held the honor of being Washington's, and probably the nation's, foremost hostess. With some regrets, I am one person who can say that I turned down an invitation to one of her parties.

NOTES

1. A copy of this resolution is in the Appendix. The resolution was negotiated and adopted at the 1952 Democratic National Convention with the help of Blair Moody to resolve the conflict between Northern and Southern delegates and keep the party together. The historic debate is part of the convention record printed in the *Official Report of the Proceedings of the Democratic National Convention, Chicago, Illinois, July 21–26, inclusive, 1952* (Published under the direction of the Democratic National Committee, Stephen A. Mitchell, chairman, and William J. Bray and Venice T. Spraggs, editors). The text of the resolution is on p. 55; discussion and action on the resolution continue through page 76.

2. Detail on this convention is found in the *Official Report of the Proceedings of the Democratic National Convention, Chicago, Illinois, July 21–26, inclusive, 1952.*

3. The convention speeches in support of Mennen Williams are in the *Official Report of the Proceedings of the Democratic National Convention, Chicago, Illinois, July 21–26, inclusive, 1952.* Copies are among Helen Berthelot's papers in the Michigan Historical Collections, Bentley Historical Library, University of Michigan, Ann Arbor.

11

WHAT DOES
A DIRECTOR OF ORGANIZATION
DO, ANYWAY?

I N POLITICAL CAMPAIGNS, as in almost everything else, a title doesn't necessarily explain what someone does. My title in the 1952 campaign was "director of organization." What I was actually doing was setting up and running the first full-time campaign office for the entire Democratic ticket. The office would house all the campaigns: the governor's, Blair Moody's for the U. S. Senate, Adlai Stevenson's for the presidency, and the campaigns for State Administrative Board positions.

Neil Staebler, the state party chairman, had talked Walter Schaar, our Michigan CWA district director, into giving me a leave of absence from my job in Lansing. In March, the party rented a whole floor of the Book Building on Washington Boulevard in downtown Detroit. Mary Wottawa, a superb secretary who had worked in the CWA office in Detroit before it was moved to Lansing, agreed to work for me again. Together, we opened a campaign office.

Lawrence "Larry" Farrell, the governor's executive secretary, had never gotten over his suspicion of the new Democratic group that had been formed and now was running the party. Larry had been Mennen's boss in 1946 when Mennen joined the Office of Price Administration in Detroit as deputy director. They had become friends, and Mennen listened carefully to what Larry had to say. Larry was from the Upper Peninsula and had been in politics long enough to have developed strong ties to the old guard. He was positive that this new group would ruin Mennen Williams's chances of being reelected.

Larry's first attempt to get rid of Berthelot before she did any great damage to the governor's campaign was to send another Democrat of the old school to the Detroit office. For a month, until I had completed a couple of CWA projects, I had to run the office by phone from Lansing. Poor Mary Wottawa was caught in the middle. She would get a project from me over the phone. Larry Farrell's cohort would immediately change it or cancel it altogether. Before the month was out, I got a tearful call from Mary telling me she couldn't stand it any longer and was quitting. She didn't tell me the reason until I got there, and by then it was too late.

After I arrived to work full time, we limped along with temporary help for a couple of weeks. It didn't take me long to realize that everything I was trying to organize was being sabotaged. Knowing what was going on, I tried to ignore the troublemaking and went ahead as best I could. Not making a big issue of it paid off. One night the two of us—Larry's "plant" and myself—went out to dinner. After a little liquid courage, my "enemy" told me he couldn't take it any longer. He said I was too nice a girl to have her throat cut at the start, and he was quitting. (His name was Andy Donovan, and we became good friends after that.)

Then, happy day, the next person Larry Farrell sent down to keep me on the straight and narrow was John Murray, a former *Detroit Free Press* reporter who had covered city hall, among other things. He was to be public relations director for the Democratic State Central Committee. It was the best thing that had happened to me, and to the party, for a long time. John and I had a straight talk right at the start, and we remained good friends from then on. Sid Woolner, John, and I formed a crack campaign team. Each of us had special talents that complemented the others'. We survived what seemed, at the time, insurmountable obstacles.

The various campaign staffs were soon put together. Blair Moody was in a tough fight to keep the U. S. Senate seat that had been Arthur Vandenberg's. Half of his staff remained in the nearby federal building, but his scheduler, Marian Lacey, his press secretary, Bob Ball, and one of his administrative assistants moved to the Democratic headquarters office. It worked very well until Marian and Bob fell in love. (They were married after the campaign.) Although they were very loyal to Blair and did their work well, the scheduler too often found time to travel with the candidate and, of course, the press secretary. That created jealousy among the rest of the staff. I often found myself in the middle trying to keep peace.

When Blair was in the office, the place became a madhouse. He could make more telephone calls to important people than anyone I ever knew, one call after another. If one person didn't answer, he would immediately place another call. Then, of course, everyone he had called would return his call at the same time.

We had only one switchboard. The operator was an older woman and easily upset. One day I went by her desk and found her in a flood of tears. When I asked her what was wrong, she said, "The senator yelled at me." His light on the switchboard was flashing impatiently, so I had the operator move over and I took her place. Answering his signal in an ugly tone of voice, I demanded, "What do you want?" Blair immediately flared up and asked, "Who is this?" "This is Helen," I said. "You have upset our switchboard operator badly." He was immediately contrite, as he always was, and came out apologizing so sweetly to the operator that she again burst into tears. From then on, the telephone calls went more smoothly.

The fact that Senator Moody had his staff in two separate buildings created difficulties for all of us. Straightening out his various problems took time that I could ill spare. After I'd solved a particularly troublesome one, Blair burst out, "My God, Helen, you are my buffer against the world." Then he snapped his fingers. "That's it!" he said. "We'll call you Buffy." Neil Staebler heard that, and from then on he called me Buffy. So did several close friends, although the staff never called me anything but Helen or Mrs. B.

Several times Mennen heard Blair and Neil call me Buffy. Curious, he asked Blair why. The next letter I received from Mennen was addressed "Dear Buffy," and he seldom again called me by any other name.

Margaret Price's "Stevenson for President" staff also had moved into the office with us. Some of them were strangers to us and felt that the presidential candidate's needs should come before anyone else's. Mennen's campaign, which I was handling with Sid and John, was in the process of getting petitions circulated. Blair's staff was doing the same thing. A very capable woman was checking Mennen's petitions for me as they were returned.

The petitions were coming along fine, but other things were becoming chaotic. The Lansing office was in charge of Mennen's schedule. Since most of the invitations came into my office, we had to work together on the phone daily. Not only did we not have any fax machines then, the equipment we did have was primitive and barely workable. We had one temperamental mimeograph machine and a beat-up Addressograph that I learned to start by kicking it gently in the right place. Our mailing list consisted of one set of address stencils. Naturally everyone wanted to use the machines at the same time.

The results were predictable. An office manager, hired by the State Central Committee, quit in a temper. The next one left in hysterical tears. A meeting was called for the party officers to discuss the problems. After what seemed like endless discussion with no agreement, I spoke up: "If none of you objects, I will be the office manager. But if I am manager, I am *going to be* the manager, and you will all have to give me your priorities and wait your turn." If I had known what I was taking on, I might not have offered. There were many times late at night when I questioned my sanity.

The first thing I did was draw up a set of rules for using the office machinery. Next, I made a deal with the mimeograph man to rent me a new machine with an option to buy. Until I could break the news gently to Neil Staebler, I made the payments out of petty cash. (We still had the old Addressograph that needed a kick in the sides every time we used it.) Neil went along with my recommendation to rent a postage meter to save time and effort—but that turned out to be a mistake. Adlai Stevenson had attracted so many volunteers, I soon had to shut up the machine and have them seal and stamp envelopes to keep them all busy. We still found great use for the meter in emergencies.

One of my big problems was getting the various staffs to prepare the materials they wanted sent out in plenty of time and not to wait until the deadline and expect miracles. Borrowing a leaf from big companies, I drafted a one-page "Work Requisition" form and made everybody use it. It was so bureaucratic that it was almost funny, but it worked miracles. We knew who the work was for, whether it was a rush job, whether it needed to be folded, and so forth.

The office was a beehive of activity from early morning till late at night. The priorities got tougher and tougher to handle. John Murray finally resorted to putting his press releases in my big chair to make sure the others did not hide them under another project. He would sign them "The Gremlin."

We were very fortunate to have people who worked beautifully throughout all the turmoil. Paul Weber, Mennen's press secretary and trusted adviser, had called early on and asked if I needed a secretary. It was through Paul that I had first learned, years earlier, of the talents of Virginia Calamia Ryan. Her husband was William Ryan, one of the most beloved and effective speakers of the house that the Michigan House of Representatives ever had. Virginia was quietly efficient and never got ruffled. She could do anything, even little illustrations at the top of a stencil. In 1949, she had worked with me at the CWA in Detroit. When we moved to Lansing, Virginia stayed in Detroit. It was fortunate for me that she was temporarily unemployed in 1952 and was delighted at the idea of working for Mennen's reelection.

One time, early in the campaign, we had rented a TelePrompTer for one of Mennen's speeches. Our speech typewriter broke down as we were rushing to finish a speech he had written for a particular appearance. Virginia suggested that we call Chrysler Corporation and ask if we could use theirs. Off she went to type the corrected copy. Paul Weber had sent it down at the very last minute because the governor had held it up, as he often did, to make corrections. (Interpreting Mennen's heavy scrawl was a challenge under the best of circumstances. On a speech, marked up all over the place, it was nearly impossible. Mennen never complained, but I often wondered if I had put the right words in his mouth.) It was a long speech. Virginia arrived at the television station with just minutes left for the governor to run through it quickly before the broadcast.

The TelePrompTer was one of the first models, with the speech typed on a roll of paper attached to a cylinder. An operator used a foot pedal to control the speed at which the speech was read. The little man who was going to operate the machine was very nervous at serving the governor. He tried to attach the speech to the roller, but his hands were shaking so much he couldn't get the screws in properly. "Give me that screwdriver," said Virginia. She took it and click, click, click, click, all four screws were solidly in place. Thankfully, TelePrompTers were quickly improved, so we didn't have to go through that often.

It was about this time that I decided to try to get the governor to use makeup for his television appearances. He was opposed to it, so I knew he wouldn't come around easily. On the day I had decided to try to talk him into it, I had the makeup technician standing by, because I knew we would have to move fast if I managed to persuade him. He had a few minutes before he was to practice, so I asked him if he wouldn't try just a little makeup. He agreed. Everyone complimented him afterwards on his appearance, so that was another hurdle passed. He used light makeup for television from then on.

The Good Lord has looked after me in more ways than I can count in all the campaigns. In 1952, Virginia ended up working for Sid on the coordinated campaigns, because she was needed more there than in the governor's campaign. At the height of my need, I got a phone call from a young woman asking if we needed secretarial help. Although I didn't know her at all and no one had recommended her, I was so desperate that I asked her to come over for an interview. She replied, "Before I come, I had better tell you that I am colored." "That doesn't make any difference here," I answered. "Come in as soon as you can for an interview." That's how the Democratic party, and later the UAW, got Madge Cruce, one of the most competent secretaries in the business.

After I hired Madge, I never had it so good, and people in the field never had their mail answered more promptly. As soon as the mail was sorted, I would call Madge in and shut my door, and we would get to work. Soon I learned that I could hand her a letter, give her an idea of what to say, and she would write the response. It was amazing how fast we could get through that pile of mail, and then Madge could turn her attention to other campaign projects. She would whip out the mail, letter-perfect, and give it to me for my signature. Her letters were a little more flowery than mine, and I am sure some of my regular correspondents wondered what had happened to me.

Campaign offices are not easy places to work. Over the years, when I hired secretaries, I would explain that emergencies were to be expected. If it upset them to start and stop several projects in a given hour, yet have them all finished by the end of the day, they didn't want to work for me, I would tell them. My manner was abrupt, and my voice often sounded cross when I was in a hurry. Because I was concentrating on getting the work done, I wouldn't always take the time to say "please" and "thank you." At least I warned them.

The campaigns for Stevenson, Williams, and Moody brought out more volunteers than we knew what to do with. We never had a staff with more degrees after their names. Two were professors at Wayne State. One of them ran our packages room, a stupendous task because of all the material that went in and out. The other was a German woman who taught languages. She loved to run our decrepit Addressograph machine. Her aim in life right then was to beat her own time in getting out a mailing list. One day I had to stop her because her face was getting so red.

We were very proud of our devoted errand boy, Joe Bauer. He was so tall, I didn't realize that he was under sixteen and we had to hurry him out to get a work permit. A couple of years later Joe proudly told us that he and a buddy in his neighborhood were the only ones to stay in school. He gave us credit for giving him the inspiration.

Another person who remained close long after the 1952 campaign was Joyce Curtis, a volunteer who came to us from Maine. Joyce's brother, Kenneth Curtis, was governor of Maine for two terms. She showed up at the office one evening and said she would like to volunteer for Stevenson. Before she knew it, she became my evening secretary.

Being blessed with good health and thoroughly enjoying my work, I kept going for hours with little sleep. My biggest problem was learning to never let on when things had gone awry. One day I let my face show that we were in trouble. The whole staff sensed it and everything seemed to fall apart. "Look at Helen," one of the volunteers said. "Something awful must have happened." From then on, if I couldn't smile, I tried to keep a poker face. "That's why I live by myself," I told Neil Staebler. "My face hurts from trying to keep smiling. I can go home and kick the furniture and make faces at it, if I want to." Generally, however, I just fell into bed.

The volunteers got a glimpse of my tough side one day, and it delighted them. One of the louder-voiced UAW staff came in to get material for the 17th District. In a belligerent, rough tone, he demanded twice as much material as the 17th District was entitled to have. (A scarcity of funds had forced us to dole out materials strictly on a quota basis.) "The UAW is paying for this material and I want it now," he blustered. Calling him by name, I addressed him sternly: "Go back to your district headquarters office and tell them when they can send someone who politely asks for it, I will give it to them. They will get their quota and no more. Today you don't get any material when you talk to me like that."

The volunteers, who had been a little intimidated by the voice and the fact that he had banged his fist on the desk, were relieved and pleased when I sent him away. That afternoon another man from the 17th District came in and put his arm around me and said coaxingly, "We need that campaign literature to pass out tonight." "Of course," I said. "You don't have to soft-soap me, either. You are entitled to it and I'll give it to you gladly. But don't ever send anyone down here again, demanding more than your share." There was no more trouble like that. The volunteers were surprised that I could get so tough with the UAW, of all organizations.

My own district, the 17th, gave me more problems than all the rest put together. When we didn't get our full supply of bumper strips, I found by accident that one of the men from my district had come in and helped himself at the printer's. Complaining to the shop foreman didn't work, so one day I called the owner. "This is Helen," I said. "Who okays your bills for payment?" "Why, you do," he answered. "All right," I said. "Until you stop letting people help themselves to my order, I'm not okaying any bills for you, and I mean it." Before he could argue I hung up. He called me right back and assured me he would stop the pilfering. We got full shipments from then on. Building a reputation for being tough and fair served me well in later campaigns and saved me a great deal of trouble. They all soon learned that I was helpful and not unreasonable—but that I meant what I said.

Recruiting volunteers and paid staff called upon every skill I could muster. Dedicated volunteers are the backbone of any campaign. In Detroit, the congressional district party chairmen naturally wanted to keep their best volunteers working in their own districts. But they were often the same people I wanted. At the start of each campaign, I wrote every congressional district chairman, saying that skilled volunteers were badly needed for the state campaigns, especially the governor's. By then, I knew the people well, and I asked for particular workers by name. The chairmen would grouse privately about losing their best volunteers, but they never did anything to stop me. They also never answered me—most of them, anyway. Louie McGuinness, the 15th Congressional District chairman, was the only one who ever answered my letters. His answers never varied. He would tell me I was asking for his best volunteers and that his district would suffer for it. Reluctantly, he would give me permission to call the people I needed. Since the others never bothered to respond, I would wait a little while, then recruit the people I wanted.

Much of what goes on in a campaign office is done out of sheer, gut instinct. Jim Lincoln, the young lawyer in the Griffiths law office who had handled postcards for us in that first campaign, was our unofficial registration chairman in 1952. Ever since the 1950 defeat of our Administrative Board candidates, he had spent his spare time studying the Michigan Manual, which is full of statistics. He always had that red book in his hand. If anyone would listen, he would recite the population of a particular town or county and the Democratic vote. "That's a working man's town," he would say. "They all ought to be voting Democratic, and they are not even registered. We've got to get them registered." His enthusiasm was catching. Although Mennen was the only one of the state Democratic candidates to win in 1952, and then only barely, Jim set the stage for 1954. Without his pushing all of us to work harder on the registration drive, we might not have won so handily in 1954. Jim's help could very well have made the difference in those early elections.

He wasn't the only member of the family who helped ensure Mennen's success. Through the skillful efforts of Jim's wife Kim, the governor was always well represented if he couldn't appear before a group. Kim, along with several others, had a knack for smoothing things over and finding just the right person to speak for Mennen. It wasn't easy, because each group had different concerns, and they all wanted the governor. Kim and her cohorts performed scheduling chores and other demanding tasks with good humor and kept everyone's spirits up. That kind of behind-the-scenes work isn't particularly glamorous. It is, however, essential to winning elections.

Jim Lincoln's later contributions came in a different arena. He devoted much of his life and his work as a judge to helping troubled young people. He made substantial improvements in the way the Wayne County court system handled cases involving young people and their many problems. Through his fairness and firmness, hundreds of young men and women put their lives back on track. Jim became nationally respected for his knowledge, his juvenile court work, and his courageous efforts forcing the state to improve the system for juvenile offenders in the 1960s. A tangible symbol of his accomplishments—a beautiful building in Detroit housing the court for his beloved young people—was most fittingly named after him: the James H. Lincoln Hall of Juvenile Justice.[1]

NOTES

1. Excerpts from James Lincoln's letter to Helen Berthelot, describing his struggle with Governor George Romney over providing adequate facilities for juveniles in Michigan, are among Helen Berthelot's papers in the Michigan Historical Collections, Bentley Historical Library, University of Michigan, Ann Arbor. Other pertinent correspondence is also on file there. Judge Lincoln's own papers from the Mennen Williams era and from the judge's efforts to improve the juvenile system are indexed under "James H. Lincoln" in the Bentley Historical Library and in the Burton Historical Collections at the Detroit Public Library.

12

EXPANDING OUR HORIZONS
WITH KOOL-AID, HELEN'S BOYS,
AND THE CLERGY

SID WOOLNER, John Murray, Adelaide Hart, and I made it our business to spoil Mennen Williams and Neil Staebler in that 1952 campaign. No matter what ideas the two of them came up with, Sid and I, in particular, made sure they were carried out. We never let on that sometimes we had to burn the midnight oil and a few other things to get them done. Sid and I stowed some of Neil's more complicated plans in our bottom desk drawers. To Neil, once they were down on paper they were as good as done, and generally they were.

Only once did I try outright rebellion. It was in response to a project Neil gave to John Murray and me. John and I got together and formulated a long list of reasons why it wasn't a good idea, why the research and writing couldn't be done on time, and so on. Neil came bounding in, all smiles as usual, and started to talk about the project. John and I took turns making our case against it. No matter what our objections were, Neil kept saying: "I don't understand. What's the problem?" We went round and round. With a deep sigh, I finally gave up and said: "All right, dammit. We'll do it." And we did. From then on, we did what we could handle and, once in a while, "lost" a project or two.

My only attempt at defying Mennen Williams was a huge joke in my beauty parlor. It was early in the 1952 campaign, and I had been concentrating on getting in the nominating petitions from the various county organizations. The governor wanted to qualify for the primary in as many counties as possible, to show the support he had across the state. The law didn't require him to qualify in every county, but I knew that nothing would do but for him to qualify in all eighty-three. The largely Republican counties had not been coming in very fast, so I had deliberately avoided the subject of the petitions in my conversations with him.

One morning I had gotten away, or so I thought, for a much-needed shampoo and set. In the midst of my shampoo the receptionist came in, all excited, and said, "Governor Williams is on the phone and wants to talk to Mrs. Berthelot." With a big towel around my head and water dripping down my neck, I answered the phone.

Mennen didn't waste any time. "Helen, are we going to qualify in all eighty-three counties?" he asked. Right then, I was far from sure we could, but I answered, "Oh, yes, I think we will." Mennen replied, "But that isn't what I want you to say." Next I declared, "I'm sure we will." Again, Mennen responded: "But that isn't what I want you to say." After two or three attempts to satisfy him with fairly confident answers, I got my back up. Of course I knew what he wanted, but I wasn't going to say for sure we would qualify and then not be able to deliver.

Everything stopped in the beauty parlor as we went back and forth a few more times. Mennen's voice carried, even on the phone, so everyone could hear him say over and over, "But that isn't what I want you to say." Finally I gave in, and in a loud, disgusted voice said: "All right, yes, we *will* qualify in all eighty-three counties." There wasn't even an answer from the other end. He knew if I said I would do it, I would—or die in the attempt. To the amusement of everyone in the beauty parlor, he then hung up, satisfied.

We did qualify in all eighty-three counties, but I had to send one of our staff members out to get the last few signatures. Our staff helped Blair get on the ballot as well. He sent me a nice letter giving me much of the credit, and it pleased me that he added a handwritten note: "To be filed under the heading of superfluous and obvious statements."

Mennen qualified in all the counties every year from then on. One year I had to go to our CWA national convention before all of them were in. Sid Woolner phoned to tell me we had qualified but that they had had to relay the petitions from two counties directly to Lansing to get them there on time. In later campaigns, when the politics got rougher and we had to be on our guard against thefts, I rented safety deposit boxes for the petitions and put them in myself every day.

Once the petitions were filed and Mennen had no primary opponent, we went to work on the 1952 fall campaign. We knew we had a real battle on our hands to keep Mennen in office. We had to work very hard to turn out the Wayne County vote for Mennen to offset the heavy Republican voting in outstate Michigan.

Adelaide Hart and Nancy Williams came up with a plan: we would ask precinct delegates to invite their neighbors to their homes to meet

Nancy, Ruth Moody (Blair's wife), or Adelaide. The invitations were dainty little notes, mimeoed on pastel paper. Virginia Ryan used her talent to make eye-catching designs. Mary Gilmore was given the task of getting the invitations out and scheduling the meetings. The idea caught on. We ran off invitations by the hundreds, and most of them were used. Mary Gilmore would follow me up and down the hall and ask, in her gentle but persistent way, "Helen, is it my turn now?" She made good use of that mimeograph machine.

Mary was married to Horace Gilmore, who began circulating petitions for Mennen in the 1948 campaign, when Horace was fresh out of law school. He continued to be active in later election years. Meanwhile, Horace's law practice grew, and so did his reputation in the classroom as a teacher of the law. Those early days were the start of an exceptional career in which he served as a judge in both state and federal courts.

Both of the Gilmores excelled at politics. Mary was a genius at organizing the women's meetings. She delivered the invitations to the hostesses in person so she could size up the situation. If she could see that the people involved were on limited budgets, she diplomatically suggested that Kool-Aid and cookies, or even just Kool-Aid, would be just right. In many cases, Mary saw to it that we furnished the Kool-Aid. This suited Nancy and Adelaide just perfectly, because they were anxious to reach as many people as possible.

Their schedules began to fill up. Nancy, Ruth, and Adelaide learned to sip a little at each gathering, then to put the paper cups down and greet people. Once in a while the three of them would meet in the office to talk over the issues. They also would trade stories about all the shades of pink, orange, and purple Kool-Aid they consumed of an afternoon. Their stomachs were sloshing. These gatherings were not as elegant as the tea parties the Kennedys had in later years, but I believe they were as effective in getting out the vote. Our hostesses were proud that their neighbors came to their homes, and many of them followed up to make sure that everyone went out to vote.

The 1952 campaign saw the strengthening of minority and ethnic support for Governor Williams. It was my job to find the leaders of the various groups and enlist their help. When we had started out in 1948, I knew four or five black leaders, two of them in the labor movement, and two people from the Polish community. Thanks to Stella Lecznar and Antoinette Stanis, I learned fast. Stella was especially helpful; she knew people from a wide range of groups. With her assistance, I made the contacts. I am sure those people got tired of my asking, "Who do you know?" and "How can we get them to support Mennen Williams?"

Ethnic celebrations were what I enjoyed the most in the campaigns. Mennen had made it a point to learn about the various ethnic celebrations. We had to ask to be invited at first, but it wasn't long before invitations started pouring in. Mennen joined in the festivities and learned their national dances. It became my responsibility to block off the dates of all the ethnic national holidays so that he would be able to attend. Mennen took Nancy and me with him whenever we could go. The people were warm and cordial, and they were genuinely proud to have Mennen and Nancy in their midst. In my purse I always carried a little notebook. One by one, I painstakingly compiled lists of leaders in each group. Mennen often would give me names, and then it was up to me to make sure the spellings were right and track down their addresses.

Going to all those ethnic affairs did nothing for my figure. Everyone insisted that we eat and would get upset if we didn't. It wasn't hard to go along. On Columbus Day, I went with Nancy to an Italian dinner on the east side. We were served huge plates of the most delicious spaghetti we had ever tasted. Knowing that in less than two hours we were due at an even bigger dinner on the west side, we ate very sparingly. The Italian ladies were afraid we didn't like their spaghetti. We tried to explain that it was delicious but that we had to go to another big dinner right away. They were disappointed, but they understood. When we got to the second dinner, there was a lot of food, but the spaghetti was only a side dish. Nancy and I looked at each other and wished we were back on the east side.

The 1952 campaign saw the start of a group of young lawyers who became known as "Helen's Boys." Although we had a big staff and lots of volunteers, I told the governor we needed a special group to answer children's mail and to help when crises arose in the evenings. Mennen took care of it in his usual way—as soon as the opportunity presented itself. It happened to be during the State Fair parade. Seizing the chance to buttonhole some likely candidates to help me, Mennen held a quick conference in the street in front of City Hall in downtown Detroit, holding up the parade for a few minutes. When the short meeting was over, he had recruited Ted Souris, Joe Pernick, and a couple of other young lawyers. He asked them to get together a group of their lawyer friends and set up a schedule so I would always have someone to call on in the evenings, if I needed them. A group of fifteen or more responded, and some even brought secretarial help.

There was plenty to do. The kids' mail was always piled up. Lots of children asked questions, no doubt suggested by their teachers. It wasn't easy getting this group to give short, direct answers. The first night, one of them typed three pages in answer to a simple question. He had written a whole civics lesson—I should have kept it. It didn't take me long to learn which lawyers couldn't adapt to writing to kids, and I found something else for them to do.

Not one of them ever refused to do whatever I asked, even when it was the tedious job of tying up bundles of campaign material to mail. We couldn't have managed without them. Some of the ones who came in for the four o'clock shift would bring me a candy bar or a malted milk, no doubt in response to a remark I'd made one time that 4:00 P.M. was my low period.

Decades later, their names read like a who's who of the Michigan legal profession, and the list includes a judge or two. Among the "boys" from those early campaign days are Vic Baum, Charlie Brown, Bob Chase, Rex Eames, William Elmer, Phil Gillis, Harman Hitt, Pete La-Duke, Bill Merrill, Ted Monolidis, Joe Pernick, Red Roche, Ted Sachs, Ted Souris, Dave Southern, Fred Wilson, and John Young.

Adlai Stevenson was stirring up a lot of interest in the campaign that year. Despite the skirmish over civil rights at the convention, Stevenson had gained national renown as governor of Illinois and was widely respected for his positions on the issues. He was seen as a thoughtful alternative to the war hero, General Dwight Eisenhower. That year, especially, it was easy to interest people who had never been active in politics before. In 1950, we had contact with some of the religious leaders in the city. This time, Sid and I thought, we might be able to generate real support. We approached some ministers we knew and asked them if they would be willing to urge their people, on a nonpartisan basis, to register to vote. We found a number of them who considered it their civic duty, and who did just that.

The Reverend Mallary Fitzpatrick of the Mount Hope Congregational Church and Sheldon Rahn, a regional official for several Methodist churches, were particularly interested. They invited us to make a presentation at a monthly issues forum they had been having with several Detroit colleagues. Sid prepared well, and was planning to chair the session. Unfortunately, this was the night Sid's wife Doris picked to finagle her husband's presence at home.

Campaigns are particularly hard on the families of dedicated candidates and workers. Doris Woolner found herself home alone most of the time with their two small children. Sid was a devoted and concerned husband and father, but he was immersed in the campaign.

The night of the meeting rolled around, and we were elated at the number of ministers who had responded to our invitation. About 5:00 P.M. Doris called and told Sid she was seeing spots before her eyes. Sid hurriedly cleared his desk, gave me the notes he had made, and said: "I have to go home. Doris is ill, and you will have to chair the meeting."

We had talked the agenda over enough so that I was familiar with what Sid had planned to say. After the first few difficult moments, I got right into it and enjoyed the meeting. Mallary Fitzpatrick sent a note of thanks, remarking that the evening was a high point for the ministers' sessions. The clergy kept in close touch with us and prompted many people in their churches to become familiar with candidates and issues.

It was a good thing the meeting was a success. A few days later, when Doris Woolner and I were talking, she laughed and said, "I got Sid home for dinner the other night, didn't I?" "Doris," I said, "Do you know what you did to me?" She said she was sorry, but that she hadn't lied. "I was ironing my white dress with the blue dots on it, and I really did see spots before my eyes."

13

In 1952,
a Recount Saves
Mennen Williams
But No One Else

A S WILD AS OUR OFFICE was every day of that 1952 campaign, you could have heard a pin drop the nights that Adlai Stevenson was on the radio. Everyone gathered around to listen to his speech—we didn't have a television set then. He was an intelligent man who offered well-thought-out solutions to the problems of the time. We in our Michigan office could never understand why he didn't win. Apparently the appeal of the D-Day war hero, Ike Eisenhower, was just too much for the people to resist. Stevenson's loss, along with the defeat of everyone else we had worked for except Mennen, had a devastating effect on us all. Mennen's and Blair's votes were the only ones that were even close.

Blair Moody had a much more difficult campaign than Mennen. The old-line Democrats resented the fact that Mennen had appointed Blair to replace Senator Vandenberg. They ran Louis Schwinger, husband of the former Democratic national committeewoman, in the primary. Although Blair had been senator for more than a year, he was not too well-known around the state. We were afraid of the old-line Democratic appeal. Blair campaigned hard and won easily.

The final election was a different story, however. The winner of the Republican primary, Charles Potter, had lost part of a leg during the war. On all of his television appearances he limped—quite deliberately—from one end of the stage to the other before he spoke. Senator Moody couldn't help it that he was the picture of health. It didn't even matter that he had been a war correspondent. It was whispered that Blair could easily go back to a high-paying job at the *Detroit News* while his opponent really needed a job.

The truth was that Potter was a well-entrenched member of the U. S. House of Representatives. He was from Cheboygan, where he had helped oversee welfare programs before the war. After he was wounded in Europe, he came home and began working as an administrator of vocational rehabilitation programs. When the incumbent representative from the 11th Congressional District died, Potter ran and won a special election in 1947. He was reelected in 1948 and 1950.

All of us did our best, but I don't believe anyone suffered more than Senator Moody's wife, Ruth. She had a wonderful working knowledge of national issues and was able to discuss them intelligently and simply enough to reach her audience. She also had a way with fashion and always looked stunning. It was not without a great deal of effort. Every public event was pure torture for her, and she was always soaked with perspiration at the end of any appearance, no matter what the temperature. She had to buy more clothes than most people because hers were so often in the cleaners, and she always had to carry a complete second or third outfit with her. Her schedule had to be arranged to give her time for a shower and change of clothes between each major appearance.

Ruth had her fun, too. During the 1952 presidential campaign, Pat Nixon, wife of Richard Nixon, made a great show of the fact that she always wore a cloth coat. On cold days during the campaign, Ruth wore a beautiful fur coat and made it a point to tell everyone that her husband had bought it for her. She even had the bill made into a fancy corsage and pinned it to her coat. It drew many laughs. Everyone knew that Richard Nixon, a lawyer and a member of Congress, could well afford a fur coat for Pat.

We just couldn't overcome the effects of national politics on our elections that year. Dwight Eisenhower's war reputation was not lost on a voting populace made up of many returned veterans. In his running mate, Nixon, Eisenhower had a Californian who had made a name for himself as an anti-Communist crusader on the House Un-American Activities Committee. It was quite a potent combination. The team of Stevenson and John Sparkman of Alabama attracted less attention, but they were concentrating on the issues.

Mennen concentrated on speaking out for the needs of Michigan. In a message to the legislature, he reiterated the pent-up problems facing the state at that time. He pointed out that people and services were strained beyond the limit. The demands of two world wars had stimulated industrial growth and helped cause a twenty percent increase in population, as people came to Michigan to work and make their homes. Mennen wanted the Republicans to wake up and realize that the needs could no longer be ignored.[1]

It was a good thing Mennen had no primary opponent to distract his attention and divide the party. With a tidal wave of Republican votes headed his way, and with a solid Republican majority in the legislature, he needed every vote he could get. His strategy, as usual, was to get his message to the people.

In a campaign flyer, Mennen's accomplishments were toted up under the heading, "Building the people's plant." Among the listings: 1,380 new mental hospital beds; thirty-seven new community hospitals; new medical school facilities at Wayne University and at the University of Michigan; new buildings of every description at every state college or university; an increase from $50 to $70 a month for old-age assistance, and an average of about $13 a month more for family grants; an increase in unemployment compensation from $20 to $27 a week; forty airport additions; the launching of plans to improve state highways; and the completion of plans and beginning of financing for the Mackinac Bridge. The flyer noted that:

> When he took office in 1949, the state had let its physical plant run down. It was inadequate to service the needs of an ever-expanding population. Governor Williams has reversed that trend, with a 'Build Michigan' program in which forward-looking citizens of all political faiths have joined. New hospitals, new public buildings, improved transportation, new schools—all these are important to Michigan's well-being. . . .

> On these cornerstones of progress, Governor Williams and his Democratic administration are building a greater Michigan.

That is the closest the flyer comes to lambasting the Republicans. In a similar listing of the governor's accomplishments, the party line was unmistakable: "In spite of bitter opposition from a small Republican policy clique in Lansing, the administration of Governor Williams has taken giant steps to bring Michigan government in line with the state's expanded needs."[2]

Once again, three Republicans ran in the primary for governor. The winner, Fred M. Alger, Jr., was a neighbor of Mennen's from the Grosse Pointes and came from a similar background, although he was ten years older than Mennen. He had gone to prep school in the East and to Harvard and had served in the Navy during World War II. He was the grandson of Russell A. Alger, who had made his fortune in lumbering and who had been governor in 1885 and 1886 and a U. S. senator at the turn of the century. Fred Alger was in his third term as secretary of state. He campaigned on the claim that Mennen had deserted his wealthy heritage while he, Alger, was loyal to the principles of the Republican party.

The battle among the three candidates quickly became bitter and, again, that was to Mennen's advantage. Alger received 384,532 votes in the primary, with his nearest opponent, Donald Leonard, getting 253,703, and the third, William Vandenberg, 231,461.

In the primary, at least, Michigan Republicans clearly were divided. But sometime between then and election day, momentum built for the Republicans—and their strategy included some dirty tricks the weekend before the election.

That year, the Stevenson campaign had produced some excellent, and expensive, campaign booklets. As always, they were in short supply. Paul Willis, who had charge of the distribution of literature for the Democratic National Committee, was a friend of those of us who were running the Michigan campaigns. He knew he could trust us to use every piece he sent us. In plenty of time for us to receive the literature—at least a week before the election—he shipped us literally a ton of the best Stevenson campaign material. Where it was waylaid, no one could ever find out, but we didn't receive the literature that our people were begging for until two days after the election. We gave everyone who wanted one a copy as a souvenir, but we were forced to sell most of the campaign literature as scrap paper to pay the bills.

As it turned out, Stevenson and all our candidates except Mennen were swept away in the torrent that elected Eisenhower and Nixon. In Michigan, Stevenson was far behind both Mennen and Blair. The final presidential tally in Michigan was Eisenhower 1,555,529 and Stevenson 1,230,657, giving Eisenhower a margin of almost 325,000 votes. Blair lost narrowly. Mennen won, but barely. The margin was so thin in the governor's race that another recount was inevitable. As it turned out, the way the votes fell, Blair probably would have been elected if a senatorial race recount had been allowed.

The senator's election night headquarters were in the Hotel Fort Shelby, while Mennen's were in the Book Cadillac. A steady stream of supporters traipsed between the two hotels, which were within easy walking distance of each other on the west side of downtown. Late in the evening Blair Moody called me and asked if I'd come over and try to comfort Ruth. We had become good friends. She was in bed, weeping, and was inconsolable. All she could say was: "Oh, Helen, I tried so hard and it wasn't enough. . . . I tried so hard." All that I could tell her was that it had been impossible to beat the appeal for sympathy their opponent had made as he limped painfully before the television camera, reminding everyone he was a wounded World War II veteran. Blair Moody was a newspaperman who did not need to be a senator, people had said. She finally sobbed herself to sleep.

There were some hard lessons to be learned from that election. It showed plainly that we had been talking to ourselves too much and had not been close enough to the people. But we hoped we could salvage something. We began making plans to see that all of the votes for Mennen would be honestly and fairly counted. Because Blair's vote was just about as close as Mennen's, he appealed to Congress for a recount. It was denied.

Even before we knew for sure that we would have a recount in the governor's election, Neil Staebler sent out an urgent letter to county party leaders and members of the State Central Committee. The letter pointed out that the party was expecting another recount and urged everyone to be prepared. Neil spelled out the volunteer help that would be needed and even set up a training session:

> We expect definite word on the recount shortly after November 26. Assuming that one will be requested, it will be necessary to bring our people together for a training session on Sunday, November 30. On that day we will meet in some 16 cities throughout the state. You will be notified of the meeting nearest you. As soon as we get word that the recount is going to be held we will advise you by telephone and you can then notify your workers. Meanwhile, have them hold open that Sunday afternoon.

> Enclosed is a form and stamped return envelope for your convenience. Please return it to Detroit by Wednesday, November 19th, listing your county recount supervisor, the attorneys who will be available, and the number of challengers available part time and full time.

George Edwards could no longer help because, as a judge, he had to forego partisan politics. Tom Downs took his place. Tom and Sid Woolner reviewed all that had been done so successfully in 1950 and outlined our plan of attack. My group of young lawyers formed a good nucleus of supervisors for the ballot counting. Several of the people who had worked in the 1950 recount volunteered. Tom and Sid ran instruction classes while Neil, Adelaide Hart, and the county chairmen signed up volunteers by the hundreds.

Again I was assigned to run the Democratic party's recount office. The night before the recount was to begin we had one last meeting with our group of lawyers. Neil made sure that they all had big enough cash advances to carry them through the week in the various counties where they were headed. Arrangements were being set up for the lawyers to call Sid and Tom every night, so they could report the errors they found every day. Often the same mistakes cropped up in different places. After every report had been analyzed, Sid and Tom would phone them all back on a conference call and give them the word as to what to look for the next day. Both Sid and Tom were convinced that strategy is what led to success. Once our team knew what mistakes to look for, they weren't hard to find.

A bad ice storm started shortly after my "boys" started out. Knowing bad weather was predicted, I asked each of them to call me as soon as they got in safely. It was a long and anxious evening for me before the last of them called in. The driving had been very hazardous and some of them had narrow escapes, but they all arrived safely.

A lack of finances had forced us to lay off our exceptional secretary, Madge Cruce, after the election. When she came in to volunteer for the recount, I was able to hire her back. Madge and I had not had time to get acquainted during the campaign. During the recount, our desks were next to each other, and there weren't many of us in the office. We became good friends.

The 1952 recount was serious business throughout—no lighthearted banter as we'd had in 1950, when we were "ahead by a slight margarine." George Edwards and several others have said that it was the 1952 recount that brought Democrats together in Michigan. People were determined to work as a team to see justice done. Even Democrats who lived in the more sparsely populated, heavily Republican areas became convinced that much could be accomplished if we pulled together.

As the recount continued, Mennen picked up more votes; errors were discovered all over the state. In the end, we won again. The percentage was only a fraction of a point higher than Mennen's thin margin in 1950, while the total vote was one-and-a-half times greater. The final tally after the recount was 1,431,893 for Mennen and 1,423,275 for Alger. None of the Democrats who ran for the State Administrative Board made it this time, so Mennen faced another lonely two years. He even had a Republican, Clarence Reid, as lieutenant governor. The 1963 Michigan Constitution now requires the governor and lieutenant governor to be elected together. Any governor who had to deal with having the opposition as a stand-in knows what a wise decision the revisers of the constitution made when they fixed that.

Blair's vote in the final election had been 1,383,416, while Potter got 1,428,352. The percent of difference was slightly greater than in the governor's race but still less than one point. It was too bad the Senate turned down Blair's request for a recount. Judging by the errors found in Mennen's votes, Blair might well have won.

When it was all over, I was exhausted. My son talked me into driving to Massachusetts for a family Christmas, complete with little children and lots of happy relatives—as far away from a campaign as I could get. Before I left, I apologized to Mennen and told him I probably would miss the inaugural. He understood, but he said it wouldn't be the same without me. Massachusetts and the family were fine for a while, but at the last minute I knew I couldn't miss the inaugural. My son drove all night to get me back in time. It was fun going through the reception line and seeing the surprised look on the governor's face. Weeks later Mennen sent me a picture that had been snapped at just that moment.

NOTES

1. For the full text of this and other messages to the Michigan legislature, see the papers of G. Mennen Williams in the Michigan Historical Collections, Bentley Historical Library, University of Michigan, Ann Arbor.

2. For examples of campaign material and insights into the Williams administration, see the Michigan Historical Collections, Bentley Historical Library, University of Michigan, Ann Arbor. In addition to the papers of Governor Williams and Helen Berthelot, the Bentley Library has several collections from other party leaders and officeholders, including Adelaide Hart, Neil Staebler, Margaret Price, Carolyn Sinelli Burns, Tom Downs, Martha Griffiths, John Swainson, and George Romney. Oral histories of many of the principals in this book and of other public figures from this period may be found in the Bentley Library; in the Archives of Labor and Urban Affairs at Wayne State University, Detroit; or in the State Archives, located in the Michigan Library and Historical Center, 717 W. Allegan, Lansing.

Mennen and Nancy Williams in January 1949. (Helen Berthelot's personal collection.)

Labor leaders unite behind Williams in the 1948 campaign. Back row: Hicks Griffiths, G. Mennen Williams's campaign manager, and Frank Martel, chairman of the AFL of Detroit and Wayne County. Front row: Gus Scholle, president of the Michigan CIO; G. Mennen Williams; and Helen Berthelot, secretary-treasurer of the Michigan Telephone Traffic Federation (later known as Communications Workers of America). (Helen Berthelot's personal collection.)

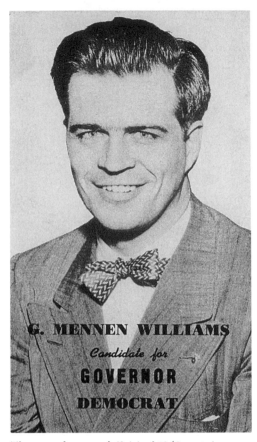

The power of a postcard. (Original 1948 campaign materials. Helen Berthelot's personal collection.)

Dear Friend,

I am writing you concerning G. **MENNEN WILLIAMS, DEMOCRATIC** candidate for GOVERNOR.

These are the things he will do for us and our families:

Housing for All
Civil Rights
Improved Schools and Teachers' Pay
Better Roads

Adequate Social Security and Unemployment Compensation
State Veterans' Service
Coordinated State Administration

Boosting Home Farm Products

This is what he has done in the past:

Liquor Control Commissioner, Michigan
Milk Marketing Study Commission, Michigan
Ass't Attorney General, Michigan

Deputy Director OPA, Michigan
Special Ass't to U.S. Attorney General
Attorney Social Security Board

With G. **MENNEN WILLIAMS** the **DEMOCRATIC PARTY** will win in November.

P.S.—WIN WITH WILLIAMS in the **SEPTEMBER PRIMARY**—Sincerely,

22

The soon-to-be-first family goes Christmas shopping for dad, December 1948: Nancy Williams, with Gery, Wendy, and Nan. (Detroit Free Press).

Mennen attends a picnic in August 1949 with members of Walter Reuther's home local, Local 174 of the United Auto Workers union. Front row, left to right: Walter Reuther, George Edwards, and Mennen Williams. (Photographer: John Pratt. Detroit Free Press.)

Mennen Williams shakes hands with George Edwards after appointing him to the Wayne County Probate Court in 1951. (Archives of Labor and Urban Affairs, Wayne State University.)

Whenever there was an emergency in the campaigns of Mennen Williams for governor, Peg Edwards was first on the spot. (Detroit Free Press.)

Governor Williams swears in Blair Moody as U. S. senator from Michigan in the spring of 1951. (Photographer: Pat Mitchell Pictures. Helen Berthelot's personal collection.)

A neophyte in campaigning, but knowledgeable in national affairs, Ruth Moody quickly became an able aide to her husband. (Helen Berthelot's personal collection.)

The Michigan delegation shows its colors—green-and-white bow ties and "Win with Williams" buttons—in Chicago at the 1952 Democratic National Convention. (Photographer: Tony Spina. Tony Spina's personal collection.)

The Michigan delegation proudly presents Mennen Williams as a favorite son candidate for president at the 1952 National Convention. The governor is at the far left. On the right, holding a "Williams for President" placard, is Adelaide Hart. (Photographer: Tony Spina. Detroit Free Press.)

Senator Estes Kefauver and Governor Williams at the 1952 Democratic National Convention. (Photographer: Tony Spina. Helen Berthelot's personal collection.)

Governor Williams and Nancy Williams sent pictures of the family each Christmas to their many friends. This was taken in their Lansing home in the early 1950s. (Helen Berthelot's personal collection.)

*Governor Williams cuts the ribbon for the successful 1959 Michigan
State Fair, with members of his administration and State Fair staff and
board members sharing the moment. (Helen Berthelot's personal
collection.)*

*Jim Hare, manager of the State Fair, and Helen Berthelot, vice
chairman of the State Fair Board, view the progress of one of her pet
projects—repair and renovation of the grandstands and coliseum in
1954. (Helen Berthelot's personal collection.)*

Nancy Williams adjusts an Indian headdress worn by her husband at a
sport show at the state fairgrounds in early 1949. (Photographer:
Vincent Witek. Detroit Free Press.)

A proud student in the 1952 State Fair cooking school shows a cake he
baked to Governor Williams and his mother, Mrs. Elma Williams.
(Helen Berthelot's personal collection.)

City man Blair Moody cautiously approaches a newborn calf at the 1952 State Fair, as Helen Berthelot, board vice chairman, and Harry Wright, chairman of the Fair Board, look on. (Helen Berthelot's personal collection.)

Vice Chairman of the State Fair Board Helen Berthelot rides in the State Fair parade with the Michigan Bean Queen. (Photographer: Marston A. Pierce. Helen Berthelot's personal collection.)

Mennen Williams rides in a parade in downtown Detroit in the late 1950s. (Helen Berthelot's personal collection.)

Adelaide Hart, Margaret Price, and Helen Berthelot join the 1953 inaugural well-wishers in the governor's office. (Helen Berthelot's personal collection.)

After a dynamic speech at the Jefferson-Jackson Day dinner in Detroit early in 1953, Eleanor Roosevelt greets Governor Williams and Nancy Williams. (Helen Berthelot's personal collection.)

Sidney Woolner coordinated many campaigns and was always a trusted campaign adviser for Mennen Williams and, later, Phil Hart. (Sidney Woolner's personal collection.)

Helen Berthelot managed Governor G. Mennen Williams's
campaigns from 1954 on. (Helen Berthelot's personal collection.)

John Murray reminisces with then-Supreme Court Justice
G. Mennen Williams during John's retirement reception in
1985 at Michigan State University, where John had a long
career as a journalism and communications professor.
(Photographer: Michael Kitchen, MSU School of Journalism.
John Murray family.)

Horace Gilmore worked with Helen Berthelot
and Sid Woolner in the early campaigns to
elect precinct delegates. In 1954, he joined Sid
as co-coordinator of Democratic campaigns.
(Horace Gilmore's personal collection.)

Paul Weber was the governor's close adviser. Their daily and sometimes
hourly exchanges helped shape Mennen Williams's vision for Michigan.
(Photographer: Ray Glonka. Detroit Free Press.*)*

After a stormy start, Neil Staebler, left, chairman of the Michigan Democratic party, and Senator Pat McNamara became the best of friends and worked together for Michigan. (Photographer: Tony Spina. Detroit Free Press.)

Thanks to the 1954 Democratic sweep, Governor Williams had a full Democratic Administrative Board and a U. S. senator. From left, Sanford Brown, state treasurer; Victor Targonski, auditor general; Thomas Kavanagh, attorney general; Governor Williams and Senator Patrick McNamara at the head of the table; James Hare, secretary of state; and Phil Hart, lieutenant governor. (Photographer: Snuffy McGill. Helen Berthelot's personal collection.)

14

NEW RESPONSIBILITIES
A JEFF-JACK DINNER, A SPRING CAMPAIGN,
LOBBYING FOR LABOR

WHEN THE 1952 CAMPAIGN was all over, I went back to the strangely quiet Democratic headquarters in downtown Detroit troit to pack up my belongings and get ready to go back to my job in Lansing with the CWA. Neil Staebler came in, all smiles as usual. "I've talked to Walter Schaar," he said, referring to my CWA boss. "And he has reluctantly agreed to let us have you for another few months." When I looked surprised, Neil said the party leadership had met recently and had some more work for me to do. "We unanimously agreed that you should be given the honor of being the first woman chairman of the Jefferson-Jackson Day dinner," said Neil, still beaming.

It was quite a tribute. When I learned that the speaker was to be Eleanor Roosevelt, the former first lady and great humanitarian, I was even more thrilled. With the chairmanship also came the responsibility of organizing the dinner. Money was hard to raise after the costly 1952 campaign, so it was no easy task to get a big crowd. Somehow, we managed to pack the Masonic Temple for the dinner and speech. My knees were shaking as I took the microphone to get things started. After I had made a couple of remarks, Nancy Williams leaned over and discreetly whispered, "Helen, the mike isn't turned on." It didn't help my nerves to have to start all over again, but I got through it.

Mrs. Roosevelt gave a powerful speech that offered hope and encouragement that we would somehow prevail. After the election we had just been through, it was exactly what we needed to hear. To this date I have not forgiven the man hired to photograph Mrs. Roosevelt and the people at the head table. He completely ignored my efforts to attract his attention so I could have my picture taken with Mrs. Roosevelt. At least he got a very nice photograph of Mennen and Nancy with her.

Before going back to the CWA, I stayed in Detroit to manage the 1953 spring election campaign. The Democratic State Central Committee had chosen me to be the campaign manager for the statewide candidates. It was the loneliest and most discouraging campaign I can imagine. At that time, elections were held in the spring for the superintendent of public instruction, highway commissioner, Board of Education, supreme court, and several other state offices. After the disheartening fall results, we had trouble getting people to run.

Enough loyal Democrats finally came forward to fill out the ticket, but the hundreds of volunteers we had worked so hard to keep busy in 1952 were nowhere to be found. Only a few of the very faithful showed up. It really didn't matter too much. There was so little money to buy campaign material that distributing it was a simple task.

My hardest problem was persuading the discouraged party people to get out and hear the candidates. Groups which had welcomed our candidates the year before were seldom interested in our spring candidates. After 5:00 P.M. most days, I was usually alone in the campaign office. That wasn't like the revved-up Democratic party I had become accustomed to. And not one of our candidates won. It was my first taste of complete, bitter defeat.

When I finally went back to my CWA office in Lansing, I had been on leave for a year and a half. It wasn't easy to get back into the routine of not being the boss and not having a hundred things to worry about at once. That spring, Neil Staebler, as chairman of the Democratic State Central Committee, wrote a courtesy letter to Joseph Beirne, the national president of the CWA in Washington, thanking him for letting me work for the party for so long. Neil was generous in his praise and noted that I had made history by being the first woman of either party in Michigan to manage a statewide campaign and the first woman to chair the Jefferson-Jackson Day dinner in Michigan:

> Helen has exemplified the very finest type of union member—deeply devoted to the Union and deeply devoted to the Party. It has contributed greatly to the development of the kind of harmonious relations between Democrats who are union members and Democrats who are not union members, which all of us hope will be the pattern for the future.

Those words meant a great deal to me, especially since they describe the kind of broad-based party that Mennen was trying to build.

A friend of mine in CWA's national office wrote me that there was going to be a vacancy in the department that oversees legislation. "It would be just the job for you," he declared. Not telling anyone, I flew to D. C. and asked Joe Beirne to consider me for the vacancy. It appealed to Joe that I would be the first full-time woman lobbyist in the labor movement. It won't be an easy job, he warned me. All the other union lobbyists will be men, he said. Working with men didn't frighten me—I was used to it, I told Joe.

"One thing," I said. "I'd want to take a leave of absence every other year as long as Governor Williams ran for office." Joe agreed to consider me. In his mind he only anticipated one leave of absence. Like many other people, he didn't expect Mennen to survive as governor. As it turned out, I had a leave every other year until I retired in 1969. When Mennen no longer ran, someone else wanted my help.

The job was thrown open for applications, but no one of my seniority or experience put in a bid. So I had the honor of being the first full-time woman lobbyist in the labor movement. Walter Schaar felt so sure I'd be discouraged and come back to Michigan he held my job open for six months. It wasn't easy. It took a long while before the men—even in my own CWA Legislative Department—accepted me. When they found I was going to hold up my end of the work and ask no favors, they finally accepted me as just another member of the group.

The move to Washington gave me a broader perspective of politics and issues. It also afforded me many opportunities to share what we had learned in Michigan with people all over the country. One of the first things I did when I got to D. C. was to volunteer my services at the Democratic National Committee. My other outside activities included the Women's National Democratic Club and several civic groups. The contacts I made in Washington would eventually help me in my work with Michigan campaigns and the national party.

Later that year, I attended my first Democratic Midwest Conference, in Milwaukee. One of the members of the press at the conference was a young man on the staff of the *Congressional Quarterly*, the journal which records what goes on in the Capitol. Someone told him I knew many of the people at the meeting, and he sought me out. We had met a few times before because the *Congressional Quarterly* was one of the best sources of information for someone in my line of work. He promptly reintroduced himself and asked if he could tag along with me to get to know people from the various states. From then on, this young man— David Broder—was my shadow. He wanted to know all about everyone, where they were from, what they did in their home states, their importance at the conference. Somehow, I was able to answer many of his questions to his satisfaction.

In the very next Michigan election he showed up at our campaign headquarters, still asking questions. By then, he was rising to prominence as a national political journalist based in Washington. Our relationship at the time was cordial and based on mutual respect, and we remain in touch. It is a pleasure to receive occasional notes from him and to read the nationally syndicated political column he writes from his base at the *Washington Post*. Years later, long after that Michigan election in which we got to know each other, I introduced him as a speaker at the Women's National Democratic Club in Washington. When he came into the campaign headquarters, I told the audience, he saw all the things I didn't want him to see and asked all the questions I didn't want to answer. However, I said, he always wrote a straight story.

Working with the CWA over the years, most of my energies were directed toward issues and legislation. (In 1954, after he became president of the CIO, I got a letter from Walter Reuther. He addressed me as "Dear Sister Berthelot" and thanked me for "excellent and effective work" and "the fine contribution you are making" on behalf of national legislation for working people.) In my work with the Democratic party, I was happy to leave the issues to the people who made up what I called (to myself) the "brain trust." It wasn't that I didn't understand the issues and voice my opinions frequently. It was simply that my delight was making the wheels of the campaign go smoothly. Mennen often called me his catalyst. The "Nuts and Bolts Girl" is my description of myself. If someone intimated that I just couldn't do that, that it was too hard, I made sure that was what I accomplished.

During my early days in D. C., I got exposed to the issues, along with a dash of the political nuts and bolts, most Sundays. Following his defeat in the 1952 election, Blair Moody was back in Washington. One of the things he was doing was hosting a popular weekly television show called "Meet Your Congress." Each week he featured interviews with one or two senators or congressmen who were in the limelight at the moment or in the circle of top leaders. Often, Blair would bring his guest or guests of the day home for dinner. Ruth Moody was great at putting together a delicious informal dinner, and everyone enjoyed good food and a stimulating discussion of problems or pending legislation. They almost always included me, so my legislative education was greatly broadened. It also gave me a chance to meet many of the leaders in Congress in a way that otherwise would have been impossible.

After the first few invitations, I never made any plans for Sunday. It became a ritual. About 10:30 A.M., the telephone would ring, and a sleepy Blair would ask, "What are you planning to do today?" My answer was some variation of "Oh, nothing in particular." Then he would suggest I come over and watch his show with Ruth and then stay for dinner. He always added, "I have a few questions about the Michigan campaign I want to ask you."

After Blair's guests left, the questions would start. It was like an inquisition. David Broder is the only person I know who could ask as many questions as Blair did. Blair was already planning to run for the Senate again in 1954, and he wanted to be prepared. He picked my brain on every aspect of Michigan campaigns. One by one, he asked about the various sections of Michigan and what appealed to the voters in each place. This would go on until Ruth would fall asleep, either in Blair's lap or in a big chair. After asking him several times to call me a cab, I would finally reach for the telephone and call one myself.

In early December of 1953, Blair decided he wanted to send Christmas cards to his huge political mailing list. He had two different pictures taken—one of himself, Ruth and their two sons, and one of him as the moderator of his television program. Two weeks before Christmas, he called me on a Saturday afternoon and said the cards were ready, but he wanted me to help him decide which picture he should send to various people. When I got there, Senator Bill Knowland, a prominent Republican from California, was there, his sleeves rolled up, ready to help get out the cards. He and the Moodys had been close friends for years.

We formed a production line. Blair would read the name of each person and then ask me which picture to send. Somehow he had a very exaggerated opinion of my knowledge of the people in Michigan. Quickly, I learned to answer with a voice of authority—"They'd like the family picture," or "I think they'd appreciate the 'Meet Your Congress' picture." Some I felt sure about. With others, I just guessed at their preference. To lend an air of authenticity to my suggestions, occasionally I would say, "I really don't know but I think either one would do." Then, I would put them in the envelope, Ruth would seal them, and Senator Knowland would lick the stamps.

It was 3:00 A.M. before we finished that huge pile of cards. We were all exhausted, but Blair was elated. He felt he had a good beginning for his election campaign. Although I felt like a hypocrite, I consoled myself with the knowledge that Blair had felt so good about personalizing his Christmas cards. No matter which one people received, they would be happy about getting a holiday greeting from him, I knew. Many people mentioned that to me later. And after the first of the year Blair started to campaign in earnest.

15

CAMPAIGN MANAGER
FOR GOVERNOR WILLIAMS

T HE MICHIGAN PRESS, controlled largely by Republicans, did its
best to portray Mennen Williams as a dancing, square-dance-
calling lightweight without a serious thought in his head. He
also was described as the lackey of organized labor—Walter Reuther and
Gus Scholle in particular—and therefore as someone who could not be
trusted to represent all the people. Of course, neither image was correct.

Many of Mennen's views on social problems and solutions were
shared by labor leaders, including Gus and Walter Reuther, but Mennen
made up his own mind. Speaking at Princeton University in 1984, Mennen pointed out that the relationship between the candidate and the labor voter is more important than the one between the candidate and the
union leader: "As Walter Reuther himself said, neither he nor anyone
else could deliver the labor vote. They could and did render invaluable
services and did open many doors. But for the most part, like the Smith
Barney ad, I had to get my votes the old-fashioned way—I earned them,
one by one."

Anyone who ever talked with Mennen Williams knew that he
thought things through. Although he never flaunted his academic honors, he was a Phi Beta Kappa at Princeton and had graduated cum laude
from the University of Michigan Law School. His broad perception of
the issues and his insistence on hearing all sides was brought home to me
at the beginning of the 1954 campaign.

It was early in the year, long before the campaign actually got
started. Mennen had called together a cross-section of about thirty peo-

ple. It was truly a representative group. There were people from small towns, big cities, and farm areas. There were labor leaders of all kinds as well as liberals and conservatives, some of them not at all friendly to Mennen. There were a few teachers and at least one housewife. This was definitely not the group of loyal supporters usually invited to the governor's meetings. Adelaide Hart and I whispered indignantly about this to each other as people arrived for the meeting and we saw who some of them were. "What is *he* doing here? He doesn't go along with anything we believe in," we said as we spotted people we thought didn't belong.

The governor chaired the meeting himself. It was quickly evident that he had given a lot of thought to this meeting and to the issues he felt were urgent. It also was quickly evident that there was a wide range of opinion. Mennen introduced subject after subject. We were all encouraged to say what we thought. The points were at times a little hotly discussed, but things never got out of hand. Mennen chaired a well-controlled meeting, yet we all felt free to express our views. It wasn't until nearly the end of the meeting that the impact of what he had done dawned on us. In no other way could all the facts, arguments, and problems have been brought out more forcibly.

Mennen hadn't written down a single word, but he summarized the consensus of the meeting to everyone's satisfaction. The purpose had been to discuss the problems he felt were urgent and to talk about possible solutions. It wasn't the task of this committee to decide how to pay for any new programs. That was the job of another group that Mennen convened a little later. He was well on his way to formulating his list of programs for the 1954 campaign.

Some of the problems we discussed at that meeting aren't too much different from those of today: the need for better housing for the general public and for the aged; inadequate schools; overcrowded prisons and other state institutions; the need for strict inspection and minimum safety codes, as well as better unemployment compensation, for workers; an improved road system; help for the farmer in getting produce to the marketplace and in spreading the word about Michigan farm products; more state efforts to protect civil rights; and a program to combat pollution of our waterways.

When the time came to get the campaign started, Joe Beirne kept his word and gave me a leave of absence to go back to work for Mennen. No one, least of all myself, ever gave a thought to what this did to me financially. Although I was able to rent my apartment in D. C. at a reduced rate, I had to find my own place in Michigan. My friends and family chipped in with the bare necessities, and I rented an unfurnished apartment as cheaply as possible. When it came to expenses, I had to pay my own way. That included cab fare home when I worked late, which was just about every night.

That year, especially, I was in considerable debt by the time the campaign was over and I was heading back to D. C. It was my own fault; I was too proud to mention my financial difficulties. It was a little discouraging at times when I saw the paychecks and expense reimbursements that went to some of the men working for me. CWA continued to pay me, but it was straight pay, with no reimbursement for expenses. In each of Mennen's campaigns, I was the CWA's contribution to Governor Williams's reelection. Despite occasional concern over my financial straits, I was proud to have such a responsible position, and I genuinely wanted to assist Mennen Williams's efforts to build a great state. The opportunity to do that made up for a lot.

When I arrived in Michigan in the spring of 1954, Sid Woolner and Neil Staebler told me that they had met with the governor and all three of them agreed that this year I should be the governor's campaign manager. As far as I know, I was the first woman in the country to hold that title for a major candidate. Women were not as prominent in politics then as they were later.

Most of the responsibility for the governor's 1952 campaign had been mine, so it was not that much different. My duties also included being the office manager. In addition, they wanted me to assist Sid Woolner, who would coordinate all the Democratic campaigns and handle television programs for the governor and the rest of the ticket. Television was something we were getting into more than we had in 1952.

In the 1954 campaign, I had more authority in preparing the governor's schedule and in making other decisions. We had decided that I would have to be the bad guy in the campaign, particularly with the schedule, and say "no" whenever it was necessary. That would leave Mennen free to say he would like to attend whatever event it was, but they would have to check with me. Mennen knew that I would schedule him to meet with as many people as possible, without overlooking any group crucial to the campaign. The other candidates on the state ticket would be asked to speak at many functions the governor had to miss. As the election drew near, no time would be wasted.

My reputation for efficient scheduling had been well established two years earlier. One Saturday afternoon in October during the 1952 campaign, I was at home watching the Michigan-Michigan State football game on television. At halftime, I saw Mennen make his customary walk across the field. It was he who started the governors' tradition of sitting first on one side, then the other, during this annual rivalry. Imagine my surprise to see him accompanied by one of our candidates on the state ticket. The man was supposed to be at a chicken dinner that very afternoon. Not long before my halftime discovery, I had received a worried phone call from the women who were putting on the dinner. They had been cooking chicken all day, and were desperate for the whereabouts of their guest. At the time, I hadn't known what had happened. Now I knew—and I was furious.

The next day, when Mennen showed up at the office to begin his Sunday campaign schedule, I confronted him. "Why did you let him go with you to that football game?" I demanded. Mennen looked a little sheepish as he answered. "Well, he *told* me he didn't have anything scheduled." "Mennen Williams," I said, shaking my finger at him, "You know very well I wouldn't waste a Saturday afternoon for one of our candidates this close to the election!"

Mennen had learned to leave matters of scheduling to me. Because he trusted me and gave me the authority to act, the campaigns ran more smoothly. Most of the problems could be solved with a little thought, and everyone was happy with Mennen.

Even by 1954, however, Larry Farrell was still afraid I would do great harm to Mennen's campaign. Larry's whole political life had been with the old guard, and he found it hard to trust me. This became obvious when the list of ethnic radio programs—a mainstay in Mennen's efforts to communicate with all the people—went to the governor's Lansing office by mistake. Larry, who was the governor's executive secretary, must have felt this was where he could be of great help. He proceeded to schedule the radio talks before checking the schedule for Mennen that we had already outlined for the month. Naturally, Larry's decision created a number of problems. Mennen got wind of it and asked the man who directed the radio programs to call me.

The director phoned and said: "I think I should tell you what the governor said. He told me to call you to straighten out the schedule and that if you couldn't do it, no one could." Those words, when I had so little personal contact with the governor during the long campaign, kept me walking on air the whole week—or at least until the next crisis. With considerable effort, I was able to schedule all the radio programs but one, and we did that one later in the campaign.

Our 1954 campaign headquarters were on the thirty-second floor of the Union Guardian Building in downtown Detroit. Oddly enough, we were in what had been a huge ballroom. We put up partitions at the back of the ballroom to create separate offices for Sid Woolner and Horace Gilmore, and one for Neil Staebler and Adelaide Hart to share. Mine was a little box outside Sid's office, giving me easy access to the typists and the long tables of volunteers. The switchboard and reception desk were at the other end of the huge room.

Of all the campaign workers I ever hired, I only had to fire one woman. She was forced on me in 1954 by one of the district party people and created problems from the very first. She was put in charge of keeping up the address changes in our books and the Addressograph files. The complaints doubled after she took over that job, and I spent a lot of time I could ill spare following up on her errors. One of the boys in the stockroom told me she was telling them not to bother doing what I had asked them to do—that I would forget about it after I'd given them the order. If I did forget it, it was because my boys were trustworthy and did follow through. They knew I appreciated it, and that was why they told me what she was doing. After I started turning up unexpectedly when she went into the stockroom, things settled down. Then one day, I saw her slap one of the clerks on the face. The clerk was a very young, bright, independent black woman. She could be impertinent, but I have no idea what went on between them. The only thing I could think of that would really upset both of them was to take them to Sid Woolner.

Everyone in the office respected and adored Sid. He never had to give the orders and was always kind and courteous. With both of the women in tow, I marched into his office and told him what had happened. Sid looked pained and gulped a couple of times. He eyed them sadly without saying a word. After a few moments, I rescued him, and told them to come out and go to work. Outside Sid's office, they both wailed, "Why did you have to tell *him!*"

The young clerk quit shortly after that, for reasons related to her home life. But the troublemaker was still around. One day, she practically defied me when I brought her still another complaint. That did it. "Don't bother to finish the day," I said. "We will mail your paycheck to you. I don't want to see you around here again." She left and immediately went to her political patron, but I had called him before she got there. He admitted he hadn't known what to do with her. "I thought you could handle her," he told me. When I cleaned out her desk, I found the drawers stuffed with address changes she was supposed to have taken care of. No wonder we had had so many complaints.

Steve Yokich and Paul Seldenright more than made up for her. They had both been laid off from their auto plant jobs, and I promptly hired them to take charge of the package room. They were great. By the time the 1956 campaign arrived, Steve was on the staff of the UAW. George Merrelli, a UAW regional director, complained bitterly but let Steve come to work for the next two campaigns. Steve Yokich was an intelligent and hard worker. He was quick to see what needed to be done and became my able assistant. Hard work only whetted Steve's appetite for doing what he could for a cause in which he believed. He later became a UAW vice president and one of the most highly regarded leaders of the union. Paul Seldenright also came back to help out in subsequent elections and became a trusted campaign driver for the governor. For Paul, too, the campaigns were an impetus. He became an assistant to the president of the Michigan State AFL-CIO and a faithful labor leader.

We also had a few very faithful workers who came in at great hardship. Cornela Sess from a west side Polish neighborhood was a prime example. Rain or shine, if we were getting out a big mailing, she was there. Someone found out later that she hardly had bus fare at times.

Early in the campaigns, I realized the volunteers wanted to feel they were a vital part of the campaign. Every so often, I would go in and work with them, stuffing envelopes for a few minutes and telling them about something that had happened, or was going to happen, that no one outside the office had heard.

One day I was able to demonstrate how valuable our volunteers really were. A brash, well-dressed young lady fluttered in and announced, in a supercilious voice, that she wanted to volunteer. It was a good thing I happened to be right there. "Good," I said. "We are getting out a big, important mailing. There's a place for you—right over there." "Oh," she said in a tone that implied she was doing us a favor, "I don't want to do anything like *that*. I want to work on policy." Smiling, I said: "I am sorry but we don't need help in that area. We already have a committee that handles policy. The people working here getting out this mailing are the most important people we have." She turned on her heel and flounced out. We didn't need help like hers, I told the long table of volunteers, but we couldn't get along without their assistance.

One of my best envelope-stuffers was a stout woman who had just walked in one day. When she sat with other people she giggled a lot, so I found a special spot for her by herself, not far from my office. One day, Jack Wuthrich, one of the governor's state police aides, dropped in to bring me a message just as I was giving her another pack of envelopes to stuff. Jack grabbed me by the arm and pulled me into my office.

"What's that woman doing here?" he asked. "What woman do you mean? The one I was talking to is one of my best volunteers," I said. "Get rid of her right away," Jack insisted. "Suppose the governor had come in." "What's the problem?" I asked. "She is just out of a mental hospital," he said. "She keeps calling and writing the governor and Phil Hart. She sent them both the keys to her house. She even got in Phil Hart's house the other night and they had to call the police to get her out."

I later told the woman, very reluctantly, that I would not have any more work for her and not to bother to come back. Two days afterward Jack told me she had been picked up and put back in the hospital. She had seemed almost normal when she had been stuffing envelopes. She had done it very rapidly and neatly. It had been good therapy for her.

Normally, the governor attracted excellent volunteers, and we tried hard to keep them happy. Sid Woolner's mother, Olive, had a remarkable talent for keeping the volunteers busy and contented. Olive and a man we knew only as Mr. Renny ran our mimeograph and postage meter

131

machines. They both were in their seventies and were perfectionists. Every day they had some sort of clash over little things that were not done to suit the other, but no one else could criticize either of them in their presence. They started complaining about each other to Sid, but I soon learned I could soothe their feelings by just talking to them. They were both wonderful helpers and it was well worth my time. Elmer Martel, the seventy-year-old brother of Frank Martel, the president of the Wayne County AFL, was in the same room with them every day. He just kept right on working and never said a word.

16

ENTERTAINING ISN'T EASY

For years, whenever I would complain about anything, Sid Woolner would say, "Okay, but remember the Tubman reception." The memory always put the current problem, no matter how frustrating, into perspective.

Mayor Albert Cobo, the man for whom the Detroit hall and convention center is named, started it all. It was 1954, and President William Tubman of Liberia was coming to Detroit with a group of Republicans. Mayor Cobo, also a Republican, announced he was having a reception for the Liberian dignitary. Apparently the mayor was already thinking about the campaign of 1956, when he would run against Mennen: He wasn't going to include the governor of the state among his fifty guests, until he got too much flak about it from the press.

It was early in the campaign, and I was having a rare moment's quiet in my office when Mennen called. "President Tubman is coming to Michigan. He has entertained me and I want to give him a nice reception here and I would like to have you handle it," he said. "When do you want it?" I asked. He named a date less than two weeks away. "How many do you want to invite?" was my next question. "About fifteen hundred," the governor answered. "Whom do you want to invite?" I asked timidly. "Oh, everyone," he replied nonchalantly and hung up. That was that.

The first thing I did was call Eddie Fishman, the printer I had used in CWA and to whom I turned in every printing emergency. He was one of the unsung heroes of all the campaigns. I asked him if he had two thousand special, large, deckle-edge envelopes and paper to match. He did. I asked him to send the envelopes over right away. They arrived that afternoon. Then I called and reserved the ballroom at the Book Cadillac Hotel.

So far so good. Pat Taylor and Peg Edwards, those stalwarts, were in the campaign office doing a special project, so I asked them to call people who had lists of names that we needed. We would ask those people to come in, get envelopes, and address them. The governor's affair, at least, was to be a nonpartisan event. We got wonderful cooperation. I am quite certain that not one active leader or official in Wayne County was left out.

The bomb fell on the Saturday morning before the reception, which was to be on Tuesday. The invitations were beautiful and were all ready to be stuffed and mailed. They were on gray paper with the state seal in green at the top. As often happened on a Saturday, I was alone in the office. The manager of the Book Cadillac called me and said there had been an error in the scheduling and we could not have the ballroom on Tuesday. He was very evasive in answering my questions.

Moving fast, I called every place I could think of that would be big enough for the reception. The only place available was the basement ballroom at the Detroit Leland, a third-rate substitute. Everyone was out campaigning, and I couldn't find anyone to help me out of my dilemma. Finally Paul Weber, the governor's press secretary, answered my call. His advice was to confront the manager and see if he would help.

Help was the last thing he intended to give me, I was sure, but I had little choice. Luckily, I was all dressed up to go to a luncheon. Gathering up copies of our most impressive VIP names on the guest list and a copy of the invitation, I headed straight for the hotel. Fortunately, the manager's secretary was away from her desk. With my head high, I marched—and I mean marched—right into his office.

"I am Mrs. Berthelot, Governor Williams's campaign manager," I said in my most authoritative voice. "Here is a copy of the two thousand invitations we have sent out, and here are a few samples of the lists of people we have invited. The invitations cannot be recalled and you will have to explain to these people why there is no reception." Turning on my heel, I started to stalk out. My knees were shaking so much that I had to walk straight and tall to keep them from buckling.

The names on the first list I handed him must have given the manager pause, because I was just going out his door when he called me back. He tried lamely to apologize. As he went on and on, I listened in stony silence, then asked him questions. "Who is renting the ballroom? Could they be reached? Would they postpone their affair if they knew about the reception for President Tubman?" The answers he gave were no answers at all. This went on for several minutes.

He hadn't asked me to be seated, but I had sat down and stared at him accusingly. Finally, after what seemed an eternity, he said grumpily, "You can have the reception but I won't be able to let you serve refreshments." "All right," I answered. "We won't have refreshments." Gleefully, I thought to myself, "there's at least six hundred dollars we will save." When I was convinced we had the ballroom, I got up, bowed frostily, and thanked him for his cooperation.

He tried again to stop us on Tuesday morning. He called me and said we would have to cancel the reception—President Tubman had received a threat on his life. "Tell them to double the Secret Service protection," I said, and hung up. My adrenaline had worked again.

That we were able to have the reception at all was a miracle. Without Peg Edwards and Pat Taylor, the invitations never would have gotten out. As the envelopes came back from the volunteers who were addressing them, we checked them against the guest lists and then put them in alphabetical files so that any duplicates could be thrown out. It was Sunday morning before all the envelopes were received. A small army of volunteers worked all day to stuff envelopes. At 4:30 P.M., Pat Taylor took the invitations over to the post office substation. She walked around the back until she found the supervisor, a good Democrat, who smiled and said: "Leave it to me. They'll get out." They did.

The assistant manager of the hotel was so embarrassed about how we had been treated that he did everything in his power to make the ballroom attractive. To add to the elegance of the occasion, I had hired a string trio to play soft music in one corner and ordered several bouquets of flowers to be placed near the receiving line. The assistant manager saw to it that we had a number of potted palms in bare corners.

The manager, however, still did his best to make the reception a flop. He informed me that people could not congregate on the ballroom floor, but would have to line up outside the room to go through the receiving line. The assistant manager arranged for red velvet ropes to guide the line. There were a number of Secret Service men in the open space in the ballroom. The security men and the red velvet ropes conveyed a sense of importance. Somehow, everything the manager did to hinder us made the affair more impressive.

The invitations were delivered on Monday. Ninety percent of the invited guests showed up on Tuesday afternoon. Because they had to line up single file, people wound their way clear around the outside of the hotel, giving the impression that this was truly a big event.

When President Tubman came in, the mystery was solved. The Republican party had put pressure on the hotel manager to sabotage the governor's reception for him. Right beside President Tubman was the Republican candidate for the U. S. Senate, incumbent Homer Ferguson.

The party had been taking President Tubman all over the country with Republican candidates, to show their rapport with black people. They had to import someone from Liberia to do it. President Tubman was perfectly aware of what the Republicans were doing, but he needed financial support for his country.

Because Mennen had wanted this to be a nonpartisan affair, we had made the receiving line rather small and had not included Pat McNamara, our candidate for the Senate. When Margaret Price saw Senator Ferguson in the receiving line, she had Pat McNamara added to the line before anyone knew what had happened. One step down from the foyer leading to the ballroom, Sid Woolner and I had our own little receiving line. Sid could assume a poker face when he wanted to, and no one ever would have accused him of mischief. He drove the Secret Service crazy trying to find out who was passing out Mennen's little bow-tie campaign pins. The people who got them from Sid were leaving them in Senator Ferguson's hand after greeting him. Some of our staunchest supporters also had fun by saying, "Hello, *Mr.* Ferguson" and then, in a loud voice, "Hello, *Senator*" when they got to Pat McNamara. Pat, of course, was not an incumbent.

Everyone had a fine time, except me. When it was over, I went home with a sick headache, emotionally exhausted. Mennen never knew a thing was wrong until years later when Sid Woolner ragged me about the Tubman reception because I had complained about something. Mennen said: "What do you mean? That was a fine reception." Sid then told him what had happened. Mennen said: "But I didn't know anything about it." "You weren't supposed to," I said. "That's why I am here."

We were always wary of attempts by the opposition to sabotage our best efforts. Even in non-election years, we had to be careful. It was one of those years, and I was back in D. C. when Sid Woolner called and told me Mennen wanted me to come to Michigan and put on a big reception for King Hussein of Jordan. Because of my activities with ethnic groups during the campaigns, Mennen thought I would work well with Arab Americans. Joe Beirne just shook his head. "Not again," he groaned. "You spend more time in Michigan than you do in D. C." He was pleased that I had been asked, however, and let me go.

The governor sent out invitations for a planning meeting to all the Arab-American leaders. Sid Woolner arranged to have it in the upstairs banquet room of the Sheik restaurant.

My plane had been delayed by a storm, and I arrived late for the meeting. Everyone was sitting there, waiting for me. In the front row were a number of friendly faces. On the plane I had had time to plan, and I was prepared. Smiling warmly, I started by saying what a wonderful opportunity we had to entertain King Hussein, and that we would plan an affair that would make us, and the governor, proud.

Glancing around as I spoke, I spotted where my problems could arise. Before asking for suggestions, I decided to test the waters by throwing out an idea. The man I expected to heckle me—a man whom Mennen had passed over for a judicial appointment—poked the man in front of him. That man stood, asked to be recognized, and, in a nasty tone, tore down what I had just suggested. Two more times I offered an idea, and two more times the man who had wanted to be a judge poked his friend, who got up and ridiculed what I had said. In the meantime, my friends in the front row were getting angry. Every time the heckler had asked for the floor, I had recognized him pleasantly. Now, I figured, I had given him and the poker behind him enough rope. The next person I recognized was a friend in the front row. One after another, my friends moved to their feet fast enough so that I was able to recognize them and ignore the pair in the back.

The rest of the meeting went smoothly. The group asked me to take charge of the details but pledged to help whenever I needed them. At the end of the meeting, Sid Woolner grinned and said, "Does this remind you of a meeting in the Seventeenth District?" Once again, I was glad that I had learned long ago to let hecklers talk until they made the rest of the people angry.

We had two weeks to do everything. Plenty of help arrived to put together the list and get invitations out. As always, Eddie Fishman had done me proud with the invitation.

A week before the reception, one of my friends told me the disgruntled applicant for the judgeship was calling all the Arab Americans he knew and urging them not to come. Something clicked in my memory, and I checked the list of consuls in Detroit. Just as I thought, the man who was telling everyone to stay away from the reception was the local consul for Lebanon. Mustering my best manner, I called him up and said: "I understand you are the consul for Lebanon. Wouldn't you like to be in the receiving line with King Hussein as an official representative of your country?" He was delighted to be asked and very quickly accepted.

The night of the reception, I had a few quiet chuckles as I stood back and overheard indignant comments from some of the guests. "Look at him," they said. "He told us that we should not come to the reception and there he is, in the receiving line!"

Not all problems were so neatly handled—especially when it came from within our own ranks. The cartoonist Walt Kelly, creator of Pogo, said it well: "We has met the enemy, and it is us."

Everyone in the party was always on the lookout for promising new candidates. It was common practice to give them assignments that would bring them before the public. One time in 1953 Neil Staebler came up with a bright prospect. The State Central Committee officers decided to ask him to be master of ceremonies for the Jefferson-Jackson Day dinner early in 1954. Neil asked if I would take him under my wing and brief him on what was expected of him.

At the same time, Will Muller, who wrote about politics for the *Detroit News*, had been sent to Washington, D. C. Carl Muller, no relation, took Will's place. It had been years since Carl had covered politics, and he didn't know any of the new leaders. Will Muller and I had worked well together, so he suggested to Carl that I could help him learn who was who in the Michigan Democratic party. Carl was a delightful man, and I told him I would be happy to help him. He made it his business to stop by my office often, and I always would give him a tidbit of news. "When we hold the Jeff-Jack dinner, I'll sit beside you at the press table," I assured Carl. "In that way, I can point out the people you should get to know."

To help our master of ceremonies, I made out cards for each person at the head table. The cards included their names, titles, and one small fact about their backgrounds. The master of ceremonies could read from these as he introduced people. After the seating arrangements were finalized, I put the cards in sequence, marking them for the left and right sides.

When I went over all the cards with him, I noticed he seemed extremely nervous. He thanked me warmly and said he would be fine. We were all seated, with Carl Muller and me at the press table facing the speaker's table. Carl was busy making notes as I explained who each person was. Imagine my shock when I spotted the master of ceremonies shuffling the cards as if they were playing cards.

It was no easy task to get to the head table and get them away from him without making a scene. Moving discreetly but quickly, I put them back in order just in time for him to introduce the head table. Heaving a deep sigh of relief, I sat down beside Carl—only to see the poor man nervously shuffling the cards again. When he introduced the people at the head table, they had sense enough to get up and take a bow when their names were called, even if the sequence was all out of whack. The master of ceremonies gave me a pitiful look, asking forgiveness.

My appeal to the reporters not to mention it worked. They all liked Carl and appreciated what I had been able to do for him. The bumbling dinner chairman never was promoted as a candidate. In fact, we saw very little of him after that.

The way a politician conducts himself or herself at any kind of dinner is very revealing. People in the audience can see right through someone who is insincere. Mennen never had any problem that way because he was naturally interested in people. He knew how important each one of these affairs was to the group that was holding it, so we were always careful about how we handled invitations.

Later in 1954, I got a call one day from the pastor of the largest downriver Hungarian church. They were celebrating their fiftieth anniversary as a church and wanted the governor to speak at their dinner. It was impossible because he had a firm schedule that took him all over the Upper Peninsula that same week. After explaining the situation, I told the pastor the governor would send a message to be read at the dinner. He didn't seem at all satisfied. The pastor phoned every day. Each time he called, he sounded more desperate to have the governor attend their dinner.

We were very wary of sending substitute speakers to ethnic affairs. We felt it better for the governor to send a personal message pertinent to the occasion. Finally, after so many frantic calls, I looked at Nancy Williams's schedule and found she had some free time that Sunday. When I got the next call, I asked the pastor if they would like to have Mrs. Williams there. He nearly leaped through the telephone, he was so pleased. Nancy agreed to go if I would go with her. When we arrived, we found out why the pastor had been so desperate. The other guest of honor was Senator Ferguson, the Republican who was running for reelection. Since many members of that parish were staunch Democrats, I'm sure the pastor had found himself in hot water.

For many reasons, I will never forget that dinner. It was a bad day for Senator Ferguson all around. He did everything Mennen Williams would not have done. He was nervous, I am sure, but he also was impolite and thoughtless of the women in the kitchen who were trying to keep the dinner hot. The food had been cooked by the women themselves. Even now, I can taste the delicious liver dumplings in the clear soup they served first. After that wonderful first course, Senator Ferguson demanded that everything stop—no tables cleared, nothing more served—so that he could speak and go on to another meeting. The gist of his speech was "I did this and I did that for the Hungarian people." He didn't acknowledge the pastor or a visiting bishop from Washington. He didn't even mention the anniversary.

Each time the senator ticked off something he had done for the Hungarian people, Nancy Williams seemed a little more perturbed. In a stage whisper, the bishop leaned over to Nancy and said: "Do not be disturbed, Mrs. Williams. Humility, too, is a virtue." Several of us couldn't suppress a little laugh, prompting the senator to turn around with a furious look. He quickly ended his speech and left without thanking the people for inviting him.

Nancy Williams never did a better job of representing the governor. She waited until the entire dinner had been served before getting up to speak. She had read the information the pastor had sent me, and, with her remarkable memory, was able to talk with knowledge and respect about the church and the anniversary. She told them how much the governor wanted to be there, and that she brought warm greetings from him. She said how sorry she was that she had to go to another meeting, and asked them to excuse her. She thanked them for inviting her and, once again, wished she could stay.

The young man who escorted us to the car told Nancy not to worry. These people would support the governor and the Democratic ticket, he said. "The senator did not fool us. We know he has not done a thing for us. If he did introduce all those bills he talked about, nothing ever came of them."

17

THE PEOPLE
OF MICHIGAN GAIN
A GREAT FRIEND AND
LOSE A DEAR ONE

RYING TO HELP manage Phil Hart's 1954 campaign for lieutenant
governor would have been a nightmare if he hadn't been such a
wonderful man. It was in that year that I really became acquainted with him.

It is a wonder we remained such good friends, for I nagged him unmercifully about his modesty. He opened every campaign speech with an apology for being a candidate. Time after time, when I got him alone, I would put my hands on his shoulders and read him a lecture. He would grin and sometimes say "okay," and next time he would do it all over again. When he would get tired of listening to me, occasionally he would conk me on the head with his knuckles, laugh, and walk away. He got the same lecture repeatedly from Adelaide Hart, too. (Adelaide and Phil were not related, even if their families did come from the same county in Ireland).

Finally, after racking my brains as to how to get across to him, I said: "So you think Governor Williams and all of us are a bunch of stupid people?" He looked indignant but didn't bother to answer. "You must," I said, "Because that's what you are really saying every time you apologize for running for office. We picked you, you know." That did it. A couple of times he started to apologize, but after spotting me in the audience, he quickly changed the subject. After that, he never did it again.

Whenever my help was needed, it was a pleasure to do research on legislation Phil Hart was sponsoring. In late 1957, when he was still lieutenant governor, he gratefully accepted a study I had completed on the history of civil rights legislation and used it to help him get started in that area. Of all the thank-you letters I received over the years, a little handwritten scrawl from Phil Hart after the 1958 election touched me deeply. "Dear Helen: If I was a songwriter I would make it sound better, but it wouldn't be any more sincere. Yours, Phil."

Phil Hart was full of contradictions. He was kind and gentle, but once he had made up his mind nothing could get him to change it. When a decision had to be made, he never came up with an answer immediately. He debated every possible angle to the solution before he would tell you his decision. Often, if you didn't press him hard, he would never tell you what he had decided. He was extremely modest, but he had a brilliant mind. He was tolerant of everyone's right to follow his or her own conscience.

Phil Hart created friends wherever he went. All kinds of people wanted to work for him. Phil owed an enormous debt of gratitude to Sid Woolner and Carolyn Burns, who carefully examined every campaign contribution before turning it over to the finance committee. Sid and Carolyn returned many checks that could have caused Phil embarrassment or legal problems. He never knew how well they took care of him. Sid joined Phil's Senate staff a few years after Mennen left the governor's office. Carolyn worked on all of the campaigns, and she and Sid became a good team. Phil trusted them completely.

Carolyn Sinelli Burns had been a valued and skilled worker in campaigns long before I became involved. She was always extremely proud of her Italian background and her family, who had come to this country during the Great Depression. Tall and statuesque, Carolyn was beautiful. Her husband was in a specialized construction business, and Carolyn busied herself with political activities. When I met her, she was a younger edition of the old guard in the Democratic party. It took a few years for Carolyn to be accepted by our group, and for her to accept us. She and I eventually became close friends. Carolyn was a perfectionist and very able, and she worked tirelessly and devotedly on Phil's campaigns.

The voters of Michigan took to Phil once they got to know him. His quiet and shy way of campaigning appealed to people. He was elected lieutenant governor in 1954 and again in 1956. In 1958 he and Mennen had to make the momentous decision as to which of them should run for the U. S. Senate and which should run for governor. They probably made the right choices, Mennen for governor and Phil for the Senate. Not many people ever knew it, but Phil once told a close friend that under no circumstances would he want to run for governor. Too many quick decisions would have to be made.

Phil Hart had served with distinction as an army officer in World

War II. He was honorably discharged after his arm was badly injured in the war. He was decorated for bravery in action and eventually spent time recuperating in the veterans hospital at Battle Creek. He was very quiet and reserved following his release from the service. Phil's entrance into politics was partly due to his wife, Jane, who told Mennen Williams that Phil needed something to reawaken his interest. Like Mennen and many others who knew Phil well, she realized her husband was a genuine humanitarian who would take the words "public servant" to heart.

In 1950 Mennen and Neil Staebler persuaded Phil to become a candidate for secretary of state. He campaigned valiantly, but that was the year everyone lost except Mennen, who won only after a recount. After that, Phil was appointed to one position after another. He first served as director of the Michigan Corporation and Securities Commission, with Sid Woolner appointed as his deputy. In 1954, Mennen again talked Phil into running for office. That's how he became the candidate for lieutenant governor who nearly drove me crazy at first. He was elected, and never lost an election from then on.

When he was elected to the U. S. Senate in 1958, Phil found his real spot in history. From then until his death from cancer on the day after Christmas in 1976, he was known as a tireless advocate for the people, always aboveboard and always modest about his accomplishments.

His wife, Jane Briggs Hart, was a big help to Phil. She was from Detroit's well-to-do Briggs family and had met Phil through her brother. A devoted wife and mother to their four sons and four daughters, she was also an experienced pilot, able to fly helicopters as well as planes. She often flew Phil around the state for public appearances. When Phil and Janey would land at a picnic in a helicopter, it would create great excitement, especially among the children.

In the 1954 primary, the old-line Democrats and the Teamsters weren't about to let Phil run unchallenged. They backed George Fitzgerald as lieutenant governor. This was the same George Fitzgerald who had been supported by the Teamsters in the struggle for control of the party in the late 1940s. He was elected national committeeman in 1948, but four years later he lost to Ernest Lacey. (Ernie was active in Wayne County politics but was not related to Mike Lacey, who had led the UAW's challenge to our 17th District leadership in 1950.) Ernie's victory was a message to the Teamsters that the party was firmly in the hands of the people. That didn't stop the Teamsters and the old guard from trying once more; they put George Fitzgerald up against Phil Hart in 1954.

Mennen, on the other hand, had no opposition in the 1954 primary. There were four Republicans running in their primary, however. Each time the Republicans had so many people running for governor—five in 1950 and three in 1952—it helped Mennen greatly. Almost at once, the 1954 Republican quartet became so engrossed with running against each other that Mennen had free rein to campaign for his own program.

Like Phil, Blair Moody had a real battle on his hands with the old-guard Democrats. In the spring of 1954, things were going well for Blair, and he had no opposition in the primary at that point. By early summer, however, a group of Wayne County government people and others who never had accepted the upstart group that was now running the party talked Pat McNamara into running against Blair.

Pat was well liked by the AFL, particularly the building trades. He had served many years as president of Pipefitters Local 636 of the AFL. He had been a member of the Detroit Common Council and chairman of the Rent Control Advisory Board. At the time, he was on the Detroit Board of Education. Pat was a smart and effective advocate for the little people. He made a formidable candidate.

The Republican incumbent, Senator Homer Ferguson, had no opposition in his primary. He was a former Wayne County Circuit judge who had conducted one-man grand juries looking into misdeeds in Detroit and Wayne County governments. He was in his second Senate term, and was a staunch opponent of the New Deal programs.

The campaign went on, hot and heavy, and Blair pushed himself hard. Somewhere along the way, during an extensive tour of the Upper Peninsula in late June, Blair contracted a bad cold but would not cut down his heavy schedule. All I had heard was that he had a cold and wouldn't go to the doctor. Then, suddenly, he was taken to the hospital in Hancock, just across from Houghton. He had such a bad case of pneumonia, we were told, that he might not survive.

His son, Blair, Jr., and I met Ruth Moody at Metro Airport. Her friends had put her on a plane from Washington shortly after Blair was hospitalized. We arranged for a private plane to Houghton so we could get there quickly. Blair, Jr., was a young lawyer working in downtown Detroit. He and Ruth were both in a state of shock and numb with worry, so I had my hands full.

Just before the plane took off, I was paged. It was Sid Woolner telling me to get the plane there as quickly as possible, since Blair was sinking fast. Without letting on to the Moodys, I whispered to the pilot to do his best to get us there quickly. When we got to Houghton, I was the first one off the plane, so I could gauge what we were facing. Never was I so glad to see a familiar, smiling face. With a broad grin, Billie Farnum told me that Blair had rallied and was doing well.

Ironically, as a U. S. senator, Blair Moody had been responsible for congressional action that helped build the little Catholic hospital, St. Joseph's, where he had been taken. The only single room available was in the maternity ward, so they had put him in there and were watching over him carefully. The mother superior took us all into a little room to give us tea and a report on Blair's condition. We had no sooner gotten seated than a petite nun rushed in and said: "Do you want the senator using the telephone? He has already called his mother and now he's trying again to reach his wife." It was so typical that we all laughed, sort of hysterically. The mother superior rushed Ruth up to his room. She assured us later she would see that the telephone was removed until Blair was out of danger.

Back in Detroit, Mary Gilmore, the wife of Blair's co-campaign manager, Horace Gilmore, hurriedly put out a statement to Democratic leaders throughout the state. "Blair has asked me to write you to reassure you concerning his condition. The report from his doctors indicates that his difficulty is pneumonia and that a full recovery is only a matter of a few weeks. . . . Blair, of course, remains in the race and will be in your area before the campaign is over," the letter read in part. Attached to Mary's letter was a mimeographed copy of a statement from Blair's doctors, specialists from Ann Arbor and Cleveland as well as from St. Joseph's: "The primary difficulty is pnemonia which produced some heart symptoms which have now subsided. He has dramatically improved. We have every reason to believe he will recover strength rapidly and continue his campaign." The physicians said Blair did not have a heart attack, and they attributed his heart symptoms to overstrain rather than to any organic condition.

After a few days, Blair seemed to be out of danger, so Blair, Jr., and I flew back to Detroit. Billie Farnum, who was managing Blair's campaign with Horace, stayed to look after Blair and Ruth. It would be a few weeks before Blair would be able to leave the hospital. It seemed best to have him recuperate in Michigan, rather than at their home in Washington. When Margaret and Hickman Price offered their spacious Ann Arbor home as a comfortable place for Blair to rest and get well, plans were made to fly him there by private plane. There was great rejoicing among Blair's many friends throughout the state and in D. C. when we learned that he had weathered the trip beautifully and was settled in at the Prices' home. Ruth was with him.

He hadn't been there long when he started to say something to Ruth and gasped. His breath failed, and he died instantly. It was July 20, two weeks to the day before the primary. The autopsy revealed that he had had a lethal type of virus. His lungs were damaged in such a way that, had he lived, he would have been a respiratory cripple.

Ruth called to tell me and asked me to break the news to Blair, Jr. At the time I was alone in my campaign office, and the emptiness of the ballroom seemed overwhelming. For a few minutes, I just sat there until I could get control of myself. Then I asked Sid Woolner to come in. After I told him, we called and asked Blair, Jr., to come over. Together we broke the news to him. One by one we brought the staff in and told them.

Telling Neil Staebler turned out to be hardest of all. He and Blair were great friends. They had plans for the next twenty years and had been completely convinced that, together, they could implement their ideas. Those plans included electing Mennen Williams president—a dream that Mennen had, too—but it was not to be. Into that huge ballroom came Neil, bouncing on his tiptoes as always, and smiling and bowing to everyone as he came toward our offices at the back of the room. We knew the reason he was so happy was that he had received word of Blair's safe arrival in Ann Arbor. To this day I don't know how we got the courage to tell him what had happened. Neil was absolutely heartbroken.

That night, Mennen Williams asked our small group—including Sid, Horace, Adelaide Hart, John Murray, and myself—to go out to dinner with him and Nancy. In the privacy of a small meeting room, we talked and told stories about Blair and laughed and cried together.

We all felt a little better, but the next few days were a nightmare. Blair Moody's body lay in state at the old City Hall for twenty-four hours before the funeral. Adelaide Hart and I each took Neil Staebler by the arm and walked those long blocks to City Hall, all of us in tears.

After the funeral, the governor—still grieving and somewhat in shock—let a whole week go by without doing anything to pick up the pieces of the Senate campaign. He didn't make a single overture to Pat McNamara. Feelings were running high. Many people wanted the party to pick a new candidate to run against Pat in the primary. Finally, after a great deal of thought, Mennen insisted that Pat was a good man and would make an excellent senator. We should not hold it against him that he had run against Blair Moody, Mennen said. Adelaide Hart, with the able help of Frank Martel, president of the Wayne County AFL, worked with the labor movement to try to bring people together. The UAW was the hardest to convince, since their leaders had been especially close to Blair.

For several days it seemed impossible to carry on, but life—and the campaign—had to go on. The knowledge that the primary was fast approaching gave us the needed impetus to go back to work with renewed vigor. Everyone worked hard to get out a good primary vote to strengthen the party and help the other candidates who had primary contests. The people finally rallied around Pat McNamara and campaigned valiantly for him. It had been too late to take Blair's name off the ballot, and he got 126,335 votes. Pat received 226,686—only about 100,000 more votes than Blair, even in death. Obviously, something had to be done; it was Pat who was running now.

18

ONE PARTY,
TWO PENINSULAS,
A GLORIOUS VICTORY

NOT LONG AFTER the 1954 primary, the governor called a small group of party leaders to his Lansing home for a meeting with Pat McNamara. Pat came alone, which was wise. His old-guard, Wayne County government supporters were neither trusted nor respected by Mennen's "new" Democratic group. The feeling was mutual.

Both Sid Woolner and I, as well as Adelaide Hart, had worked closely with Pat in city politics. Adelaide and I had served with him on the Rent Control Advisory Board. We admired him, personally, and had been good friends. As luck would have it, Mennen was late getting downstairs for the meeting. When Pat arrived, the first people he saw were Sid and me. It helped him to see friendly faces as soon as he came in, and we did our best to make him feel welcome. Adelaide joined us shortly afterwards. It wasn't easy, for we all had loved Blair dearly,[1] but we liked Pat McNamara and knew what he could do, so we swallowed hard and did our best for the party.

Mennen Williams was never better diplomatically than when he chaired that meeting. He made it clear to Pat what the party now stood for and what was expected of him. He was kind but firm. Pat McNamara was a good soldier and conducted himself admirably in what was, mostly, a hostile group. It was hardest on Neil Staebler. He placed his chair so that he wouldn't have to face Pat. I don't believe Neil said a single word at the meeting. Gradually the wounds healed, and, in later years, Pat and Neil became fast friends. Neil eventually admitted to

Adelaide and me that we had been right when we tried to tell him that Pat McNamara had the potential to be an excellent senator.

The press soon learned of Mennen's meeting and realized the governor was pulling the party together in the first big test of the mettle of the "new" Democratic party. Owen Deatrick of the *Detroit Free Press* wrote: "Michigan Democrats promised the people and then threatened the Republicans with 'the best co-ordinated campaign we have ever waged in Michigan.'" Owen's story carried a headline saying "Democrats Outline Campaign for State—We See Issues Alike, Williams Says After Talk with McNamara." The story quoted both Mennen and Neil and described the plan to use the central campaign office to work for the election of the entire state ticket as well as local candidates. The story said at least one of the party's statewide candidates would visit every county, city, and township in Michigan before the November election. In a flush of optimism that turned out to be justified, the governor predicted "complete victory" for the state Democratic ticket in the November election.

Even though he was unopposed in the primary, Mennen received 426,660 votes—a good sign that he was succeeding at building up the Democratic vote. The Republicans running for governor attacked each other quite severely, and the splintered vote reflected that. The winner was Donald Leonard, who received 188,054 votes. His closest opponent was D. Hale Brake, the state treasurer and former state senator from Stanton in Montcalm County, with 112,797 votes. Two other candidates, Owen J. Cleary and Eugene Keyes, received fewer than 100,000 votes each.

In the Democratic primary for lieutenant governor, Phil Hart easily defeated George Fitzgerald, 301,820 to 93,001. Clarence A. Reid, the Republican lieutenant governor, drew only 375,655 votes, against no opposition, in the primary. In the Senate race, Senator Homer Ferguson made an impressive showing: 419,729 votes, with no Republican primary opposition—a sign that we couldn't let up, especially in our efforts to elect Pat.

Despite Mennen's three victories and the rising respectability of the Democratic party, we knew we had to work hard. As always, I was a candidate for precinct delegate. A campaign flyer I used that year is a good example of how bluntly we stated our case. It reads in part:

Dear Neighbor:

Are you as disgusted as I am at the Republican sideshow that passes for government in Lansing and Washington? Are you tired of Republican promises and lack of performance in Congress? As a citizen of a great nation, are you as disturbed as I am about the recent nauseating spectacle between the United States Army and the very junior senator from Wisconsin? Are you concerned about the effect this mess has had on our relations with friendly nations? [The reference is to Senator Joseph McCarthy and the televised hearings on his allegations that some American army officers and civilian officials were agents of the Communist Party.]

Are you disturbed by mass layoffs in Detroit and Michigan and the refusal by Republicans to do anything about them?

Do you believe that wage or salary earners should receive tax cuts as well as corporations or coupon clippers and that Republicans should have considered the small fellow first?

Are you disturbed by the giving away by the Republicans of our natural resources such as offshore oil, timber and grazing lands and water reserves? . . .

> Democratically yours,
> Helen Berthelot,
> precinct delegate candidate

Except for the reference to the McCarthy hearings, my flyer could have been written for a campaign in the 1990s. It shows that many of the problems we battled back then were bigger than even we could have guessed at the time. When the primary votes were counted, I was re-elected as precinct delegate. The hard work lay ahead, in the fall campaign.

Horace Gilmore and Billie Farnum, who had been co-chairmen of Blair Moody's campaign, had been looking forward to joining him in Washington after the election. They were devastated by Blair's death, but the party soon found ways to use their considerable political ability. Neil appointed Billie to run the State Central Committee office and asked him to concentrate on organizing outstate Democrats and getting out the vote. Mennen Williams brought Horace into his campaign as a partner with Sid and me. Horace was particularly helpful to Sid and John Murray in organizing the governor's television appearances.

One thing Mennen Williams had taught us was to pay strict attention to the smallest details. We soon learned to be especially attentive whenever Mennen's beloved Upper Peninsula was involved. He was a stickler for always thinking of Michigan as the big beautiful state that it is: both peninsulas, from lakeshore to lakeshore, top to bottom.

Exactly how strongly he felt about that became as clear as Lake Superior to us during one of Mennen's television broadcasts. With the help of Sid and Horace, John Murray put together an exceptional program describing Mennen's accomplishments for the state. Someone—I never did know who—made an excellent map of the state to be used on the program. But whoever did it forgot to get the correct measurements to have it projected on television. The map didn't arrive in the studio until just before rehearsal time. To Sid and Horace's dismay, it was too big, and

150

they couldn't include the Upper Peninsula on the screen. There were references to the map throughout the script, so they couldn't just scrap it. In the end, the map was shown on the air without the UP.

The show went off perfectly. Sid and Horace had done a fine job of outlining Mennen's improvements for Michigan. When the program was over, those of us in the studio rushed to congratulate them. Glowing with our praise, Sid and Horace turned to meet Mennen Williams's accusing face. "Where was the Upper Peninsula?" he demanded. Adelaide stepped forward and shook her finger in Mennen's face. "That was a wonderful show and there is a valid explanation why the UP was not included," she said. The governor relented and told Sid and Horace they had made an excellent presentation. They explained the problem, and Mennen gracefully accepted their story. But no one ever left the Upper Peninsula off any piece of Mennen's campaign material again.

After the primary, and after the meeting at Mennen's residence in August, Democrats all over the state seemed to come to life. They were determined to win and cooperated with great enthusiasm. The state ticket was top-notch. Our candidate for attorney general was Thomas M. Kavanagh, a fine lawyer who had a long career on the bench following his service as attorney general. Tom was born near Carson City, just about in the middle of the mitten of Michigan. He graduated from the University of Detroit Law School in the early 1930s and practiced law in Detroit for a while before returning to his hometown to serve his community in government and the law. Partly at my urging, the state party convention had chosen Jim Hare as the candidate for secretary of state and Sanford A. "Sandy" Brown to run for treasurer. At the time, Jim was still manager of the State Fair and had won wide acclaim for cleaning it up and making it profitable. Sandy Brown had an exceptionally brilliant mind when it came to finances. He discovered that the previous treasurer, a Republican, had been keeping state funds in checking accounts. That changed when Sandy took over; he put the public funds into interest-bearing accounts to let the people make a little money on their money. The Wall Street bankers and investment people soon learned that this friendly man from rural Michigan knew what he was doing. He enjoyed their respect and admiration throughout the more than ten years that he handled the state's money.

Sandy was born and grew up on a farm in Bay Port, a town in the Thumb near Saginaw Bay, and left as a young man during the Great Depression. After finishing night school in Detroit and working at a variety of jobs, he returned home to work the farm. He became school board president and helped organize the local chamber of commerce before he joined Mennen's team. Sandy and his wife Millie continued to run the family dairy farm during the time he served as state treasurer.

More and more, the party was looking carefully at the spouse of any potential candidate, to make sure that the "better half" would be at least helpful. This was the campaign in which all the Administrative Board candidates' spouses—Anne Hare, Agnes Kavanagh, wife of Attorney General candidate Thomas M. Kavanagh, Millie Brown, and Jeanne Targonski (married to auditor general candidate Victor Targonski)—began to carry schedules almost as heavy as those of their husbands. Nancy Williams, Adelaide Hart, and Margaret Price took turns heading up teams of two or three of the Ad Board candidates' wives. Nancy, Adelaide, and Margaret were all experienced at these things, though none of the others had made a speech in their lives. The meetings were kept small, and the newcomers soon became adept at discussing the issues.

Donald Leonard, the Republican candidate for governor, wasn't much of a politician. Before the campaign, Mennen had inherited him as state police commissioner. Mennen ignored Leonard and his lackluster effort and talked instead about the hospitals, schools, and social services that had been improved through the Democratic program. The Teamsters didn't like Leonard and concentrated on Ferguson, whom they quietly backed. Pat McNamara campaigned strongly against Ferguson. The papers supported both Republicans, but were not as vicious against Mennen as they had been in the past.

Everything was going well, but we were too busy working on the campaigns to have time to guess how we would do. We knew we would do better than in 1952, but we weren't prepared for a sweep. When the votes were counted, however, the Democrats had made a clean sweep of the statewide offices and had made some inroads in both houses of the Republican-controlled legislature.

Even before the election, Mennen sensed what was coming. On October 29 he wrote me a letter indicating he realized how much work had gone into building the party and the campaign organization:

> Personally, as a candidate, let me thank you for developing the most tremendous supporting organization that Democratic candidates have ever enjoyed. Not only have we had candidates for all of the state positions who can command the enthusiasm and respect of their community, but we have precinct workers and other workers to carry the message to the people and get the people to the polls. This certainly is a tremendous step forward in establishing the kind of two-party government that you and I believe is in the best interests of all our people.

The November victory was the result of teamwork up and down the line in the party. That sounds like a cliché, but it isn't. There simply is no other way to say it. Horace, Sid, and I had no illusions about ourselves; we knew it was a team victory. We had one more task: thanking the people.

Not everyone in politics understands the importance of a follow-up letter thanking the workers when a campaign is over, win or lose. It is one of the most important things to be done. The people are usually volunteers, and they feel appreciated when they get a thank-you letter.

Sometimes these letters are hard to write. In 1954, ours was easy. It was with genuine gratitude that we wrote a letter of thanks to the many who worked on the campaign. It began "Dear Fellow Democrat," but the tone was warm and personal, because all three of us really meant it. All three of us signed it, too:

> When elections are over all of us are generally so busy trying to adjust our lives back to normal living that we never seem to find time to say the things we feel so deeply.

> This year we just can't let the occasion pass without telling all of you how much we appreciate the wonderful cooperation we received in everything we attempted to do.

> All campaigns are made up of just one emergency after another. This campaign seemed to have more than the usual number and there were a couple of days that all we seemed to be doing was calling 83 counties.

> The wonderful part of all this is that no matter how many times we called or what had to be done, you all came through with a response that kept all of us in the headquarters' office encouraged to believe that this year we would really win.

> Without the help of all of you, the job could not have been done.

The final vote gave Mennen the victory over Donald Leonard, 1,216,308 to 963,300. It was with relief that we realized there would be no recount this time. Phil Hart defeated Lieutenant Governor Clarence Reid, 1,158,276 to 974,120. Thanks to the Teamsters, Pat's victory over Senator Ferguson was a narrow one, 1,088,550 to 1,049,420.

All of the other Ad Board candidates were elected, but not by landslides. Jim Hare defeated incumbent Owen Cleary to begin a sixteen-year career as "James M. Hare, Secretary of State." Tom Kavanagh defeated Attorney General Frank G. Millard. Sandy Brown defeated State Treasurer D. Hale Brake and began a decade of service in that job. And Vic Targonski defeated Auditor General John B. Martin, Jr. Mennen finally had his administrative team.

At last we could have an inaugural that was a real Democratic celebration, and we didn't have to share it with the Republicans. We formed a big inaugural committee, with people from all over the state, and started planning our party.

Mennen and Neil decided that I should be the chairman. The governor's office would handle official details, but the Democratic celebration was in my hands. Mennen was completely immersed in planning his legislative program for the next year. To get his attention on the inaugural was impossible. Remembering Adelaide's advice to put it on paper, I wrote out a program so full of activities that it would scare any ordinary person to death. It went from 7:00 A.M. to midnight, starting with a church service and ending with the inaugural ball. In between were open houses, breakfast, lunch, and dinner, plus receptions of all descriptions. Each member of the Administrative Board had a separate open house. My proposed lineup offered child care for small children, a teen center for the older ones, and a television set at the open house in the Masonic Temple in Lansing for any diehards who wanted to watch the Rose Bowl game.

Carefully, I put little yes and no boxes by each affair. Handing it to Mennen, I asked him to check the yes or no boxes. In about an hour, he gave it back to me. "But you haven't marked any of the boxes yes or no," I said. "It's fine," he declared. "Do the whole day just as you have outlined it." The whole day! Quickly, we had to create more committees and recruit hundreds more people to help, but at least everyone who wanted to work on the inaugural got a chance to do so. If anyone was left out, I never heard about it. Everyone who had worked in the campaign was rewarded by having a role in the inaugural.

Our old reliable, Eddie Fishman, came through with the seven thousand invitations we ordered. We did our best to come up with a list of everyone who might want to come, but we were concerned that people who hadn't received an invitation would be hesitant about joining the celebration. So in early December I wrote a letter to Democratic officers across the state, letting them know invitations were on the way and that they were "not intended to shut out anyone, but to let more people know about the various events."

Mennen wanted this to be a people's party, and it was. The budget was under $13,000 and was completely covered by modest admission fees. People paid $3.50 for the luncheon, $5.00 for the dinner, and $2.50 for the inaugural ball. We counted fifteen hundred at the dinner and one thousand at the ball. Hundreds more came for the ceremony itself. The day started with 7:00 A.M. services at St. Paul's Episcopal Church in downtown Lansing and ended at midnight with the last dance of the inaugural ball at the Masonic Temple.

Mennen loved tradition, and when we won again in 1956, he wanted to repeat the whole day's program for the January 1, 1957, inaugural. Mennen, Neil, and Adelaide wanted me to be chairman that year, too, and again in 1959. Luckily for me, Mennen decided to cut down the program considerably for the 1959 inaugural, his last. There was a recession, and many people were out of work.

Amid all the jubilation in early 1955, there was a serious reminder of the challenges that lay ahead. In a message to the people and the legislature, Mennen made a plea for help in meeting Michigan's needs:

Despite the progress we have made, our physical plant, our working forces, and in many cases our laws, remain inadequate for this expanded task. We simply cannot serve Michigan adequately with the forces and equipment that we have. . . .

Building Michigan is, therefore, the main task of this Legislature and of every official of this government. We are not in a period when government can be judged by mere maintenance of its services. We are in a period when government must be judged, and will be judged, by its capacity to meet tremendously expanded needs, and to plan effectively for even greater needs which can be seen in the near future.[2]

NOTES

1. A resolution of tribute to Blair Moody, describing his accomplishments and life history, was adopted by the Democratic State Convention August 14, 1954. See Appendix for the text of the resolution.

2. For the full text of this address and other speeches and messages from the governor, see the papers of G. Mennen Williams, Michigan Historical Collections, Bentley Historical Library, University of Michigan, Ann Arbor.

19

DON'T FORGET THE PEOPLE

WORD BEGAN TO SPREAD around the country about what Mennen Williams and the Democratic party were accomplishing in Michigan. Not long after our 1954 Democratic victory, Neil Staebler wrote to Joe Beirne, my boss at the CWA:

> You have seen the newspaper figures on Michigan. It appears that we have had the greatest Democratic sweep of any state in the country—Mennen elected to an unprecedented fourth term by the biggest margin he ever received, a complete sweep of all our elective state officials, the re-election of all our previous Democratic congressional seats (one of them by a new congressman, Charlie Diggs, Michigan's first Negro congressman) and the election of two new congressmen (one replacing the odious Clardy),[1] the near capture of a gerrymandered state House of Representatives, good gains in our state Senate. This will be the first time the state has had a Democratic Administrative Board since the early days of the New Deal. The fight was done in the face of the most intense Republican campaigning including visits from Eisenhower and Nixon and a good share of the Cabinet and Senate. . . .
>
> This was the greatest off-year Democratic victory we have ever had in Michigan and, except for 1932, the greatest ever.

Neil attributed our victory "in large part" to me. He told Joe Beirne I had done a "magnificent organizing job" and had helped develop strategy, choose and assign personnel, decide on campaign materials, and handle the media. He also told Joe I had worked with the various ethnic groups and made them a significant part of the campaign for the first time. Neil sent me a copy of the letter and, impishly, attached a tiny note at the top: "Dear Helen, Don't blush! Neil."

It was nice to hear such praise, but the important thing was that Mennen's people-oriented approach was a proven winner. Now, it was time to start spreading the word across the country to the people who could make it happen in other states: Democratic party workers.[2] After the 1952 defeat of Adlai Stevenson and so many Democratic candidates, the whole party, nationwide, was at an all-time low. It took a couple of years before rebuilding really began.

Early in 1955, Democratic National Committee Chairman Paul Butler appointed Mennen as chairman of the Nationalities Committee, whose function was to try to enlist the support of various ethnic groups. Mennen's success among ethnics and, for that matter, all voters, was a major reason why Paul looked to Michigan for the chairman of a committee created to rebuild the national party. Mennen took the work seriously. He pushed Paul to give the committee a working budget so ethnic groups could be brought into the next campaign in force.

The governor needed a strong representative to stand in for him at the meetings he could not attend. Because I had had almost daily contact with the ethnic groups during the campaign in Michigan and because I was based in D. C., Mennen chose me. It was a frustrating experience. The previous chairman had let the committee run without any supervision, with a strictly New York executive committee and staff. Traditionally, a big fundraising dinner was held every year in New York City to reach out to ethnic groups and raise funds for Nationalities Committee operations. It was nearly impossible for me, even representing the chairman, to get a word in on how the dinner should be planned. But since I was representing Mennen, I wouldn't give up.

The executive committee and staff ended up working as a team with me. We did it my way—Mennen's way. That year's dinner, in the Waldorf-Astoria Hotel, was a financial success and made new friends among the nationalities groups. Many of them had formal organizations that could be very helpful at election time. The affair also brought Mennen new respect in the national party and made Democrats from other states start listening more to what he had to say.

Mennen's advice was simple: Find out who the leaders are in the various groups, make contact with them, let them know you care, and indicate you would welcome invitations. When you get them, go and speak from the heart. Then, represent their interests in programs and policies wherever possible.

He practiced what he preached. One of his most successful campaign devices was a series of radio programs, each geared to a different group. He would discuss issues of particular interest to that nationality and answer questions. On the programs and in person, he always tried to greet the people in their own language. He worked hard at it, and the words came out okay, but always with a Williams accent. If he mispronounced a word, he carried it off with a laugh, saying something like: "I didn't do that very well, did I? But I meant it anyway." The people loved it.

Paul Butler also appointed Neil Staebler, the Michigan Democratic party chairman, to lead the fifty-member National Advisory Committee for Political Organization. The charge was to look at what was going on in the party and figure out what needed to be done. Steve Mitchell, the previous national party chairman, had done his best to rebuild after the 1952 fiasco, and he had made some progress. However, it took Paul Butler and the committee he had set up to bring new life to the party all over the country.

Most of the members of the political organization committee held party office in their home states. A number of them were later elected governors, U. S. representatives, and U. S. senators. Among the committee alumni are Patrick Lucey, who later became governor of Wisconsin; Kenneth Curtis, who went on to become Maine's governor; and George McGovern of South Dakota, who became a U. S. senator and the Democratic presidential nominee in 1972.

Since 1952, I had been the speaker's bureau representative in Michigan for the Democratic National Committee. Even after I went to Washington, I took on the responsibility of getting good Democratic speakers from around the country into Michigan. The DNC staff in Washington knew me well because I was always volunteering for whatever needed doing.

Because of my activities with the national committee, Neil thought I might be interested in the new political organization committee. He asked me to become the volunteer secretary. Joe Beirne again agreed, and I was delighted at the chance to work with so many Democrats who could teach me so much. When Neil said secretary, he meant secretary. My notes from every meeting—I don't think I missed a single one—are in my handwriting, complete with my own personal abbreviations, since I didn't know shorthand.[3] Later, Paul Butler made me a full-fledged member.

The committee was in existence from 1955 to 1960. It is my firm belief that John Kennedy, no matter how appealing he was, never would have been elected without the work of that committee. It is ironic, and also too bad, that the committee was disbanded not long after Kennedy took office. He didn't want to entrust political strategy to a large group so far removed from him and his close advisers.

This committee definitely outlined new approaches. After looking at all phases of party operations, its members decided that basic organizational skills and procedures were lacking. A political manual was written for use at the neighborhood level on up. The committee analyzed and argued over every section. It was a time-consuming but successful cooperative effort. Tom Downs of Michigan wrote the first draft, which I reworked because the lawyer's language needed simplifying. A little touch of personal pride made me use the street address of my girlhood home in Massachusetts—1664 Pleasant Street—on a sample file card in the chapter on precinct organizing. That manual was rewritten many times over the years, but I got a chuckle out of noticing that no one ever changed the address. They probably thought it was made up.

After the manual was printed, the next step was to sell the ideas. With Paul Butler's blessing, the committee got a grant from the DNC to hold regional seminars for party officers all across the country. Neil worked out a sales pitch and chaired each meeting. He prevailed on Joe Beirne to let me attend all the meetings. Over the years, we saw with pleasure that party organizations had some successes using the methods we suggested.

At the time Neil got the grant, the chairman appointed Venice Spraggs, a former newspaperwoman from Chicago, to be Neil's Washington representative and to handle all correspondence. She became the keystone for the committee and was personally responsible for much of its success. She had most recently been a DNC staff member and was very knowledgeable on the issues, especially as they affected her and other black people. She was a tremendous speaker and took the committee message to many small groups who wanted help in their campaigns.

When we were on the road, Neil made time for congressional candidates to meet privately with me for advice on making best use of the money and people available to them. Drawing on experience and on lessons Mennen and I learned from Stella Lecznar, our west side Polish friend, I talked about everything from schedules to handshakes.

No matter how sophisticated campaigning may become, the handshake will never lose its importance in politics. Estes Kefauver had a good method. He reached out, grasped the other person's hand fully, gave it a quick shake, and let it go. For that brief moment, he looked the other person straight in the eye and gave his undivided attention. He moved on quickly, but he had made contact with that person. A candidate who greets one person while looking to see who is coming next doesn't impress anyone.

Marie Stark, who worked in all of Mennen's campaigns, understood the power of a handshake better than many candidates. Marie may not have gone to college, but she had more political sense in her right hand than most people have in their heads. Pushing her grandbabies in a buggy half-filled with campaign literature, Marie scrupulously canvassed not only her own precinct, but several others as well. Her finances were often tight, but she always found a way to attend local meetings and congressional district conventions. Someone always saw to it that she got a ride to the state conventions as well.

In doing her canvassing, she talked to all the people in her area. If Marie told us we were on the wrong track, it behooved us to pay attention. Adelaide Hart and I were trying to size up a new candidate one day. We were not quite sure of his leanings on civil rights but were giving him the benefit of the doubt. Marie looked at us and nodded solemnly. "When I shake his hand, I will know," she said.

Mennen's handshake won him many friends because his interest in people was real. As tiring as his schedules were, he was never happier than when he was out among the people. He often showed up at plant gates at 5:30 A.M., whether or not it was an election year. There are thousands of Michigan communities, churches, clubs, and organizations of all kinds whose members remember to this day that Governor Williams came to their dinner. He wasn't put off by the modest size of an event, or by the fact that he wouldn't get any coverage by the press. Never before had the people of Michigan had a governor who accepted so many invitations to speak. Mennen felt very strongly that any group whose members invited the governor deserved consideration, and he or Nancy would attend if at all possible.

During the campaigns, it was understood that Mennen wanted his fellow Democratic candidates for the State Administrative Board to represent him when he couldn't make it himself. It was his way of helping his team gain visibility among the people. In addition, a speakers' bureau was formed during the campaigns to provide knowledgeable people all over the state who could represent Mennen on particular subjects as needed. These people served loyally and admirably over the years. Their task was doubly difficult. First, they were faced with disappointment from people who expected Mennen or Nancy, or an Ad Board member. Then, they had to deal with difficult questions on the issues of the day. That meant they had to be up-to-date on the problems and on Mennen's proposed solutions, not to mention the political obstacles Mennen faced with the legislature.

People trusted Mennen. He had a program to help postwar Michigan cope with the baby boom and provide for modern needs. He accomplished much of it: new hospitals; better mental health care; dozens of facilities for research, studying, and learning at state colleges and universities; and, for local educational needs, more money for teachers and classroom work as well as help financing badly needed new buildings. And, of course, there is the Mackinac Bridge. For a century it was believed impossible and—until it was finally built—was sneered at by many as "Soapy's Folly."

160

Mennen always talked in terms of "we" and "the Democratic party" when he was pushing his programs. He saw the party as the basis of support for what he and others were trying to do. During the twelve years he was governor, the voters developed a loyalty to the party and its candidates that went beyond Mennen's popularity. That's the way he wanted it. Without a doubt, though, the party was the result of Mennen's vision. It was he who inspired the people who did the work. It was his program that the party embraced. It was his people-to-people approach to politics that became the party's.

Mennen Williams knew, and we all learned, that successful campaigns are not built entirely by huge rallies and big contributions—or, to put it in contemporary terms—by image consultants and media packages. They are, even now, made up of a myriad of small incidents involving the candidate and the people.

Early in Mennen's tenure as governor, a farmer in the Upper Peninsula began to tell this story:

You know, when Kim Sigler was governor, he always came to the Upper Peninsula State Fair. But who did he talk to? He marched in with a full retinue of state police, all in uniform. He must have sent word ahead that he was arriving because the mayor, the fair manager, and a few select citizens met him at the gate. He shook hands with them and then marched around the fair, his state police behind him, as if he were on parade. Then he marched right out again.

Just a few of the more wealthy farmers got to shake his hand, but by and large the people just nodded to him as he passed by.

Now, last year, I came into the fairgrounds. Behind one of the barns was a whole group of farmers, all hunkered down, talking up a storm. Who was sitting on his heels in the middle of the group, listening and asking questions? None other than our new governor, G. Mennen Williams. He was listening carefully to all the tales of woe that the farmers had to tell him and was in no hurry at all. He listened and he answered questions. Then he toured the whole fair. It took him a long time because he took time to speak to everyone and shake their hands. That's our kind of governor.

There were few people in the Upper Peninsula who did not hear some version of that story.

The importance of people-to-people relations came home to me in a poignant way one Saturday during one of Mennen's early campaigns. One of our most devoted volunteers that year was Betty Pippins. She was poor and black, but she was determined to do what she could. She organized a group of neighborhood women into a club that worked very hard to spread the word about the candidates and then get out the vote.

Her group put on a chicken dinner one evening. My wonderful secretary at the time, Madge Cruce, went with me, and we brought greetings from Governor Williams and from Adelaide Hart's Federation of Women, as well as from the State Central Committee. Madge and I arrived early. It was plain to see that the dinner was far from ready. Betty greeted us warmly and asked us if we minded paying for our dinner then. The dinner cost $3 apiece, and we paid her immediately.

We decided to go and sit in the car for a while so the busy women wouldn't feel they had to entertain us. Madge happened to look back as we crossed the street, and there was Betty hurrying into the grocery store next door. She was using our money to buy the first batch of chicken. We watched as people began to arrive. As soon as they had entered, more trips were made next door.

When Recorder's Court Judge Elvin Davenport arrived, we decided it was time to go back. Judge Davenport and I were seated at the speakers' table all by ourselves. Our dinners were served immediately. It was very embarrassing; most of the people had not yet been served. When I had come in, I had told Mrs. Pippins I had three donations for her club. Now, after I had eaten just a couple of mouthfuls, she clapped her hands for the group's attention.

She introduced me and told them I was representing Governor Williams. Setting aside fork and napkin, I stood and gave the speech I had learned to give for the governor in all sorts of situations. At the end I said I knew they would do everything they could to support him. Then I told them the Williams Campaign Committee appreciated all that the club was doing and wanted to make a small contribution toward its activities. To polite applause, I then presented Mrs. Pippins with a check for $10. She thanked me warmly, and I sat down.

After a few more bites of chicken, I heard myself being introduced as bringing a message from the Democratic State Central Committee. My speech was shorter but expressed the party's appreciation of the club's work. Mrs. Pippins was presented with another $10 check, which she again acknowledged warmly.

The judge, who was running for reelection, was then called upon. He gave a good campaign speech, not only for himself but for Mennen, the rest of the Democratic team, and other judges who were running for office. With a twinkle in his eye, he reminded the group that this was Saturday night, and he hoped he would not see any of them in his court on Monday morning.

By this time, I had finished my dinner and was happy to see everyone had been served. For the third time, I was introduced. This time I represented our "beloved vice chairman, Adelaide Hart, the head of the Federation of Democratic Women." For the third time, I expressed appreciation for the work of the club, this time in Adelaide's name, and presented Mrs. Pippins with still another $10 check.

This may not seem a very essential meeting to attend to get votes. There were only twenty-five people there. However, we knew that even if all the people in the neighborhood could not afford to come to that dinner, they eventually would learn we were there and had honored the club for its work. We also knew that, on election day, everyone belonging to that club would start early and work late getting their friends and neighbors to the polls to vote. And when those people entered the voting booth, they would have a copy of our Democratic slate in their hands.

NOTES

1. Kit Clardy was a native of Missouri who remained in Michigan after getting a law degree at the University of Michigan. His legal specialty was the trucking business. He lived in East Lansing and was elected to the 6th District seat in Congress in 1952.

2. Helen Berthelot's step-by-step guide to the nuts and bolts of running successful campaigns is among her papers in the Michigan Historical Collections, Bentley Historical Library, University of Michigan, Ann Arbor. Other papers in her collection there might also be useful to students of politics and to candidates. The first is her March 1971 letter to Blair Moody, Jr., in response to his request for political advice from the woman who had helped and advised his father so many years earlier. (The younger Blair was elected twice to the Michigan Supreme Court. He died suddenly on the day after Thanksgiving in 1982, only about three weeks after winning his second term. He was only fifty-four.) The second useful piece is an undated letter written by Helen Berthelot in the 1990s to Democratic leaders in a western state who had heard of her success with state and national campaigns in the 1950s and 1960s and requested her advice on selecting candidates and organizing campaigns.

3. Notes from these meetings of the National Advisory Committee for Political Organization, from 1955 until its demise in 1960, are among the papers of Helen Berthelot in the Michigan Historical Collections, Bentley Historical Library, University of Michigan, Ann Arbor.

20

THE 1956 CAMPAIGN
WILDFLOWERS, NANCY'S SCRAPBOOK,
AND THE SORE FEET VOTE

ARLY IN 1956, Mennen asked a few of us to gather for a campaign
session at Haven Hill, a lodge nestled in the woods in western
Oakland County. It was located on grounds adjoining Dodge
Park and was an ideal place for a private political summit.

The governor had gone to great lengths to keep word of the meeting
away from the press. Will Muller, one of the most astute of the news reporters, had ferreted out the fact that such a meeting was being held. He
called Haven Hill and asked to talk to Paul Weber, Mennen's press secretary. Will did his best to find out what the meeting was all about. Paul
told him over and over the same thing: "The governor has called in the
manager of the park, who is now giving a lecture on the rare forms of
flora and fauna to be found in the park. He has brought in samples of the
flowers that are in danger of extinction and the group is examining
them."

Will didn't believe him, of course, and hung up in a huff. The joke
of it was that, at the very moment Will called, it was absolutely true.
Mennen never missed an opportunity to broaden our knowledge of the
state and had called the park manager in to brief us. He had brought
about a dozen specimens of rare plants most of us had never seen. During
the entire length of the phone call, we were looking with interest at various plants and listening to the park manager. When Paul came back and
told us how angry Will was, we had a hearty laugh and couldn't get back
down to business for quite a while.

In 1956 we really had fun. By this time, we had a reputation for knowing what we were doing. As a matter of fact, we *were* getting pretty good.

The most successful program in the 1956 campaign was the brain-child of Nancy Williams and John Murray. As a former newspaper reporter, John was aware of the importance of the governor's image as portrayed in the press. So was Nancy. From the first day Mennen decided to run for office, Nancy had us clipping all the newspapers. She wisely insisted that we clip not only articles on our candidates, but also on the opposition. Over the years, we accumulated a great deal of information. Nancy kept the clippings in a series of scrapbooks, with everything carfully labeled and dated. Out of this came the idea of using Nancy and her scrapbook clippings on television.

Nancy has a wonderful memory and was very knowledgeable about the issues. With the help of John Murray and a couple of volunteers, she was able to pick out statements made and positions taken, sometimes a year or more ago. She and John then decided what issues and candidates to single out for each program. Nancy would introduce the subject and talk a little bit about it, explaining what was at stake and what Mennen was trying to do. Then she would say what the other side had done, or not done. The actual news clippings were used to back up her explanations. Many of our opponents wished they had never made the statements she read from the newspapers.

Together, John and Nancy made "Nancy's Scrapbook" one of the most effective parts of the 1956 campaign—and again in 1958. The show was aired once a week during the day and was aimed at women. Back then, they were often at home with the children. Nancy came across as a warm and friendly wife and mother, which she certainly was. She also was razor-sharp on the issues, a whiz at politics, and a real trouper.

Nancy always did a short rehearsal at the television studio just before air time. We would all go to see how it went. John would come out shaking his head, his face white with anxiety. "This one's going to be a dud," he'd say glumly.

Not Nancy's program! The rehearsals may have been terrible, but the minute the camera was pointed at her and the "on" light glowed, it was a different story. Nancy smiled and "just walked right into our living room," was how it was described by women all over the state. She would start out with a story or two about her kids or her husband, then move into the issue of the day. Then—POW!—out came a Sunday punch at the opposition. Nancy always managed to deliver a strong message without appearing vindictive or petty.

She remained cool, no matter what happened. Once, her daughter let go of the family's black cocker spaniel, who was being held in the wings. Viewers saw a streak across the stage and then, suddenly, a dog curled up on the couch beside Nancy. She just laughed and said, "This is another member of our family who wants to be in on the act," and went right back to her discussion.

Perhaps the secret to Nancy's success with the show is that she really did identify with the people who were watching. Like Mennen, she was born into a well-to-do family with a strong sense of social responsibility and concern. Nancy attended public schools in her hometown of Ypsilanti, then went to private high school in Dobbs Ferry, N. Y., and returned to study social work at the University of Michigan in Ann Arbor. After she and Mennen were married and he went off to war, she became active in civilian efforts to help the troops. Her contribution was to drive ambulances here in Michigan. She also spent two years as a Red Cross nurse's aide.

After the war, like many women of her time, Nancy helped her husband as much as she could and cared for her children. She was involved in Boy Scouts and Girl Scouts and helped out at church. She volunteered her time with various organizations devoted to patriotic causes and to education, farming, gardening, and conservation. She had to sit on speakers' platforms for such long periods of time that she took up needlepoint in the early 1950s and began making purses for family and friends. Later, she made needlepoint covers for all of her dining room chairs. (There were at least twelve of them.) Always active and athletic, Nancy enjoyed golf, tennis, and bowling when she could squeeze in the time.

In many respects, the Williamses lived as an ordinary family. The state had no official governor's residence in Lansing at the time, so Mennen and Nancy bought a comfortable older home not far from the capitol. There, for twelve years, they lived with their three youngsters, Gery (Gerhard Mennen, like his father), Nancy Quirk, and Wendy Stock. The family included the cocker spaniel, Torchy, and, later, toy poodles.

Mennen usually went home for dinner with the family. If he didn't have a meeting, he often went back to his office in the capitol in the evening. After the first of the poodles joined the family, he would tuck the little dog under his arm when he went back to the office. In winter, the dog would be in his overcoat pocket with only its little head sticking out. While he worked at his desk, she would snooze contentedly until about 10:00 P.M. Then, as if an inner alarm had sounded, she would wake and pace the floor until Mennen quit working and took her home.

Mennen and Nancy raised their children to be tolerant, inquisitive, and responsible. They imparted to their youngsters the global sense of family they both had. Mennen and Nancy had a deep appreciation for different cultures and people. Nancy was willing to go anywhere and do anything as Mennen's partner, whether his work took him to Africa or the Philippines, as it did later, or to the far reaches of the Upper Peninsula while he was governor. She was extremely resourceful and able to juggle her many responsibilities with apparent ease. She really enjoyed driving and chauffeured herself and others, including me, whenever possible.

During the summers when she had her television show and the children were staying at the state-owned summer residence on Mackinac Island, Nancy would drive down to Detroit to do her program, then drive back the same night. She was on the road alone for hours, driving after dark through miles and miles of woods and open land, with no houses as far as the eye could see.

One day, late in the 1958 campaign, Nancy made the long drive from Detroit to Escanaba with Mary Farrell and me to represent the governor at an important Democratic luncheon that he had to miss. Because it was a seven-hour trip, we left long before daybreak and arrived just in time for Nancy to make her speech. She stayed as long as she could and graciously greeted everyone before excusing herself to make the long drive back. She explained that she had to do her "Nancy's Scrapbook" show first thing in the morning at a Detroit television studio. It snowed hard almost all the way to Detroit. Nancy only had time to catch a little sleep at her hotel before her show, but John Murray said it went on without a hitch.

Once I asked her if it bothered her to drive alone as much as she did, especially at night. She said, nonchalantly: "Oh, I have a state police radio in the car." Without saying anything, I wondered to myself if that radio was strong enough to get through to the police if she ever really had needed them on those lonely stretches of road in the woods. The Good Lord looked after her and she never had a problem, but some of us got gray hairs, especially during her long drives back and forth from the summer residence. We were all mighty relieved when the family moved back down to Lansing in the fall.

By the autumn of 1956, the campaign was going full tilt. Mennen had established himself in Michigan politics, and he wasn't challenged in the primary. There wasn't an election for the U. S. Senate that year, so we were able to concentrate on the races for governor, lieutenant governor, the rest of the Ad Board, and congressional and local offices.

It was a good thing we were able to focus on the general election. One of the Republicans in the primary, Donald Leonard, had been beaten by Mennen quite handily in 1954. The other Republican was Albert Cobo, the mayor of Detroit. Mayor Cobo was a clever politician and popular public figure. It was he who pushed for the development of the convention center that later bore his name—Cobo Hall, now expanded and referred to as Cobo Center. At the time, Detroit was a bustling city of about 1,750,000 people, and Cobo was a powerful figure. He was backed by Teamsters President Jimmy Hoffa, who hadn't given up on the idea of defeating Mennen. Cobo won the primary with almost seventy percent of the vote.

Like Mennen, Phil Hart was unopposed in the primary. However, Phil's Republican opponent, Clarence A. Reid, drew more votes in the primary, where he also was unopposed, than Phil did. In 1954 Phil had defeated Reid in the lieutenant governor's race. Reid was a lawyer who spent several years in the state senate. He represented a west side Detroit district but was originally from Ohio. In fact, his official state biography in the 1953–54 Michigan Manual said that he was "born in a log cabin in Pickaway County, Saltcreek Township, Circleville, Ohio." Phil Hart's vote compared to Clarence Reid's gave us fair warning that we would have to concentrate harder to get him reelected.

In the race for governor, "Al" Cobo proved to be a most vocal opponent. One of the things he said was that Mennen bought handmade shoes from outside the state. Obviously, Cobo hoped to discredit Mennen with working people who were loyal to Michigan-made products.

That was just down Paul Weber's alley. Paul, a former newspaperman, had been active in his union and was outraged at the mayor's attempt to discredit the governor. Mennen had a television appearance coming up, and Paul seized the opportunity. He wrote a masterful piece of script to be added to the program at an appropriate point, after Mennen had talked about some of the issues.

Paul had Mennen explain on the air that he had trouble with his feet and that he couldn't wear ready-made shoes. As a master touch, we showed a pair of his specially made shoes. My contribution was to turn the soles to the camera so you could see how wide his feet were. We lost count of the number of letters of sympathy from people with sore feet. Mennen certainly got their vote.

President Harry Truman and Mennen Williams celebrate Detroit's 250th birthday in 1951. (Photographer: Tony Spina. Tony Spina's personal collection.)

Governor Williams at the 1956 Democratic National Convention with Mildred Jeffrey, left, and Phil Hart. (Photographer: Tony Spina. Tony Spina's personal collection.)

Governor Adlai Stevenson greets his final Michigan rally of the campaign at the Fox Theatre in Detroit two days before the 1956 election, with Senator Pat McNamara and Governor Williams at his side. (Helen Berthelot's personal collection.)

Governor Williams presents Venice Spraggs with an award for outstanding contributions to the Democratic party. (Helen Berthelot's personal collection.)

Labor Day, 1957. At left is William C. Marshall, one of Mennen
Williams's supporters, who became president of the Michigan State
AFL-CIO. Next to him is Ed Carey, who was a state representative and
a Detroit Common Council member and always an ally of Governor
Williams. (Archives of Labor and Urban Affairs, Wayne State
University.)

Among the stalwarts attending the June 1958 dedication of the
Mackinac Bridge were: far left, Bill Cochran, chairman of the
congressional district party in the Upper Peninsula; next to him is
former Governor Pat Van Wagoner; Nancy Williams and Governor
Williams's are in the center; behind Governor William's shoulder is
John C. Mackie, the highway commissioner. (Photographer: Mickey
Duggan, St. Ignace. Helen Berthelot's personal collection.)

Nancy Williams designed her own needlepoint patterns and produced lovely handbags for gifts. Shown here in May 1958 are, from left, Ruth Adams, wife of attorney general Paul Adams; Anne Hare (standing), wife of Jim Hare, secretary of state; Millie Brown, wife of Sandy Brown, state treasurer; Burnette Staebler (standing), wife of party chairman Neil Staebler; Nancy Williams; Adelaide Hart (standing), state Democratic party vice chairman; and Helen Berthelot, Governor Williams's campaign manager. (Photographer: Leo Knight, Detroit. Helen Berthelot's personal collection.)

Mennen Williams's last Administrative Board prepares for the final campaign with him in 1958. From left, standing, Jim Hare, secretary of state; Sandy Brown, state treasurer; Frank Szymanski, auditor general; Paul Adams, attorney general. Seated, from left, candidate for lieutenant governor John Swainson, then a state senator; Governor Williams; and Lieutenant Governor Philip Hart, who was running for the U. S. Senate. (Helen Berthelot's personal collection.)

Mennen Williams's final campaign for governor in 1958.
(Helen Berthelot's personal collection.)

The Michigan Democratic party leadership makes plans for Harry
Truman's 1958 appearance in Michigan. From left, chairman Neil
Staebler; alternate national committeewoman Mildred Jeffrey; Thomas
H. E. Quimby, national committeeman; Margaret Price, national
committeewoman; Helen Salamon, party secretary, and Adelaide Hart,
vice chairman. (Helen Berthelot's personal collection.)

Former President Harry Truman with Governor Williams and Helen
Berthelot during the 1958 campaign visit. (Helen Berthelot's personal
collection.)

Phil Hart displays the paper describing his hard-won 1958 election to the Senate and Governor Williams's victory for a sixth term. (Detroit Free Press.)

Janey Hart, wife of Senator Phil Hart, used her newly acquired helicopter license to fly her husband all over the state. In early 1959, she shows their children how a helicopter works. (Associated Press photo. Detroit Free Press.)

John F. Kennedy came to Mackinac Island in June of 1960 to discuss his national program with Governor Williams. Nancy Williams rode with them to the governor's official residence on the island. (Associated Press wire photo. Detroit Free Press.)

Even in 1960, when he wasn't a candidate himself, Mennen Williams paid careful attention to business at the Democratic National Convention in Los Angeles. (Photographer: Tony Spina. Tony Spina's personal collection.)

"More than any man in America," Mennen Williams said, "Kennedy combines the ability to see the challenges and opportunities in our world today and to do something about them with the support of the people. He will, I believe, inspire and regenerate America." (Photographer: Tony Spina. Tony Spina's personal collection.)

Senator Pat McNamara, left, with Robert Perrin, who joined McNamara's staff and became respected for his work with legislation and constituents. (Detroit Free Press.)

Julie Lawler was Governor Williams's personal secretary for many years. (Photographer: Pat Mitchell Pictures, Lansing. Detroit Free Press.)

Although Hickman Price, a successful businessman, never held office in the Democratic party, his support enabled his wife Margaret to serve ably and effectively for many years as an officer of the state and national party. This photograph was taken in the garden of their Ann Arbor home in 1958. (Helen Berthelot's personal collection.)

21

The Principle Was Invincible

MENNEN WILLIAMS had more to worry about in 1956 than Al Cobo. Once again, the governor was in the thick of it at the Democratic National Convention. Once again, he made a strong stand for Estes Kefauver. This time, it was a fight that added Kefauver to the national ticket as Adlai Stevenson's running mate.

Remembering the Michigan delegation's favorite son nomination of Mennen and then our strong backing of Kefauver in 1952, Adlai Stevenson sent letters to many of us just before the 1956 convention, asking for our support:

I want to write you in your capacity as a delegate to our party's national convention. The role you'll play in shaping our party's course in this fateful year is most important.

We must have a Democrat in the White House because the times are too perilous and the stakes too high to run the danger of further Republican part-time management by people who do not represent all of us.

I realize that you support the candidacy of Governor Williams. I respect your preference and only want to repeat what I have said before: that *who* leads us is less important than *what* leads us—what new ideas, what faith, what convictions. I'm confident—as I know you are—that 1956 is going to be a Democratic year. But let *our* victory be achieved through a courageous and constructive campaign on the great issues of our time. Our victory must benefit not our party alone but our country and people as well.

I'm ready to do what I can for our entire ticket either as a worker in the ranks or as the nominee if our party sees fit to so honor me.

We in the Michigan delegation again made our favorite son nomination of Mennen but switched to Stevenson before the roll call was over. He was nominated with ease.

It was a different story with the vice presidential nomination. Contrary to custom, Governor Stevenson left the choice of his running mate up to the convention. There were many candidates—including John F. Kennedy—and it was a wide-open contest. At the height of the battle, the convention aisles were crowded with delegates, shouting support for their particular favorites with as much fervor as if they were candidates for president.

Mennen Williams of Michigan and Hubert Humphrey of Minnesota had worked closely together all through the convention. Mennen's Michigan delegation was strongly in favor of Kefauver, but the Minnesota delegation was divided, mostly between Kefauver and Kennedy. Mennen soon persuaded Senator Humphrey that Kefauver was the man. Once Humphrey was firmly for Kefauver, he battled royally to convince his delegation and finally was able to swing a majority to support Kefauver. Eugene McCarthy, then a Minnesota congressman, was on the other side, as usual.

Mennen had been waiting for word from Humphrey, hoping they could stick together as the roll call was read. Just before it was time for Michigan to vote, someone in our delegation spotted Humphrey, standing on a chair, waving wildly to get Mennen's attention. Humphrey mouthed the word "Kefauver" and Mennen gave him the high sign. Both states voted for Kefauver for vice president, and tipped the scales for his nomination. Any differences were soon forgotten in the face of the enormous task that lay ahead—the campaign against President Dwight Eisenhower and Vice President Richard Nixon.

Not long after the convention, Adlai Stevenson sent short personal notes of thanks to many of us who had backed him and Estes Kefauver. His note to me read in part: "As I said last week, I pledge to you every resource of mind and strength that I possess to make your deed a good one for our country and for our party."

Kefauver's note of thanks came shortly after Stevenson's. It began "Dear Helen: You have been a wonderful friend and I want to thank you for your support and loyalty all the way through. I hope I can show you my appreciation by making a real contribution to the Democratic cause and the party in your state. In Adlai Stevenson we have chosen a great leader and I am proud to be on the same ticket with him."

Traditionally, Democrats kicked off the campaign in Michigan on Labor Day, with big rallies in Detroit and Flint. It was in Flint in 1952 that Stevenson's shoes became famous. As he sat on the platform with his legs crossed, an alert photographer noticed that a hole was almost worn through the sole of one of his shoes. Four years later, Stevenson was wearing a miniature of that shoe in his lapel when he came to Michigan. The little silver shoe with the thin sole became a good fundraising gimmick. The pins were eagerly sought and worn by Stevenson supporters throughout that 1956 campaign.

Not long after Labor Day, Stevenson and Kefauver were both planning campaign trips through Michigan. Stevenson's itinerary was not firm. Kefauver was to tour the Upper Peninsula, where Mennen was popular and where Democrats had strong support among the mine workers and many other groups.

Over the years, it had become second nature to us to develop thumbnail sketches of cities and towns for candidates and their staffs to have before they visited. Working with our people, I would see to it that all the important facts about an area were summarized neatly. A candidate would know what was big locally before setting foot there.

After we had sent Kefauver and his staff our usual report on the UP towns he was to visit, I received a grateful letter from Ken Hechler, executive assistant to Stevenson, asking if we would do the same for Stevenson once his tour was set. Ken enclosed a one-and-a-half page list of questions to be answered about each place. It was one of the most impressive, issue-oriented lists I had ever seen. They wanted to know everything, from what the farmers thought about Eisenhower's policies to local views on the administration's handling of defense and foreign affairs. Pat Taylor and Peg Edwards did a wonderful job of compiling the information. Afterwards Ken sent another letter of thanks, telling us how much easier campaigning would be if every state party would cooperate as well as we had.

Kefauver's UP trip also caused me some chagrin. Indirectly, it prompted an uncharacteristic outburst from me toward Mennen—in public, mind you. We had some new state and national campaign material and had decided to send packages of it by Greyhound bus, timing it to arrive at each place before Senator Kefauver was to speak. It had just been delivered to our office, and I had all my lawyers—"Helen's Boys"—doing the very un-lawyer-like work of counting and packaging the material in time to make the last bus to the Upper Peninsula on a steamy summer evening.

In the middle of the frenzy the governor called and said that he and his state police aides were at Berman's Restaurant, a popular steakhouse a few blocks from the office. He wanted me to join him for dinner. Normally, I would have been delighted at the chance to talk, but this could not have been a more inopportune time. Giving hurried instructions to my volunteers, I arrived at the restaurant out of breath, after they had started to eat.

Looking back now, I can't even remember what it was all about, but Sid Woolner had been getting a bad deal in some way, and I was very upset about it. Although I am not much good at fighting for myself, I can be a tiger for my friends. No sooner had I sat down when Mennen said the wrong thing about Sid's situation. He didn't know for a minute or two what hit him. Not only did I feel strongly about whatever it was that people were doing to Sid, I also was hot, tired, and frustrated. Mennen got it from me with both barrels. The state police boys didn't know where to look. They practically had their faces down in their plates.

Mennen was a gentleman, and patient with me. When I finally stopped for breath, he asked me questions that would give him what he needed to know, and then changed the subject. He took care of the situation the next day, and never said a word to me about it again. Mennen knew from experience that I wouldn't have said anything if I didn't think he needed to hear it. Fortunately, there weren't very many times when I had to make my point so strongly with him.

The 1956 campaign was nothing like the previous ones. It seemed that we suddenly had grown into a big operation. There was a lot of interest in the campaigns, both state and national. People expected us to deliver what they wanted when they wanted it, which usually was yesterday. At the governor's request, we finally opened a second office in Lansing to handle the growing volume of work for his campaign. That office, too, was my responsibility.

We made particular efforts to organize Mennen's supporters within the ranks of ethnic groups and within special interest groups, such as builders and real estate people, farmers and small business owners. That, too, fell under my wing. Once again, we reached out to the clergy. Wade H. McCree, Jr., who later became solicitor general for the United States and a federal appeals court judge, drafted a simple, nonpartisan letter for the governor to send to religious leaders. It urged them to remind their congregations of the importance of voting and to point out that it would be a shame to forfeit that right just by failing to register.

With the tide swelling for the national Republican ticket, we did what we could to get the voters out. Tragedy marked the end of the national campaign for us in Michigan, however, and almost made the outcome seem unimportant. Venice Spraggs, the former newspaperwoman who had joined the Democratic National Committee staff, was a good friend of mine. In addition to her able assistance to Neil Staebler on the committee that Paul Butler had created to rebuild the national party, she was the committee's liaison with the DNC. She was a tireless worker for Stevenson and helped his campaign immensely among black people and everyone else she met. Venice was an engaging speaker and had the gift of inspiring others to work as hard as they possibly could.

As usual, Venice was pushing herself too much. She was traveling the country with the Stevenson campaign on a tour which was to end in a huge rally at the Fox Theatre in Detroit. She had caught a heavy bronchial cold and could hardly talk. We tried to persuade her to go to the doctor and just cancel her speech. We would find a substitute, we assured her. She was so dedicated to Stevenson that she wouldn't listen. She insisted on making her appearance and forced her voice to carry to the remotest area of that huge theater. She was coughing constantly when it was over. Instead of staying overnight, she wanted to take a late flight home to D. C. No one realized how desperately ill she was. When she got home, she assured her husband, William Spraggs, that she was okay. In the morning, she entered the hospital, but it was too late. The coughing had ruptured her esophagus, and she died in great pain.

When I reached the funeral parlor in Washington, the director called me into his office to answer a telephone call from Detroit. It was Neil, in tears. The planes were grounded by fog, and he could not get to D. C. for the funeral. "I was to give her eulogy," he said. "Helen, you will have to do it for me. No one else knows her as well as you do."

The funeral was delayed a little to permit Representative William Dawson, Venice's hometown congressman, to arrive from Chicago, so I had a few minutes to get my wits together. The parlor was filled to capacity, but I didn't really see anyone. The funeral director led me to a low podium a few feet from Venice's open casket. Seated there, all alone, were her husband and her mother. As I began to speak, I just looked at the two of them, who also had become my good friends. Looking back, I have no recollection of what I said. All I did was talk directly to them from my heart, telling them what a wonderful person she had been and how much we all loved her. The tears were rolling down my cheeks but somehow I was able to talk for several minutes. Many of the people later told me I had said just what needed to be said, and they knew I had talked from my heart. How I ever did it, I will never know.

We had to cope with another devastating experience before the 1956 campaign was over. Although we were always geared for a dirty trick the last weekend before election day, this time it went beyond our worst imaginings.

One Saturday near the close of the campaign, I got a call from Ed Winge, a *Detroit Free Press* reporter who was looking for an officer of the party. Ed told me that a pressman had brought in a letter he had received that morning, and Ed said it was political dynamite. A messenger from our office went to the *Free Press* and got a copy for me. When I read it, I could hardly believe my eyes. The letter was addressed personally to, we later learned, many black people, including our pressman friend. It was written in intimate and friendly terms, urging a vote for Adlai Stevenson because he would appoint people like Jim Eastland and Strom Thurmond to the Supreme Court if he were elected president. It was signed by "Friends of Jim Eastland and Strom Thurmond." Since Senators Eastland and Thurmond were both staunch Southern segregationists, we knew this letter was a political dirty trick.

After Ed Winge phoned me, he called John Murray for a comment from the Democratic party itself. John immediately saw the significance of the letter and alerted Paul Weber. At my end, I got on the phone and found Neil Staebler and Adelaide Hart. We got together and composed a telegram to black clergy and community leaders. Congressman Charles Diggs agreed to let us use his name in the telegram. Paul Weber called the UAW, which immediately put its communications network into operation. It didn't take me long to find that the best list of black leaders I had ever compiled was missing. So was a young Southern white boy who had worked in the office. We later saw him on television at a right-wing rally in Atlanta. The letter sent to black voters in Michigan was postmarked Atlanta.

We all spent the rest of the day and evening telephoning as many people as possible to watch for that and similar letters. As luck would have it, Mennen's schedule on Sunday had him speaking at several black churches in the area. He was able to assure people that it was an ugly hoax.

The letter had the opposite effect than had been planned by its instigators. Voting in the black areas was heavier than usual. People were angry that a trick like that could be played on them and the candidates they believed in. But if that letter had been received on Monday instead of Saturday, and if the pressman and Ed Winge had not acted so quickly, we couldn't have counteracted the impact before the polls opened Tuesday. There simply wouldn't have been enough time to use the methods available to us then; television wasn't the instant and universal communicator it is today.

Ed broke the news story in the *Detroit Free Press* Sunday editions, two days before the election. The letter was part of the "reverse English" bigotry campaign, which consisted of last-minute mailings that appeared to be favorable but which actually were vicious and slanderous. The mailings went all over the country, but Michigan was a particular target because of the popularity of Mennen Williams and Adlai Stevenson in this state.

After a long investigation, it was found that a Republican public relations man from Oakland County had his people prepare the letters and envelopes, using the list of black leaders stolen from my office. The big question, as always, remained unanswered: Who in the higher ranks of the Republican party authorized, condoned, or at least knew of this underhanded activity? Most people believed that the PR man took the rap for someone much higher up.

All the Democratic candidates on the statewide ticket won. Mennen's total was 1,666,689 votes to 1,376,376 for Republican Al Cobo. Stevenson not only lost the election, he also lost in Michigan, much to our sorrow. We had had enough sadness to last us for several elections.

The spring election of 1957 cheered us up because Mennen gained two more members on his Administrative Board. Lynn M. Bartlett was elected superintendent of public instruction and John C. Mackie highway commissioner. Both these men brought great ability to two of the areas that Mennen was interested in improving. They made great strides and were reelected several times.

22

THE TWO
PENINSULAS BECOME ONE

O F ALL HIS ACCOMPLISHMENTS in office, none was more satisfying to Mennen than the Mackinac Bridge. When he was first elected governor, public transportation between Michigan's two peninsulas was by ferry between Mackinaw City and St. Ignace. The distance across the Straits of Mackinac is less than five miles, but the trip took about an hour, and often there was a much longer wait. A twelve-hour holdup waiting to get on the ferry was not unusual, or even an overnight delay if the ice was too thick. The situation was so frustrating that some motorists would drive all the way around Lake Michigan and up through Wisconsin to get to and from the Upper Peninsula.

There had been talk of building a bridge since the nineteenth century, but the skeptics said it was impossible. Mennen didn't believe that. Shortly after he became governor, he began the long process which would result in the building of the bridge. It wasn't easy, and Mennen's first steps were ridiculed unmercifully. "Soapy's Folly" was mild compared to some of the vicious things that were said about his plans. Years later, I am sure many of those critics crossed the bridge numerous times without even reflecting on their shortsightedness.

When engineering studies proved that it would be difficult but not impossible to build a bridge over the Straits of Mackinac, Mennen pushed and prodded until he finally had the project started. With the help of people from both peninsulas who wanted a bridge, Mennen persuaded the legislature to create the Mackinac Bridge Authority in 1950. The governor appointed the members of the authority, who then went to work on the project. Years later, in a foreword to a book about the bridge, Mennen somewhat triumphantly described the authority as "a group of citizens who put an end to doubts that a bridge could be built, by actually building it."[1]

It was mid-1954 before construction actually began. Mennen was determined not to miss any of it whenever he was at the summer residence on Mackinac Island. He had some small trees and bushes cut back so he could watch the construction crews at work. Like a small boy, Mennen was thrilled every time a new support was riveted into place. He often pulled visitors aside to show them exactly what was going on as the project progressed. The bridge took more than three years to build, so Mennen got in a lot of experience as a sidewalk superintendent, although he was quite a distance away and there was no sidewalk. On November 1, 1957, the bridge was finally opened. Nancy and Mennen led a small group that held a modest ceremony before traffic began to cross the bridge. Mennen and Nancy were to drive the first car over the span. Mennen climbed behind the wheel and then remembered that he didn't have a valid driver's license anymore; as governor, he couldn't really drive himself anywhere anyway. Just imagine what would happen if the governor were to be accused of driving without a license, he told Nancy. Nancy, who loved to drive and had her license with her, took the wheel. They paid their toll, "and I got to be the first person to drive over the Mackinac Bridge!" Nancy laughed. Mennen didn't mind. He was so thrilled that the bridge was finally a reality that nothing could dim his enthusiasm.

It truly was a marvelous sight. The span of the bridge draped by the graceful suspensions is more than a mile and a half long. The cables themselves are more than two feet around and weigh several tons each. At the center of the bridge, the road surface is almost two hundred feet above the straits. The two towers, from their foundations underneath the water to their soaring heights, are taller than the Westin Hotel on Detroit's riverfront. Measured only from the water's surface to their tops, the towers are still considerably taller than the four Renaissance Center skyscrapers that surround the hotel.

In the foreword to *Miracle Bridge at Mackinac*, written by the bridge's architect, David B. Steinman, and John T. Nevill, of nearby DeTour Village, Mennen reveled in what he called "the world's greatest bridge." He wrote in part:

The people of Michigan were faced with an apparently insoluble geographical problem—a barrier of deep and turbulent water which cut the state in half. This same water barrier served as a fluid highway on which the mineral and timber riches of the Upper Peninsula were carried to the mills and factories at the foot of the lakes. But insofar as land transportation was concerned, the four miles of deep water between Mackinaw City and St. Ignace choked off commerce and culture. The geographical fact of the straits dictated that our great transportation routes should run across lower Michigan, from east to west, rather than along the logical north-south route from Lake Erie to the American and Canadian Northwest. The difficulty of transportation oriented half of the state to Wisconsin, and tended to draw very thin the cultural ties between Michigan's Northland and the great metropolitan cities of the south.

The people of Michigan saw that this barrier must be bridged. They saw that a bridge at the straits would create an entirely new trade route, a new Northwest Passage. They saw that a bridge would open up the magnificent northern Michigan vacationland, with its immense potentialities for those who live in the cities of the Middlewest.

Today the Mackinac Bridge stands as a fitting symbol of the spirit of Michigan—a spirit which has never found any job too big, if the job needed to be done.

Because the weather in late fall at the straits can be unpredictable, the dedication ceremony was set for June of 1958. It was to take place right in the middle of the bridge, with traffic temporarily halted. Invitations to the dedication were hard to get and jealously guarded by anyone lucky enough to receive one. This was a nonpartisan affair. Some of the members of the bridge authority were Republicans, and members of both political parties were involved in planning the dedication.

The original plan was to set up tables on the bridge and serve box lunches to celebrate. But the first of that day's disasters was an accident involving the truck bringing the tables. It was hit broadside before it reached the bridge, and the tables were strewn all over the highway. It was impossible to retrieve them in time for the luncheon, so the party planners decided to put the lunches on the buses that brought the guests onto the bridge. The guests then could take the food back to their motels when the ceremony was over. The Democratic State Central Committee had rented a motel meeting room in Mackinaw City, and we were all to meet there for our own private celebration afterward. (The company that had charge of the box lunches was not very well organized. In the last-minute distribution of the box lunches, some buses got two sets of lunches and some got none. It was probably just a coincidence, but several of the buses carrying the Democrats were the ones left out.)

The dedication ceremony was planned to allow several speakers—members of the bridge authority, local officials, and others—a chance to say a few words. When everyone else was finished, Mennen was to give a short speech and then pull the cord that would reveal the plaque permanently dedicating the structure and naming it, officially, the Mackinac Bridge.

178

Imagine Mennen's great disappointment when the man who introduced him reached over, pulled the cord revealing the plaque, and said that he officially dedicated the Mackinac Bridge. Gasps of astonishment could be heard throughout the crowd. The bridge had been the governor's dream, and he had made it come true. Everyone knew it had been his deep desire to pull the cord and dedicate it. Somehow, Mennen swallowed his disappointment and anger. He made the speech he had so carefully prepared, omitting the final paragraph that would have dedicated the bridge.

It was a good thing we had a private retreat for the Democratic party after the ceremony. Mennen paced up and down the room, indignantly recalling what had been done to him and denouncing the people involved. Never before—and never again—did I ever see him that angry. Never had I seen him show his feelings so openly among his fellow Democrats.

Not long afterward, I thought I would surprise Mennen with some stationery honoring the Mackinac Bridge to use in the 1958 reelection campaign. Poor Eddie Fishman. He had great difficulty producing an image of the bridge from the only picture I could find. He came through, of course, and I had several hundred pieces of letterhead stationery made and ready to use. With a big smile on my face, anticipating a happy surprise, I showed Mennen the finished product. He didn't say a word. He looked at it carefully for hardly a minute and then he made a pen mark on the outline. "We can't use this," he said. "This support on the bridge is not right. I've made the correction and it will have to be redone." So much for surprises.

A few months after Mennen's undeserved comeuppance in the middle of the bridge, I had one of my own—in Escanaba, west of the bridge. Normally, I tried to stay in the background in public, especially with Mennen or Nancy. They were the ones people were coming to see, after all. In Escanaba that day, I found myself in the spotlight and in a nasty situation to boot, and it was Nancy who rescued me.

The local Democratic party traditionally put on a big luncheon for the precinct workers just before the election. It was always the political event of the year in Delta County. All the major state candidates were invited. The governor usually attended. This year, however, it was on the same date as a Wayne County day that he couldn't miss. (During the closing days of all of Mennen's campaigns, every Wayne County congressional district party organization got one day of the governor's time, all day and all evening. They each picked their own days and usually kept the same ones for every campaign. We didn't dare tamper with them.) The Delta County chairman insisted that the governor's wife, at least, come to the luncheon. Nancy agreed and asked me and Larry Farrell's wife, Mary, who was from that area, to go with her. Nancy and I picked up Mary in Lansing at 7:00 A.M. and drove almost nonstop to get to Escanaba on time. Even then, we were late.

When we arrived at the luncheon, the people at the speakers' table were all seated. The table stretched the length of the room. Nancy was asked to sit near the middle, close to the podium, while I was shown to a seat at one end. Mary, who knew many people at the luncheon, was seated at a table nearby.

The county chairman introduced the people at the speakers' table. He had flowery compliments for everyone until he got to me. He almost sneered as he introduced me as "a spy from the Lower Peninsula." Trying not to look shocked, I stood, smiled, and waved at the guests. The chairman moved on without further comment, introducing the next person in the same lavish way he had the others. It couldn't have been more noticeable.

While this was an insult to me, it also was a slap at the governor, since I was his campaign manager. Nancy was not about to let this go unnoticed. Senator Pat McNamara's administrative assistant, Hal Beaton, was a native of Delta County and the next person scheduled to speak. Nancy leaned over and whispered pointedly to him just before he got up to speak. Hal found a way to mention me again and made some gracious remarks about my loyalty to the party and my campaign experience.

The county chairman, a prominent local businessman, never did speak to me all the time I was there. It was not until long after the election that I learned that he blamed me for sabotaging his attempt to get Mennen to appoint him to the U. S. Senate vacancy that had been given to Blair Moody. Why the man thought I had that much influence I never will understand. If only he had known that I was as much in the dark as he was as to who would be appointed. At the time of the appointment, I barely knew Blair Moody. In the years that followed the unforgettable luncheon in Escanaba, the chairman and I worked together in relative harmony to get out the vote for the Democratic ticket. The incident was never mentioned.

NOTES

1. This is from Steinman and Nevill's *Miracle Bridge at Mackinac*. See also Lawrence A. Rubin, *Mighty Mac: The Official Picture History of the Mackinac Bridge* (Detroit: Wayne State University Press, 1958), and *Bridging the Straits: The Story of Mighty Mac* (Detroit: Wayne State University Press, 1985). Rubin was executive secretary of the Mackinac Bridge Authority from 1950 to 1983. For more background on the building of the Mackinac Bridge, see the papers of G. Mennen Williams, Michigan Historical Collections, Bentley Historical Library, University of Michigan, Ann Arbor; and the State Archives, located in the Michigan Library and Historical Center, 717 W. Allegan, Lansing.

23

MENNEN'S
LAST CAMPAIGN
FOR GOVERNOR

T HE CAMPAIGN OF 1958 was a more serious one, without as much of
the hilarity and lightheartedness as we had enjoyed in the past.
First of all, it was the year of the great decision: Who would run
for governor, and who would run for the U. S. Senate? The two candidates in question were Mennen Williams and his lieutenant governor,
Phil Hart. It was taken for granted that they would both run, but for
which office?

We all had different ideas as to which man should run for which position, and why. It was my strong opinion that Phil Hart would make a
better senator than he would a governor. He didn't find it easy to make
decisions quickly. He wasn't an administrator, I felt sure. With the
number of appointments the governor has to make, to say nothing of the
battles with the legislature, I could foresee many controversies and problems for Phil in that office.

Yet if Mennen did not run for the Senate that year against the Republican incumbent, it would be several years before he would have another chance, since Pat McNamara was the other senator from Michigan.
While I knew Mennen would make an excellent senator, I felt it would
be very difficult for him to become a junior senator after having been a
governor. As chief executive of an important state, he was a powerful figure. As the lower-ranking Michigan member of a legislative body of one
hundred people, he would be very small potatoes until he could prove his
leadership ability.

When I sat at the meetings Mennen held to discuss the matter, I listened to all the pros and cons. As I often did when a decision was to be made, I listed the numerous arguments on both sides as best I could. No question about it, it was easier for me to think of reasons why Mennen should run again as governor. However, I did try to list all the opinions that had been voiced. Mennen had my list copied and distributed to the group. Neil Staebler was the strongest advocate for Mennen running for the Senate. He held onto a dream that someday, Mennen would be the popular candidate for president.

What Mennen's private reasons were, I never knew. But those of us who were in favor of having him run again for governor were pleased when he decided to do so. That cleared the way for Phil Hart to run for the Senate.

It is still debatable what would have been in the future for Mennen if he had run for the Senate that year. In 1981 I heard him say that if he had run for the Senate, he would still have been there then. Perhaps that's true, but I feel strongly that he contributed greatly in that last term in the governor's office, in Africa and in the Philippines under appointments from Presidents Kennedy and Johnson, and later, especially so on the Michigan Supreme Court.

Once Mennen had made his decision to run for reelection, we had another concern—getting him to announce his candidacy. It wasn't the lack of campaigning or publicity that troubled us; we were worried about the petition drive to get him nominated. Because Mennen always insisted on having enough signatures to qualify in all eighty-three counties, we had to start early and work hard and long. We had to get the petitions out in time for them to be circulated, signed, returned, and checked over for errors before we filed them with the secretary of state. It was no small task to get people lined up to do the legwork.

In Mennen's previous campaigns, we usually had the nominating petitions out by February or March. This time, he wanted to delay things as long as possible. The political situation was tense, and the legislature was being especially uncooperative. Mennen knew that as soon as he became a candidate, his best efforts would be thwarted. He would be accused of electioneering, and the Republicans would block anything of importance that he tried to do. Mennen really thought he might get some of his tax changes through before the politicking got impossible, but it wasn't to be. In the meantime, we waited, getting more nervous every day.

As the campaign manager, I was the most unnerved of all, but I forged ahead and began planning anyway. The advertising agency and I had worked on designing his petitions. This year I wanted a slogan on them. "Why?" everyone asked. "Just because," I would answer. When they realized I meant it, I got one—"Keep Michigan Strong."

The petitions were printed. A letter was written, telling the people that Mennen appreciated their help, and that, once again, he wanted to qualify in all eighty-three counties. The petitions, with my letter enclosed, were all addressed and sealed. We were only waiting for the official word from the governor that he was running to put them through the postage meter and mail them.

Every day I would tell Paul Weber, Mennen's trusted confidante and press secretary, about my worries. Finally Paul called me. "The governor is going to announce his candidacy tomorrow," he said. "Are you sure?" I asked. "Yes," he replied. "He has agreed to do it at his morning press conference." "Can I put the petitions in the mail?" I asked. "Sure," Paul said. "Go ahead." Into the mail they went that night.

This was one time the mail was delivered too promptly. One of the reporters happened by on his way to Mennen's press conference the next morning while Mary Margetts, Paul Weber's secretary, was opening the mail. (In the governor's office in Lansing, all the secretaries' desks were in a hallway outside the offices of the governor's staff, and the press people often stopped to chat.) Out of one of the envelopes came the governor's petition and the accompanying letter that I had sent Paul for his information. The reporter just had time to see it was a nominating petition and that my signature, as campaign manager, was at the bottom of the letter.

Into the press conference he went, and waited rather impatiently for the governor to make his announcement that he was running. It never came. Finally, the reporter spoke up: "Governor, when are you going to announce you are running again?" "I'll get around to it one of these days," Mennen responded. The reporter, thinking he was calling the governor's bluff, then said triumphantly, "Your nominating petitions are out." Mennen was startled. He mumbled something about having friends and cut the press conference short. Paul called me right away and told me what had happened. "If the governor says anything to you about it, you can blame me," he said. "But he did tell me he was going to announce today." If Mennen was upset about being put on the spot, he never mentioned it to me. Actually, he got unexpected publicity because the reporter wrote quite a story. When I read it, I was even more glad I had insisted on having a slogan on the petition, because he quoted it. He also printed my letter, almost in its entirety. It was one of my better letters, if I do say so myself. The story went out across the state. The *Detroit News* on April 22 quoted the slogan in the second paragraph and printed passages from my letter:

Mrs. Berthelot's letter, with a salutation to "Dear Friend," said many dedicated Democrats work at each election for their favorite candidates.

"I know that you will be happy to be in the group working for the re-election of our great governor, G. Mennen Williams," the letter continued.

The *Detroit News* story went on to say that I had enclosed an order blank encouraging requests for more petitions and that we had set a May 23rd deadline for return of the petitions.

Two days after the press conference, Mennen made his official announcement, and there was more coverage in the papers. Many people thought we had planned the double announcement in order to get extra publicity. Several people complimented me on it. Even though it all happened by accident, I accepted the congratulations without saying a word.

In most of his campaigns, Mennen had left the filing of the petitions up to the staff. This year, he decided to bring his petitions into the secretary of state's office himself while his son, Gery, and grandson, also named Gery, watched. The three generations together made a wonderful picture for the newspapers.

For the first time since 1948, Mennen Williams had an opponent in the primary. William L. Johnson, owner of a radio station in the western Upper Peninsula, filed as a candidate against him. It was really no contest; Mennen even beat him in his home area of Gogebic County.

With Phil Hart running for the Senate, Mennen chose John Swainson as his running mate. Because of the way elections were held then, John had to run on a separate ticket, but at least he had no primary opponent. He was one of the young Democrats who had been elected to the state senate and who were struggling to help Mennen with his programs. John was a veteran of World War II and had lost both of his legs below the knee. Anyone who didn't know him well never would have realized the extent of his injuries.

This time around, Mennen decided to have his staff in the governor's office report to me, as campaign manager, for activities related to the campaign. This was new. My worst problem was getting them to finish the drafts of the governor's speeches in time for Mennen to work on them for the television shows, particularly after the primary. Over and over, I would ask Larry Farrell, Mennen's executive secretary, where they were. His answers varied: "Oh, I gave it to so-and-so." Several times, the so-and-so of the day was out on the golf course. More than once I had to call a couple of the staff members at home and prod them to get their speeches written. It was a strange experience for me. The men on my campaign staff had never shown the slightest reluctance to work for or answer to a woman boss. In fact, one of them had sent me a lovely letter at the end of an earlier campaign, confessing that he had been skeptical at first but ended up pleasantly surprised at how much he enjoyed working for me.

In 1958, with the governor's office staff to cope with and a campaign to run, I didn't have much time to focus on the office itself. Luckily for me, Helen Bevans was the office manager. She had been active in 17th

District politics from the beginning of Mennen's campaigns, so she knew how to handle the unexpected emergencies. She managed to keep the office humming and the staff happy at the same time—not an easy feat, especially that last year. Her skillful management was something I appreciated, since I faced enough of my own challenges outside the campaign office.

The differences between the campaign office and the governor's office became obvious early in the campaign, when Mennen called a meeting of his staff and invited me. It had just been announced that his staff was to report to me for any campaign work. (From the start, Mennen augmented his staff year-around as well as during the campaigns by hiring people whose salaries he paid with his personal funds). Mennen began the meeting by sketching out ideas for the campaign. The plans that came out of his mouth did not jibe with anything he had ever advocated before.

We were seated in a circle and I sat on his left. Starting with the person on his right, Mennen went around the room, asking everyone to respond to the ideas he had presented. It was a good thing he wasn't looking at me. My mouth must have dropped open. The answer from each staff person was some variation of "Yes, Governor. That's a fine idea." "Yes, Governor. . . . Yes, Governor. . . ." from each and every one.

Mennen then turned to me and asked me what I thought. Quietly I said: "I am sorry, Governor, but I will have to disagree with your staff. I don't think the ideas you have presented fit in with the type of campaign we have found to be effective." While the others had been talking, I had been outlining in my mind the reasons why I should disagree, and I stated them as I thought of them. Mennen didn't comment on my answers. He went on to other subjects without again asking our opinions. Later, when we were going out of the room, I heard him tell Frank Blackford, a trusted adviser for many years, "I don't always agree with Helen but she always tells me the truth." We ran the campaign according to our tried and true methods, by the way.

There was at least one other time when Mennen and I really had words. He had gone to a dinner with a group that I felt might tarnish his reputation because some of their business dealings were questionable. After I heard about it, I told him I thought he should not have associated with that group, and why. He didn't reply, but later he told Adelaide Hart that I looked at him as if he had spit on the Bible. Two years later, Hicks Griffiths went to a dinner with the same group. Mennen Williams confronted me: "Your friend Hicks Griffiths went to that dinner. What do you think of that?" I replied, "I don't like it any better than when you went."

Even after ten years of working with Mennen in all sorts of situations, it wasn't easy for me to get him to do something he had made up his mind not to do. That became painfully obvious to me near the end of the 1958 campaign. One tradition that carried through all the years was to assign each Wayne County congressional district a whole day of Mennen's time the last week or so of the campaign. Each district chairman seemed to have a special preference that worked out very well. The 13th District always wanted Sunday. That gave the governor the opportunity to speak in most of the black churches. One time, neither Mennen nor Nancy could make it to one of the churches, and the minister asked me to come and speak for the governor. If the subject had been anything but Mennen's campaign, I don't believe I could have done it. The congregation gave me a warm welcome and seemed to like my speech. The fact that it was short and to the point probably helped.

John Schneider always prepared the schedule for Louie McGuinness, chairman of the 15th District. John was an elderly lawyer who had been an active volunteer in the 15th District for many years and always could be depended upon to fill in wherever needed. John always wanted to please everyone. There were many groups in the 15th District, which covered part of western Wayne County. Most of them wanted a personal visit from Mennen and were reluctant to combine with other groups.

Because John accommodated them, the 15th District day was always overloaded. Louie used to tease me by saying, "Now, John . . . ," because I was always admonishing, "Now, John, you'll just have to cut this schedule down." John would dutifully go back at it, but he always added one or two more instead of taking some out. "How do you expect the governor to go to this many meetings in one day?" I would ask. "Oh, I timed it," John would reply. "It worked out perfectly." "John," I would say, "how many hands did you stop and shake on the way?" He would always admit that he had just walked and driven the route. This went on year after year. It took a great many telephone calls and much persuasion to get the schedule down to a workable size. The other Wayne County districts dutifully combined their groups, so their schedules weren't such a problem.

The 14th District was invariably the victim of a last-minute television show. Sid Woolner always managed to come up with the money for one more television appearance. He would insist that I produce Mennen for the occasion. Because of the timing, it would mean breaking some of Mennen's commitments in his home district. Lucien Nedzi was district chairman in 1958. Later on, as a congressman, he was widely respected for his understanding of national defense issues. He took good care of his constituents while he was in Congress, just as he had done as district chairman. When we had to cancel some of Mennen's 14th District appearances, Lucien always groaned but gave up his time with grace. "You just do this to me because I'm good-natured," he would tell me.

Mennen was never happy about having to ditch some of his time in his home district. In 1958, it turned into a battle of wills. It was the night before Mennen was scheduled to visit the 14th District groups. Sid Woolner called me to break the news that the campaign had acquired a couple of minutes free time on a major television station in strategic thirty-second spots. It had been decided that the best way to use the time was for the governor to appear on camera and simply ask people to get out and vote. When I told Mennen that evening, he remonstrated and suggested several people who he thought could do it much better. They want you, I told him. He was late for his next meeting so could not stay and argue with me.

Mennen's state police aides were some of my best friends in all the campaigns, but they loved to play tricks on me and got a kick out of watching me get out of difficult situations. The next morning, George Kerr, Mennen's senior state police aide, came in early. With an impish grin, he told me, "The governor says he's not going to make that TV tape this a.m." He quickly left, knowing he had me buffaloed. Dashing into Sid's office, I told him what George had said. "What am I going to do?" I asked. Sid didn't hesitate. "Berthelot," he said, "You are the governor's campaign manager. It's up to you to get him there. I'll have the agency waiting to cut the tape at 11:30 A.M." Then he, too, hurriedly walked out of the room.

There was no doubt what I was up against. Mennen was a strong-willed person. My only other attempt to change his mind had ended in complete defeat. In that instance, he had been campaigning steadily and I knew he was very tired. Without saying anything to him, I took a small meeting, one I had used as a time filler, out of his final schedule. Unfortunately, he had seen the first draft, and in nothing flat I got a telephone call. "Where's the meeting?" he asked, referring to the one I had cut so judiciously—or so I had thought. I told him that I knew he was dead tired and I had tried to reduce his schedule in a way that would not hurt anyone's feelings. That was the wrong thing to say. He put the appearance back in—and added another one that I had never even heard about.

Remembering that episode, I was not very optimistic about getting Mennen over to the station. He disliked making speeches on television under any circumstances, and when he was tired he had trouble with his voice. Double trouble. The night before, I had been able to cancel the necessary time from the 14th District day with no problems. Lucien was even relieved to have a little leeway in the tight schedule. The meeting Lucien and I canceled was only a time filler anyway, but I wasn't going to tell Mennen that.

After Sid left me to my devices, I looked over the morning's appearances and discovered that at that moment, the governor was in the lunchroom of a small factory, greeting people as they came off the shop floor in groups for their breaks. Paul Silver, the union steward who had arranged the meetings, was a friend, so I had no trouble getting into the lunchroom.

Mennen was not a bit happy to see me. He knew why I was there. He did his best to ignore me but I didn't let him get away with it. There were brief lulls between each group, and I made the most of the time. With my best smile, I said, "Mennen, we really need you to do those TV spots." There was no time to say any more than that. Before he could respond, another group came in. The next time, I told him that Sid Woolner and the ad agency were waiting for him. Another group arrived. Next, I assured him that he would not be missing a meeting in the 14th District since Lucien and I had agreed to cancel it. Lucien was glad to have the extra time, I told him. It dawned on me that I was like a pesky mosquito, buzzing around his head and not letting him alone. That made me laugh, and I thought up new things to say as he shook hands with the workers.

My positive attitude that he *was* going to do the tapes finally penetrated to him. Time was getting very short. When I finally said, "Mennen, we will have to leave now," he grumpily mumbled something to the 14th District volunteer and signaled to a disbelieving George Kerr that it was time to go. Knowing I was not very welcome, I went right along, too, and gave George directions to the television station. When we arrived, Sid looked enormously relieved. "I didn't think you could do it," he said to me later. "Hmmph," I said, "no thanks to you."

The taping started out to be a fiasco. Mennen was very tired and irritated at having to make the tapes. He made a couple of attempts but could not get his voice to sound convincing. Thinking there was nothing more to lose, I stood in front of him and made a complete fool of myself, twisting my face into the worst contortions I could manage. He had to laugh, and that did it. The taping went smoothly, and he completed the rest of his 14th District day while I went back to the office. That night, the 14th District had a big banquet to which I had been invited, too. Lucien Nedzi gave me a very nice introduction, and the audience dutifully applauded. Mennen then got up and said: "I am glad you like my campaign manager. It is not always easy to manage me," and then he looked over at me and grinned.

By this time, we all knew each other very well. The years had taught me to sense when Mennen's incredible strength began to wane, and I found ways to rejuvenate him when he needed it most. My best ally in that was Frank Szymanski, a delightful man who was so modest about his effect on people that I am sure he didn't realize how much he helped boost Mennen's spirits. When Mennen was tired and had a hard schedule I often sent Frank along with him. The governor always came back looking like a different person after a day with Frank because he had laughed so hard.

Frank, who was at the time auditor general, was one of the most popular members of the Ad Board. He was friendly, warm, and funny. Frank had been an All-America football player at the University of Notre Dame and later played pro ball with the Detroit Lions, the Philadelphia Eagles, and the Chicago Bears. Like so many men who came of age under the cloud of World War II, he had interrupted his life to enlist in the military. Frank's story of how he wore down the Navy's objections to allowing him to enlist made Mennen laugh until tears ran down his cheeks, no matter how many times he heard it. Frank would talk about his flat feet, and about how he kept taking his case higher and higher until he finally found someone who would accept him, flat feet and all. Frank was given a high rank, to boot, when all he wanted was to get in. As a Navy veteran himself, Mennen really appreciated Frank's description of his little campaign to win over the poker-faced authorities.

The campaign staff had a lot of fun planning an event that turned out to be the highlight of the 1958 campaign: a day-long visit by former President Harry Truman. He was so down-to-earth that it was hard to remember that he had been president during such a crucial period in history. Of course, he gave a few speeches on behalf of Mennen and the entire Democratic ticket, but it was at the informal receptions that he really shone. He was like an old family friend, greeting everyone warmly and chatting easily.

Because he was the former president, all of our volunteers wanted to be photographed with him. He posed for a number of pictures. Late as usual, I came into the room where the pictures were being taken, my arms filled with copies of the schedule, my purse, and my stole. The governor called me over to have my picture taken. President Truman took one look at me and, in one motion, took all the things from my arms and tossed them over to the sofa. "Give Governor Williams your right hand and give me your left hand," he ordered. He waited until I crossed my arms over each other to do as he commanded. Though I felt a little foolish, it did make me laugh. "Now, isn't that better?" he said with a grin.

24

MENNEN
IS A SURVIVOR, PHYSICALLY
AND MENTALLY

I WOULD HAVE WORRIED more about Mennen's safety over the years if I hadn't been so busy with the problems of campaigns. He was on the road so much that it was fortunate that he was never in a serious car accident. But in the summer of 1950, Mennen's concern about a problem almost cost him his life.

At the time, there were many stories out of Marquette Branch Prison about bad conditions and poor food. The prison, one of the oldest in the state, had been operating for more than sixty years and housed some of the most dangerous criminals. In typical fashion, Mennen decided to see for himself. He informed the prison authorities that he was coming, but they knew he would set his own agenda when he arrived.

As soon as he got there, Mennen asked to be taken to the kitchen. He spotted a kettle of beans and ham and walked over for a taste. George Kerr, Mennen's state police aide, and two other men were with him. What they didn't know was that, somehow, the prisoners had advance knowledge of the governor's visit. An enraged lifer was waiting for Mennen in the kitchen and lunged at him with a very long, razor-sharp knife.

If George Kerr had not been cool and collected, Mennen could have had his throat cut. Two other prisoners immediately moved in. One of them stabbed George in the back. George managed to get the knife away from him, even though it cut his hand very deeply. Drawing on his great physical strength, Mennen managed to hold back the first attacker when his attention was distracted in the melee. The other prisoner who had moved in attacked a guard and broke both his arms with an iron potato masher. At another door leading into the kitchen, guards were struggling to keep a number of prisoners from pushing their way inside. George finally was able to draw his gun. He shot and killed one of the first attackers and warned the others he would shoot again if they came closer. Finally, the situation was under control.

Word of the attack leaked out at once. Nancy had heard a distorted story over the radio by the time Mennen was able to get her on the phone and reassure her that he was all right. "Divine Providence saved his life," Nancy told the reporters when they asked her for comment.

As soon as everything at the prison was under control, the governor went on to his next scheduled meeting, minus one state police aide, and made his prepared speech without mentioning the harrowing incident. George Kerr was sent to the hospital for treatment of his stab wounds. He later received a citation and a promotion for saving the governor's life. If Mennen, too, had not had presence of mind and strong arms, not even George could have saved him.

The governor immediately ordered a housecleaning at Marquette and warned the other wardens to put their prisons in order.

Fortunately, nothing of the kind ever happened to Mennen again. But by the 1958 campaign, there were other sorts of difficulties to be faced, particularly because it was a transition year for the Michigan Democratic party. Mennen had not come out and said he wouldn't run for reelection in 1960, but most of us assumed he wouldn't. Since there didn't seem to be any question that he would win the 1958 election, his usual supporters didn't put forth as much effort as they had in the past. The fact that he trounced his primary opponent, William Johnson, by almost six-to-one contributed to the impression that Mennen could not be beaten.

The chance to elect Phil Hart to the U. S. Senate was foremost in many people's minds. Phil easily defeated Homer Martin, a former UAW president, in the primary. In the general election, Phil had to take on Charles Potter, the incumbent Republican war veteran who had defeated Blair Moody in 1952. Although Phil would soon become a popular public figure, he was still relatively unknown. He had a small campaign staff and not much money to spend. Phil would never seek contributions and was still shy about asking the voters to support him.

We all helped as much as possible. Carolyn Sinelli Burns, who by now had become a good friend of mine, handled Phil's Senate campaign schedule and assisted Sid Woolner, the campaign manager, in many ways. Because of the broad territory Phil was trying to cover, it was especially hard to get the schedules done ahead of time. More than once, I stayed late to keep her company and walked with her after midnight to deliver the schedules to the newspapers and television stations in downtown Detroit.

Phil had a special place in my heart. It was hard not to like him—he was so sincere and had such a sense of purpose. In 1956, after Mennen and Phil and the rest of the members of the State Administrative Board were reelected, I got a handwritten note from Phil:

Dear Helen,

How do you put it into meaningful sentences?

For *all* you did, I'm grateful. That covers a mass of detail and a whole campaign full of imaginative management.

The alleged experts will assign a dozen reasons for the successful result. I'll start the list with *you*, and keep my fingers crossed I can look to you for "the same" two years hence!

Gratefully,

Phil

How could anybody not want to help a man who wrote a note like that?

Phil's unassuming ways won out in that 1958 election. Without calling attention to his own World War II arm injury, Phil defeated Senator Potter, who was still using his battle injury as a ploy for votes thirteen years after the war ended.

That victory was the beginning of a noteworthy career for Phil in the Senate. And although we didn't know it at the time, the 1958 election marked the end of Mennen's candidacies for many years. He wasn't planning to leave politics. Quite the contrary. He had done so well in Michigan, despite an uncooperative legislature, that he was considered a good prospect for national office. The idea of running for president, or perhaps vice president, was in the back of his mind. No one, not even Mennen, talked openly about it.

For one thing, he had an election to win. The Republicans were lying in wait in hopes of tripping him up before he could even get his big toe into national politics. The 1958 Republican candidate for governor was Paul D. Bagwell, a professor of speech, drama, and radio at Michigan State University. Professor Bagwell had had no opposition in the primary, and he was an articulate and popular spokesman for the grumbling Republicans, who tried to convince voters that Mennen was to blame for the state's money problems.

In Michigan and the nation, the economy was in a slump. Michigan's financial problems were coming to a crisis point. Mennen had been trying unsuccessfully for a decade to get the legislature to approve the corporate profits tax. As the historian and author, F. Clever Bald, wrote in 1961, the state treasury was dependent on nuisance taxes on such products as beer, cigarettes, and gasoline. Whenever the need for money became desperate, the legislature would increase those taxes or impose new ones. Economists who studied the state's tax structure concluded that people with incomes under $2,000 a year were paying twenty percent of their income in state and local taxes, while residents with incomes of more than $10,000 were paying only seven percent. There was no state income tax.[1]

Mennen's response to Republican campaign attacks was to reiterate what he had been proposing and to explain that he could not force the legislature to act. In addition, he continued to work with the groups of volunteers we had, inside and outside of the party organization, all over the state. He was determined to show his supporters that he appreciated all they had done for him through the years. No one was more aware than Mennen that it was the work of thousands of volunteers that had put him in office and kept him there.

Knowing that Mennen wanted something special, I focused on how we could thank the people who circulated his petitions. These people had always come through for him, even though it was an almost impossible task in some counties. We came up with a souvenir pin the size of a quarter that would identify the wearer as one who had helped the governor qualify for the ballot by gathering petition signatures. Imprinted on each pin were the words "Governor Williams," the year "1958," and the word "Petitioneer" underneath a green-and-white polka-dot bow-tie emblem.

Everyone who circulated a petition got a letter from the governor accompanied by a single pin, carefully wrapped in corrugated paper. We kept the extras under lock and key so the petition circulators could show off a pin no one else had. His letter to the circulators read in part: "You have participated in making history. For the first time, according to the Secretary of State, a candidate has filed for statewide office qualifying with one hundred or more legal signatures in every one of the state's eighty-three counties. Your hard work and devotion helped us to do that. My heartfelt thanks to you." Mennen told the recipients he planned to visit each county during the campaign and would look for people wearing the pins. "I want to be able to personally thank all of those who helped me with my petitions and this will enable me to spot you." It was a good campaign gimmick, and Mennen meant every word of it.

He also wanted to do something special for the ethnic groups who had done so much for him. Over the years, through much hard work on the part of Mennen, Nancy, and myself, we had compiled a good list of names and organizations and had cordial relations with most of them. After years of being a guest at their affairs, Mennen decided the nicest thing to do would be to invite leaders of each ethnic group to a series of buffet dinners with the governor. It was a delicate task to compile the guest lists. For example, the Polish groups had to be separated into east side and west side. We tried to keep each dinner to no more than thirty people but include the most active members. Still, we ended up exceeding the prescribed number of guests.

Everyone who was invited got a letter of thanks from the governor. There must have been some hurt feelings, but with the help of the leaders of each group, we did our best. It was exhausting and expensive, but the people seemed to appreciate it. The dinners were paid for by the Williams campaign committee and were held in a special room at the Hotel Fort Shelby downtown. Mennen and Nancy enjoyed the chance to play host and hostess to the people who had worked so hard to help him. Even though I had known Mennen for years, I was always amazed at how genuinely interested he was in people, and how much mutual affection there was between him and the people.

Something that had happened early in the 1958 campaign reminded me of the strength of Mennen's character. He had asked our close circle to join him for a meeting to discuss the campaign. We knew it was going to be a rough year. The day before the meeting, I gave Mennen a memo with some ideas for us to consider. Now, I can see how pragmatic it sounded:

> It is urgent that the public not realize that there is the slightest defection so far as the governor is concerned. . . . The governor has every right to expect and does know that the party, the Ad Board, and his appointees will be eager and willing to do everything that should be done. Most of them do not realize that anything needs to be done.

My memo urged him to meet with his appointees, his staff, Democratic leaders, and people from all walks of life to ask for their help and ideas in governing as well as for the campaign:

> It is my feeling that this is the very best kind of campaigning you can do between now and the primary. You are doing what you were elected for and what people have grown to expect from you. These are the kinds of activities that everyone can point to with pride. It will give the party people the feeling that something is happening, that the top man is on the job, that he is standing between them and disaster and all is going to be right with the world.

At the meeting, with Mennen sitting right there, we discussed his great strengths, but we also freely went over his weaknesses and talked about how to present him in the best possible light. (We never would have dared be so blunt had Nancy been present. We learned early in the game never to criticize Mennen in her presence.)

The next day, I was so remorseful that I sat down and wrote him a letter telling him I was proud to know him and work with him, and that he always renewed my faith in what we were fighting for. My New England background made it difficult to say such things in person, I wrote. It bothered me that we had picked him apart like a piece of merchandise, I told him, and I tried to explain:

> Everything we say or do is because we are so anxious to have you appear as nearly perfect as is humanly possible for you to be. Thank goodness you are human or we'd all be scared to death of you. . . .
>
> Do forgive us all. We do it with love and faith in your ability to lead the country out of the mess it is in.
>
> > Devotedly,
> > Helen

Mennen responded quickly:

> Thanks a million for your kind and friendly letter.
>
> I do appreciate your feelings and I am glad that you all like me well enough to help me do a better job and make more of myself. All the best.
>
> > Sincerely,
> > Mennen

Mennen's sixth victory turned out to be much easier than we expected, and a far cry from those first two squeakers. He defeated Paul Bagwell with fifty-three percent of the vote. John B. Swainson, who would be elected governor in 1960, defeated Donald Brown, a lawyer from Royal Oak who had been in the state House of Representatives, with about fifty-four percent of the vote and succeeded Phil Hart as lieutenant governor. Phil defeated Senator Potter by about the same percentage. Our candidates for the Ad Board all won by similar margins.

Mennen headed into his last term with familiar faces on the board. Secretary of State Jim Hare, who had battled back after a terrible auto accident in 1956, would remain in office until 1971. Paul L. Adams, a prominent lawyer and former mayor of his hometown of Sault Ste. Marie, had succeeded Tom Kavanagh as attorney general in late 1957. Paul, whose college and law degrees were from the University of Michigan, was on the Board of Regents of his alma mater when Mennen chose him to succeed Tom. Paul would serve as attorney general until December 1961, when he was appointed to the Supreme Court by Governor Swainson, who then named Frank Kelley the new attorney general.

Frank was a native of Detroit and a graduate of the University of Detroit and its law school. He had gone to Alpena to practice law in 1954 and became involved in local government and politics. He has served more than three decades as attorney general, his many elections earning him the distinction of being one of Michigan's longest serving and most popular public officials.

Sanford "Sandy" Brown was reelected and would remain as state treasurer until 1965. Frank Szymanski was reelected auditor general, but he resigned in the fall of 1959 when Mennen appointed him probate judge in Wayne County. Mennen filled the auditor general vacancy with Otis M. Smith, who became by all accounts the first black member of the Ad Board in Michigan history. A native of Memphis, Tennessee, he was a successful lawyer and civic leader in Flint. In 1957, Mennen had appointed him chairman of the Michigan Public Service Commission, and Otis was widely respected for his handling of that position.

Otis Smith won election as auditor general in his own right in 1960. That made him not only the first black person ever elected to a full-time, statewide position in Michigan, but also the first black person elected to a full-time state job anywhere in the country since Reconstruction. In the fall of 1961, he made history again, becoming the first black justice ever on the Michigan Supreme Court when Governor Swainson appointed him to the bench. As far as can be determined, only one other state had ever had a black supreme court member and that, too, was in the South during Reconstruction.

With his tenure in the executive office winding down, Mennen was very thoughtful of the future of his staff. He found secure places in state government for a number of them and gave Sid Woolner the honor of being his executive secretary for those final two years. He also appointed Larry Farrell to oversee the retirement system for state employees.

Mennen's final inaugural was simpler and shorter than the previous two. No one appreciated that more than I did, since I was chairman for the third straight time. Getting it together was far from simple, as usual. At ten o'clock in the morning on the Sunday after Thanksgiving, Ellen Gardner and her three small grandchildren met me in the cold, gloomy, campaign office downtown. We spent the whole day stuffing invitations into envelopes, with those little children working more diligently than most adults. By Monday morning, the invitations were ready for the post office. Liz Abernethy, one of our longtime volunteers, spent New Year's Eve with her committee, blowing up hundreds of balloons by hand (and mouth). The rented tank and hose wouldn't work, and they couldn't find another one on New Year's Eve.

While Liz and her group were blowing up balloons, Georgia Greenspan and I were having our own troubles. Georgia was in charge of the ticket files for the breakfast, luncheon, dinner, and the ball. We had talked about getting different colored file cards for each event but never got them. Later that night, how I regretted that. Georgia had them all filed alphabetically in a big box, in separate sections for each event. Some late arrivals still needed to be filed that night. After several of us enjoyed a pleasant dinner at our hotel in Lansing, I offered to help Georgia file the last cards and do a final head count for the meals.

We were almost finished when the bells and horns sounded that it was midnight. Georgia jumped up to wish me happy new year, and the box tumbled from her lap, spilling the cards all over the floor. Georgia was in the last days of pregnancy. She was exhausted, and the shock of seeing those cards scattered all over the floor was too much for her. She cried so hard she frightened me. Making light of it, I insisted she go to bed. It took me most of the night to organize those cards. (Having things in alphabetical order is critical in anything of this sort, to avoid duplication and speed things along. The only other time I saw alphabetized stacks upset that badly was in Washington, when a rickety dolly containing Hubert Humphrey's pre-addressed Christmas card envelopes tipped over after a sudden turn to avoid another rickety dolly. The envelopes literally spewed from one end of the hall to the other. The messenger pushing the dolly ran the other way. The Humphrey people never did find out who he was. They probably didn't want to know.)

The next morning, I awakened to find that I would have to carry that box of inaugural tickets across a glare of ice that had frosted the sidewalks and streets of Lansing. Attendance was down at most of the events during the day because people hadn't been able to get through the ice storm. By evening, though, the roads improved, and there was a good turnout for Mennen's final inaugural dinner and dance.

By late evening, I was ready to collapse. My Bentley's toe—no connection to Alvin Bentley, the wealthy Republican from Owosso who ran against Pat McNamara in 1954—chose that evening to act up. (For some unknown reason, the toe next to the little one cramps violently and sends pain clear up to the hip. It's hard to walk, much less dance.) All night, I avoided Mennen. Several times the state police told me the governor was looking for me, but I had been able to put them off. Finally, with my coat over my arm, I was heading for the door and blessed relief.

Mennen caught me before I could escape. "You weren't planning to go without dancing with me, were you?" he asked. Before I could tell him that I had a cramp in my foot, the orchestra started into the Mexican hat dance and Mennen whirled me onto the floor. My cramp having magically disappeared, I did a darn good version of that dance.

Since my light fantastic days had ended with my entrance into Democratic politics, my political friends were astonished that I could dance. They couldn't have known, because I hadn't told them, but before I became involved with politics I went dancing nearly five nights a week. Even the reporters were surprised. One newspaper carried a story saying that the governor and his campaign manager ended the inaugural ball by doing a spirited version of the Mexican hat dance.

NOTES

1. Bald was a professor of history and director of the Michigan Historical Collections at the University of Michigan. The tax study is mentioned in his description of Michigan's financial situation in *Michigan in Four Centuries*.

25

EVEN GOVERNORS
NEED MORAL SUPPORT

MENNEN'S INAUGURAL ADDRESS on January 1, 1959, was a serious review of Michigan's problems. During his previous five terms, he had been warning that the legislature was courting disaster by defying the constitutional ban on spending more than was collected. All that time, the Republican legislature had appropriated millions of dollars more each year than it provided in revenues. As a consequence, by early 1959, the state was facing a deficit of more than $100 million. In his inaugural address, Mennen explained that there was now, undeniably, a financial crisis.

Mennen had been trying for ten years to get the legislature to put Michigan on a solid foundation. At the time, Michigan's primary sources of revenue were the sales tax and other taxes that fell disproportionately on the poor and the working classes, who could least afford it.[1] Mennen had decided that a personal income tax as well as a corporate profits tax would be much fairer and more likely to provide a secure revenue base. A Citizens Advisory Committee, with a Republican from the House of Representatives overseeing it, had come to a similar conclusion.

Mennen went to the people with a special tax message a few weeks after the inauguration. He explained that a tax on personal income and a tax on corporate profits would take care of the backlog and put Michigan back on its feet. As usual, Republicans in the legislature would have none of it. They stuck with their short-term remedies, which were really not the answer, and refused to help solve the crisis. The state couldn't borrow from outside sources to get the needed cash because of a constitutional limit on such loans.

Things got so bad that Mennen finally decided the only way to get over the hump was to solve the immediate problem by borrowing from the veterans trust fund, which provided money for sick veterans. That would allow time to work out a lasting solution. The opposition wouldn't approve even that. Although Mennen didn't think the Republicans in the legislature would allow the state to drift toward disaster, he was wrong. They were firmly resolved to cause him political trouble.[2] They wanted to make sure he could never run for national office.

By late spring, the situation was very grave. The state was fast approaching the time when the cash would actually run out. Finally, in the first week of May, the state had to put off meeting its payroll. There never was a missed payday, although the whole country thought Michigan had "payless paydays." Mennen took drastic measures to conserve what money was left by postponing any spending that could be deferred. But the damage had been done. The nation knew that Michigan was down to counting pennies. There was much bad publicity about a "welfare state" that had run out of money and about "payless paydays," when in fact neither was true.

It was very difficult for those of us who were close to Mennen to see this happening, especially if we were far away and couldn't do anything about it, as I was. One night in early May, I couldn't sleep, so I got up and wrote him one of my letters, typed with two fingers and written from the heart. I tried to tell him how much his battle for the people and for good government in general had meant to all of us. The letter was much too long and rambled a lot, so I decided not to send it. But the feeling persisted that he needed encouragement from his friends, and I decided to try again:

> About two weeks ago, I wrote you a long letter, and then decided not to send it. I will talk about parts of it when we meet and the time is more appropriate.
>
> However, I wrote it very late at night and got quite serious about what this battle means to all of us who have been involved in the political wars these past years. Perhaps you need to hear what I thought that night so I will quote myself:
>
> "A number of the people who have been close to you since your advent into public life have completely rearranged their own lives to devote their time to your career. Why have they done this?
>
> Partly because of personal admiration and affection for you, of course. But that was not enough. You were the instrument through which they can contribute to the welfare and betterment of the world. It is because we all believe in you, your strength, your integrity and in your destiny.
>
> We cannot ourselves do what you are able to do, but we feel we can help you accomplish what we feel needs to be done.

All of us, even vicariously, are then servants of humanity.

Even though the people do not understand or criticize us for what we do, we are still obligated to you and to ourselves to go forward.

Therefore, we must find the courage to do what we think, in our best judgment, is right and, with God's help, do it.

Whatever your decision in the future, or how complete a sacrifice you feel you must make, you alone must decide. But, whatever you do, you must fight for what is right whether it is as the President of the United States or whether it is fighting as a citizen to awaken the consciences of the Democratic Party. You alone must make the decision but, whatever you do, some of us are involved and the decision affects us, too.

I don't mean just the running for office, but what we have been working for and what we believe we can and must do. I want you to know, and I think I speak for most of us, that you would be letting us down more, if you ran for the Presidency and neglected to fight for the people. So you really are not alone at all."

Doris Fleeson [a Washington, D. C., reporter] had a column that I sent to Neil Staebler and Tom Quimby which deplored the fact that none of the leading contenders generated personal followers to any great extent. I put a little note on the clip to the effect that this was what you were going to do, one of these days.

It must be heartbreaking to have to go through what you have been subjected to these past few weeks. But I am as sure as I am sitting here that this is going to work out to your advantage one of these days. It is easy for me to sit here in D. C. miles away and say this, but I truly mean it.

Perhaps one of the reasons I feel so sure about it is the increasing number of people who are quite familiar with what is going on and are most sympathetic. We all tell the story at the drop of a hat, but I am finding that many people are following closely what is going on and more and more people are understanding that this is a condition that the Republicans will visit on more than one state before the year is out. . . .

Hurry up and settle those Michigan Republicans so I can get your D. C. Williams for President Committee in session. . . .

Affectionately,

Buffy

His reply almost made me cry. It was a personal letter, not meant for the newspapers. The sentiments are all the more touching because they were from the heart:

Dear Buffy:

God bless you for your letter of May 12. You and Margaret Price have written me the kind of letters that would put steel backbone in a punctured rubber balloon. Not that I want you to think I am a punctured rubber balloon, but I do want you to know that you have given me strength to meet the very real challenges that confront us here.

The last ten years have been a crusade that has commanded and received the very best that is in all of us. I am really proud of our joint accomplishments. I have been most fortunate to be the visible portion of the moving iceberg, but I am conscious and rejoice in the depth of the movement.

We have worked miracles and we have made a real contribution in our time to the betterment of mankind and the world in which he lives.

The measure of this contribution is as concrete as the Mackinac Bridge and as delicate as the feeling of friendship in the hearts of human beings half way around the world for Nancy and for me who were where we were because of all of you. Frank McNaughton, who is doing my biography, has been so tremendously enthusiastic about our whole movement that I am inspired to hope that his book will give some picture of what we have meant one to another and what we all have meant to better government and better living. I really hope it tells our story because it will be a small reward, at least, for those who bore the brunt of the battle without the personal headlines that some of our group received.[3]

These last few weeks have been rugged ones indeed. They have been the kind to tie one's stomach in knots as one struggled to think out what was right and do what one thought one ought to do. We had a lot of bad public relations breaks and sometimes what we relied on most gave way at the most inopportune moment. In all of my experience I have never felt the like of it but I feel we have had the worst and are on our way up. We certainly are far from smooth sailing but at least we are moving in the right direction and the worst of the storm has done its job and we are still afloat.

Believe me, one of the wonderful experiences is to get out among the people and to feel the warm handshake and kind words when the tone of the press and the so-called statistics would prepare one for the cool glance and the rough rebuff. Thank God for these people who still have confidence and who return the love we have for them.

Naturally to have one's hand on the tiller in 1961 and thereafter, would be an opportunity to do the things we want for the people that nothing else in all probability could ever equal.

If that is the good Lord's will we will have done everything possible to be ready and worthy of it. If it is not His will, as you say, it is more important as Alvin [sic] Barkley used to say: "It is more important to be a servant in the house of the Lord than to sit in the seats of the mighty." I still believe and always will believe that there is the same law in politics as there is in physics and that no action is ever lost. Just what the results of that action will be or what form it will take, the good Lord alone knows, but I have every confidence that the good that we do will add up in the service of humanity for better living for all and that we have nothing to lose.

When the dust settles we shall have some hard decisions to make and I trust that all of my friends will have the courage to tell me what they honestly know and think. As you say, we have a contribution to make and we will make it with all our hearts and joyfully be it on Pennsylvania Avenue or in some place we do not yet dream of.

In any event, we will go after the main job right here to get our fiscal situation straightened out and the Republicans as educated as we possibly can.

Believe me I am grateful to Almighty God for the love and support you have given me and for the opportunity to be the spearhead in our efforts to do good. Neither the slander nor the grinding down will for one minute make me unhappy in the life that I chose and I shall forever be grateful for my companions in arms. Somehow or other I can't help but feel that the good Lord must have some purpose in all of this. I remember Lincoln went through many personal and public defeats and even our good friend, Harry Truman, failed in his business.

By this I do not feel necessarily that I am guaranteed the heights but I do feel it is all in the day's work and that there will be good innings coming up.

Again, many thanks for your fine letter. I hope to see you at the JJ Dinner and at other times too.

> Affectionately,
> Mennen
> Governor

All that spring and summer, the state limped along. It became a battle between Mennen and the twenty-two Republicans in the Michigan Senate, who stood together against him. The Republicans, of course, were being coached by leaders of the big corporations and businesses who didn't want either a corporate profits tax or an income tax. But even the Republicans and the leaders of industry were embarrassed when a memo was leaked to the press, showing how the Republicans were willing to damage the state's future for the sake of hurting Mennen politically. It was written by Joseph Creighton, the lobbyist for the Michigan Manufacturers Association, to all the Republicans in the state senate: "You have him [Mennen] over the barrel for the first time in ten years. Keep him there 'till he screams 'Uncle.' God bless each of you."[4]

Mennen finally had no choice but to cry uncle. The Republicans were destroying Michigan's reputation. There was nothing wrong with the state's credit rating, and the state wasn't in debt—it was simply a matter of a cash crisis that the Republicans wouldn't solve. The whole country was laughing at Michigan.

What the Republicans wanted to do was what they knew Mennen wouldn't let them do—shove the problem onto the working class. The Republicans wanted to increase the sales tax, but the constitution prevented any increase in the sales tax without a vote of the people. So they adopted a one percent use tax on top of the three percent sales tax. Mennen and Paul Adams, the attorney general, warned that the use tax was illegal. By late August, Mennen felt he had to sign the bill for the sake of the state. He was confident it would be struck down in court. Indeed, in late October, the Michigan Supreme Court declared the tax unconstitutional.[5] Michigan was in trouble again.

Mennen took the unusual step of calling the legislature back into session. The Republicans did what they had done in previous years: They passed several additional taxes that would require working people to pay more than their share. That produced about $70 million. Then the Republicans proposed to take tens of millions of dollars that previously had gone to local schools and use it to supplement the new taxes to pay the state's bills. That idea was a mistake. The schools already had had to make do with less because of the state's fiscal problems. All over Michigan, there was an uproar. Suddenly, Mennen had a few more people on his side.[6]

What was really unfair about the whole mess was that Mennen was blamed for the financial crisis, when in fact his Republican predecessor, Kim Sigler, had called attention to the problem. Frank McNaughton, in his biography of Mennen, writes: "Actually the storm was a long time building up. When Williams was elected in 1948, the outgoing Republican governor, Kim Sigler, in his departing message, sternly warned his party in the legislature that it was running into deficits, and that it must either reduce its appropriations or levy more taxes."[7]

Despite the damage to his own political future, Mennen's main concern was that the state got an undeserved bad reputation in the eyes of the nation. Michigan's economy was basically solid at the time, despite the recession that had hit the state and nation in 1958. Yet a lasting impression was created that the state was falling apart. Over the next few years, that undoubtedly cost the state some businesses and investments that might have brought jobs and capital to Michigan.

Mennen had been wrestling with the question of whether he should try to win the presidential nomination in 1960. The news of Michigan's financial disasters quickly ruined his chances in that respect, but he didn't make his decision until early in 1960. In midwinter of 1959, when Mennen's hopes were still very much alive, I decided to have a dinner party to introduce Mennen to some of my Washington contacts. Mennen and Joe Beirne, my CWA president, had birthdays ten days apart. This made a good excuse to invite people to dinner. Mennen and Neil Staebler were in town for the Democratic National Committee meeting, so I seized the opportunity. With forty people on my guest list, it was going to be a squeeze to get them all into my apartment for dinner.

My CWA executive committee members, their wives, and several other guests arrived right on time. It was a good thing I had made plenty of hors d'oeuvres. Mennen Williams, the guest of honor, was late. So were Senator Phil Hart, Michigan Democratic Party Chairman Staebler, and National Committeewoman Margaret Price. They were late—and later. The hors d'oeuvres began to disappear. Finally, Margaret called and told me what had held them up. The Democratic National Committee had selected Los Angeles as the location for the 1960 national convention. She apologized but said they would all have to drop in on an impromptu celebration thrown by the ecstatic California people. She said they would come as soon as they could get away. Mrs. Conway, my cleaning lady's mother-in-law, was handling things for me in the kitchen. She was a wonderful cook and managed to make some adjustments so the dinner wouldn't be ruined.

Two hours late, Mennen, Phil, Neil, and Margaret arrived, bringing with them four Michigan delegates Mennen had invited. Dinner was served, the cake was cut, and "Happy Birthday" was sung with gusto. It was no small task to see that Mennen got to talk to all the heads of the organizations I had invited, but I managed to do it. Later I heard expostulations from the kitchen. "But my hands are all wet," Mrs. Conway was protesting. It was Mennen as usual, out in the kitchen complimenting the cook.

NOTES

1. For more background on the fiscal and political situation in the late 1950s, see Bald, *Michigan in Four Centuries*, pp. 484–88. See also Dunbar, *Michigan*, pp. 631–46, and McNaughton, *Mennen Williams of Michigan*, pp. 9–25.

2. McNaughton, *Mennen Williams of Michigan*, pp. 12–19.

3. The book Mennen Williams refers to is the McNaughton biography, *Mennen Williams of Michigan*.

4. This telegram is discussed in McNaughton, *Mennen Williams of Michigan*, p. 9, and in Bald, *Michigan in Four Centuries*, pp. 485–86. Articles about the telegram and the uproar it created appeared in newspapers during the height of the crisis in the spring, summer, and fall of 1959.

5. McNaughton, *Mennen Williams of Michigan*, pp. 23–24.

6. McNaughton, *Mennen Williams of Michigan*, p. 25.

7. This reference is found on page 11 of McNaughton, *Mennen Williams of Michigan*. Governor Sigler's messages to the Michigan legislature and other official correspondence may be found among the papers of Kim Sigler, Michigan Historical Collections, Bentley Historical Library, University of Michigan, Ann Arbor.

26

MENNEN AND JFK
FROM MACKINAC ISLAND TO AFRICA

MENNEN WILLIAMS'S ONLY SERIOUS ATTEMPT to recruit D. C. support for his presidential campaign was a fiasco. In spite of the broad range of organization leaders he had met in my apartment, I don't think he realized how many influential people I knew in Washington. At any rate, in May of 1960 he sent Tom Quimby, our national committeeman, to D. C. to test the sentiment for a Mennen candidacy for president.

Tom had instructions to work with me and did. Together, we compiled quite a large list of people he should contact. With a few of them, I asked him to take me with him for the meetings, but he couldn't wait until I had time to go. It wasn't long before I began receiving phone calls from people who were curious to know why a strange man from Michigan had contacted them about Mennen instead of me. No serious harm was done, but the support was not as solid as I would have liked.

Whether at Mennen's suggestion or someone else's, I will never know, but for some reason, Tom contacted India Edwards and asked her to host a dinner for prospective supporters of Mennen Williams. If they had consulted me, I could have told them she was inclined to support Lyndon Johnson. India had been appointed vice chairman of the Democratic National Committee under President Truman. Because of her wide support in the party, India was very much in demand as a speaker in behalf of potential candidates. She had been nominated for vice president in the early balloting at the 1952 convention. Every candidate called on her for help, and Mennen was no exception.

India was always willing to help a potential candidate, and she agreed to host a gathering for Mennen. The invitation list was compiled before I knew much about the affair. When I saw the list, I knew we were in deep trouble. The list included two political economists, Leon Keyserling and John Kenneth Galbraith. Keyserling was an old-school conservative, while Galbraith was ahead of his time. They had never been known to agree on anything. There were about twenty people invited besides the two potential combatants and Tom Quimby, India Edwards, and me. I was not familiar with most of the people. Mennen would not be there.

The dinner was elaborate and the atmosphere pleasant until India made her pitch for Governor Williams. She offered a few welcoming remarks and mentioned that Mennen Williams was toying with the idea of becoming a presidential candidate. She then made a short speech on his behalf. It was more or less the same speech she used for all the candidates. India asked what people thought of the idea, and a few of the guests made favorable comments about Mennen's work as governor.

Someone then raised the question of the nation's financial problems in light of what was going on in Michigan. From then on, the evening turned into a full-fledged debate on fiscal policies between the two economists. No one else had a chance to speak. It was acrimonious to say the least, in spite of India's attempts to pull it back together. People left without knowing much more about Mennen Williams than they had before they arrived.

Shortly after this party, John Kennedy began to take the limelight. Mennen announced that he would not seek reelection. After a few more attempts by Mennen to gain recognition as a candidate, we all realized that it was useless. By spring, it was painfully apparent that for the first time in twelve years, Mennen's name would not be on any ballot.

The state party convention that spring was to be Mennen's last public appearance as the key figure. The fall convention would focus on the new candidates for governor and other offices. Everyone wanted to put on a big demonstration for Mennen at the spring convention, which was held in Lansing. The district organizations showed up with placards of all sorts honoring him, expecting a gleeful celebration with bobbing signs and happy faces.

Instead, there was nothing but sobbing and sadness. No one wanted to cheer about anything. At the end of the convention, Nancy Williams, standing beside Mennen, was weeping openly. Adelaide Hart and I were also on the platform, behind Mennen and Nancy. Adelaide was crying so hard half the people who came up to shake Mennen's and Nancy's hands stopped by to give her a loving pat. It was just dawning on all of us that this was the end of an era and that the governor—there is only one "governor" as far as I am concerned—was not going to be there to lead us anymore. When Mennen finally left the platform, Nancy, Adelaide, and I were weeping uncontrollably and couldn't move. He threw his arms around all three of us and swept us off the platform.

Long before the rest of us recovered from our disappointment, Mennen was reconciled to the fact that he would not be a candidate in 1960. He began to realize that John F. Kennedy, the charismatic young senator from Massachusetts, offered the party's best chance of reclaiming the White House.

A delicate courtship took place between Mennen and JFK, with Donald M. D. Thurber, an old friend of both, playing matchmaker. Don was a businessman who devoted his time and talents to a wide range of humanitarian causes in the Detroit area. He worked tirelessly on behalf of history and the arts, youth programs, mental health services, and helping children and adults stricken with polio and other crippling conditions. Knowing of Don's dedication, Mennen appointed him to replace Paul Adams on the University of Michigan Board of Regents in early 1958. Don remained on that board for several years and later served on the state Board of Education.

Don and Mennen had been friends for years. He was among Mennen's early backers and remained helpful and supportive throughout the time he was governor. Don had also been a classmate of Kennedy's at Harvard and had kept in touch with him over the years. At that time, of course, Kennedy was far from a political superstar and had to work to build a name for himself nationally.

Here is Don's account of how he brought the two men together:

Late in 1959 or early in 1960, I received a telephone call from Jack Kennedy. He said he wanted to consult me about the Michigan situation and asked if I could come East and meet with him. I, of course, said I would go and worked out the details with one of his aides.

On a Sunday morning I flew to White Plains, N. Y. and met with Jack for lunch in his hotel suite. We ate fish chowder and oyster crackers on a small table set between us. He was coatless but wore a tie and was his usual affable and animated self.

After a few catching-up remarks he got right down to business. He asked me to review the Michigan situation for him. I replied that the state was in good shape for the Democrats and that the party was united, its leadership experienced and quite accustomed to giving a good account of itself in elections and to winning most of them. That state of affairs had been brought about by Mennen and the team he had assembled around him. I immediately said that Mennen enjoyed the complete support and loyalty of nearly every Michigan Democrat. He asked how serious Mennen was in seeking the nomination. I replied that he was very serious and that we were all committed to helping him achieve that goal.

"He has no chance," Jack replied.

"You may be right," I said, "but that is a premature conclusion at this point. Michigan remains absolutely committed to Mennen unless or until he releases the delegation, after concluding the nomination cannot be his."

I added that I definitely would not advise Jack to come into Michigan and attempt to capture Mennen's delegates or potential delegates.

"Such an effort," I said, "would be bitterly resented and would not succeed."

He said he had no such intention but that Michigan should not remain locked into what he regarded as a hopeless candidacy and thereby lose its chance to play a timely and perhaps decisive role in the nomination. I told him I thought there would be real enthusiasm for him as the second choice after Mennen and that he should not lose that underlying goodwill by doing anything rash.

Jack said he did not feel he knew Mennen at all well and asked me to describe him. I did so in very positive terms and concluded by saying that undoubtedly Mennen did not know Jack well, either. I suggested it would be a good idea for the two men to get on more comfortable terms with each other, since it was likely their political paths would cross in one way or another in the next few months. I offered to work toward better acquainting them with each other. Jack welcomed the idea and thought I was the right one to carry it out. He cautioned that he did not want to be in the position of begging Mennen for a meeting or a series of meetings. The arrangements would have to be casual and natural, so as not to seem that there was extreme urgency on either side. I observed that such a low-key rapprochement would probably best serve Mennen as well, and I agreed to look for opportunity to bring it about.

Jack said he was content to leave the matter there for the present. He said whenever I had anything of importance to communicate, I should speak with either Ted Sorensen or Steve Smith, his brother-in-law. He then called both of them in and introduced me (I already knew Ted but not Steve) and briefly explained the substance of our conversation. I then said good-bye and left. The meeting took about 45 minutes. Jack's attention had not wandered at all. He was very focused and I knew he was decidedly interested in the subject of our talk.

Shortly after returning home, I got in touch with Mennen and offered to make available to him whatever knowledge I had about Jack Kennedy, gleaned from my long observation of him. Mennen confirmed that he did not know him at all well and welcomed the opportunity to have me tell him about Jack. We met at the Kellogg Center at Michigan State University early one Sunday afternoon. We were in a private room and only Mennen, Nancy and I were present. I did almost all the talking and had several books and articles to leave with them. Both Mennen and Nancy listened intently, Mennen asking a number of questions as I went along. Nancy said very little but was thoughtfully attentive. At the end Mennen said he was pleased with what I told him. He anticipated there would probably be an opportunity, perhaps more than one, to meet with Jack in the months ahead, and he felt much better prepared for such meetings than he had been before seeing me. I offered my help in arranging any such meetings between Mennen and Jack. Mennen thanked me and said it might well be helpful down the road, if he could call on me. We left it at that, but I felt some important ice had been broken, even though I did not feel free to reveal to Mennen my recent meeting with Jack or its confidential details. I sensed Mennen was not prepared to go further at this time and I did not press the matter.

I did, however, report the outcome of the meeting to the Kennedy people, I think to Steve Smith. They felt encouraged and requested that I watch developments and report anything important to them. Mennen and Jack met briefly and informally once or twice in the ensuing months. I remember Steve Smith telling me the meetings were cordial but in no way definitive. I urged him not to press matters or force anything unduly.

His attitude was that Jack did not need to do so, since things were continuing to break well for him. Steve continued to stress that Michigan should not wait too long, for fear of losing its chance to play an important, even decisive, role. I told him I felt Mennen and his chief advisers would be well aware of that consideration in the event it became a factor as the convention neared. I emphasized that the secondary support for Jack was very strong in Michigan and that he should not jeopardize that position by being overzealous at this point.

As the convention approached, it was apparent that Mennen's efforts were falling distressingly short and that Jack was close to a breakthrough in delegate strength even before the convention convened.

It was really a case of now or never for Michigan. It had to move. My real worry was that perhaps Michigan had already waited too long, that other states might move to Kennedy and make Michigan's delegates immaterial to him. I expressed those fears in some conversations with Neil Staebler, who first revealed to me that Mennen had decided to release the delegates and to pledge the support of almost all of them to Kennedy. He said a meeting between the two men had been tentatively set for Mackinac Island on such-and-such a date, but definite confirmation had not been received from the Kennedy people. I saw at once what I should do, while completely respecting the confidentiality of what Neil had revealed to me of Mennen's intentions. I spoke with both Smith and Sorensen and said as

210

strongly as I could, "Get Jack there. It is vital that he attend." I held my breath that they would say to me, "Well, he's not going to. We don't need Michigan at this point."

Though they did not say that, it was clear to me they were uncertain and wavering. "What did Soapy want to talk about? Jack does not need to beg at this point and does not want to put himself in that position. Would the trip be a wild goose chase? We'd like to know in advance what Soapy is likely to say so that Jack will not be taken by surprise and caught off balance," they said.

In my opinion, the meeting was in the balance at this point and I then played my last card. Without disclosing what Neil had told me about Mennen's intentions since it was up to Mennen alone to do so, I said the meeting would provide the culmination of what we had talked about several months ago in White Plains and I urged Jack's attendance in the most urgent terms. Smith and Sorensen said they needed 15 minutes to consider everything and would call me back. I assumed they wanted to reach Jack.

Naturally, I waited by the telephone. When they called again, they agreed that Jack would drop everything, rearrange his schedule and be at Mackinac Island. I reported to Neil that I had every reason now to believe that Jack would attend and that Neil would hear accordingly. He was much relieved and encouraged. He did hear, and the meeting took place.

I was in the lobby of the *Free Press* Building to buy one of the first copies of the early edition, the one that came out at 8 P.M. It had a headline story about the Mackinac Island meeting, together with the joint press statement of Mennen and Jack. I went to a telephone and immediately called Sorensen and Smith and read them the *Free Press* story. They were delighted, of course, that Michigan had moved toward Kennedy in time to be the decisive state in giving him the majority of delegates in advance of the convention.[1]

There were others besides Don who were working hard to bring JFK and Mennen together, but the Kennedy people gave Don much of the credit. It was a delicate balance of timing, with the added complications of political egos and aspirations.

Frank Blackford was one of the other people who had a hand in bringing together Mennen and JFK. Frank had previously handled legislative affairs for Mennen and served on the Liquor Control Commission under him. Frank was named state insurance commissioner early in 1959. He worked closely that year with Robert Kennedy and Pierre Salinger while the state conducted an investigation of the Teamsters Union's major insurance provider. After extensive hearings, the insurer's license was revoked. (The man later was murdered in a Chicago parking lot.) For more than six months, Frank was in close touch with Salinger, who later became JFK's presidential press secretary, and with Robert Kennedy. Both of them were working closely with a congressional committee investigating Teamsters and corruption.

The next year, 1960, Frank was attending an insurance conference in San Francisco when Salinger contacted him and said he and John Kennedy were in town and would like to talk with Frank about Mennen. Frank, like Don Thurber, was glad to oblige. It was just before the meeting JFK and Mennen had on Mackinac Island. Frank, Salinger, and JFK had a two-and-a-half hour meeting. Kennedy and Salinger asked for a few logistical details, such as the best way to get to Mackinac Island. But what they were really interested in, according to Frank's recollection, was Mennen. They asked questions and listened eagerly. They were glad to hear about Mennen and JFK's common bond as Navy men during World War II. They were interested in Mennen's strong position on civil rights and in his legislative programs. They were particularly impressed that Mennen's attention toward building a strong party and a strong program had paid off in the election of so many Democrats to the State Administrative Board.

They wanted to know about state party people and Mennen's staff. Frank told them Neil Staebler probably had the greatest influence with Mennen, followed by Paul Weber, as "a close second," as Frank put it. Frank described Larry Farrell, Mennen's executive secretary for many years, as the link to the older party people who had been in power when Pat Van Wagoner was governor.

Frank said Salinger and Kennedy were intrigued to learn of Paul Weber's extensive knowledge of the papal encyclicals on the rights of working people and organized labor. Many years later, Salinger told Frank that Kennedy had talked to Paul about those encyclicals and later had used that information very effectively. People, especially in the labor movement, were impressed with Kennedy's knowledge of the papal pronouncements on unions.[2] It seems appropriate that one of the things that Kennedy gleaned from his contact with Mennen and his staff was a better understanding of the moral foundation of the rights of working people. Mennen was always thorough in his study of the issues; the people he chose as his closest advisers were too.

Mennen approached the Kennedy candidacy as he did everything else—by considering the issues before deciding what was best. The Kennedy people, apparently accustomed to more pragmatic politics, asked Mennen what he expected in return for his support. One of the participants in the Mackinac meeting told me that Mennen's response was, "Good government." Not the usual answer, I'm sure.

Early on the day of the Mackinac Island meeting, Mennen wrote me a letter, reminiscing a bit: "Along about this time ordinarily you and I would be planning our campaign for governor." Mennen had given a great deal of thought to the "Kennedy situation," as he referred to it. Further down in that letter he wrote:

> As you by now know, I have invited Jack up to Mackinac Island for a little talk. We have been working together on the issues and I am quite convinced that he is the kind of man we need.
>
> I have been reading his book, *The Strategy of Peace*, and this really elates me. I feel in such sympathy with what he writes. With all his idealism and I think broad comprehension of the moving factors in the world today, he seems to have a pretty hard-boiled sense of how to get things done. By this I don't mean he has any lack of courage. Quite the opposite. He seems to be able to determine what has to be done and then if it is a big job he takes it on nonetheless. I do think he is going to tend to break down the big job into manageable proportions so that we will have a reasonable but frontal attack on the problems of our day.
>
> Just what the mechanics of handling this is going to be, we are going to have to work out. We have been doing some thinking about it and I believe we can make some contribution to the overall effort.

Mennen went to great lengths to gain support for Kennedy from Michigan delegates. By the time we went to Los Angeles, all but a few die-hard Stevenson supporters were solidly behind Kennedy. Jack Kennedy paid a visit to the Michigan delegation during one of our major caucuses at the convention. He thanked us for not supporting him in 1956 for vice president because he would have been defeated with Stevenson. Now, he told us, he could go on to win the presidential election. Most of us believed he would win, too.

After Kennedy was nominated, he chose Senator Henry "Scoop" Jackson of the state of Washington as chairman of the Democratic National Committee. Scoop wanted Margaret Price to be the party vice chairman and, as a courtesy, asked Mennen's permission. Mennen was delighted at Scoop Jackson's recognition of Margaret's ability.

It was a very busy convention, and, as always, Mennen insisted on keeping us informed. Whenever anything important was going on, we were under the stairs of the podium, deeply engaged in a caucus. The Minnesota delegation had its caucus room just across from ours. It was torn apart by internal battles, with Senator Hubert Humphrey and Governor Orville Freeman on Kennedy's side, while Eugene McCarthy supported Stevenson. More than once I was stopped by Minnesota's national committeewoman in tears. "Helen," she would say, "what am I going to do with these men? They are tearing our party apart with their fights." All I could do was put my arm around her and tell her I was sure it would all work out in the end.

To tell the truth, I wasn't really sure it would work out. In light of McCarthy's political moves in later years, I'm not sure it did. During the decisive roll call for president, McCarthy unexpectedly nominated Adlai Stevenson. Then, when Kennedy was fast going over the top, Minnesota had to pass when it was their turn to vote because the delegates couldn't agree. Later, even though Humphrey was waving the state sign frantically in hopes the delegation could clinch the nomination for Kennedy, the magic number had been reached and Minnesota lost out.

From then on, everyone's attention was turned to the vice presidency. Who would it be? Humphrey, Stevenson, Johnson? No, not Johnson, Michigan said. Mennen and the rest of us were suspicious of Johnson and his wheeler-dealer style of Texas politics. Mostly, we feared that Johnson did not have a strong stand on civil rights—a fear that turned out to have been unfounded.

This is one time I wish we hadn't been so adamant. Mennen came into the Michigan headquarters suite and told a few of us that he had heard it was going to be Johnson. None of us could believe it. Just then, Jack Kennedy called the governor on his private number and told him that Johnson was his choice for vice president. We could tell from Mennen's answers that he was disagreeing with Kennedy. In the background someone yelled, "Tell him we will walk out." Mennen Williams finished the conversation abruptly and hung up.

Immediately afterward, Bobby Kennedy, his face pale and solemn, walked in. They adjourned to Mennen's private caucus room, which, incidentally, was the bathroom—the only place he could talk in private. The meeting was over in a very few minutes. Bobby Kennedy strode out quickly, not looking at any of us as he left. Mennen then called a caucus and broke the news to the delegation that, yes, it was Johnson. It was a strategy to get the Southern vote, he explained. Our cries of indignation could be heard outside the caucus room. A delegate, just coming in, told us several reporters were listening just outside the door. Mennen polled the delegation. It was almost unanimous to vote "no" for Johnson.

The Kennedy people feared a floor fight over Johnson from Mennen Williams of Michigan and Joe Rauh, Jr., of D. C. and their delegations. Joe was chairman of the national ADA. Like Mennen, he believed deeply in liberal causes and principles. They were both worried that the Johnson candidacy might hurt progress on civil rights and other important issues. It was the same thing Mennen had stood up for at the earlier conventions.

Just before Michigan's name was read in the roll call, there was a prearranged move to choose Johnson by acclamation and a quick voice vote. Mennen and Joe leaped up angrily to vote "no." Johnson was declared the winner. A picture which was to cloud Mennen's political future for many years was on the front pages of the Detroit papers and appeared in many magazine reports of the convention. It showed Mennen standing 6-feet-4 with his mouth wide open yelling "No!"

In the campaign and the November election that year, Michigan was a staunch supporter of JFK. Knowing Mennen's great ability, we were all waiting anxiously for the big appointment he would be given in the new administration. Kennedy had first thought of Mennen as secretary of commerce, but the family business created a possible conflict-of-interest. According to two of Kennedy's close aides, Kenneth P. O'Donnell and David F. Powers, Mennen also was considered for secretary of state.[3] Instead, Kennedy decided to make Mennen assistant secretary of state for African affairs. That decision turned out to be one of the wisest he made.

That job was probably the last thing Mennen wanted at the time, but he hid his disappointment and soon realized what a fascinating assignment it was. Every year while Mennen was governor, he and Nancy had hosted informal buffet dinners at their Lansing home for foreign students at Michigan State University. The students sat on the floor, ate home-cooked food, and talked all evening. Many of them said that experience was the highlight of their stay in the United States. Later on, as adults, many of these students held important positions in African nations. They enjoyed renewing old acquaintances with Mennen and Nancy and paved the way for them to meet the people and learn the customs of their countries in a way that would not have been possible for most visitors.

Mennen and Nancy toured Africa as they had toured every county in Michigan. No African nation was too small or politically insignificant for them, just as no Michigan town or county had been too small for the governor to visit. During the 1960s, Africa was changing rapidly and gaining the world's attention. Mennen and Nancy made many friends there on behalf of the United States.

Only once while he served as assistant secretary for African affairs did Mennen cause the president any problem. Taken out of context of a speech, his term "Africa for the Africans" created a big furor in the press. It is hard to understand how a phrase like that could cause such controversy. Kennedy had the right response. When he was taxed with Mennen's remark, he replied: "Who else would Africa be for?"

Mennen's good sense of humor showed that Christmas when he had silver ashtrays inscribed "AFTA." He gave one to the president, one to Secretary of State Dean Rusk, one to Nancy, and one to me. Mennen had such a look of hurt and disgust on his face when he gave me my ashtray and I didn't get it. We were standing in the aisle of a plane headed for D. C., and he had to tell me what the initials meant. He never told me how the president and Dean Rusk reacted, or whether they understood the significance right away. Perhaps he didn't have to explain "AFTA" to them. Mennen himself could never forget. He named the next poodle in the family AFTA.

In 1968, Mennen was named ambassador to the Philippines. That appointment came from President Lyndon Johnson. Apparently LBJ had mellowed enough to overlook Mennen's staunch opposition to his nomination as vice president.

NOTES

1. The original of this narrative from Donald M. D. Thurber, along with the typed statement of G. Mennen Williams, dated June 2, 1960, announcing his support of John F. Kennedy for president, are among Helen Berthelot's papers in the Michigan Historical Collections, Bentley Historical Library, University of Michigan, Ann Arbor.

2. Frank Blackford's account of his role in bringing together John Kennedy and Mennen Williams is among Helen Berthelot's papers in the Michigan Historical Collections, Bentley Historical Library, University of Michigan, Ann Arbor.

3. Kenneth O'Donnell and David Powers discuss the controversy over Johnson's selection in their book, *Johnny, We Hardly Knew Ye*, with Joe McCarthy (Boston: Little, Brown and Company, 1970). See pp. 182–200 for their description of the Johnson furor. Mennen Williams's role is described in detail. The reference to Mennen Williams as a candidate for secretary of state is on page 236.

27

THE KENNEDYS
COME TO MICHIGAN

L ONG BEFORE MENNEN decided to support John Kennedy for president, Kennedy had been making careful overtures to the Michigan delegation. In May of 1959, as he was testing the waters for his candidacy, he and Jacqueline Kennedy traveled to Detroit for a visit. During that weekend, he met many of us who were close to Mennen and also talked to leaders of the state's major labor unions.

After his return to Washington, he wrote short but politically astute notes to each of us, showing good staff work and smart political instincts. He addressed us by our first names and personalized the content. Mine read in part: "You have done marvelous work, not only for the Communications Workers and for Governor Williams, but also for the entire Democratic Party in Michigan. It was certainly a pleasure for us to be with you." He added that he was glad the news stories picked up by the wire services and sent throughout the country emphasized his praise of Mennen and his leadership in Michigan. "He certainly deserves great credit in this regard," Kennedy wrote.

The next year, shortly after Mennen's endorsement of JFK in June, I got another letter from Kennedy, again full of praise for Mennen:

Dear Helen:

Governor Williams' endorsement of my candidacy has been one of the most heartening developments of my campaign for the Democratic nomination for president.

I cannot tell you how much I value his support and his generous appraisal of my qualifications. This support, coming as it does from one of the great liberal leaders of our Democratic Party, has given important new strength to my campaign. . . .

Sincerely,

John F. Kennedy

Kennedy then made a pitch for our votes at the convention, explaining that he had refrained from approaching us in Michigan until now out of respect for Governor Williams. In the same letter, Kennedy said he understood that Mennen had given me a memo on Kennedy's positions on the issues as well as a copy of his book, *The Strategy of Peace*, which Kennedy described as "a collection of my speeches over the past seven years." He certainly got his mileage out of that book.

Once the convention was over and Kennedy was nominated, our next concern was the traditional Labor Day Democratic campaign kickoff in Detroit and Flint. As usual, details were not decided until the last minute. The Democratic State Central Committee was planning the day with the Kennedy staff. There was much to be done. Careful decisions had to be made about seating at every event. The state central committee had to determine who would ride in which cars in which order in the caravan that would take Kennedy and his entourage from Detroit to Flint. Once all that was settled, our office had to type the VIP seating and car arrangements. We could expect members of the Kennedy staff and all their many problems to arrive on Saturday of that weekend. That was less than a week away when I was called in to get things going.

My first move was to call Roy Reuther, Walter Reuther's brother, and beg him to allow Madge Cruce to work with me for the Labor Day weekend at least. She had been a valued member of the UAW Political Action Committee staff for many years by then. Because she was responsible for so many facets of the UAW PAC, Roy was reluctant to let her come, but he finally agreed.

There still wasn't anyone to even answer the telephones. By this time, every line was ringing frantically. Billie Farnum and several committee people dashed in and out, but they had no time for my problems. They were setting up Kennedy's campaign itinerary, which had to be ready for his staff to okay when they arrived.

Finally, in the middle of the week, relief appeared in the form of a volunteer who walked in to get some Kennedy material. She could see the trouble we were in, so she asked if she could volunteer to help. "Can you type?" I asked. "Oh, yes," she said. She told me she was Taimi March and that she had worked for Congressman Thaddeus Machrowicz. That's how I got my secretary for that campaign.

There was much to be done. Madge Cruce came over on Saturday to help me. We worked all day and again on Sunday, right through the

218

night until just before dawn on Monday, Labor Day. The Kennedy campaign had opened its headquarters in a suite of the Book Cadillac Hotel. Our Democratic campaign office was a short walk away in the Book Building. The Kennedy people had to approve everything, but the State Central Committee was responsible for all the arrangements. There were too many people trying to decide who should sit where, which cars the top people should ride in, and even who the top people were.

Madge and I spent all Sunday night getting the car lineups and seating arrangements typed for the parade cars and the podium appearances. Then we assembled hundreds of copies of both lists, each with many pages. We did all of this not once, but three times. Someone would remember a VIP who had been left out, or disagree with the arrangements, and the list had to be started all over again. Marty McNamara from the Kennedy campaign took pity on Madge and me. He walked back and forth to deliver the lists and stayed with us throughout the night to help us collate and staple the copies.

It was 4:00 A.M. before everything was finally finished and okayed. Madge and I got a few minutes of sleep before the calls started to swamp our switchboard. There was little we could do except soothe the egos that were bruised and calm people down as best we could. All the decisions were being made in the Kennedy suite in the Book Cadillac. Unless it was extremely urgent, I did not refer any calls over there.

In spite of the lack of sleep, I enjoyed the rest of the day. From the back of the platform I was able to see everything and hear the Kennedy speech. There was, even then, a sense that this was history in the making.

Our biggest problem was the press. Please deliver me from the majority of the national news media, especially the crew from the *New York Times*. The Kennedy staff had thoughtfully set up an ample buffet table for the press and the television crews at the Book Cadillac Hotel. One of the top reporters for the *Times* nearly knocked me down as he pushed me aside to get to the buffet table. All I had been doing was checking to see that the press had enough to eat.

Thank goodness I didn't have to deal with a caravan of national press very often. Whoever it was who was driving their bus, I never found out. What the reporters may have done to egg the driver on, I never learned either. All I know is that at every opportunity, the bus, which had a defective exhaust pipe, pulled in front of the cars in the long entourage headed to Flint. The police moved them back repeatedly, only to have them push in ahead of the car I was riding in. Apparently, they were trying to take pictures of Kennedy. We were nearly asphyxiated by the exhaust fumes. In spite of the warm weather, we had to close the car windows—and there was no air conditioning, so we really suffered.

Within a few weeks, Jack Kennedy was back in Michigan, campaigning with his wife. He was scheduled for only one major appearance, a speech and rally in the auditorium on the state fairgrounds. We learned once again how important it is to plug all the holes for skulduggery. Jerry Bruno, the advance man for that affair, was devastated by what happened that night. He felt he would probably be fired, although he wasn't.

As Kennedy began his speech, we noted with dismay that there were vacant seats on one side of the auditorium. That didn't make sense. We had expected thousands of people to pour into the fairgrounds in their cars to see Jack and Jacqueline Kennedy, and Don Swanson, the State Fair manager, had found every available place to park them. What we had failed to do was station Democratic guards at the far gates to the street. Those gates were supposed to be open, and there were plenty of Detroit police there to handle the traffic. We had told the police we had room for everybody, but we found out later that the officers at those far gates had refused to let people come in. We always suspected that the Republicans had passed the word through the police department to be as uncooperative as possible. The Democratic State Central Committee officers made a complaint to the police department, but it was ignored. It was too late, anyway.

That night I met Jacqueline Kennedy. After the rally, Mennen was standing in the hallway talking to Jack. Although I didn't want to interrupt, I had a message to deliver to Mennen. It seemed best to stand off to one side and wait. Jackie was also waiting. She walked over to me, held out her hand, and said, with that sweet smile, "I don't believe I have met you." When I explained that I had been Mennen's campaign manager, her response was warm; she said she was aware of Mennen's accomplishments in Michigan. For the life of me I can't remember what she was wearing, but I was impressed by her sincerity. She was even more beautiful in person than her pictures would suggest. When Mennen was through talking, he moved over with Jack and introduced me as his former campaign manager. Jack smiled and acknowledged me warmly. Before I could say anything, Kennedy aides hurried Jack and Jackie out to their car.

Several other members of the Kennedy family campaigned in Michigan in 1960. One of the biggest attractions was Jack's mother, Rose Kennedy. The staff handling Mrs. Kennedy and Jack's sisters was very different from Jack's professional staff. They were all women, and most of them were cousins or other close relatives. With one or two notable exceptions their attitude was that we should be honored that Mrs. Kennedy would deign to speak at our functions.

Adelaide Hart was handling a reception for Rose Kennedy and found it very difficult to get firm commitments from her staff. One day

Adelaide came to me and said: "I am too angry to talk to them. Will you please call them for me and tell them that Senator McNamara is running for reelection and that we insist he be in the receiving line with Mrs. Kennedy when she comes to Detroit?" Dismayed by the lack of political sensitivity, Adelaide exclaimed: "Their rule is that no one be in the receiving line except Governor Williams and Mrs. Kennedy. I can't argue with them any more, but we can't leave Pat out of that receiving line."

Assuming my most "professional" manner, I called and said: "This is Governor Williams's campaign manager. I understand you refuse to allow Senator McNamara to be in the receiving line with Mrs. Kennedy. We do things differently in Michigan, and there will be no receiving line unless Senator McNamara is included." The woman at the other end of the line sputtered incoherently for a minute or so. Then she said, "If you insist, perhaps Mrs. Kennedy should not come to Detroit after all." Quietly I told her: "I can't believe you would hurt Jack's campaign to that extent, but that is your decision to make. We will discuss the matter more later if you wish," and I hung up.

Without wasting any time, I called my friend Larry O'Brien, Jack Kennedy's campaign manager, and told him our problem. He said he had heard the story and was sure we could handle the problem our own way. "I am betting on you girls," he said. He wasn't about to enter into that altercation.

In a little while, a very subdued staff woman called me back and said they would make an exception to their rule in our case, and that Senator McNamara would be welcome in the receiving line. To give Mrs. Kennedy credit, I don't believe she had any idea of the rules her staff had made. She was graciousness itself all through the affair, and stood in line much longer than we felt she should.

The other appearance by Rose Kennedy was scheduled for Flint. It was to be an invitation-only affair for local Democratic women and their friends. Adelaide was ready to give up, with all the problems she encountered. This time, the Flint people could not agree among themselves on where the reception should be held.

The invitations were nicely printed, and we in the campaign office had just finished putting them in the addressed envelopes when Adelaide called in despair. "There is a mistake in the address printed on the invitation," she said. "We will have to reprint them." Luckily, we hadn't yet sealed the envelopes. While the volunteers were pulling out the old invitations and destroying them, I called my friend Eddie Fishman. "Eddie," I said, "I've got another emergency. Do you have a printer who can work overtime tonight? We'll gladly pay for it." "What now?" he asked with a sigh. After I told him what we needed, I explained they had to be in the mail by midnight that night. Eddie's printer stayed, and so did some of my volunteers. The ink was hardly dry on the invitations before we were stuffing them into the envelopes.

Eddie was a lifesaver, and it didn't hurt Mennen at all that Eddie's work always carried the union bug. That symbol made it clear for all to see that Eddie employed union printers—and that Mennen patronized businesses that used union labor. That little bug was often inconspicuous —especially on invitations—but it was always there. In later years, the people handling the bills for the party decided not to use Eddie as much because they said his rates were higher than the other printers. When I heard about it, I explained that he had raised his prices to us in self-defense. Not only had we forced him into many expensive rush jobs, but campaign committees are not always prompt in paying their bills. At the end of a campaign, the people who do not complain loudly are the last to be paid—and sometimes get overlooked altogether. Eddie Fishman's campaign contributions to the Michigan party were never recorded as such, but they were considerable.

Candidates in 1960: from left, standing, Attorney General Paul Adams; T. John Lesinski, candidate for lieutenant governor; Secretary of State James Hare; and Auditor General Otis Smith. Seated from left: State Treasurer Sandy Brown; John Swainson, the nominee for governor; and Ted Souris, candidate for state supreme court justice. (Helen Berthelot's personal collection.)

Labor Day 1960: Lieutenant Governor John Swainson, candidate for governor; Senator John Kennedy, the presidential candidate; and Senator Pat McNamara, running for reelection. (Helen Berthelot's personal collection.)

Gery Williams enjoys a light moment in his father's office near the end of Governor Williams's administration. (Associated Press photo. Detroit Free Press.*)*

Mennen Williams always saw endings as new beginnings. As he cleaned out his desk in the capitol on the last day of the year in 1960, he looked forward to whatever new adventures lay in store. (Photographer: Pat Mitchell Pictures, Lansing. Detroit Free Press.*)*

As President Kennedy's assistant secretary of state for African affairs, Mennen Williams the diplomat describes the tour of Africa which he made in early 1961. (Detroit Free Press).

Mennen Williams calls a square dance—something he had done often in Michigan—for a gathering of African diplomats and their guests in Washington. (Associated Press photo. Detroit Free Press.)

*Adelaide Hart, vice chairman of the Michigan Democratic party, gives
Mennen Williams a warm welcome after his return from Africa in
1961. (Photographer: Pat Mitchell Pictures. Detroit Free Press.)*

*On behalf of the Democratic party, Michigan's two U. S. senators—Phil
Hart and Pat McNamara—show their appreciation for the hard work
of Adelaide Hart and her sister Helen by hosting them at a lunch in
1962 in the Senate dining room. (Helen Berthelot's personal collection.)*

Former Governor Williams, Nancy Williams, and their daughter Wendy make a sentimental journey across the Mackinac Bridge on Labor Day 1963. (Associated Press wire photo. Detroit Free Press.)

In 1964, former Governor Williams introduces his good friend, candidate for governor Neil Staebler, at far left, to the intricacies of campaigning at the State Fair. (Helen Berthelot's personal collection.)

Mennen Williams, surrounded by his family, announces his candidacy for the U. S. Senate in 1966. From left, Gery; Nan Williams; Nancy Williams; the former governor; Gery Williams's wife, Lee Ann Monroe (Lannie) Williams; and Wendy Williams. (Photographer: Fred A. Plofchan. Detroit Free Press.)

G. Mennen Williams with Rev. Martin Luther King, Jr., March 14, 1968, at Grosse Pointe High School, where Dr. King spoke to a crowd of 2,700. (Archives of Labor and Urban Affairs, Wayne State University.)

*Mennen Williams in the fall of 1966 during his campaign for the
U. S. Senate. (Photographer: Walter Steiger. Detroit Free Press.)*

*In 1966, during his Senate campaign, former Governor Williams shakes
hands with children whose parents were about their age when he was
first elected governor. (Photographer: Jimmy Tafoya. Detroit Free
Press.)*

In 1981, Mennen Williams joined the Wayne State University Board of Governors and then-President Thomas Bonner to reenact the moment twenty-five years earlier when he signed the bill making Wayne a state university. (Photographer: Taro Yamasaki. Detroit Free Press.)

Here, in 1987, Supreme Court Justice Williams participates in the "growth of excellence" celebration on the Williams Mall/Governor's court on the Wayne State University campus. Left to right, Wayne State University President David Adamany; Mildred Jeffrey, then vice chairman of the WSU Board of Governors; Nancy Williams; and Mennen Williams. (Photographer: Hugh Grannum. Detroit Free Press.)

Mennen Williams continued his tradition of campaigning at plant gates in the 1966 Senate campaign. (Photographer: Jerry Heiman. Detroit Free Press.)

Nancy Williams, always a trouper, picked up portions of Mennen's Senate campaign schedule when he was recuperating from surgery in 1966. (Photographer: Jimmy Tafoya. Detroit Free Press.)

Larry O'Brien's many years of service to the Democratic cause spanned the eras of John Kennedy, Lyndon Johnson, Robert Kennedy, George McGovern, and Hubert Humphrey. (Helen Berthelot's personal collection.)

Billie Farnum worked for the UAW before turning his talents toward politics and the Michigan Democratic party. (Detroit Free Press.)

Jim Lincoln demonstrated keen foresight and played a
major role in Mennen Williams's first three elections.
Later, Jim became a judge and an authority on juvenile
delinquency. Here, he stands before the courthouse built
in his name. (Helen Berthelot's personal collection.)

During Tom Kavanagh's eighteen years on the Michigan
supreme court, Republicans and Democrats alike knew
him as a real fighter for justice. His colleagues elected
him chief justice for three terms, allowing him to make
great strides in streamlining the courts. (Associated Press
wire photo. Detroit Free Press.)

Mennen Williams, as chief justice of the Michigan supreme court, addresses the Michigan legislature in 1983. (Photographer: Dale Atkins of the Associated Press. Detroit Free Press.)

John Swainson and Mennen Williams at the capitol in June 1986 for the Soapy Williams Day festivities. (Photographer: Thomas M. Farrell, Michigan supreme court.)

Chief Justice and former Governor G. Mennen Williams, age seventy-five, at a farewell press conference December 30, 1986. (Photographer: George Waldman. Detroit Free Press.)

28

PAT MCNAMARA
UNDER THE ROUGH EXTERIOR,
A PEOPLE'S CHAMPION

BESIDES THE PROBLEMS of the Kennedy campaign staff, I had my hands full with Pat McNamara in 1960. Pat was very different from Mennen Williams. He was quite direct and could be blunt, especially in his dealings with the ethnic groups that Mennen had so carefully cultivated. Pat was Irish, and, of course, the Irish are an ethnic group. Still, he believed firmly that people are people no matter what their nationality and that none of them should be treated differently. Mennen, on the other hand, was careful to respond to each group in keeping with the particular interests of its people. Stella Lecznar had helped Mennen understand that each nationality group had its own concerns. He quickly learned how to keep them all happy.

Pat had no patience for such painstaking attention. Because Mennen had worked so hard to honor all the various ethnic groups' personal feelings, Pat's casual treatment was all the more noticeable and was hurting his chances for reelection to the Senate. The situation was especially worrisome because Alvin Bentley, the wealthy Owosso businessman who was Pat's Republican opponent, was trying to imitate Mennen's success by wooing the ethnic groups. He was particularly effective with the Polish people, whose support could make the difference between winning or losing in Wayne County. Representative Thaddeus Machrowicz, a Democrat from the 1st District, was conservative in his views and was leaning toward Bentley.

Mennen got so many worried inquiries from the Polish leaders that he decided he had better do something before there was a large-scale

223

defection. He asked me to compile my best list of influential Polish people. Then he wrote each of them a personal letter and invited them to a dinner to meet with Senator McNamara and himself.

The night of Mennen's meeting with the Polish leaders, I was seated peacefully at the head table at our annual State Fair dinner. It was one of our better dinners. Before I had enjoyed so much as a forkful of steak, I was called to the telephone. Sid Woolner, then Mennen's executive secretary, was calling from Lansing. "The governor is in bed with a migraine headache and can't make the meeting. Can you handle it?" What could I say but yes? We certainly did not dare postpone it. The election was only two months away.

Back to my seat I went, thinking I would eat a few bites before I had to leave. No such luck. No sooner had I sat down than Governor Williams called. "Will you take my place at the Polish meeting?" he asked. "Yes, of course I will," I answered. "What do you want me to tell them?" He gave me a short synopsis of the ideas he wanted to get across to them, and I told him I would do my best. Though I tried hard to sound confident, my heart was down in my boots.

Forty-five Polish leaders had accepted Mennen's invitation to the dinner. It was up to me to recognize each one and to pronounce their names correctly. I started at once for the meeting hall. Since I had planned to join Mennen there later, I had the guest list with me and was able to go over and over the names. After several attempts to pronounce them out loud to myself, I was pretty sure I would be able to do it. It was a good thing I got there early because the guests all came early, too. Putting on my best smile, I greeted each one at the door and was able to call them all by name. Pat came late, with Bob Perrin, his administrative assistant.

The speakers' table was a small one. There was just Pat, myself, T. John Lesinski—our candidate for lieutenant governor—and Congressman John Lesinski, Jr. Congressman Machrowicz sat nearby. Small though our group was, it wasn't short on political experience. T. John had been a member of the Michigan House of Representatives for nearly a decade. John Lesinski, Jr., was a longtime member of Congress from the west side. Congressman Machrowicz had represented his east side district for many years.

So much was at stake I felt I should have some support from the floor. Also, I wanted to find out where Congressman Machrowicz really stood. He was seated at one of the front tables. Paying him a compliment about his long service in Congress, I told him I would like to call on him to speak first to the group. He consented, not too graciously. Then I told Joe Wisniewski, the longtime chairman of the 1st District, that I was going to call on him to speak for the east side Poles. Frank Szymanski was always an enthusiastic speaker who could be depended upon to put everyone in a good mood. So I asked Frank, the former auditor general who had become a Wayne County probate judge, to give the wind-up speech. That was all very well, but that left Senator McNamara as the next-to-the-last speaker. Again, I was not destined to get any dinner. It was probably just as well.

Soon after the food was served, I opened the meeting, trying my best to convey the message the governor had sent. As sincerely as I could, I told them of Mennen's strong support for Senator McNamara and asked, on Mennen's behalf, that all of the group give Pat their support. My remarks were short but as persuasive as I could make them. Then I called on Congressman Machrowicz. He had not quite finished his dessert and grumbled a little, but he made quite a passable speech. Then I opened the discussion to the floor.

To this day, I don't know how I did it, but I was able to recognize each speaker by name. That group could be very rough when questioning a candidate. This time they tried their best to tell Pat the things they wished he would do. They complained he did not answer their invitations. Right away, I knew what had happened. A mimeo'd, hand-scrawled notice of a meeting was often sent to a candidate. We had learned through sad experience that this would be the only invitation we would receive and that the group expected us to acknowledge it and come to the affair. In the senator's office, something like that probably went into the wastebasket. At this dinner, they were saying: "Mr. Pat, please answer our invitations. Mr. Pat, please come when you are invited."

The group was critical, but they were being very polite and kinder with their criticism than I had ever seen them. Pat's Irish temper was simmering more with each plea. Sensing it was about time for a break, I called on Joe Wisniewski. Joe was always very dependable. He delivered a good plea on behalf of John Swainson, our candidate for governor, and Pat, as well as the entire Democratic ticket.

We had a few more comments from the floor before I introduced the senator and asked him to respond to the group. By this time, Pat was ready to tell them all off. The essence of his speech was that he did, too, answer his mail. He turned to Bob Perrin and asked, "Isn't that so, Bob?" and Bob agreed. Pat didn't quite say that he didn't believe in ethnic groups anyway, but he may as well have.

Congressman John Dingell, Jr., who has a lot of good Polish blood in him, had arrived as dinner was being served. Over the years, John has proved that he inherited his late father's political sense, first by filling the congressional seat left vacant by his father's death, and then, over four decades, becoming one of the most powerful figures in Washington. On this particular day early in his tenure, John would show that he had good, common sense as well. There was no other place at the small speakers' table, so I had put him in my place and taken a seat on a bench just behind the table.

As Pat kept talking, John Dingell began pulling at me on one side while T. John Lesinski pulled at me on the other. "Stop him, stop him!" they insisted. It wasn't easy, but I managed to make my way discreetly to Pat's side and thank him for coming. Frank Szymanski had a few words to say, I announced. Poor Frank. He did his best, which is very good, but you could tell that he was upset.

As I closed the meeting I felt I had to repeat practically everything I had said in the beginning about the governor asking for their support for John Swainson and Senator McNamara. Then I thanked them for coming and for all their helpful comments, and said that I knew what they had told us would be of great help in the campaign. When the meeting was over, Pat didn't shake a single hand or greet even one friend. He just got up, walked over to the corner, and entered into a conversation with Bob Perrin as people mingled a bit before leaving.

Rushing to the door so I wouldn't miss a soul, I made it a point to greet and thank everyone personally for coming. It was hard to do after what had happened. Antoinette Stanis, another good friend from the west side Polish group, and three or four other loyal supporters were waiting for me outside. "What are we going to do when the senator talks like that?" they asked me. My response was quick: "It's just like this. You can support your senator who votes right every time and in Congress does many things for the working people even if he does talk tough—or you can support a smooth-talking Republican who won't do a thing for you when it comes to votes." They understood immediately. That fall, they did use their great influence to support the senator. Later, they often mentioned how much he did for them.

Reporting to Mennen about that meeting was one of the hardest things I had to do in all the years I worked with him. Thankfully, Frank Szymanski had called the governor before I talked to him and told Mennen I had done a very good job under trying circumstances. Mennen followed up with a letter of thanks to me. He penned a personal message at the bottom, reiterating his appreciation for representing him so well— his words—and letting me know that he had been working with the Polish leaders since that night. "Understand Pat is beginning to move," Mennen's note concluded.

Frank also took the time to send me an encouraging note, in his own handwriting:

May I congratulate you on the handling of the meeting the other night with Pat McNamara. The mere fact that the people invited showed up to participate would indicate that things are not as bad as I personally thought they were. The suggestions I am sure were well taken by Senator Pat, and I can't help but admire an Irishman who would take so much from the people assembled.

There was a great deal to like about Pat when you got beyond his sometimes rough exterior. It couldn't have been easy for him to replace Blair Moody, who had made many friends in Washington and Michigan. The task was made all the more difficult because Blair's death had been so untimely and shocking. Pat had battled his way up through the labor movement and had been working hard at making his own place in the Michigan Democratic roster by the time he became a senator. His approach was that he wanted to get the job done. His friendly attitude helped him over the rough spots, and he became one of the most respected members of the Senate. He was not the most diplomatic of people, but he was at heart a warm, kindly friend.

In the 1954 campaign, it hadn't been easy for us to make the transition from working for Blair to working for Pat. It helped that I had served with him on the Rent Control Advisory Board in the late 1940s and knew how strong an ally he could be. He, Adelaide Hart, and I represented the tenants on that board, which was a Wayne County branch of the federal agency charged with monitoring problems with rental housing. We had many difficult cases to handle. Pat never could be bothered to sit through our long meetings while the friends of the landlords battled with those of us representing the tenants. Sometimes, when a particularly nasty case was going to be heard, we knew we might need help to protect the tenants' interests. When that happened, which was not often, Adelaide would call Pat and give him the facts, then ask him to help. He would show up and take charge. Quickly, he would cut through the arguments, and the case was usually easily settled in our favor.

Pat had always been a passionate defender of the little people. The son of Irish immigrants, he grew up in Massachusetts before coming to Detroit in 1920 as a journeyman pipefitter. As a young man, Pat fought for passage of the state's first old-age pension law. He became active in the labor movement and served many years as the unpaid president of Pipefitters Local 636 of the AFL. Pat eventually went into the management side of the construction business, but he kept in close touch with his union. After World War II, he became a member of the Detroit Common Council and later served six years on the Detroit Board of Education. While on the school board, Pat was supportive of the move that elevated Wayne University from a city institution to a state one.

During the first year of Pat's Senate term, when I was in D. C., I tried to be as helpful as possible so that he knew he had a friend around. It wasn't difficult. Pat was funny and very human. He had the ability to laugh at himself and make everybody feel good. Our rum pie ritual got to be a joke between us. The Senate dining room served that dessert only on Wednesdays. We were both very fond of it. If I ran into Pat on Wednesdays—and I certainly made an effort to do so—he would almost always invite me to lunch. He would then order one piece of rum pie and two plates. "It's too rich for us to eat a whole piece," he would say. We were so predictable that the maitre d' never even bothered to ask. The dining room sometimes ran out of it, but the maitre d' made sure we never went without.

In the Senate, Pat put his humanitarian instincts as well as his tradesman's skills to good use. He distinguished himself in the areas of public works and highway programs, needs of the aged, labor relations, and civil rights.[1] In 1955, Pat's office was greatly strengthened when Bob Perrin became his administrative assistant. Bob had been a labor writer and reporter at the *Detroit Free Press* and, before that, a reporter for what was then called United Press Associations. Bob knew how to get information and answers from anywhere in government, and his knowledge of the issues was excellent. A deep friendship formed between them. Bob often was able to protect Pat without his ever knowing it. Sometimes Pat could be his own worst enemy.

One Sunday evening after John Kennedy and Lyndon Johnson were elected, Pat and I rode the same plane back to D. C. from Michigan, as we often did. He began to chuckle shortly after we were buckled in. "You remember a couple of weeks ago I wrote a strongly critical letter to Vice President Johnson?" he said to me. "I released it to the press at the same time I sent it to him. I didn't know that he had already gone to Texas, or I wouldn't have sent it until he got back." Pat related. The letter made quite a stink; it looked as if Pat had waited until LBJ left town before sending it. The vice president knew the ways of the Senate well, having been majority leader for many years before assuming his new duties, which included presiding over the Senate.

Pat continued:

Mr. Johnson told me I had hurt him deeply. This last Friday when I was getting ready to leave, he came over to me and put his arm around me and said, in that coaxing voice he has: "Pat, I am tired, Lady Bird is tired, and we are going down to the ranch for the weekend to rest. You're not going to send me another nasty letter while I am gone, are you?"

Pat laughed loudly, and his voice carried. People all around us heard him tell me his answer to LBJ: "'I don't know why I should write you another letter, Mr. Vice President. You haven't answered the first one yet.'"

That was Pat. To him, everyone was a fellow human being, no matter who it was. Despite what happened at the meeting with the Polish leaders, Pat was generally good with people before an audience as well as one to one. Many times, when I was giving a friend, a relative, or a CWA visitor a tour of the Capitol, he would come out at just the right moment. He would stop and talk and usually tell some little story about whatever was going on at the time. The people loved it, and it helped raise my stock in their eyes.

Pat was like a rock on the things he stood for. The people lost a loyal friend when he died. With the 1966 election fast approaching, Pat learned that he had cancer and could not run for another term. Knowing that Mennen Williams wanted to be a senator, Pat announced early in the election year that he wouldn't run, giving Mennen a head start. Pat died on April 30, 1966, a little more than two months after he made his announcement.

Bob Perrin wrote a memoir about Pat which was published in the *Muskegon Chronicle* on May 4, 1986, to commemorate the twentieth anniversary of Pat's death. Bob maintained a home in western Michigan. Immediately after Pat died, Bob stayed on to serve the federal government for several years before becoming a vice president of Michigan State University during the 1970s and later, vice chancellor of the State University of New York system in Albany.[2] In the 1986 article, Bob pointed out that Pat was a defender of the environment before it became a popular cause. As chairman of the Senate Public Works Committee from 1963 until his death, he created the first subcommittee specifically for environmental matters and produced two film documentaries on the effects of air and water pollution.

LBJ, who by then was president, flew to Michigan to attend Pat's funeral. Pat wouldn't have let it go to his head. As Bob Perrin pointed out in the essay, Pat often wore a little lapel pin of a miniature section of railroad track to remind him on which side of the tracks he had been born.

NOTES

1. Pat McNamara's correspondence, photographs, and memorabilia are part of the collection of the Archives of Labor and Urban Affairs at Wayne State University, Detroit.

2. The full text of Bob Perrin's essay on Pat McNamara and his legacy, published in the May 4, 1986, *Muskegon Chronicle*, is in the Appendix.

29

COACHING
A NEW TEAM TO VICTORY

THE 1960 CAMPAIGN FOR GOVERNOR was unusual. It was the first time since 1948 that there was a serious contest in the Democratic primary. Many people assumed that John Swainson, the lieutenant governor, would be the party's candidate for governor. He was a candidate, but he wasn't the only one. Ed Connor, a longtime member of the Detroit Common Council, decided to run. Jim Hare, the secretary of state, also entered the race.

Jim had been part of Mennen's circle since the early days. His decision to run for governor surprised us all. Ever since his auto accident, Jim seemed to have drifted away from many of his friends. The accident happened near the end of the 1956 campaign. While Jim was driving to his hotel after an evening campaign rally, his car was hit broadside by someone who ran a red light. Jim nearly died, but he pulled through and was elected that year and again in 1958. To the voters and people who were not close to him, he appeared to be the same person he was before the accident. Those of us who knew him well saw a big difference in his approach to life. When he and Ed both decided to run for governor, we all began to worry. Unity among Democrats had helped us win elections.

Mennen's strong leadership in the party was clearly missed, and he hadn't even left office yet. He knew it would hurt the party if he endorsed a candidate in the primary, so he didn't. He asked the rest of our little group not to take sides, either. It was agonizing for him, and for the rest of us, to watch Democrats attack each other. We knew that in the long run, the candidates and the party programs would suffer.

230

Neil Staebler, still the state party chairman, was at his wit's end during the weeks before the primary. He did his best to keep all three of the candidates from tearing each other apart and get them instead to concentrate on the Republicans. It was no easy task, since John and Jim were quite evenly matched and were tempted to take potshots at each other. More than once, Neil called all three of the candidates together and read them the riot act.

When the primary was finally over, Neil did what he could to heal the wounds. John, too, worked hard at trying to mend the party. He had won easily, with 274,743 votes to Jim's 205,086. Ed Connor drew only 60,895. Ed Connor went back to his Detroit Common Council job, since he had not resigned. Jim Hare was again nominated at the state convention for secretary of state. Other members of the Ad Board—Attorney General Paul Adams, Auditor General Otis Smith, and State Treasurer Sandy Brown—also were renominated at that fall state convention.

One new face was added to the ticket. T. John Lesinski was the candidate for lieutenant governor. He was a brilliant lawyer who had been elected to the Michigan House of Representatives every two years starting in 1950. He grew up in Hamtramck, where he graduated from St. Ladislaus High School and then went on to the University of Detroit and to U-D Law School. His long service in Lansing had given him valuable political experience, but most of his involvement had been with civic and Polish groups in his area. He was new to statewide campaigning and to our group of Mennen's original supporters. He seemed a little uncomfortable, probably because Neil was the only one of us he knew well. We all tried to make him feel at home.

Even before the primary was over, Neil insisted that all three candidates for governor agree on who should be the campaign coordinator for the fall election, no matter who won. They all wanted Sid Woolner, but Mennen needed him as his executive secretary. The only person they could all agree on—who was available—was me. Neil talked to Joe Beirne even before he talked to me. There was no question about my accepting. Like an old fire horse hearing the alarm, I was ready to go to work.

As soon as I got the word, I started writing memos to Billie Farnum, who was running the State Central Committee office. It would be a while before I could get away to start working in the campaign. My idea was for Billie to give us a head start by getting the telephone system we needed, the secretaries I wanted him to hire, and other necessities. Because I had been through this so many times, I was even able to tell him where to get the best deal on office furniture. Early in the campaigns, I had found a Democratic friend in an old gentleman who ran a second-hand store specializing in office furniture. He would sell us equipment

231

each election year at rock-bottom prices, throwing in extra chairs and odd pieces of furniture. After the campaign, he would buy back the equipment, barely making a profit on the deal.

After the first campaign, I had learned to be quite good at scrounging for what we needed. Al Gregory, whose family ran a large stationery store, more than once cleared out the store basement of odd supplies for us. Early on, one of the Wayne County Building men sent me a huge, overstuffed leather office chair on casters. From campaign to campaign, that was acknowledged to be Helen's chair. It was a life-saver, considering the number of hours I had to sit in it. In 1958, I was devastated to find it had fallen apart.

Despite my urgings, the Democratic State Central Committee was late in renting the campaign offices in 1960. What a shock it was to walk in ten days before Labor Day expecting to find the furniture in place, the telephone system all installed, and Madge Cruce waiting to be my secretary. Nothing was set up, and there was no secretary. Everyone had been too busy with the forthcoming Kennedy visit to pay much attention to the campaign offices. There was only one telephone hooked up, and the furniture was in a pile. Billie Farnum broke the news to me that Madge was working for the UAW's political action staff and was not available. It was then that I contacted Roy Reuther and persuaded him to let Madge work with me, at least for the Kennedy visit. Billie quickly sent over a couple of workers, and I soon had the furniture in place. The telephone installers were old friends, so that was no problem.

The 1960 campaign was an exciting time, and I enjoyed most of it very much. The logistics were old hat to me, and the Administrative Board candidates all had excellent campaign staffs. The only hard part was overcoming the suspicion of some of John Swainson's staff. His campaign manager, John J. "Joe" Collins, was an ambitious young businessman, still in his twenties. Joe had made a name for himself as a campus leader at the University of Michigan and had a growing insurance business in the Ann Arbor area. He was an astute politician, but he didn't have much experience in campaigns at this level. Joe was friendly, and I had no problems with him—except that he believed he could be of more help to John in the field. Joe never spent any time in the office after 6:00 P.M., so the rest of his staff left also. Several times I tried to explain to him that many of the worst emergencies arose in the early evening. He was quite content to let me handle them. Luckily, the majority of the people calling in were used to my being there. They wanted to talk to the campaign manager directly, however, and I didn't blame them.

After hearing from various people the problems John Swainson faced in that campaign, I began to think it was a wonder he didn't hate the very name of G. Mennen Williams. It was "but Governor Williams did it this way" or "Governor Williams never did that" wherever he went. John told me once that the crowning insult had come from a waitress in Traverse City, during the National Cherry Festival. He had duly eaten his cherry pie after lunch and had been given an official badge to prove it, as was the custom. At dinner, he ordered a piece of apple pie for dessert. "Governor Williams would have known to order cherry pie," the waitress said with a flip of her skirt, and she refused to bring John his dessert. "I just don't like cherry," John told me. "I never thought a thing about it. I was tired and didn't realize I had lost my badge."

John Swainson was a devoted campaigner. No one ever knew how much he suffered to keep going. He had enlisted in the Army as an eighteen-year-old, right out of Port Huron High School, where he had been captain of the Big Reds football team and an Eagle Scout. Not long after D-Day in 1944, he landed in France at Omaha Beach. Some weeks later, he was with a small group of soldiers taking food and ammunition to other men when their jeep hit a mine near a small village. Some of his buddies died in the blast. John lost both of his legs below the knee. He spent many days in hospitals in France and Wales, where there was an American hospital, before being returned to the United States. After surgery, excruciating therapy, and many more days in hospitals, he learned to walk with artificial legs.

John tells his story in the November/December 1991 issue of *Michigan History Magazine*, a special expanded issue published by the state's Bureau of History to commemorate the fiftieth anniversary of Pearl Harbor. After the war, John attended college on the G. I. Bill. He had hoped to be a dentist, he explains in the article, but he showed an aptitude for law, and it was much more compatible with his new legs.[1]

By 1958, John had established himself as one of the bright young members of the state senate. He had moved to the Detroit area and built a law practice. He was thirty-three when he joined Mennen on the ticket. After his service as lieutenant governor and governor, he went on to become a Michigan Supreme Court justice. Later, he became a member of the Michigan Historical Commission. His hard work and enthusiasm brought him much respect and well-deserved credit for raising the public's awareness of the importance of Michigan history.

After John recuperated from his war injuries, he decided to make it a point whenever he could to visit and encourage children and adults who were struggling with disabilities, particularly the loss of a limb. Hundreds, perhaps thousands, of veterans and civilians alike have benefited from his generosity over the years. His interest was genuine, without any thought of publicity. "The loss of my legs gave me more empathy than I otherwise would have had to people with disabilities," John says in the *Michigan History Magazine* article. "Not everybody operates the same way; everyone has different problems you may not be aware of. But that was then. I never paraded my disability."

Not only did John not play on his war injuries—as Blair Moody's opponent had done so shamelessly many years earlier—he also did his best to keep a tight schedule in that 1960 campaign, no matter how much his legs hurt. There was, I am sure, no one in Michigan who could keep up as tough a campaign schedule as Mennen Williams had done. When he was governor, he had had to double and then triple his staff of state police aides. He wore them out, too. It's no wonder John Swainson couldn't match that pace.

Later in the 1960 campaign, I would get call after call asking why John had not done this or done that. It got so most of my evenings were spent educating the people that they could not expect anyone to do what Mennen Williams had done—certainly not a man with two artificial legs. Time after time the callers were shocked. They had never known that John had lost parts of both legs. "Isn't he wonderful? How does he do it?" they would say. John would have been very unhappy with me if he had known I told so many people that he had two artificial legs and that he suffered greatly when he was on his feet all day. Once I practically ordered him to cancel his schedule and go to bed. His stumps were raw from walking so much and were in danger of ulcerating. My orders really didn't mean anything, but I did persuade him, with the help of his aides, to stay in bed for a couple of days.

T. John Lesinski, our candidate for lieutenant governor, was a trouper. One Saturday, I got him out of bed at seven in the morning to send him to an 8:00 A.M. meeting with a huge teachers' group in Dearborn. His wife, Carol, told me later that he hadn't returned from a campaign trip until four that morning. When it was over, he came into my office and said, rather accusingly, "Pat McNamara wasn't there. Why didn't you call him, too?" "Because," I answered, "I'm not responsible for Pat McNamara, but I am responsible for you." He grinned, and we became good friends from that point on.

It was a tough campaign. Paul Bagwell, the MSU professor, was back and running a hard campaign against John for the Republicans. Even though some of the Republicans were suspicious of Professor Bagwell because of his academic background, they all saw their first chance in a decade to take back the governor's office. He hadn't even had any primary opposition.

The political turmoil over Michigan's sorry financial situation had helped convince some people that it was time for the state to write a new constitution. Although it was the Republicans, not the state constitution, that created most of the obstacles for Mennen, the 1908 constitution did have built-in limits that had made it all but impossible to maneuver.

The Republicans in the legislature balked at the idea of a ballot proposal that could lead to a constitutional convention. Through the efforts of civic and citizen groups, the question ended up before the voters anyway. The Republicans did put an amendment permitting a sales tax increase on the 1960 ballot. Both amendments passed.

George Romney, a strong-willed Republican who had helped turn around American Motors Corporation, was one of the leaders behind the drive for Con-Con, as the constitutional convention came to be called, and was elected a vice president of the convention. Romney became John Swainson's opponent in 1962 and ran, successfully, on the platform of the new constitution and the citizens movement that had brought it about. Romney was against special interests—which he always defined as labor, never business.

That was still two years away, however. Election night in 1960 was the most exciting one since Mennen's early campaigns. Pete Buback, the Wayne County clerk, had been extremely helpful to me for several years, and on that evening, he gave me passes to come into the County Building. Because I was very careful not to get in anyone's way, he let me work in his own office.

The key Detroit precincts already had reported by the time I got there. They showed a good margin of victory for our ticket. The Wayne out-county votes were what I had come over to check. The heavily Democratic areas were coming in slowly, but they were following the Detroit trend. Hamtramck and several of the Democratic out-county cities had not yet reported, but I had seen enough to know we were well ahead, and in my mind victory was certain.

Our campaign office was heavy with gloom, however, when I returned. "What's wrong?" I asked. Someone said that John Swainson was losing, and so was the presidential ticket in Michigan. Ed Winge, the former *Detroit Free Press* reporter, was by then on the State Central Committee staff. He was on the phone giving the bad news to John. Immediately I dashed over to Ed and said: "Give me that phone, please. [I probably didn't say please.] We are winning okay."

Taking the phone, I said: "John, I don't know where Ed got his report, but it is way off. I just came back from the County Building. We are winning heavily enough in Wayne County to go over the margin we need to overcome the outstate vote." "Are you sure?" he asked. "Ed Winge was positive we'd lost, and he had seen the latest TV reports." "I'm sure," I answered. "The TV reports are behind. The County Building can't have given them the latest figures yet. When I left, we were way ahead, and some of the downriver reports were not in, and Hamtramck was not in either. Go to bed and get some sleep," I advised him. "You will have to make a victory statement in the morning." "Thanks, Helen," said John, sleepily, "I will."

235

After John hung up, I turned to Ed. "Why did you call him before I got back from the County Building?" I demanded. "We were so far behind on the TV reports, I didn't think we could catch up," Ed said. "John had asked me to call and wake him when I knew any definite results."

Everyone's face lit up when I gave them my latest report. Just then, Neil Staebler came out of his office. He and Sid Woolner had been tallying the Kennedy reports from all over the country. "What can you tell me about Kennedy?" Neil asked. "John Swainson's okay," I said, "but Kennedy's vote is slightly behind John's. I think he's okay but I can't say for sure yet that he's going to take Michigan. I will go back to the County Building and see if I can get any later results." After checking more out-county results and with Hamtramck still out, I came back to report to Neil.

Kennedy's national campaign staff had been on the phone constantly from the time I had left. Neil was cautiously optimistic but couldn't give them a definite yes. When we finally got the Hamtramck vote, we were sure that Michigan was going for Kennedy. Neil let me listen in on another phone when he gave the word—"Michigan's okay for JFK." We just missed putting Kennedy over the top. Neil was sorry we didn't have that honor, but still felt he could not afford to report an error.

The turnout that year was phenomenal. The vote for governor was about forty percent higher than it had been in 1958. John Swainson's victory was a narrow one, 50.6 to 49.4 percent; T. John's was only a fraction better. By comparison, Mennen's win over Paul Bagwell in 1958 had been the narrowest in years for him—53 to 47 percent.

NOTES

1. The question-and-answer interview with former Governor John Swainson, by Dr. Roger L. Rosentreter, editor of *Michigan History Magazine*, appears on pp. 50–52 of the November/December 1991 issue. Papers and correspondence from the administration of Governor Swainson are in the Michigan Historical Collections, Bentley Historical Library, University of Michigan, Ann Arbor.

30

THE KENNEDYS
(AND, IT SEEMS, EVERYONE ELSE)
GO TO D. C.

A S SOON AS I got back to the CWA office in Washington after the 1960 election, Joe Beirne called me in and said: "Don't bother to start work. Margaret Price called me and asked if you could help during the Kennedy inaugural." Margaret, the new vice chairman of the Democratic National Committee, needed someone to handle all the problems of finding places for people to stay—the Housing Committee's responsibility. To say there were problems was putting it mildly. It had been so long since there had been a Democratic president, and Kennedy was so popular, it seemed that every Democrat in the country wanted to come to his inaugural.

The 1961 Inaugural Committee worked out of the Liberty Loan Building, a ramshackle old structure on 14th Street. It was just below the entrance to the 14th Street bridge, where questionable looking people would occasionally hang around. As usual, I often turned out to be the last person to leave the office. Many times, no cab would answer my call. More than one night I walked several blocks, all alone, before I could find a taxi. They wouldn't even come close to that neighborhood.

The three major hotels in the city each sent a full-time representative to work with the Housing Committee. After I carefully explained that we had to make sure that everybody had lodging that came close to meeting their needs, the hotel people just held their heads and laughed. These professionals were used to housing big crowds. We finally laid out a wonderful working arrangement that enabled me to solve most of the problems.

Late one evening, I got a call from the man handling housing for Missouri. He started yelling at me as soon as I said "Hello." He was frantic. Not one of the Missouri people had received a confirmation from the Housing Committee and everyone was furious with him. He called me all sorts of names and never stopped long enough for me to say a word. Finally, I managed to get him calmed down enough to find out what had happened. Knowing there was no one around and nothing could be done until morning, I assured him I would check into it and call him back in the morning. "Morning!" he roared. "I want action right now." When I explained I was a volunteer, he swore at me. "Volunteer!" he exploded. "Tell them to get rid of you and hire someone who knows something."

First thing in the morning he was back on the phone, a little more rational. Finally, I got out of him what I needed to know and began the search for his Missouri guest list. When I tracked it down, I found that he had paid no attention to the instructions sent out by the Inaugural Committee. The DNC chairman's secretary, Loretta Larkin, came from Missouri, so the Missouri man had thought he'd get special service from her. He had sent her no cover letter with his list, and she didn't know what to do with it. Eventually she sent it to the Inaugural Invitations Committee. When I finally found it there, it was in a pile that no one knew what to do with. After looking at his list, I understood why it had been shoved aside. There were pages and pages of mimeographed names and addresses, many of them barely legible.

My years of work on Capitol Hill came in handy in such instances. One of my friends was Stanley Fike, administrative assistant to Senator Stuart Symington of Missouri. "This is just a reproduction of our state Democratic directory," he told me when he saw it. "All these people are not coming to the inaugural. I'll take care of it." Several days later, we got a neatly typed list of the Missouri people who were requesting hotel space.

Another kind of emergency hit on the eve of the inaugural—an unbelievably heavy snowstorm. The parties and festivities the night of January 19 went on anyway, but D. C. was one snowy mess. The Army and local road crews worked all night to clear as much snow as they could from the Capitol and the White House area.

The next morning was bitterly cold. Adelaide Hart and her sister Helen were staying with me. We gave up the idea of taking a cab or driving when we saw cars abandoned all over the city. We took the streetcar, only to have salt from the streets stop every streetcar in the city. We took a bus as far as we could, then plowed the rest of the way to the Capitol on foot through waist-high snow, with me lugging a blanket.

Adelaide and Helen were to sit with Mennen, Neil, and Margaret in the Michigan Democratic party section, and didn't want the blanket. On

238

the way to my seat, I ran into John Abernethy, who had been active in our Michigan campaigns for years. We decided not to go any further and huddled together under my blanket. Not all the foot stomping during the inaugural speech was for the new president. We were all grateful for any excuse to stand and get some blood circulating in our feet.

After the ceremonies, Michigan guests were invited to Senator Mc-Namara's and Senator Hart's offices for hot coffee and pastries. There were so many people there that I offered to stay and help clean up, so I missed the Michigan bus to the White House to watch the inaugural parade. It was fortunate that I did. As I walked the two miles down Pennsylvania Avenue to the White House, I had a fine view of the whole parade and the exercise kept me quite warm. Even CWA had a float, its first, in the parade: an elaborate depiction of pole climbers and a switchboard. Jane Palmer, a close friend of mine who had helped design it, was at the switchboard. Bundled up as she was, Jane still looked cold.

The Harts and I went to a couple of receptions before making our way back to my apartment, giving my well-developed cab-hailing skills a real workout in the crush. That evening, we put on our long dresses and headed out to the inaugural ball at the Sheraton Park Hotel. It was the only time I can remember wearing snow boots with an evening gown. We carried dressy shoes, of course. Being sensible has its limits.

Finally, after the inauguration, I was back at my old job with the CWA, lobbying on Capitol Hill. Much of my time was taken up with getting to know new members and their staffs and renewing old acquaintances. For once, I didn't leave all my old friends behind in Michigan. After Mennen received his appointment from Kennedy, he and Nancy bought a house in Georgetown. The house was all in order, but Nancy was still in Michigan, tying up their affairs there. Mennen wanted to have a dinner at their new home for Dean Rusk and his wife. Nancy wouldn't be able to get there soon enough to get things planned. Would I make arrangements?

It was like old times to be setting up an event for Mennen and Nancy, and thanks to my D. C. contacts, it was easy. The Brauns, who had been catering CWA affairs for years, helped me plan a dinner that drew admiring compliments from everyone. The food was marvelous and beautifully presented. Ruth Braun made a lovely ice carving for the table. She was as talented artistically as she was in the kitchen and was well-known to her clients for her graceful ice sculptures. Secretary of State Dean Rusk's wife took Nancy aside and asked her for the name and telephone number of the caterer. Many times after that, Mrs. Rusk used them for State Department dinners. The Brauns were very grateful to me. They had been trying for years to get contacts in the State Department.

When Nancy and Mennen moved in, they brought with them the female poodle puppy Mennen had named AFTA, for the "Africa for the Africans" incident. In good time, AFTA produced four lively babies, and the little family settled in happily in an upstairs bathroom. AFTA needed help feeding the puppies. Nancy would sit on the toilet seat with a towel over her lap and a dish of well-ground hamburger at her side. One by one, she would pick up the pups and poke a small ball of meat into its mouth. She would let it sit there for a minute, then pick it up and burp it just like a baby. No wonder they were such healthy dogs. Adelaide and Helen Hart had one of AFTA's babies, McDuff, for many years. Nancy and Mennen kept one and named it Buffy Berthelot Williams. Oh my.

More and more members of our old circle were spending time in Washington, either to work in the Kennedy administration or to attend party meetings. Mennen and Nancy were always opening up their home to everyone, as they had in Michigan. Early in 1962, a group of us thought it was time the Michigan–Washington transplants, as Helen Hart called us, should put on a party for Mennen and Nancy. It was close to Mennen's birthday, so we decided to make it his birthday party. Since none of us could think of anything Mennen needed or wanted, we each brought him a joke gift. We took an old nominating petition, rewrote the words as a tribute to him and signed our names.

The card that accompanied my gift to Mennen referred to our telephone conversation at my beauty parlor: "Dear Mennen, I said I would try; you said we must. I said we'd do our best; you said that is not enough. So we did qualify in all 83 counties and now it can be told how we did it. Yours, in servitude, Helen B., campaign manager." My gift was a replica of Tom Downs's "Jim Dandy" lifetime precinct circulator bag, which I filled with all the items I could remember Tom had included. Sid demonstrated it for me, since Tom could not be there, and did so with gusto. By this time Sid was a Washington transplant, too, having been given a federal appointment by Kennedy. We laughed hard and enjoyed ourselves that evening. Unfortunately, it was not often that we all got together again. We were all busy with our work and our outside activities.

Kennedy's election had put the Democratic party back in power for the first time since 1952. The elation was felt all over the country and gave the state organizations new life. Everyone wanted an excuse to come to Washington. As vice chairman of the Democratic National Committee, Margaret Price was in charge of activities for the women. Intrigued by the new president, the women began clamoring for a national women's conference in Washington. There would have to be a reception in the White House Rose Garden, of course.

Margaret began working on the idea almost immediately and was able to schedule the conference in the spring of 1962. She asked many of the wives of members of the Kennedy administration and Congress to serve on committees for the event. It was a foregone conclusion that I would chair the Housing Committee. Quite a number of people showed up with no reservations, hoping someone would take care of them. By now, I was used to that, and we found rooms for them all.

Plans for rebuilding state party organizations were discussed at length at the conference. For most of the women, however, the Rose Garden reception was to be the highlight—a chance to see the president and first lady up close. Several of the congressional and administration wives volunteered to help me load the women on buses for the ride from the conference hotel to the White House. Most waited, more or less patiently, to get on the buses, but there was a small group of overzealous Kennedy fans who were determined to get on the first bus. In their grand rush, they shoved the committee members aside. Lindy Boggs, wife of Congressman Hale Boggs of Louisiana, landed in a hedge beside the driveway. To help get the handicapped mother of one of our VIPs on the bus, I had been trying to keep the crowd back a little and had hold of the door handle when the onslaught overran me. My arm was not broken, but it was mighty sore for days. We all got a little chuckle out of the fact that President Kennedy didn't come out to the Rose Garden until the last bus was being unloaded. The women who had waited most patiently turned out to be the people he greeted first.

31

NEIL STAEBLER
FOR CONGRESS AND
JOHN SWAINSON
FOR GOVERNOR

J OE BEIRNE probably wouldn't have known what to do with me if I had spent the entire spring, summer, and fall of an election year in the D. C. office. As the 1962 election approached, he needn't have worried.

An increase in population had given Michigan an additional member of congress. The state legislature, however, had been unable to come to an agreement on the revision of the district boundaries in time for the election. The solution was to elect a congressman-at-large for one term. The Democratic party leadership agreed that Neil Staebler should be the candidate. Neil got Joe Beirne's approval for me to run his campaign. As usual, it was taken for granted that I should be the office manager for the entire group of Democratic candidates.

It was a lonely campaign, at least in the beginning. None of the people I had worked closely with in the past were available to help. Sid Woolner was in Washington, where he was overseeing a Kennedy administration program helping colleges and local communities finance public works. John Murray was working for the highway department in Lansing. He had moved from the party staff to Mennen's office during the last few years Mennen was governor. John was a great help with speeches and other public presentations. Paul Weber was now with Michigan Consolidated Gas Company. Paul was the one who knew how to find the right words or the right tactic to solve any problem. They were my constant helpers, and I missed them terribly.

There were new people and new ways of doing things in John Swainson's campaign. Neil had told me at the start that John's reelection was the top priority and that I should try to be helpful in his campaign whenever I could. When I told Neil I needed an assistant in his campaign or I would not be able to help John, he agreed I should have one. He persuaded Marilyn Cochran to work full time as my assistant. Her husband Bill had been the 11th District chairman for a number of years, and the Cochrans both knew a great deal about the whole state as well as northern Michigan. They had always been available to help in an emergency. Here they were, living in Lansing when we needed them. Marilyn was so efficient that when I told her what needed to be done, I could rest assured it would be done promptly and correctly. The Cochrans' involvement in Neil's campaign gave me more time to help in John's campaign and still know that Neil was not being neglected.

Leonard Woodcock, who was then vice president of the UAW, took a firm hand in John's campaign. Unhappily, the rest of the staff did not form a cohesive group. Each one had definite ideas on how the campaign should progress. The results were chaotic. More and more of my time was spent trying to avoid disasters, many of them caused by the dissension on John's staff. The poor young woman who was trying to set up John's schedule was getting orders from at least three different people. By working carefully at night, I was able to help her put together a logical schedule. The next day, I would casually mention in the right places what a good schedule had been worked out.

It wasn't possible to head off every disaster. After it was too late, I discovered that John hadn't even been scheduled to go to the Upper Peninsula State Fair. Alice, his wife, was sent in John's place, but she was called away early to go to another campaign event in Wayne County. Missing the UP State Fair was a dreadful mistake. The people depended on having the governor, no matter who he was, attend every year. Even Governor Kim Sigler went, although he only walked through with his state police aides. Just as stories of Governor Sigler's standoffishness had circulated throughout the UP, word that Governor Swainson missed the fair altogether spread widely. It was all very frustrating.

Zolton Ferency, who was John Swainson's executive secretary at the time, had the reputation of being difficult to work with. However, he needed me then—desperately—and I found him to be most cooperative. There were countless times when he called and said, "Helen, I don't know how you are going to do this, but this is what we need done."

It was like walking on eggs, but generally I was successful. Most of John's staff knew my record as a campaign manager, even if they hadn't previously worked with me. Soon I found that if I would suggest something in a pleasant voice and with a positive attitude, I would be able to get the idea across.

One of the worst problems was that each person on the staff wanted to be the one closest to John. Instead of solving problems as a team and keeping the candidate above the fray, these people saw each crisis as a way to maneuver closer to him. As a result, each staff member kept pulling John into making decisions on problems he should not have even known existed. This, in turn, created more personality conflicts. It got so bad that John had to give up one whole precious Sunday of campaigning to sit down with his staff and make them work out their differences.

One of the biggest bones of contention was his long-range schedule. On yet another Sunday afternoon midway in the campaign, I found myself chairing a meeting of all the staff even remotely connected with the schedule, including Leonard Woodcock and two other UAW people. Leonard is one of the most talented negotiators in the labor movement, but he couldn't possibly know the problems involved in keeping the party people happy with the governor's schedule. That was one of the longest afternoons I have ever spent. We literally negotiated a workable schedule. Part of the time I spent kicking the young woman in charge of the schedule under the table, so she would be quiet and not upset it when we were close to agreement on a segment of the schedule.

Every talent and bit of experience I had had in negotiations came into play that afternoon. The only thing that saved me was that while Leonard often disagreed with me, he had confidence in my experience. He treated me as an equal, which gave me the courage to openly disagree with him. And I was careful to have good, logical reasons for not conceding that he was right. It was after 7:00 P.M. when our meeting finally broke up, but we had a workable schedule for the rest of the campaign. And we stuck to our agreement, partly because I was around the office enough to make sure we did.

The only thing that had kept me from giving up several times that Sunday afternoon was the knowledge that John Swainson trusted me. That trust had been hard-earned. In his 1960 campaign, I stayed around in the evenings and answered all the calls that should have been taken by his staff, who were always gone by 6:00 P.M. After he was elected, two of his former staff members told him lies about me. They said I had spent all my time running him down and heaven only knows what else.

A good friend told me what was happening. The news made me sad as well as angry; I had worked too hard and was too fond of John to be put in that position. Before I left for D. C., I went right into the capitol and to John's office. He had seen me coming and was almost out the door when I got there. Taking him by the arm, I said: "John, please don't go away. I want to talk to you." He had been very hurt by what he had been told and really didn't want to talk to me. He did go back and sit down, however. I said, "John, have you ever known me to lie to you?"

244

He had to agree that he didn't believe he had. "All right," I replied, "then please listen to what I am telling you and believe it." Honestly and firmly, I laid it on the line that I knew what he had been told. Then I said: "Let me tell you my side of the story. I can give you the names of a dozen people who can verify what I am telling you."

John could hardly believe what I had to say. There had been several instances in which his staff had created problems. It had been up to me to convince the people who called to complain about a problem that John never would condone such actions, and that I was certain he knew nothing about them. He hadn't known. Most of the problems were with small meetings originally on the schedule and then inadvertently left off. In each instance, the people expected a speaker who didn't arrive. His staff would tell him I had changed the schedule deliberately to make him look bad. Thinking it over, John could remember a number of times when he, himself, had called his office and I had been the one to answer the phone and handle his problem. We had a long talk and parted good friends.

Another attempt had been made to stop me from helping him just before the start of his reelection campaign. Before I left D. C., I spent hours writing down in chronological order all the things I thought he should do to have a successful campaign. Including a page of "don'ts" that could be harmful, I sent the whole thing to him at his office in the capitol. There was no response. One day when I saw him at a meeting, I asked him if my memo on campaign strategy had been helpful to him. He looked blank and said he had never seen it. Sadly he said, "Helen, if you have something you really want me to get, send it to my home." Because I had kept a copy of what I had written, I was able to reproduce it and send it to John. He was so pleased he gave copies to the two people in charge of his campaign.

Why I was the subject of such deception by some of his staff I have never known, whether it was to cover their own activities or whether they just plain didn't like me. No matter what the reason was, I have always been glad I made John listen to me, for we became lasting friends. His gratitude came through in a warm thank-you note he wrote after he finally saw my ideas. "I certainly appreciate your kindness in putting forth so much effort to gather this information for me. Believe me, we are more than grateful to receive your helpful suggestions."

As Neil's campaign manager I had enough problems without worrying about John Swainson's staff. It's never easy to run a campaign when some of the people have already started and settled into their own routine. This is what happened to me. Two people had been handling the campaign, including the scheduling, for several weeks in the primary before I was free to come to Michigan. One of them, Bernie McQuiggan, had been Neil's assistant in party work and, I am sure, felt he should have been the campaign manager.

When Neil first talked to me about managing his campaign, he was aware that there might be friction. He assured me he had taken steps to smooth things out and told me to contact him immediately if I had any problems. Knowing Neil as well as I did, I knew he shied away from personality conflicts among his friends and that I would be on my own to work out any problems.

It was not very long before I discovered that the schedule I had recommended and outlined for Neil had been altered before it was finalized. When I asked the scheduler about it, I received a hostile response that I could not understand. One day I overheard what was going on. The scheduler was being told to disregard my written instructions and to do it her own way. She really had no idea what to do. She was from New York and just out of college. Her husband wrote for a national magazine and had a good knowledge of Michigan, but she hadn't absorbed it very well.

The orders to ignore me came from Neil's former Democratic party staff assistant, so it was understandable that they carried considerable weight with the scheduler. When I casually mentioned to Neil that I was having a few problems, he shook it off as a minor personality clash that would blow over. It was then that I knew I would have to face the scheduler and the saboteur. Although I was diplomatic, by the end of our meeting there was no doubt left in either of their minds that I was the campaign manager. Their help and advice were valued, I assured them. However, when a decision was made, I told them, I expected to have it carried out.

Even after that, there were one or two minor attempts to change a finished schedule. Expecting some backsliding, I was careful to check each schedule. Difficult as it was, I did my best never to show that I knew that everything was not running smoothly. After a while, it was. Marilyn Cochran's pleasant disposition and cooperative attitude helped immensely. Once that was done I could put more effort into John Swainson's campaign, where it was becoming obvious that we needed all the help we could get.

The 1962 campaign for governor became entangled with the politics of the constitutional convention. After a petition drive, the voters had amended the constitution in 1960 to make it easier to call for a convention. Then in the spring of 1961 they approved the convention itself. Delegates were elected that summer and fall. Con-Con convened in Lansing in October 1961 and continued into 1962. The convention adopted a proposed new constitution in August.

Although the new constitution didn't go to the voters for approval until the spring of 1963, it was a big issue in the 1962 campaign. Adelaide Hart had been elected as the leader of the Democratic delegates. However, more than two-thirds of the Con-Con delegates were Republicans, largely because of the way the state was divided into districts. John Swainson and many of the state Democratic party leaders opposed the constitution because of the makeup of the convention. As John put it, there was nothing wrong with rewriting the constitution as long as the group that did so was representative of all of the people of the state.

John's Republican opponent, George Romney, had quite a following because of his involvement with Con-Con. Rather liberal for a Republican, Romney was outspoken and very quotable, and he began to make a name for himself nationally. Born in Mexico, where his American parents were forced to seek temporary refuge from persecution for their Mormon beliefs, Romney grew up out West and started his business career in the aluminum business. He moved into manufacturing and was chairman and president of American Motors Corporation from 1954 until early 1962, when he resigned to run for governor. He was a leader in the Mormon church and active in volunteer causes after he left the governor's office. His wife, Lenore, was badly defeated when she ran against Phil Hart for the U. S. Senate in 1970.

In 1962, with a huge campaign fund and with Con-Con momentum on his side, George Romney presented a strong challenge. John Swainson had an uphill battle all the way. It didn't help that he had to take a courageous stand that year on a city income tax proposal. He vetoed a bill to allow Detroit to impose the tax because an amendment had been added that would have undercut it by exempting suburbanites who worked in the city. Voters in the suburbs interpreted his veto as a maneuver against them; they were angry and blamed John, when it wasn't his fault at all. He was put in that position by people who knew the quandary would cause him trouble. A few years later, the tax was approved for non-residents employed in the city as well as residents, although people from the suburbs were to pay less than city residents.

When the 1962 campaign was over, we were happy that Neil Staebler, the other Democratic congressional candidates, and Lieutenant Governor T. John Lesinski had won, but sad that John Swainson was not reelected as governor. John did the best he could that year, and so did all the party officers and volunteers. Romney's showing was far from resounding—less than 51.5 percent of the vote. Still, the political winds had shifted. It would be twenty years before another Democrat would be elected governor in Michigan.

John Swainson and T. John, as we all called the lieutenant governor, seemed to sense that Democrats had a rough road ahead. In separate thank-you letters to me, they acknowledged the important help of the party and the volunteers in bringing them so close to victory despite the odds. Both of them said they hoped that party workers would continue their efforts to advance Democratic candidates and programs. As T. John put it in his letter, "Much labor is ahead."

Neil's election to Congress was encouraging to all of us. John Swainson's 1960 campaign manager, John J. "Joe" Collins, was state party chairman during the 1962 elections. Joe, who later became a highly successful insurance executive and businessman, wrote me an enthusiastic letter thanking me for my part in Neil's victory. It was no credit to me that Neil Staebler won. He did it completely on the love and trust he had inspired in the party faithful all the years that Mennen Williams was governor. The hard work they put in for him was their way of saying thanks for all he had done for them over the years.

Bob Popa, who at the time was a reporter in the Lansing Bureau of the *Detroit News*, wrote an excellent account of Neil's campaign. It was headlined "Staebler Finds a New Formula for Success." The story described how Neil never campaigned like the other candidates, who tried to greet and shake hands with large numbers of people. Instead, he lingered with individuals as he met them. Anyone who has ever talked with Neil knows he is nothing if not thorough, especially on a political issue. He must have made a lasting impression.

Bob took it for granted that the staff member he had interviewed—the same man who had tried to undercut me with the schedule—was Neil's campaign manager. Without realizing who was who, Bob identified my former rival as the campaign manager and me as a member of the staff and Mennen's former campaign manager. My friends took great delight in asking me what I'd been doing while Neil was out campaigning in that new successful style of his.

32

THE 1964 CAMPAIGN
ONE LOSS, ONE LANDSLIDE

E LECTED IN 1962 by a good margin, Neil Staebler had served one term as a congressman-at-large from Michigan. Now that the boundaries of the districts had finally been settled, the at-large seat was eliminated. Many people were urging Neil to run for governor, and he was trying to decide if he should enter the race.

Mennen Williams often used to call me his catalyst. Now, I thought, Neil needed me to be his catalyst. These two were gentlemen and were reluctant to ask favors of each other even though they were such good friends. When I arrived in Michigan at the start of the 1964 political year, it seemed to me that Mennen wanted to help Neil but was waiting for Neil to assure him he needed it. Neil, on the other hand, badly wanted Mennen's help and advice but didn't want to impose upon his time.

We were all together for a meeting, so it was an ideal time for me to get to work. When I was able to get Mennen alone, I told him outright that Neil wanted his help and advice very much but was reluctant to ask him. Mennen looked at me as if he couldn't believe what I was telling him. "Why don't you offer to help him today, and see what he says?" I asked. Mennen agreed and suggested I tell Neil he wanted to see him. In nothing flat, I took off in pursuit of Neil to tell him only that Mennen wanted to see him. "Why don't you ask him for his advice about running and, if you decide to run, the best way to start?" I said to Neil.

The next thing I saw was the two of them with their heads together in earnest conversation. Burnette Staebler, Neil's wife, was a good friend

249

of mine and Neil's partner in political endeavors. She was pleased at what I had accomplished and even more pleased when I showed her an outline of what should be done, step by step, for Neil's campaign. It was easy, after all those years with Mennen. She told me that a member of Neil's staff, Bernie McQuiggan—the same one I had had to keep an eye on in 1962—was supposed to be drawing up a campaign plan but had no experience at it. Neil would be pleased that I had done it, she told me. Knowing Neil, I quickly cautioned her: "Please don't let Neil add too many details to this outline. Tell him to let us run the campaign and just be the candidate. If he would be as good as Mennen was about not interfering in the details, we'll be home free."

Neil prevailed on Joe Beirne to let me manage his campaign. By this time, Joe was quite resigned to releasing me every two years. He never told me whether he regretted the agreement he had made with me. By this time, he must have realized that the contacts I made were of benefit to CWA. Also, I think he was proud that they wanted me.

They might not have been so eager if they had known how badly I was to bungle the start of the 1964 campaign. What I learned that year —and should have known before—was that someone coming in to run a campaign that has already begun should make changes quietly, without being openly critical.

The State Central Committee was in charge of running the campaign office for Democratic candidates. The office manager they had hired was new to politics. The two women who had set up the office were taking me around and proudly showing me what had been done. My mind was taking note of everything that would have to be changed and what else needed to be done. I should have kept these thoughts to myself while verbally thanking the women for all their hard work. Unfortunately, however, my mouth was saying everything I was thinking. To give myself credit, I cannot remember ever being so tactless. My only excuse was that I was dead tired. As soon as I had spoken, I knew by the looks on their faces that I had hurt them deeply. It was a long time before they trusted me again, and I had to work hard to regain their regard. The office manager picked up their cue, and my work stayed at the bottom of the pile.

Help arrived when I needed it most. Barbara McCann, a secretary I knew well from my State Fair Board days, dropped in one evening to help. When she saw my plight, she offered to come in several nights a week. She got me through the primary. Despite my careless criticism, Neil's campaign did not suffer—largely because of Barbara's help and my determination to cooperate.

When the primary was over, the office became my responsibility. To make sure everyone was getting fair treatment, I met every morning and afternoon with the office manager and set up priorities for the work everyone needed done. She was an ex-Marine sergeant whose military training was of no help in handling the office. She could get the work done, but she only took orders from the boss. Once I had the authority, she did whatever I wanted.

Neil was concentrating on outstate areas in the campaign for governor. Robert A. Derengoski, Neil's running mate, was from Manistee in western Michigan. He was spending most of his time around Detroit, where he was not well-known. This was the first campaign under the new constitution, which required the election of the governor and lieutenant governor on the same ticket. Bob was a very personable man and a skillful campaigner. He later became solicitor general for the state of Michigan. Neil, as always, was very effective in personal appearances and meetings where he had a chance to talk about the issues.

No matter how much Neil and Bob tried, however, it proved to be impossible to overcome George Romney's popularity. Governor Romney, by now well-entrenched, won with fifty-six percent of the vote. His running mate was a young Republican from Traverse City, state Senator William G. Milliken, who became governor in January 1969 when President Richard Nixon named Romney to his cabinet. Milliken was a Yale University graduate and an air combat veteran of World War II who returned to his hometown of Traverse City after the war to work in the family department store business. Like his father and grandfather, he entered politics and was elected to the state senate seat they had held before him. Milliken served two terms before he was elected lieutenant governor under Romney in 1964.

Neil's defeat was my first major loss—I didn't count my own legislative primary defeat in 1948 as much of a setback. Neil's trouncing was much harder on me than on him. He really is an eternal optimist. Next day, he was busily figuring out what the party needed to do next.

The party did well in the other statewide races. Phil Hart easily won reelection to the Senate. Attorney General Frank Kelley and Secretary of State Jim Hare won by substantial margins, too. Under the new constitution, the other Ad Board offices were changed to appointed positions. In the congressional delegation, we picked up four seats from the Republicans, as President Lyndon Johnson won in a landslide against the extremely conservative Senator Barry Goldwater of Arizona.

As soon as the campaign was over, I went sadly back to the CWA in D. C. This time I didn't even get as far as my office. Joe Beirne met me as I was coming into the building. He greeted me warmly and then started to laugh. "There's no use for you to go up to your office," he said. "Margaret Price has been calling me for a week trying to find out when you were getting back. The Housing Committee for the inaugural is having a rough time and she says they need you badly. Go ahead and help her but don't forget to come back," he said, giving me a playful swat.

It was time for Margaret to be in her office, so I hailed a cab and surprised her. To say she was glad to see me ready for work would be putting it mildly. "I don't know the man in charge of housing this year," she said, "but all I get from everyone are complaints." After President Johnson's overwhelming victory, the Inaugural Committee had much larger and pleasanter offices than the rundown place on 14th Street four years earlier. When I found my desk, I sighed. The deep pile of papers represented a stack of problems, I knew.

My friends from the major hotels welcomed me warmly and then began their tales of woe. They told me that the man in charge of housing the inaugural guests hadn't the faintest idea how to handle the job. "He has a real short fuse, and when we try to help him, he cuts us off," one of the exasperated hotel representatives told me. They were ready to walk out and leave the problems to the Inaugural Committee, which would have been a disaster.

Neale Roach, chairman of the Inaugural Committee, had overseen the 1961 inaugural. He and his wife Fran were known for their skill at handling big D. C. events. The housing director had not yet arrived, so I went directly to Neale's office and briefed him. He quickly called a meeting of all of us who were going to work on housing and made it plain that I would handle problems from the state party organizations.

From then on, things ran much more smoothly. The housing director and I had plenty of arguments when he finally showed up, but with my authority firmly established, I won at least half of them. The hotel men had helped me solve my many housing problems four years earlier. They assured me I had amply repaid them this time.

Watching the 1965 festivities was a far cry from my experience in 1961. Fred Belen, deputy assistant postmaster general and an old friend, invited a small group to join him and his wife Opal to view the parade from the second floor of the old Post Office Building facing Pennsylvania Avenue. We watched the inaugural ceremony on television. It didn't have the same thrill, but I was much warmer.

33

GMW TRIES FOR THE SENATE

FROM 1961 TO 1966, I saw comparatively little of Mennen and Nancy Williams. Mennen continued his work for the State Department, while I kept on with my CWA duties and Michigan election campaigns. Helping address their Christmas cards was one of the activities that brought us together. That was a time-consuming chore but one I enjoyed. Seeing so many familiar names brought back memories. It also was a challenge to spell the names of Mennen's new friends from around the globe. Sometimes their titles took up two whole lines on the envelope.

To help with the cards, I called on a local crew of top-notch women who volunteered with me over the years on many projects. They were so willing to help that I took to calling them my "victims." Every year I even had a "victims" party for them. Margaret Price once said, "Helen, you don't let them hear you call them that, do you?" Ruth Brooks, one of the "victims," heard her and spoke up: "She sure does. We know we are 'in' if we are 'victims.'" The next year, Margaret sent me a huge poinsettia addressed to "the biggest 'victim' of them all."

My "victims" were a group of D. C. area professional women, all of them top secretaries on the Hill or in government departments. Although their home states literally ranged from Maine to California, they had great respect for Mennen and were always glad to help out on any project for him. We worked in one of Mennen's small reception rooms in the State Department. It was easy for him to stick his head in from time to time and ask how we were getting along with the cards.

253

One Saturday, six of us were at work there. Mennen came in and insisted on taking us all to lunch. He chose one of Washington's swankiest places. When we walked in, Mennen was told that the restaurant objected to serving black people. There were black women in our group. Mennen was appalled. He demanded to speak to the manager and insisted that we be seated and treated with respect. We were, and we had a delightful meal. This incident, which took place in the early 1960s, was a sad reminder for all of us that the battle for civil rights will never end.

In the spring of 1966, soon after Pat McNamara had announced he was not running again for the Senate, Mennen began to think seriously about becoming a candidate. Typically careful and thorough, he wanted an idea of how people would respond. He talked to friends and advisers whose counsel he trusted, and then decided to send a letter to a wider circle of people and ask what they thought about his running for the Senate.

Getting those letters out was a project that really appealed to me, and I volunteered to take it on singlehandedly at the start. Collecting addresses was simple. We had all kinds of contacts and sources of information. Harking back to my early days with Mennen, I went ahead and wrote the letter myself. When it came back from the printer, I was so anxious to get it in the mail that I didn't proofread it as thoroughly as I usually do. No one else proofread it before it went out.

There were two errors in the letter, one in punctuation and the other a wrong word. Unfortunately, I missed them both. Bill Welsh didn't. Bill had been a friend since I arrived in D. C. in 1953 and started helping out with the Democratic National Committee, where he was staff research director. He served the party well over the years. His diverse responsibilities included working as Phil Hart's administrative assistant in the Senate, as executive secretary of the DNC under Chairman Larry O'Brien, and as administrative assistant to Vice President Hubert Humphrey. Bill also held several positions in the labor movement, handling legislative matters with great skill. He has a keen political mind—and a sharp eye. He sent me back his copy of the letter, corrected, with a note saying he expected better than that from me. Anyone else who noticed the errors was either too kind or too polite to say anything. Bill never let me get by with anything but my best work. If Mennen saw the errors, and I am sure he did, he was too absorbed in reading the answers to the letter to mention the mistakes to me.

(There really was no excuse. My proofreading skills were well-developed. Stenographers used to call me "Old Eagle Eye," because often I would walk by, glance over their shoulders, and spot a misspelled word. They just seemed to leap out at me. This was somewhat ironic, because my own spelling is atrocious. There is an excuse for that, however. After taking notes at so many meetings, I had concocted my own form of shorthand, which destroyed my spelling ability.)

To address the envelopes, I called on my "victims." We worked in the dining room of my apartment, and I fed them, as always. After the "victims" and I had all the envelopes ready, two of Mennen's other stalwart volunteers stepped forward—Mae Ann and Van VanBlankensteyn. Van, whose given name was Cornelius, had been in the top ranks of the Michigan State Police and was well-respected by Mennen. Mac Ann, Van, and I spent a weekend stuffing the letters into envelopes, sealing them, and licking the stamps. We sent out several thousand letters.

The response was overwhelmingly in favor, which convinced Mennen to enter the race. Although eight years had passed since his last campaign, most of the letter writers said Mennen was still their favorite candidate for public office.

The passage of so much time made it imperative that we draw up a new list of people who might help us. Computer lists were still in the future. Using my dining room as an office, Mae Ann VanBlankensteyn had made 3-by-5-inch cards for each one of the persons who received Mennen's exploratory letter. Mae Ann's cards became the basis for recruiting Mennen's campaign workers. When I went to Michigan to start work, the cards filled a huge suitcase. It was so heavy that two men had to carry it. Those 3-by-5 cards gave Mennen a big boost in that 1966 primary. Nonetheless, the campaign is one that I wish I could erase from my memory.

Shortly after the letters went out, the wonderful sense of communication that Mennen and I had always enjoyed broke down for a long period. My attempts to restore it seemed to occur at the wrong time, or else I didn't express myself well. Our contacts were always hurried, so we never really talked about the problems.

Mennen went through the procedure that was now routine, asking Joe Beirne for my release to work in his campaign, but he didn't say what my role would be. Joe had just appointed a new head of the CWA legislative department, who was pretty grumpy about my leaving.

All the pre-campaign planning had been done in Michigan before I could get free. When I did arrive, I was completely in the dark as to what was expected of me. It was a foregone conclusion that I would handle the nominating petition drive, but no one had told me who would be the campaign manager. Everyone assumed I knew all about the campaign plans. Mennen and two young aides met me at the airport. He was late for an appointment. All he said was that there would be meaningful work for me to do, then he left me with a driver to take me to my hotel.

When I came into the campaign office, I felt like an outsider for the first time in my life. Eddie McGloin, a former Detroit schoolteacher, was the campaign manager, I learned. Eddie made me feel welcome and, as I had suspected, asked me to handle the petition drive. Mennen had been gone from the state since early 1961. There was a whole new group of voters and party officers. It was a strange feeling to have to sell people on the idea of circulating Mennen's petitions. It took more telephone calls and letters than ever before to find the right people to circulate the petitions.

Mennen's opponent in the primary was Jerome P. Cavanagh, the mayor of Detroit. I first heard of Jerry Cavanagh when he was administrative assistant to the State Fair manager Mennen had had to fire many years before. Jerry was a very good-looking man in his thirties. He had a pleasing personality and a winning smile. My personal feeling is that he could have won if he had just campaigned hard. Instead, he spent all his time belittling Mennen.

Although he was a young man, Jerry was backed in his Senate race by the old Wayne County group, the building trades and the old guard who had fought Mennen since 1948. In addition, the Teamsters were quietly helping Cavanagh. The return of the old rivalries made me all the more determined Mennen should win. The group supporting the mayor was against the open party philosophy and most of the programs Mennen and the rest of us had worked so hard to establish for the people of Michigan.

In trying to develop a strategy to combat Jerry Cavanagh's attacks on Mennen, we sorely missed the talents of Paul Weber and John Murray. John had recently begun teaching journalism at Michigan State University. They were lucky to have him; he was to spend twenty years there and would become a national expert on the media and government, especially media law. John was always so good at understanding the issues and helping Mennen communicate his ideas through speeches and television programs. Paul was still with Michigan Consolidated Gas Company. Officially, he had been Mennen's press secretary, but unofficially he was so much more than that. He had a thorough grasp of government, politics, and the media, and he shared Mennen's views and principles. Mennen trusted and relied on both Paul and John. So did the rest of us. If Paul and John had been with us in 1966, I'm sure they would have found a way for Mennen to ignore Cavanagh's insults and keep talking effectively about Michigan's needs.

Jim Robinson, a former newspaper reporter, was hired as Mennen's spokesman for the campaign. Despite his good reputation as a newsman, Jim fell short of our needs in representing Mennen. The fact that he wasn't a dedicated party man showed up often. Without any previous political experience, he often gave Mennen what I thought was the wrong advice. Mennen later felt that way, too, I am sure, based on his discus-

256

sions with me after the campaign. Jim was not as polished a writer as either Paul or John, and he had had no time to assimilate Mennen's style of expression.

Even the campaign office presented problems. The only headquarters the committee had been able to obtain were on the ground floor and two of the upper floors of the Tuller Hotel at Grand Circus Park in downtown Detroit. The hotel was closed, and the setting, at best, left much to be desired. We had to watch out the window to make sure our secretaries got into their cars safely. A number of prostitutes, male and female, seemed to surround us in ever increasing numbers. Even Mennen was accosted by a female prostitute in our lobby. Our protests to the police brought very little result. Personally, I felt sure the increase in the number of prostitutes was a campaign dirty trick. After the mayor lost the primary, they all seemed to disappear, which convinced me that their presence was no accident. Jim Robinson and I both took apartments in the old Leland Hotel nearby. Whenever possible, we walked back to the hotel together. It was a joke between us as to who was protecting whom.

After the petitions were filed, everyone was much too busy to give me any particular assignment, so I filled in wherever I could. It was hard to see so many things that should be done and not be able to go ahead and do them. Eddie was happy to accept most of my suggestions, when he found time to talk to me. Often, however, he wasn't able to follow through with them. Conscious of my uncertain position, I didn't push as hard as I might have for fear of intruding upon Eddie's authority.

Mennen was working harder than ever before, and I seldom saw him. Once he came through my office and asked if I would like to attend a campaign meeting. He asked me just at the moment when I was embroiled in something I didn't feel I could leave right then, so I said no. Mennen didn't wait for me to explain why I felt that way. He must have thought I wasn't interested or was pouting. At any rate, I was never again asked to go to any of the planning sessions for the primary campaign. That was why the talk of my becoming the campaign manager for the fall election was such a shock to me.

Reports from the field gave everyone in the office a feeling that in spite of Cavanagh's nasty campaign, we were going to win the primary. Mennen did win, by a good margin—381,496 to 258,822. Everyone was exhausted when it was over.

Sid Woolner gave me the first inkling that the State Central Committee was contemplating changes in campaign personnel for the fall election. They were seriously considering making Eddie McGloin the overall coordinator for all Democratic state campaigns, the position Sid had ably filled for so many years. Eddie's pleasant personality, they said, would be the answer to the problems being created by Zolton Ferency, our candidate for governor. Zolton had no Democratic primary opponent, but he was not a team player. Because of his witty, one-line comments, he was the darling of the press. Unfortunately, many of those sharp cracks were aimed at his Democratic teammates. Whatever the reason, Zolton showed not the slightest intention of working with Mennen as a team.

"Who is going to run Mennen's campaign?" I asked Sid. "They're talking about you," he replied. "I just can't do it," I told him. "Neil's campaign in 1964 was a complete failure. That taught me that I had been out of the state too long while too many changes had taken place. They won't ask me. They haven't said a word about it to me anyway." Sid was greatly concerned about my accepting the job. While he didn't tell me not to do it, he warned me that, if Mennen were defeated, I would be held entirely responsible.

Since I hadn't gone to any of the campaign meetings, I didn't know what had been decided. I found out they wanted me as campaign manager when Mennen said to me gravely one day, "When you take over as campaign manager, I want you to do. . . ." What it was he wanted me to do, I will never remember. I was too stunned to hear it, much less answer him. Everything in me warned that I shouldn't do it, but after all my years of work and devotion to Mennen, I didn't see how I could turn him down.

Mennen invited me to send him, confidentially, a plan for the general election and said he welcomed my ideas. My written response included several suggestions, an organizational chart, and my usual plea for his ear whenever I needed it. His answer was very supportive, and he gently apologized for any estrangement I may have felt:

> You can be sure that I am delighted that you are taking over as campaign manager and that I have every confidence that you will do a good job. You may be sure that I am pleased to hear from you and that you want to give me your impressions, good or bad. I regret you felt any reluctance in the primary campaign, but when I tried to include you in some of the sessions, I gathered that it was your wish not to be included and so I respected it. But, in any event, as far as the future goes, I will be hearing from you fully now at all times. You can be very sure that I look forward to your conducting the campaign and backing you up. You may be sure that I will look to you to go ahead and make the necessary decisions and also to your carrying out the decisions which I will be making.

Mennen's letter answered many questions that I had in my heart, and I felt greatly relieved. We were going into the fall campaign with the same mutual understanding without words that we had had for so many years.

34

THE 1966 CAMPAIGN
LOYALTY AND TEAMWORK ABOVE ALL

URING THE PRIMARY, all of us had worked as never before. Jerry Cavanagh had implied that Mennen was a tired old warhorse, uninformed and behind the times. He had challenged Mennen to speak out on everything he could think of. Mennen had a broad understanding of national and foreign issues from his recent work with the State Department, from his early days as a young lawyer with the federal government, and from the inquisitiveness of his own active mind. Still, Cavanagh's tactics forced us to put more issues and complex statements into Mennen's speeches and campaign material than anyone could adequately cover. It was more than the public could be expected to absorb.

This was no campaign for a sick man. And Mennen was a very sick man. How he had gotten through the last few weeks of the primary no one will ever know. He had several violent attacks from kidney stones that would have devastated most men. Right after the primary, he was taken to the hospital and had an operation to remove the kidney stones. The fight to continue the campaign had taken a great deal out of him. The chances of his being able to campaign at all in the final election looked very slim, indeed.

How do you run a campaign with the candidate desperately ill and in the hospital? How do you combat the rumors that the opposition is spreading all over the state that your candidate has cancer and will die in office like Senator McNamara? You cannot tell people that he doesn't have cancer because, you hope, they may not have heard the rumor. You can only issue reports that the candidate is rapidly recovering from his

259

operation for kidney stones and suggest that he will be on the campaign trail before long.

Our campaign staff was very small. Only one person besides me, Ed Winge, had ever been through an entire campaign before. Early on, there was an article in the *Detroit News* in which Jim Robinson said that Paul Weber and Sid Woolner, among others, were sorely missed. "There are a lot of green hands around here," Jim had told Glenn Engle, the reporter. "This is essentially an amateur staff." Glenn singled me out as an exception in the ranks of novices, but that didn't make me feel any better. As for Mennen, he was too ill to talk about anything. So I squared my shoulders and said to myself: "Berthelot, you've got to do it. So get busy and quit worrying about what you can't do. Just do what needs to be done."

Mennen's opponent in the general election was Robert Griffin, who had been a member of Congress for ten years and who was strongly supported, for once, by the entire Republican party. Funds for anything he needed or wanted came in ample supply from wealthy Republicans. Every possible effort was made by the Republican party to see that one of their own was elected. After Phil Hart's election in 1958 and until Pat McNamara's death in 1966, Michigan had two Democratic senators for the first time in more than a century.[1]

Griffin had been appointed to the Senate by Governor George Romney after Pat's death that spring. Griffin made good use of the fact that he was the incumbent. He pointed out that he had a decade of experience as a congressman. He questioned why the voters should replace him with a man who had no legislative experience. Being a senator brought him large contributions from the big business lobbyists—to say nothing of the franking privileges that allowed him to send material to the voters under the guise of keeping his constituents informed on the issues.

Griffin was a seasoned campaigner and took full advantage of the fact that the Democratic candidates for governor and senator did not seem to be in full accord. He didn't have to mention it himself, but his people and many of the Republicans around the state kept the rumor alive that Mennen had cancer. They let that whispering campaign continue through election day.

It was most unfortunate that Mennen's doctor and the hospital where he underwent surgery were both known for cancer treatment. This gave credence to the story that Mennen had cancer. There was no way to destroy that rumor. He spent about two weeks in the hospital and then went home to recuperate. While Mennen was in the hospital, Jim Robinson seldom showed up in our office except to put out short releases on Mennen's recovery. He spent most of his time with his newspaper buddies and brought back to us the latest negative rumors.

Meanwhile, the Democratic candidate for governor was making

cracks that only helped the opposition. Zolton Ferency, though a brilliant man, seemed happiest when stirring up dissension. This was true of his entire political career. It did great harm in the 1966 campaign. He was in an uphill battle against the popular George Romney. Romney was brash and quotable, but Zolton outdid him in the area of remarks that caught people's attention. Zolton's quips made good copy. One of the nasty cracks attributed to him was repeated with glee by the Republicans. The gist of it was: "The only new thing to come out of Soapy Williams in years was a kidney stone."

Zolton was clever. In his speeches and statements to the media, he was careful not to contradict Mennen's record or criticize his accomplishments. He did leave the impression, however, that he, Zolton, could do much better as governor. When asked if Mennen would be able to campaign at all, Zolton raised his eyebrows and said something like: "Yes, of course. His campaign committee assures us that he will." Subtly, he gave the impression that we were indulging in wishful thinking. He made it his business never to appear on the same platform as the people who were representing Mennen—or Mennen himself, when he was finally able to campaign.

How do you run a party-coordinated campaign when the candidate for governor will not cooperate? My decision was to try my best to get Democrats in the various counties to work for all the candidates, from the top of the ticket to the bottom. Someone else, someone who did not have "coordinated campaigns" in her very lifeblood, probably would have broken away from Zolton and run a campaign strictly for Mennen. All the years that Mennen had run for office, he had drilled into our heads and hearts that teamwork was the key to success. We almost wearied of hearing him say that the Democratic umbrella was big enough to cover everyone, he said it so often.

No one could tell me any differently. "Make it Emphatic—Vote Straight Democratic" was more than a campaign slogan, though it was a familiar one in the 1950s. It was a way to identify candidates with a program for the state. It was a way to win elections. As governor, Mennen had insisted on cooperation with all the candidates, even though some of them were not of his choosing. Could I have him change now and say "Just work for me alone"? Of course not, and so I may have been one of the major factors in his defeat. If so, the responsibility is mine, and I just have to live with it.

Things were so bad that some of the staff actually proposed going off on our own for Mennen alone. With tears in my eyes, I told them: "We can't do that. It's against everything Mennen has stood for in building the party all these years. He can't change now because it affects him adversely." Then I added, "And I would not have much respect for him if he did."

261

Without Paul or John to help, I found myself having to worry about the media and about how Mennen was being perceived by the public. Never before had I had to handle that responsibility, and I didn't cope very well with it. Always before, I would tell Paul or John what problems were bothering us and they would come up with something that took the wind out of the sails of the opposition—as Paul had done with the criticism of Mennen's shoes. In addition, it seemed impossible to write speeches on new subjects. It had all been said in the primary. Without the candidate to at least reiterate the ideas in a new setting, the words fell flat.

We couldn't even do much campaigning with the nationality and ethnic groups who had helped us so much in previous elections. It had to be either Nancy or Mennen who attended their functions. We had always done it that way because personal attention was so important to those groups. This year, however, Mennen was home ill and Nancy was caring for him.

Even though things were discouraging, the three men in the campaign office—Mennen and Nancy's son Gery Williams, Ed Winge, and Paul Donahue—never showed it. They tried to fight the ugly rumors by being truthful and upbeat. They worked closely with the people who had urged Mennen to run. The conversations that Gery, Ed, and Paul had with these people gave us all new hope. Many of them assured us they were working hard to debunk the untruths the Republicans were spreading. They also told us they were doing their best to educate the younger generation who did not remember Mennen's years as governor. They said they were recounting over and over all that Mennen had done for Michigan and were enjoying the chance to make new friends for him.

We wrote to all the party officers at least twice a week, giving them the encouraging news that Mennen was recovering. Finally, we were able to say for sure that "the boss" was getting well enough to plan a few campaign meetings, especially the extremely important Wayne County district days that had helped so much in Mennen's elections for governor. Everyone knew how valuable it was to get out a big vote in Wayne County.

In the campaign office, we tried to tell each other any good news we heard from the field each day. While Mennen was recovering at home, the telephone was close to his side. It taxed my memory each day to give him favorable stories we were hearing. However, there were many calls to the office wishing him godspeed in recovery that I could tell him about.

One suggestion from Mennen made me feel sad because I couldn't do it, and I couldn't tell him why. He wanted me to reactivate my young lawyers committee that had been so successful in past campaigns. There was no way I was going to tell a sick man that, outside of a few faithful

262

friends, the young lawyers had been so dedicated because they had hopes of someday being appointed judges. In the senatorial campaign, he had virtually nothing in the way of jobs to offer them. There was no denying it. The number of lawyer volunteers had doubled after one of them, Vic Baum, had been appointed to the bench. True, the young lawyers made many sacrifices to work for Mennen, but it was a two-way street.

Everything seemed to be ganging up on Mennen. It was almost as if he had not been the much-loved governor of Michigan for twelve years. Among the few bright spots in the whole dismal campaign were messages of hope from Paul Weber, whose office was just down the street. Mary Margetts, Paul's secretary, was a good friend who also had worked for Paul in the governor's office. One day, Mary called on the phone and told me to go to my office window and wave a newspaper. When I did, still holding the phone, she told me where to look. There was Paul, waving a newspaper back to me from his office. He got on the phone and told me if I was in serious trouble to fly the flag upside down, and he would rush over. That would be great, I said, but it wouldn't do much good unless he could stay.

During those dark days, Adelaide Hart, still the Democratic state vice chairman, was upstairs in the general campaign office, valiantly trying to do the same thing I was—hold the party together and keep the campaign on an even keel.

But the results were as we all feared, a defeat for both the gubernatorial and senatorial candidates. George Romney and William Milliken beat Zolton Ferency and his running mate, John Bruff of Macomb County, with sixty-one percent of the vote. Mennen did much better but still lost to Griffin. Mennen had 1,069,484 votes to 1,363,530 for Griffin. Frank Kelley and Jim Hare won reelection, this time to four-year terms because of the new constitution.

Most of the Wayne County Democratic congressional delegation pulled through. However, a Republican named Marvin Esch defeated Weston Vivian in the 2nd Congressional District. They were both from Ann Arbor and had academic backgrounds. In the 19th Congressional District, Billie Farnum, who, like Wes Vivian, had been elected in the Johnson landslide of 1964, lost to Jack H. McDonald. McDonald was a former Redford Township official, a member of the old Wayne County Board of Supervisors, and a big Romney supporter.

Michigan Democrats were not alone. This election was particularly hard on Democrats across the country because it followed LBJ's landslide victory in 1964. My face must have been very forlorn at the end of election night. After starting out the door, Mennen Williams looked back and saw me. In spite of his own disappointment, he came back to kiss me gently on the forehead.

After I got back to D. C. I got a sad letter from Mennen. He thanked me sincerely and told me he was sure that, in any other year, we would have won. He complimented me on what we had done, and indicated he understood what a trying time it had been:

Dear Buffy:

.... It was just short of miraculous what was turned out of our office. I wish somebody had a log on it that I could read someday. Throughout the campaign I was constantly being surprised by some special program which I had not heard of, but which I was delighted to learn of. I know there were many, many such things that a candidate just couldn't keep up with, but which on learning, warmed the heart. I know that many of these projects came from your initiative and experience and probably most of them benefited from your guidance. . . . I am sure our efforts would have fallen apart many times, had you not been there to hold us together.

Mennen said maybe he would feel better if I sent him one of my two-finger-typed letters.

What could I say but tell him how I had felt about the campaign and that, in spite of everything, we could be proud to have stuck by our principles. Also, I assured him that I was convinced the Good Lord had a reason for his defeat and that He had work for Mennen to do. It was now up to Mennen, I said, to find out what it would be, but I had a few ideas for him to consider. The defeat of so many good Democrats in the 1966 election had convinced me that we needed to motivate young people to become involved in politics. By accepting invitations to speak to students in the schools, Mennen could inspire the younger generation as he had inspired us, I told him. First, however, he needed to recover completely and get his energy back, I said.[2] What I didn't tell him was that many of his friends believed that defeat saved his life, because he was still very ill.

Sadly, I went back to CWA and my old job. Instead of offering sympathy and much-needed understanding, my new boss—the one who had arrived just before I left—greeted me with the words: "So you're back. I had hoped you would be in the senator's office by now." It was not a happy beginning for either of us.

He had been given the assignment to work in our legislative department despite his protests. He didn't know what to do with me, since I had been allowed to define my own job by working in any legislative field where I thought the CWA could benefit. He seemed uncomfortable with that, but he had no idea what to tell me to do. The best he could do was to direct me to get specific information from the Federal Communications Commission or other government agencies when it was needed, and to work on current legislation. In spite of the lack of direction I received from CWA, I concentrated on issues that were to stand me in good stead in my next campaign.

NOTES

1. Bald, *Michigan in Four Centuries*, p. 484.

2. A copy of this letter, in which Helen Berthelot writes about the importance of political parties in developing American public policy, is among her papers in the Michigan Historical Collections, Bentley Historical Library, University of Michigan, Ann Arbor.

35

HUBERT
HORATIO HUMPHREY
FOR PRESIDENT

PRESIDENT LYNDON JOHNSON stunned the nation on March 31, 1968, by announcing that he would not run for reelection. Johnson had no sooner made his announcement than Vice President Hubert Humphrey's office was flooded with calls, telegrams, and letters urging him to run. It was a big decision to make. There already were three candidates in the race, and they all had well-organized campaigns. Vice President Humphrey was well-respected for his stands on human rights issues, but it was going to be a tough fight because of all the tumult over the Vietnam War. Entering the campaign would mean big sacrifices for him and his family. He debated every angle and consulted with a wide variety of possible supporters. Even Wall Street was enthusiastic and hinted at generous financial assistance. "Anyone but Bobby Kennedy," was the rumor. After intensive research, Hubert Humphrey made up his mind to run.

The campaign was ill-starred from the first. On the night he made his decision, he attended the annual Democratic National Committee fund-raising dinner. The vice president had said nothing yet about his plans. Not a single speech had been made before the word was flashed to the crowd that the Rev. Martin Luther King, Jr., had been assassinated in Memphis. After a moment of silence and a prayer, the group disbanded. For the next few weeks the country was torn by civil unrest and political turmoil. Finally, on April 27, four weeks after the president's announcement, a big group of Humphrey's loyal supporters organized a rally to hear the vice president make his plans known, and the campaign began. A few weeks later, in early June, came another blow. Hubert Humphrey had been invited to be the keynote speaker at the Communications Workers of America anniversary dinner in Washington. (Planning that dinner had been entirely my responsibility.) The CWA was to endorse the vice president's candidacy immediately following his speech. Two days before the dinner, Robert Kennedy was assassinated in Los Angeles after he had won the California primary. The vice president, of course, would not make his speech. He and Muriel, his wife, came to the dinner and were introduced as honored guests, with no fanfare and no speeches.

It wasn't long after that dinner that Joe Beirne called me into his office. He said that Bill Welsh, my old friend from the Democratic National Committee, had asked if CWA would let me go to work in the Humphrey campaign. They needed someone to run their correspondence section. Bill was the vice president's administrative assistant and was to be a major player in the Humphrey campaign for president. He was a close friend of mine and had dragged me into many projects from the days when I first started to work in D. C. and he was research director for the Democratic National Committee. This time he hadn't even asked me first. When I chided him for asking Joe Beirne for my release without giving me a chance to say anything about it, he just laughed and said he knew very well I would work for Senator Humphrey in any capacity. "Isn't that so?" he charged. It was.

The following week, temporarily relieved of my CWA duties, I found myself in the Executive Office Building of the White House, in the correspondence section of the vice president's office. The young woman in charge gave me samples of the responses they had been sending to people who had written to Vice President Humphrey. To say that I was appalled would be putting it mildly. They were routine answers without any depth or warmth.

I worked for a week without answering any letters—just getting the feel of the mail coming in and the replies going out. The next week, Bill took me to the vice president's office in the Capitol and introduced me to Edna Ravenholt, Humphrey's office manager. He told Edna I would be running the campaign correspondence section. She had evidently been well briefed about me and what I was going to do. It could have caused real trouble for a stranger to be introduced as the person who would be overseeing a crucial part of your office operation. She welcomed me warmly, however, and I soon found out that Edna trusted Bill Welsh's judgment as much as I did. He soon left us alone to examine their new machine marvel. An early version of computerized letter writing had just been perfected for the electric typewriter. It was ideal for handling the dozens and dozens of letters, questions, and complaints received every day.

It was amazing to me how many letters came in that could be answered with variations of the same response. By composing numerous paragraphs that answered the questions of the day and then directing the machine operator to assemble the paragraphs in varying sequences, we could put together letter after letter that seemed to be individually dictated.

The staff was as wondrous as the equipment. Edna Ravenholt was one of the most capable office managers I ever encountered in the Capitol. She brooked no nonsense, but she had such a warm personality no one resented her. Jack Limpert, who wrote the paragraphs we needed, was an exceptional writer, and in fact later became editor of the prestigious *Washingtonian* magazine. When I needed new paragraphs, I would take in a few sample letters and tell him what kind of answer I felt was needed. At first, Edna and I made the decisions, but soon she left it up to Jack and me. He would think for a minute, then in one or two sentences would have just the answer I needed.

All new paragraphs went to Bill Welsh with a summary of the questions to be answered. Sometimes I would have to goad him into giving us the go-ahead. "Do you want me to get the vice president's letters answered?" I would ask. He would laugh, stop what he was doing, and I would get my okay. In later years, Bill said our section of the campaign was run the most efficiently of all.

Cooperation made such efficiency possible, because it was fast turning out to be a difficult job. Louise Green, an old friend of mine on the staff who had been out ill, came back and began to handle legislative subjects. The political mail was my responsibility. Another person handled the volumes of children's mail. As the campaign progressed, more and more teachers assigned their students to write the vice president about innumerable subjects.

One of the other people handling the mail was a rather brash young man. It was his job to open the mail, date it, and sort it. Then he would pull out the official vice presidential mail and send it to the proper department. When I first started in the office, this young man took it upon himself to brief me on how to handle the mail. He was most condescending, and I got a big kick out of how quickly he went back to his own work when Edna came in. Louise later told me about her conversation with him shortly after she arrived back at work. She said he told her that "some older woman who did not know anything about handling the vice president's mail" had started working in the office. With a sniff, he told her, " 'She's going to handle the political mail.' " Louise asked who it was. When he gave her my name, she said, " 'Not *the* Helen Berthelot!' " She laughed as she told me how she really laid it on about how fortunate they were to have me. That did it. From then on I got real help, not unsolicited advice, from him.

The mail was a good barometer of what was happening in the campaign; I knew that from my days in Michigan. Before the convention, much of the mail came from various supporters of Eugene McCarthy, Robert Kennedy, and George Wallace. It was often vicious and never friendly. Along with every charge imaginable, they all had one theme: Get out, we don't want you. Humphrey's answer to these people by way of our staff and Bill Welsh was kindness itself. We were never allowed to say one sharp word. Humphrey finally did allow us to hit back at the Wallace people, but even then it was mildly written. Gene McCarthy was his friend, he would say to us. With friends like that, who needed enemies, I would think to myself. How I wished I could answer some of the letters the way I really wanted to. The Humphrey supporters never seemed to write, but I comforted myself with the hope that they were too busy campaigning for him. When, once in a while, I got a friendly letter, it made my day.

The number of adverse letters received in our office increased after the national convention in Chicago. Never have I been so angry at news coverage as I was at the 1968 convention. The violence was not as prevalent as the media suggested. And after I saw a television cameraman urging a group of young people to throw unmentionable objects so that he could take pictures, I found it hard to believe such televised scenes again. It also irked me that sons of some prominent Republicans were spotted by our Michigan delegates running around with aerosol cans that I imagine contained something stronger than hair spray.

Inside the convention, the coverage focused on all the arguments that were to be expected in a year like this. Any and all sharp altercations were shown over and over again on television. No one bothered to explain the end results of that process. In spite of all the commotion, the platform hammered out at the convention was a credit to the Democratic party and held much promise for the American people.[1]

We in the correspondence section were upset before the convention, but the mail we got afterward was devastating. Thanks to the news media, disillusioned Democrats wrote by the hundreds that they would never vote for the Democratic party again. Hubert Humphrey was to blame for it all.

We killed them all with kindness. We patiently explained that Humphrey was the candidate and not responsible for what happened on the convention floor. Nor was he to blame for what people thought went on in Chicago, based on what they saw over and over on television. Each letter we sent contained a résumé of the platform that had been voted on at the convention. Every night, as hard as we worked, we went home with some correspondence still unanswered, heartsick at the injustice of the letters being written to Humphrey.

Humphrey's loyalty to Johnson was a millstone around his neck. Finally we in the correspondence section could stand it no longer. We met and agreed to write him a letter which we all would sign. We had added a retired minister and several assistants to our crew by this time. Jack Limpert wrote our letter, quoting from some letters I had selected to give Humphrey an idea what people were saying and feeling. We signed it in alphabetical order. Edna was able to get our letter directly into Humphrey's hands. His staff was too protective of him, we felt. Humphrey quickly sent the letter back. His reaction was scrawled across the top: "My God, I knew it was bad, but I had no idea it was this bad."

From that time on, without actually being disloyal to Johnson, Humphrey voiced more of his own beliefs and programs. Humphrey, who had been so loyal to his president, to his colleagues, and to the people wherever he was needed, got little or no actual support from them.

After our letter to him, Humphrey made an excellent speech about Vietnam on network television. The telegrams in response to this speech were the most encouraging we had received. By the grapevine, I heard an interesting story about Senator Ted Kennedy, who wanted to hear the vice president's speech but had lost the card telling him where he could go to hear it. That evening the senator was at the Kennedy Center for the Performing Arts in Washington. The offices were all vacant, but he found some cleaning women who also wanted to hear the speech. One of them knew where there was a television set, and so Senator Kennedy and about thirty cleaning women listened to the speech together. He later told someone he had great difficulty hearing because the women made so many loud comments. Just one little interlude in the life of a senator when his staff has left for home.

It was not a pleasant campaign for loyal Democrats. Honestly, I believe Gene McCarthy still would be teaching college in St. Paul if it had not been for Senator Humphrey and Governor Orville Freeman. With their strong help and encouragement, he had been elected first to the U. S. House and then to the Senate. He showed his gratitude by being the only defeated candidate for the Democratic nomination for president who refused to come to the platform to congratulate Humphrey and have his picture taken with the group when Humphrey won the nomination.

That was not the most unforgivable thing he did. During his campaign, he had attracted hundreds of young, idealistic, volunteer workers who were devoted to him. They had slaved for him for months, often under hardship conditions. Some paid their own expenses to go to New Hampshire and work on the primary there. When he was defeated, he completely ignored them. You could see them everywhere at the convention, weeping their hearts out, not only at their idol's defeat, but more because he didn't care enough about them to even gather them together and thank them for their wonderful contributions to his campaign. We will never know how many talented young Democrats were lost to us forever because of his selfish and careless attitude.

About six weeks before the election, someone must have turned the lights on in Democratic households across America. After weeks of reading letters that tore us apart, all at once we were hearing from people who began to realize what was at stake. Old people, especially, pleaded "What will happen to us if you lose?" The letters coming into our office were almost unanimous in their support. They were harder for us to answer than the critical ones we had received for so many weeks.

We never solicited money in our department, but in one week late in the campaign, we took in $10,000 in small contributions. It all came too late. The labor movement had withdrawn financial support when it was needed the most. The labor leaders had given up on the idea that Humphrey could win. At the same time, Humphrey was risking his life flying around in the only plane—a rickety one—the campaign could afford.

When the votes were counted, Humphrey had lost to Nixon, with 42.9 percent for Humphrey, 43.5 percent for Nixon, and about 13 percent for Wallace. It was then that the hardest part of my work began. Letters of support and regret came in by the thousands from all over the world. We hardly had room to work in our office. They all had the same basic message: that Humphrey was a wonderful man, and his loss was devastating. Where were these people on election day? I wondered. We never even tried to answer all of them. For ten days three of us did nothing but open the letters, staple them to their envelopes, and stamp the date received.

In light of Humphrey's later contributions in the Senate and his devastating illness—he was diagnosed with cancer a few years later—I now feel that, for his sake at least, it might have been best that he was defeated. He was reelected twice more to the Senate and was able to remain his own man to the end, which came in 1978.

Election night, those of us who wanted to go were flown to Minneapolis. When the results were conclusive and Hubert had to make his concession speech, I stood behind the platform and was touched to see that Muriel, his wife, had her arm around him and was gently patting him all the time he spoke.

After we had cleaned up all the campaign debris, Hubert and Muriel had a nice party for his D. C. staff. When he got to me to shake my hand, I couldn't say a word. He didn't either. Just as Mennen Williams had done when he lost in 1966, Hubert Humphrey leaned over and gently kissed me on the forehead before he went on to the next person.

271

NOTES

1. A complete text of the 1968 national Democratic party platform is found in *National Party Platforms, Vol. II, 1960–1976*, 6th rev. ed., compiled by Donald Bruce Johnson and Kirk H. Porter (Urbana: University of Illinois Press, 1978), pp. 718–43.

36

THE 1972
DEMOCRATIC NATIONAL
CONVENTION

I T WAS EARLY IN 1972, and the presidential candidates were beginning their campaigns. Since I had retired from the CWA in 1969, I
had more time to spend—though certainly not as much money—
when election time rolled around. Because of a chance meeting with my
friend Don Nichol, I began working as a volunteer in Ed Muskie's presidential campaign. Don had been his administrative assistant and was
now his campaign manager. Edmund Muskie was a fine senator, and I
had always respected his work.

One day I had lunch with Edna Ravenholt, from Humphrey's 1968
presidential campaign. She told me that the Muskie people were asking
all over who had handled Humphrey's political correspondence in his
campaign. Edna said, "They'll be looking for you." That afternoon I took
something in to be okayed by one of the Muskie people. A man I didn't
know was with the Muskie person. She introduced me to him, and his
eyes lighted up. "You're Helen Berthelot?" he inquired. "And you are
over here already, working for Senator Muskie?" Laughing, I replied,
"Yes, were you looking for me?" He said that he was and that he wanted
to have a serious conversation with me when he had time.

When we finally did get together, we didn't talk for very long. One
of the first things he asked me was "What would you do if Hubert
Humphrey ran again?" "I would go back and work for him, of course,"
was my answer. That ended that, and I was never asked to work on Senator Muskie's correspondence.

What the Muskie people never knew was that I really set up their whole procedure. The person they picked to handle the correspondence section was a close friend of mine. She asked me to help her, so I worked out her schedule and showed her how to organize the work, using my knowledge of the problems we had solved in Humphrey's 1968 campaign. We never told a soul that I had done it.

The Muskie campaign had an unknown saboteur. It was the same man, I am sure, who later, in 1976, stole Jimmy Carter's briefing book and caused much embarrassment to the candidate. In 1972 he must have had a responsible position in Senator Muskie's campaign and was able to do a great deal of damage. All sorts of queer things happened. The pilot of the campaign plane, for instance, was given an incorrect schedule and took the candidate to the wrong city.

Whatever else the troublemaker was able to do I don't know, but Don Nichol, the campaign manager, was blamed for all the mishaps. He and Senator Muskie came to a parting of the ways. Don had been executive secretary of the Maine Democratic party and had contributed greatly to the national party through the Paul Butler committee chaired by Neil Staebler. The Democratic party lost a valuable man when they lost Don Nichol. He never worked in politics again. Don was deeply hurt, I am sure, that Senator Muskie didn't trust him enough to find out who was really responsible.

The culprit was almost certainly a paid agent for the Republican party. After the McGovern campaign picked up steam, the same man showed up there with a book George McGovern had written and asked to have it autographed. He wasn't able to get into the inner circle, however, and left.

By Easter, it was obvious that Humphrey was not going to run again, so I went to Florida for a vacation. Every year for the previous dozen years, I had spent two or three weeks at Easter time at the Riviera Motel on Longboat Key. It was a delightful place—the same people from all over the country kept coming back at the same time, too.

While I was enjoying the Florida shores, I got word that Dick Murphy had been named manager of the Democratic National Convention. Dick had been a friend since I first met him in D. C. in 1953, when he was executive secretary of the Young Democrats. We had worked well together on many projects, so I wrote him right away and told him I was available. Dick called me in Florida and said, yes, he wanted me, and how soon could I come?

Ten days later, I had wound up my vacation, gone back to D. C. to pack, and arrived in Miami Beach, ready to work. Dick had me check into the Fontainebleau Towers, where the convention staff and offices would be housed for the next few months. It was a good thing I didn't know it then, but I was the only person on the entire floor at the time.

The housekeeper spoke to me on the elevator a few days later. "Oh," she said, "you're the lady who is staying all alone on this floor. Aren't you nervous?" Until she asked, I wasn't. And I hadn't even noticed how deserted it had been. My room was delightful, on an upper floor, with a beautiful view of the ocean on one side and Biscayne Bay on the other.

Dick had said on the phone that he wanted me to handle the convention workshops. When I got to Miami, he never even mentioned workshops, but put me to work helping him set up the rooms for convention committees. It was a daily jigsaw puzzle to assign working space for the various committees. Dick kept getting new orders from D. C. that required changing the offices all around. My CWA friends who installed the telephone systems began greeting me every morning with "Well, boss, what have you done to us now?"

Those workers were efficient and friendly despite all the confusion. Phone installation had been a pleasure—until the day I had to get Larry O'Brien's office set up. It was my first Sunday there, and I had been looking longingly at the lovely swimming pool. With no one around and no work to do, I would spend the day at the pool and give my new bathing suit a workout, I thought gleefully. My suit got a workout all right, but I spent the day in the hotel lobby and in the manager's office.

It had seemed simple enough. All I had to do was get the key to Larry's suite in time to have the phones installed before Larry, the Democratic national chairman, checked in at 6:00 P.M.

Checkout time was 10:00 A.M., so the previous occupants should have left the suite by then. On my way to the pool, I stopped at the hotel desk. "May I have the keys to Mr. O'Brien's suite?" I blithely asked the grumpy man at the front desk. "The people aren't out yet," he growled and walked away. At noon, the telephone men knocked on the door to see what was going on and reported back to me. They said a man and a woman were eating a leisurely lunch and two young people were playing pool in the two-story suite.

It was time to find the person in charge, the assistant manager. "Mr. O'Brien's suite was supposed to be available at ten o'clock this morning," I said. "The telephone men have to install the telephone system. It is very complicated, and they will have a hard time finishing it now before Mr. O'Brien gets here." The assistant manager was sympathetic, but he explained that the man in the suite was the head of a national insurance group which had just finished a convention there, and he didn't want to offend him. The assistant manager would do what he could. Hours later, when I found him again, he still had not been able to get them to leave. The telephone men reported that the insurance man was taking a nap.

Begging, pleading, cajoling—nothing worked with the hotel management. Finally, I got a temporary suite for Larry and went with his secretary to pick him up at the airport. Larry greeted me warmly, but saw I was concerned. Reluctantly, I explained. Larry was kind but upset. When he picked up a stack of phone messages at the desk, he was even more frustrated.

At 10:00 P.M., Larry's assistant called the hotel sales manager at home. The man hurried over and went into the suite, where he found the two teenagers, still playing pool. "The man at the desk said we could stay here as long as we wanted," they said. That same desk clerk gave us trouble throughout the convention. More often than not, I was the one who had to deal with him.

A few days after that Sunday, Dick Murphy came into my office and announced, "I need an office manager for this convention, and you are it, Berthelot." He left the room before I could answer. From then on, I was given more and more responsibility. We had to get each office completely outfitted for the various committees on the day the chairmen were to arrive. That meant transforming hotel rooms into offices—with working telephone systems and desks and typewriters, but no beds and dressers—in time for the noon arrival of the plane from D. C. each day. Dick got me a young college assistant, Lynn Daniel, to take charge of setting up each committee suite. Jan Akerhielm, Larry's secretary, worked with me on assigning the offices and the space. It was a complicated arrangement that couldn't easily be changed once it was set up.

Almost all the committee suites were in place about the middle of June. When I went to get the key for Robert Strauss's eighteenth floor suite, the man at the front desk told me it was occupied by a permanent guest. He offered an identical suite one floor below. His attitude was: "Take it or leave it." Although the change would upset our arrangements, Jan Akerhielm and I decided we had no choice. We put Bob Strauss, the Democratic National Committee treasurer, on the seventeenth floor. The evening desk attendant was friendly and helpful, so that night I asked him who was in the eighteenth floor suite. He told me it was a "Mr. E. H. Hunt." A few days later, the suite was mysteriously available.

At the time, it didn't register with us because we were so pushed. Later, we put two and two together and realized with a chill that it had been the Nixon man, E. Howard Hunt, who was in the suite above Bob Strauss, undoubtedly ready to monitor all telephone calls and conversations in the rooms below. He disappeared from Florida immediately after the Watergate crew was arrested. Later I told the story to Daniel Schorr. He didn't believe that Hunt had been in the hotel, but after checking it out, learned I was right and broke that part of the Watergate story.

The Watergate break-in forewarned us. From the date of the break-in on June 17, 1972, the convention hall and all of our major convention offices were swept electronically every few days. Nothing was found in the offices, but signs of covert activity were turned up at the convention hall. Although there were none of the usual listening devices, some air conditioning pipes had been stuffed with cotton and crumpled paper. There were other indications of attempted sabotage, but our watchfulness prevented any trouble.

Management of the convention offices was now my responsibility. In the past, committees and staffs had operated independently and rather casually, buying what they required as they needed it. Dick agreed it made sense for me to handle it all through requisition forms. The staff from the national headquarters was told to report to me first thing.

One huge group came on a single plane and completely filled my office. It wasn't hard to see that they were hot, tired, and unhappy about their hotel accommodations. After greeting them warmly and telling them they were going to have fun, I turned serious and said, "You have to make a difficult decision right away." They looked apprehensive. "What now?" I knew they were thinking. "I can let you have either two paper clips and one rubber band, or two rubber bands and one paper clip. You will each have to decide which you want." That broke the ice. They all relaxed, and I assured them I was there to help if they needed it. One of the girls told me later that if I had not broken into a smile, they were all ready to go back to Washington.

During the convention itself, Dick wanted me to run the office under the podium. Since everyone who went to the podium came through my office, I had a chance to greet many old friends. An elderly guard wanted to know what I did in D. C. "Everyone seems so glad to see you," he said.

My convention week duties also included handling emergencies and assigning caucus rooms to the delegations. Several days before the convention opened, I returned to my hotel office after a brief inspection of the meeting rooms. Jim O'Hara and his staff were waiting for me. Jim was a Michigan congressman and a committee chairman. "What are you trying to do to me?" Jim said laughing. He explained that he had checked into his suite and found Harriet Cipriani, vice chairman of the Democratic National Committee, "not quite dressed." Jan Akerhielm and I had made a change in room assignments late the night before but had failed to log it with the hotel. We were able to take care of it easily, but Jim lost a little faith in my efficiency. Lucky for me that he was easygoing and that Harriet didn't rattle easily.

When I goof, I pick only important people. The only other bad error I made—that I know of—caused some inconvenience for Joseph A. Califano, Jr., another committee chairman. He had asked us to leave a bed in one room of his suite so he could sleep there. All I had to do was pass the word to Lynn, the young man who was assisting me, to leave a bed in one room for Joe Califano. Unfortunately, I forgot to tell Lynn to do it. It was late in the day before Joe's secretary alerted me to the problem. She had been calling the front desk. My nemesis was on duty, and nothing had been done. Joe needed some sleep. The overworked maintenance staff had been sent home for the night. Luckily, the desk clerks changed shifts, and the friendly clerk bailed me out with a temporary suite. Joe, who later became secretary of health, education, and welfare under President Jimmy Carter, had a good sense of humor. Every time I ran into him, he would look at me and mutter, "No beds in my room."

My days at Miami Beach were long and difficult, but everything I had learned during Michigan campaigns and with the CWA made the problems easier to handle. Dorothy Bush, the secretary of the DNC, often gave me a respite. Several times a week she would call and say, "Your lunch is ready." If I could manage it, I would drop everything and go down the hall to her office. John Bush, her husband, would have concocted lunch in their apartment and brought it down. Our favorite was hot dogs he had doctored up. She would close her door and shut off the telephone calls, and we would steal fifteen or twenty minutes to eat and talk.

Dorothy was one of the best known and loved of all the DNC members. She was a beautiful Southerner, from Mississippi, and was first elected to the national committee in 1944 at the age of twenty-seven. She was the first woman and the youngest person ever elected at the time, and she remained on the committee more than forty years. Delegates from all over the country went to her with their political problems. During those lunchtime sessions, we came up with solutions to many of them.

Many other officers and committee chairmen were old friends. It was good to see them, and I got a kick out of taking care of the emergencies they were always encountering. My old friend Sid Woolner, who was then Phil Hart's administrative assistant in the Senate, became my assistant for the convention. That was a switch—Sid working for me. In every other way, however, it was like old times.

One of my new friends was the man in charge of security. His main responsibility was the badges. Keeping the design secret until the day of the convention is one of the toughest security problems of a national political convention. Whole new sets of thousands of badges have had to be printed overnight because someone got hold of a badge and used it to print large numbers of phony ones. The color changed each day for added security. Guest badges were the biggest headaches. After much consultation, we put the security office next to mine. There was a bathroom between our offices, and we double-locked it on my side and kept the guest badges in the bathtub. No one pilfered them.

My worst emergency during the convention itself was at 9:00 P.M. the night the Kentucky Fried Chicken people had furnished box lunches to every delegate, with plenty for the staff, too. A guard appeared in my office. He said we had a big problem. "Coretta King and nine of her cohorts are at the door," he said. "They don't have any passes and also told us they had not had dinner because they heard that there was Kentucky Fried Chicken for everyone."

There had been passes reserved for Mrs. King and her group, but she hadn't received word where to pick them up. Sid Woolner jumped to the rescue. Phil Hart's box seats were just outside the door. Sid explained the problem, and Phil graciously gave up his box to Mrs. King and some of her staff. Sid somehow found seats for the rest. The chicken was long gone, but Sid went out and got sandwiches and goodies for them.

As office manager, I was also in charge of equipment that had been leased. At the end of the convention, I was proud that no typewriters or desk lamps were stolen from our offices. Every convention, they tell me, they expect to lose large numbers of typewriters. A couple hundred typewriters and at least a hundred desk lamps had been rented for our convention offices. The very idea that it was inevitable that some of them would disappear made me resolve that none of them would.

Armed with a list of every typewriter and lamp, I asked the two rental companies to have their people meet me at 7:00 A.M. the day after the convention. Lynn called at 6:30 in the morning, saying he was ill. It was up to me. We started in the basement, where it would be easiest for anyone with sticky fingers to get in and out without being seen. One by one, typewriters and lamps were loaded on the rental company dollies and crossed off our lists. We worked every office, floor by floor. At 9:00 A.M., the trucks pulled away with not a lamp or a typewriter missing. Looking back, I wish I had had charge of the convention area. Several pieces of costly equipment were missing from the offices over there.

When we had our office records packed up, Dick Murphy took a group of us to the Penthouse Restaurant in Fort Lauderdale to celebrate. We were pleasantly relaxed, with not a care in the world. Our part was done.

37

GEORGE MCGOVERN'S
RACE FOR PRESIDENT

OUT ON THE CONVENTION FLOOR, Senator George McGovern of South Dakota easily won the presidential nomination in 1972. In November, however, he carried only Massachusetts. The factors that led to his resounding defeat were evident at that convention. McGovern angered many loyal party people when he replaced Larry O'Brien with Jean West as chairman of the Democratic National Committee.

Larry O'Brien had taken the chairmanship in early 1970, when the party was divided over the issue of the Vietnam War and deeply in debt. Hubert Humphrey and other influential Democrats persuaded Larry that he was desperately needed. He was the unanimous choice of the Democratic National Committee. Larry finally accepted at great financial sacrifice and as one last favor to the Democratic party.

In contrast to Jean, who had very little national campaign experience, Larry had been the campaign manager for both John Kennedy and Robert Kennedy. He had joined the Humphrey campaign after Bobby was killed in June of 1968. Larry had handled legislation on the staffs of JFK and Lyndon Johnson and had been appointed postmaster general by LBJ. He only resigned that position to manage Bobby Kennedy's presidential campaign after Johnson decided not to run. Larry had a wonderful personality and was greatly admired by Democrats in high office as well as by thousands of volunteers throughout the country.

Jean was appointed to replace him at the urging of McGovern's campaign committee. Despite my best efforts to find out, I never learned exactly what kind of pressure prompted McGovern to replace Larry with Jean. She was the first woman chairman—or chairwoman, if it must be —of the Democratic National Committee. Jean was virtually unknown, except to the McGovern staff. She refused to talk to many of the old-time Democrats, even after she became party chairman. Her manner was very abrupt. She did everything she could to damage Larry's reputation. She made it difficult for him to manage McGovern's campaign, even though George himself had begged Larry to become campaign manager. In campaign matters, Jean would work only with Frank Mankiewicz and Gary Hart, the two who had really forced her election.

If Larry had not been such a loyal Democrat, he would have quit the campaign cold and gone back to his promising new business. He had successfully launched O'Brien Associates, a consulting and public relations business, and had been happily working at it when the party persuaded him to become chairman in 1970. His clients had included the three major television networks and Hughes Enterprises, Howard Hughes's business conglomerate. During that difficult campaign of 1972, Larry confided to me that although he was tempted to go back to the business world, he felt an obligation to the party. Larry stayed so that he could try to pacify Democrats from all over the country who had been active for years and who were now shut out by the new people.

The controversy over Jean's selection, on top of the hard feelings over the new delegate rules, made her position very difficult and tended to divide the party. The convention delegates had been chosen under a new set of rules designed to give a more equitable share of delegates to women and minorities. The rules had been discussed and argued over for at least a year before they were approved.

If the longtime party people and officers from the state organizations had studied the rules, many of the internal battles before and after the convention might have been avoided. As it was, many people who had been loyal party workers and delegates for years were not able to attend the national convention. Senator McGovern was chairman of the committee that had drafted the new Democratic National Committee rules, and his staff took full advantage of the new division of delegates to help him get nominated.

In many respects, McGovern himself wasn't to blame for the bad treatment Larry received. The senator apologized to Larry for the way he was replaced before pleading with him to become campaign manager. McGovern's press release announcing Larry's appointment stated he would be McGovern's liaison to the Democrats in Congress, to Democratic governors and mayors, and to other Democratic officials. Also, it said, he would be the foremost consultant on all policy. It was a flowery description that left Larry and everybody else a little puzzled as to his exact role in the campaign.[1]

In fact, there were two campaigns going on at the same time. One was run very effectively by Gary Hart and Frank Mankiewicz, but especially by Gary. It consisted mostly of the organization that the McGovern people had set up during the primaries to win him the nomination. The other campaign was in Larry's lap. His full-time, painful chore was to soothe the hurt feelings of the hundreds of key people who were left out as convention delegates and who were not included in the campaign itself, either. Larry begged them to help all they could for the good of the Democratic party.

It was in that spirit that I became involved in the campaign. After the convention was over, Larry had casually said to me, "I'll see you in the campaign office." He didn't mention any specific job for me to do, and he didn't give me any dates or other details. So I hadn't made any plans to join the campaign in Washington.

Immediately after the convention, I went to Michigan for a much-needed vacation. Refreshed from a relaxing day at the lake, I arrived home to a message from my son Doug that there had been an urgent call from D. C. One of my close friends was calling to ask why I wasn't in Washington. She had called the McGovern campaign office and they had given her a phone extension for me, but the person who answered had told her only that I was not there.

A quick call to Jan Akerhielm, Larry O'Brien's secretary, turned up the fact that, indeed, there was a desk and a telephone assigned to me. The campaign staff was wondering when I would arrive. The assignment they gave me was to be the receptionist and answer phones in Larry's office suite. That put me in an excellent position to observe first–hand what was happening.

Larry was the campaign manager in name only, although he was chief spokesman. Most of the decisions were made by Gary and Frank. Gary later would become the well-known senator from Colorado. Frank was an old Kennedy associate and was most closely identified with Bobby Kennedy. Both of them came out of the new group of the party. It was no wonder that so many calls from the party elders came through to Larry's office.

Many of these callers knew me. My name had become a familiar one at the convention, and I had worked with a number of state officers through the national committee over the years. These people were still hurting from their defeat under the new rules, and they were happy to talk to someone who knew them. Because I was so familiar with their roles in past elections, it wasn't hard for me to figure out which callers should get through to Larry himself.

Larry was a good political organizer, and he knew how to keep his finger on the pulse of the party and the campaign. There were times he simply insisted to Gary and Frank that something had to be done differently. They didn't always take his advice with good grace, but they were smart enough to know they should go along with him.

As a rule, Larry was much more patient with them than most people would have been. He seldom lost his cool. A difficult problem would arise and the newspapers would be calling every few minutes. He would check out the situation, consult with his media people, and then either issue a news release or call a press conference. He never talked to any of the reporters until he knew all the facts and never showed any favoritism.

Larry's skills got quite a workout in the unfortunate controversy involving Senator Thomas Eagleton of Missouri, George McGovern's running mate. News stories about medical treatment Senator Eagleton had received raised the specter of mental illness. In a statement that later would come back to haunt him, George McGovern at first backed Senator Eagleton "one thousand percent." It wasn't long before he replaced Eagleton with Sargent Shriver, the husband of Eunice Kennedy and the first director of the Peace Corps.

Sargent Shriver was an excellent campaigner and a big plus for the ticket, but it was already too late. The campaign ended in defeat, and on a sour note in terms of the party as well. The new rules had particularly affected Democrats of long standing, and there were hurt feelings in every state delegation—and beyond.

Jean West, the new Democratic National Committee chairman, didn't help matters any. She had arranged for suites at the Mayflower Hotel on election night for top DNC officers and campaign people. When the media asked which suite was assigned to Larry O'Brien, she told them he was going to go to South Dakota with McGovern. Some of the reporters didn't believe her and called John Stewart, one of Larry's campaign press aides. John told them Larry was going to stay right in his office and take calls with results from the various states. No, he had not been assigned a suite in the Mayflower. John Stewart passed it off as Larry's preference.

It was true. Larry wanted to spend the evening with his immediate staff and share the election returns with us. We had planned to send out for sandwiches and coffee. We were shocked when Larry's wife Elva arrived with a wonderful dinner for all eight of us. We had a pleasant time, sitting on the floor in Larry's office, watching television and eating our dinner.

The mood wasn't happy for very long. The results got worse and worse as the evening went on. It was a humiliating defeat for McGovern and Shriver and for the Democratic party. It was the beginning of nearly a generation of Republican politics in the White House and elsewhere.

Dorothy Bush, my friend from the DNC, wandered in later and

asked me to make the rounds of the Mayflower suites with her. There were new faces everywhere, so we didn't stay long. Dorothy paid her respects and we left. It was a new era. Just a few short years ago, I had been one of the young upstarts. Now I was an old pro, and the new ones were eager and willing to take over.

My reward was the respect and thanks of Larry O'Brien. After the convention, he had sent me a note which began: "No convention or national campaign would be complete without the outstanding efforts of Helen Berthelot. . . . As usual, you have conducted your duties with the patience of Job and the wisdom of Solomon, and through it all you have kept a sense of humor! Helen, my deep gratitude to you in a task of unparalleled difficulty." In November, he sent me another note in which he scrawled at the bottom, "you were great."

The problems of the 1972 campaign were not Larry's doing, yet he had tried his best to alleviate them. Larry had dedicated his life to the Democratic party. He had sacrificed a great deal to manage just one more campaign to hold the party together. What a sad ending to a brilliant political career.

NOTES

1. For details and insights on Democratic party politics from 1968 through 1972, see chapters 11–16 of *No Final Victories: A Life in Politics—from John F. Kennedy to Watergate*, by Lawrence F. O'Brien (Garden City, N.Y.: Doubleday and Company, 1974).

38

MENNEN
ENTERS A NEW PHASE
OF PUBLIC SERVICE

ALTHOUGH MENNEN WILLIAMS left office January 1, 1961, successful Michigan campaigns were not over for me. To my surprise and delight, they were not over for Mennen, either.

He never lost his zeal for public service. While he was recuperating from a brief illness in early 1968, Mennen was doing some thinking about his future in politics. On January 25, he wrote me a letter which strongly suggested he would be a candidate again, even after that disastrous Senate campaign of 1966:

Dear Buffy:

. . . . The loss of the Senatorial election was a shattering experience, and there were some really dark days and nights following it. I feel so confident that I could have made a real contribution, but I guess there are other places I can too. I have found some useful avenues, but I haven't got things worked out yet the way I would like and haven't been able to apply full steam yet. But, I'm going to take it easy and keep my eyes open and be ready to act when the occasion arises.

In 1970, a Michigan Supreme Court seat was up for election. Mennen took a long look at the changes that had taken place on the court since he left the governor's office. By careful use of his power of appointment, Mennen had broadened the outlook of the court, which had previously been dominated by the Republicans. The *Detroit News*, on January 8, 1964, gave Mennen credit for shifting the court's balance from conservative to liberal. The *News* pointed out that the people approved of the changes, because they ratified Mennen's choices in subsequent elections.

Now, however, the Republican influence had grown so much that the court was in danger of reverting back to the old order. Here was a way he could again serve the people of Michigan, Mennen thought. After serious consultation with party officials, friends, and many advisers, Mennen threw his hat into the ring for the supreme court nomination.

Before he formally announced he was running, Mennen wrote a short letter to his friends and potential supporters, letting them know of his plan to become a candidate:

Dear Friend,

. . . . The determining factor in my decision, after several months of consideration and discussion with many people across the state, is that I am convinced that I can offer a genuine, significant service to the people of Michigan as a justice of the Supreme Court. Throughout the entire Michigan community, and indeed the whole country, there is a growing concern about our courts and the importance of their role in the society of the 1970s. In large degree, that is where the action is today, and the action taken by the courts will affect the lives of all of us.

He pointed out that early in his career, he had been an assistant state attorney general and a special assistant to the U. S. attorney general, which gave him experience with grand jury proceedings and trials in federal court in Detroit. His twelve years as governor involved writing, interpreting, and administering the law. His State Department work had given him firsthand exposure to international law.

Mennen announced his candidacy for the supreme court in May. Mennen and Nancy's granddaughter, Lee Ann Monroe Williams, was at his side, holding his hand. She was just a tiny toddler at the time, but it was prophetic. Years later, Gery and Lee Ann's daughter was to follow in her grandfather's footsteps by becoming a lawyer.

Mennen was starting on a whole new career in public service. His many admirers in Michigan were happy to see him running again. Mennen's first campaign flyer in more than a decade collected and presented potent words of tribute from many people:

Will Muller of the *Detroit News* called Mennen "a man of independent decision" and said his real qualifications included "honesty, sometimes preserved at cost to his political fortunes," and "a sense of integrity toward responsibility."

John D. Voelker, the famous author, fly fisherman, and former supreme court justice who had retreated to his beloved home in the Upper Peninsula, said, "It is great news for the people of Michigan that Mennen Williams is offering himself for a seat on the state supreme court, a demanding job that requires high intelligence, great legal savvy and a big heart—three qualities with which this gifted man is so magnificently endowed."

Judd Arnett, writing in the *Detroit Free Press*, hailed "Soapy Williams . . . gentleman, scholar, compassionate friend of the underdog, American to the core. . . . Experience has shown that his philosophy of government is sound and his ideas practical."

Otis Smith, the first black member of the Michigan Supreme Court, who was by this time in private business, said: "Perhaps no man in the history of Michigan has contributed so much to the strength of the judiciary in this state as has G. Mennen Williams. It seems only natural that he now be elected to the Michigan Supreme Court." Otis Smith had been appointed to the court by John Swainson, but it was Mennen who, by naming Otis auditor general, paved the way.[1]

To become a candidate, Mennen had first to be nominated at a political party convention, then sever all connections with the party and campaign on a nonpartisan basis. This is the ironic situation created by Michigan law for candidates who wish to run for the state's highest court. Mennen was nominated enthusiastically by the Democratic party at its state convention. Then off he went to one of his great loves—meeting the people and shaking their hands. He campaigned hard, as he always did. It only took a trip to a friendly group of people—the larger the crowd, the better—for Mennen's enthusiasm to be completely renewed. This is probably why he wore out the rest of us while he seldom appeared tired.

As always, I couldn't miss one of Mennen's campaigns. This time, I felt as if I were going back to kindergarten. This campaign was completely out of my range of experience. The issues were legal and technical. Paul Donahue, Mennen's able campaign manager, had a group of bright young people working with him. They were all kind to me, and I did my best to fill in wherever possible. My skills in stuffing envelopes and getting out mail stood me in good stead, and I was able to hold up my end in that department with the best of them. Mennen told me later that I had kept up the morale of his staff and they had been very glad to have me around. It was a strange experience for me, however.

He won easily. At last Mennen had found that new opportunity for public service which he had wanted for so many years. In a letter to me on January 12, 1971, he was brimming with enthusiasm:

Dear Buffy:

. . . . Let me say I have found the first week on the court to be most stimulating. The intellectual challenge is great and the opportunity for social service really much greater than one could imagine. It is not only the quality of the decisions which have impact, but the opportunity to improve the administration of justice which is so exciting.

He went on to describe the "very concentrated and confining experience of sitting behind the bench hearing cases." There were the hours of reading and writing and the many conferences with the other justices to discuss the law and the cases. "But beyond that," he wrote, "there is the planning and the developing of the proper administration of justice which means the employment of all of one's administrative and leadership talents throughout the society and throughout the state."

Mennen Williams had always loved the law and had excelled in law school at the University of Michigan. On the court he gained a reputation as a scholarly jurist who was careful and fair in his interpretation of the law. He ran for reelection in 1978 and won another eight-year term by a big margin.

Everyone expected Mennen's colleagues on the court to elect him chief justice. Finally, when he was well into his second term, they did. Unfortunately, he had to have surgery shortly afterward and spent several weeks in the hospital. He told me rather mournfully, when I called him, that he had been elated when he was elected chief justice—but he didn't think he would have to spend half of his term in the hospital.

He didn't. He soon was back on the job and ready to tackle the long-overdue task of streamlining the court's procedures. Under the Michigan system, the supreme court is responsible for the operations of local courts throughout Michigan. With Mennen's vast administrative experience, this was a job right up his alley. He quickly took stock of what needed to be done to make the entire court system function more smoothly.

Just as he had done as governor, Mennen approached his duties as chief administrator of the courts with a good team. Shortly after becoming chief justice in January 1983, he realized that the court office had some excellent people from previous administrations, people who were knowledgeable and ready to do the job. He let them know right away that he welcomed and appreciated their help. His team formed quickly and became very loyal. With the skills of these people and Mennen's determination, it wasn't long before significant changes were made. The procedures put in place under his administration helped the statewide court system handle cases more efficiently and cope with continually increasing workloads. Mennen's colleagues reelected him chief justice in January 1985, and he served in that leadership role until his term expired two years later.

Without a doubt, Mennen would have run for the court a third time, because there were so many more things he wanted to do. However, he turned seventy on February 23, 1981, and was therefore ineligible to run when his term was up. According to the Michigan Constitution, a person age seventy or older may not be elected or appointed to a judicial office. It was a sad day when Mennen left public office on January 1, 1987, thirty-eight years to the day after his first inauguration as governor.

Mennen's sense of humor and magnanimous nature showed forth a few days later, when he was invited to speak at the investiture ceremony marking the beginning of former Senator Robert Griffin's term on the court. Griffin was the Republican who had defeated Mennen in that difficult 1966 U. S. Senate campaign. He was elected to the supreme court in 1986, the year Mennen was prohibited from running again because of his age. Mennen smoothed over what could have been an awkward situation: "It's a great honor for me to have been asked to address this group, and I'm highly indebted to Senator Griffin for making this possible. I also am particularly grateful to you, Bob, that you waited long enough to let the constitution retire me, rather than take more direct means.[2]

It was a warm and generous finale to a memorable new chapter in Mennen's public life. While I wasn't close to Mennen's day-to-day work on the court, it had been a great pleasure to have a hand in the campaigns that allowed him to have a hand in the campaigns that allowed him to spend sixteen years serving the people through the law. He had always taken such great pains to appoint highly qualified people to the judiciary. It was fitting that he should be able to make his mark personally.

Besides Mennen's court campaigns, I was involved in two other state campaigns in the 1970s. Neither had happy endings. The first one was in 1970, just before I went to work on Mennen's first campaign for the supreme court. Billie Farnum had been a wonderful friend to me when I needed help in campaigns through the years. When Jim Hare retired as secretary of state after sixteen years in office, Billie decided to try for the job. After all his years of service inside and outside of government, Billie had earned the position. More importantly, he had the sharp eye and top-notch administrative skills it requires. Billie was good at sizing up any situation, no matter how complicated. Years after he served a single two-year term in the U. S. House, his advice was sought on budgetary matters and other complex issues before Congress.

Billie's goal of becoming secretary of state turned out to be impossible to achieve. By 1970 the UAW had become a powerful force in the party. Unfortunately for Billie, the UAW already had agreed with the Democratic campaign planning committee that it was time we had a black man on the Administrative Board. They had found a fine candidate in Dick Austin, a certified public accountant who had founded a CPA firm in Detroit. He had had a wide-ranging career of public service and, at the time, was Wayne County auditor. It was a bitter blow to Billie not to be supported by the UAW or the Democratic party. He had given so much of his life to causes dear to the party and the union and had supported the Reuthers in every way possible.

Billie Sunday Farnum grew up in a farm area of the Thumb as the eldest of ten children. He was in the Civilian Conservation Corps in the 1930s before landing a job in the auto factories. As an auto worker, he was active in organizing the union and held many offices, from steward right on up to international representative. He had even served as a bodyguard to the Reuther brothers when their lives were in danger. Like many people, Billie felt a keen sense of personal loss when Walter Reuther and his wife, May, died in a plane crash in May of 1970.

Ordinarily I think the UAW would have supported Billie Farnum, but they didn't tell him about their plans for supporting Dick Austin until Billie had his campaign well under way. The fact that the party leaders and UAW people broke the news to him before the convention where the nomination took place didn't ease the pain of rejection very much. Billie had served his party and his government, at both state and national levels, in many difficult posts. He was state auditor general for a time and was elected to that one term in Congress in 1964. He had been a stalwart in every phase of the building of the modern Democratic party in Michigan.

Billie decided to stay in the race and give it his best. Since the nomination was to be made at the state convention, the campaign was conducted rather informally among party people. It was summer, and I was staying at my lake cottage in Livingston County, not too far from Billie's home. His secretary picked me up and drove me to Billie's home so we could work on the campaign there every day. We did our best, but it was not to be. At the state convention, Dick Austin was picked as the candidate by a rather large majority. He went on to break Jim Hare's record as longest-serving secretary of state and become one of the most popular public figures of the period.

Billie was hurt, but he remained a dedicated worker. As the secretary of the state senate during a tumultuous period in the 1970s, he gently led the membership toward reforms. His conciliatory ways and organizational ability greatly improved the senate's reputation and operations. Grateful legislators named the senate office building across from the capitol after Billie, who died of cancer in November 1979.

The other sad campaign I was involved in during that decade was, strangely, a successful one. It, too, involved Billie Farnum—this time as campaign manager for Thomas M. Kavanagh.

Tom was the highly respected chief justice of the Michigan Supreme Court. Several months before his term was up in 1974, his beloved wife Agnes died. Grieving as he was, Tom had no inclination to run for reelection. But his daughters and friends were able to convince him that he shouldn't retire, so he decided to run. Billie Farnum agreed to manage his campaign and persuaded me to come back and run the campaign office and handle the schedule.

Even though the Book Cadillac Hotel was getting rather run-down, I talked them into renting me the same fifteenth floor room I had had in the other campaigns. It still had a wonderful view of the lights on the boats on the river. In previous years, I had gotten in the habit of propping myself up so I could watch them glimmering after I turned off my lights. It helped me go to sleep. Our campaign office was just a few doors away on Washington Boulevard, so I felt very comfortable staying there. It was brought home to me just how dangerous the area had become when most of my women friends told me they were too afraid to come down and have dinner with me. It turned out to be a rather lonely campaign.

Tom Kavanagh was campaigning most of the time in outstate Michigan. He was such a good friend that it was a labor of love to make his campaign as interesting as possible. He didn't have a strong opponent, so I could schedule him into places where I knew he would find friends. He looked better and happier each time I saw him, and I knew he was enjoying himself. He won with a comfortable margin. Election night, a large group of Tom's close friends gathered at his home in Lansing to celebrate. He tried to hide my purse to set up a surprise but couldn't pull it off, so he just presented me with a lovely black leather bag as a thank-you gift.

After the campaign, Tom took a trip out West and had a fine time. When he came back, he went to the doctor for a routine check-up. It disclosed that he had cancer. He had surgery, but the cancer was so widespread that he never left the hospital. He died in the early spring of 1975.

While Tom was hospitalized, all I could think to do was write him cheery letters. The letters turned out to be the adventures of the little black bag he had given me—where it had gone, who it had seen, and what it had heard. As usual, I was attending a large number of political affairs in Washington, and they formed the basis for most of my letters. Tom would know the people I saw. When my week had not been interesting enough, I delved into my imagination, and the little black bag had some exciting adventures. Billie Farnum told me Tom got a big kick out of my letters and showed them to his friends.

Luckily, the medical people were able to contain Tom's pain, but he failed rapidly. His election was all in vain, but he had had a happy time campaigning.

NOTES

1. A campaign flyer showing endorsements of Mennen Williams's candidacy for the supreme court in 1970 is among Helen Berthelot's papers in the Michigan Historical Collections, Bentley Historical Library, University of Michigan, Ann Arbor.

2. Mennen Williams's remarks on the occasion of the investiture of Robert P. Griffin as state supreme court justice may be found under "Griffin Investiture Ceremony" in the January 6, 1987, record of official proceedings of the Michigan supreme court, which is kept in the offices of the Michigan Supreme Court, Lansing.

39

THE 1976 CAMPAIGN
FROM SARGENT SHRIVER TO ROSALYNN CARTER

T HE SUMMER OF 1976 would have been a perfect time for me to forget elections and bask in the sun on the beautiful Cape Cod beaches near my girlhood home. As the presidential campaigns were getting under way, I wasn't inspired to volunteer for any of the candidates. As it turned out, I missed my first national political convention in twenty-four years, but not the campaigns. My year started in Sargent Shriver's campaign and ended in the presidential transition office, helping Rosalynn Carter and her staff deal with sacks of mail.

A friend from the 1972 convention, Ed Cubberly, called to tell me that Dick Murphy, who had lured me to Miami Beach to work for him that year, was managing Shriver's campaign. Ed was working in the Shriver campaign and said Dick needed me. After the third call from Ed, I agreed to volunteer two days a week. The campaign was based in D. C., where I was still living, even though I was retired. When I put my head in the door, there was a roar that startled everyone. "Buffy," Dick Murphy yelled. "You came to help."

"Buffy" is all anyone in the office ever called me. Six weeks later, the campaign treasurer and I were working alone. "Do you know anyone by the name of Helen Berthelot?" he called to me. "This man insists she works here." "That's me," I told him. He was flabbergasted. "I never knew that was your name," he said.

Two days a week quickly turned into six days a week, twelve hours a day. Dick was using a T-shaped table for a desk. He put me on the right-hand side and moved the telephones over to me. "You answer my calls, please," he said. "Handle them yourself as much as you can. Tell them you are my assistant."

Seeing Dick's mail start to stack up, I offered to help and got the whole pile. From then on, I handled all but the most personal mail. He never read any of the letters I wrote for him, but I did make him sign them. Once I threatened to write a nasty letter, calling Sarge Shriver all kinds of names, over Dick's signature. He just laughed. He knew I wouldn't do it. Before long I was running the office. Sargent Shriver had a great staff, and we all enjoyed working together.

Dick Murphy spent a great deal of time trying to persuade officers of various state Democratic organizations to work for Shriver. Ed Cubberly, the workhorse of the group, handled the schedule, the campaign material, and many of the irksome details. His wife Loretta helped handle the media. Several times when we had had a difficult week, I would have Dick Murphy and the Cubberlys over for a home-cooked meal. One night, I made a beef stew which Ed Cubberly never stopped talking about. Because of what was to happen later, I never forgot about that stew, either.

Ed had been feeling out of sorts for several weeks, although he never complained. Loretta finally persuaded him to go to the doctor. The next thing we knew, Ed was in surgery. He was so filled with cancer that there was nothing more to do. He never knew, I hope, how bad he really was. They kept him sedated, so he felt no pain. We called him several times a day and always found him cheerful—full of questions and suggestions about the campaign. One day, he told me he expected to leave the hospital soon. He made me promise to make him beef stew with dumplings, first thing. He died quietly in his sleep that night.

With that news, the office fell apart. The whole heart of the campaign was gone. Somehow, we went on, but every day we were reminded of something Ed Cubberly had done or said we should do.

Working for Sargent Shriver—whose wife Eunice Kennedy Shriver was the sister of Jack, Robert, and Ted—was enlightening. One night the Shrivers invited the whole Democratic National Committee and D. C. members of the influential convention committees to their home for a cocktail party. Dick Murphy insisted I should act as a hostess since I knew so many of the people. In her absent-minded way, Eunice Shriver thanked me for helping her, but didn't even recognize me a few minutes later in the next room.

The same was true of the whole family. Years earlier, I had met Sarge Shriver when he came to the CWA office at my request to speak at one of the informational meetings I had arranged for CWA staff. In the 1976 campaign, I sat right beside Dick whenever Sarge Shriver was in the office, but Sarge looked right through me and probably wouldn't have acknowledged me on the street. It was a strange feeling after having been so close to the people I had worked for in other campaigns.

The Iowa caucuses were the end of the Shriver campaign for president. The story of what happened there has never been resolved to my satisfaction. All we knew was that Shriver was ahead when, for some unknown reason, the counting of the outstate votes came to a halt. It was days before we got the final tally, which showed Jimmy Carter had won. We muttered and sputtered, but I never heard any satisfactory explanation for the mystery.

Mulling over my experiences and treasuring my new friends, I went off to Massachusetts. Dick Murphy was once again involved in the upcoming national convention. He and convention chairman Azie Taylor Morton wanted me to help, but the party couldn't afford to put up all the volunteers—and I couldn't afford to pay my expenses in New York City. So for the first time since 1952, I missed the national convention. I wasn't around when they nominated Jimmy Carter and Walter Mondale in New York. It was a strange feeling, and I was a little lost, but I decided it was time for others to take over. That resolution didn't even last through New Year's 1977.

Finances for the Carter campaign in Michigan had been handled by Carolyn Sinelli Burns, my hardworking friend from many Michigan campaigns. After the election, she spent a week in Georgia, going over her meticulously kept records with the Carter people. Carolyn was a brilliant woman and very much aware of the problems that can result from improperly kept financial records. She told me with horror that some of her counterparts from other states dumped boxes of disorganized records in the Georgia office and took off.

Plans for the inauguration were equally disorganized. The Carter people had appointed someone new to handle all the details, and he was in deep trouble. He would have remained in trouble if it hadn't been for Salome Williams, the longtime assistant to Sam Fishman, the UAW's political action director. Because Salome had a reputation for being able to handle any situation, the UAW loaned her to the Inaugural Committee as assistant to the chairman. Before Salome knew it, the chairman was spending only a couple of days a week in the office, and Salome was, in effect, in charge.

Carolyn had ridden to D. C. with Salome so she could visit me. The second day she was in town, we went to the Inaugural Committee office to see Salome. Carolyn called Rick Hutto, a young man she had met in the Carter campaign, to find out what he was doing in the transition office. "Oh, Carolyn," he moaned. "I'm in the worst trouble. They have given me Mrs. Carter's mail to handle. There are bags and bags and bags of it, and more coming every day. What am I going to do with it?"

When Carolyn offered the help of "a couple of experienced volunteers," Rick gratefully accepted. She hadn't even asked me.

The next morning, we headed for the old Health, Education, and Welfare building where the transition committee was working. Rick Hutto greeted Carolyn with outstretched arms, flashed me a warm smile, and gave us both badges reading "R. Carter Staff." When we got inside Rosalynn Carter's office, we saw why Rick had panicked. It looked like the Humphrey office after he was defeated. Carolyn and I started opening the mail and soon found it would fall into many categories. Carolyn was an experienced scrounger. She disappeared and came back loaded with empty stationery boxes. We consulted for a few minutes, put labels on the boxes, and continued sorting the mail. We piled the boxes alphabetically by category on the broad windowsills. It took us a week of hard work to catch up with the backlog.

The very next day, when everything was in excellent order and ready to send to the proper people to answer, in came Rosalynn Carter, followed by an entourage of reporters and television cameras. She introduced Rick as her assistant, and he introduced his two volunteers. He was able to give the reporters an excellent briefing. The reporters were very interested in the type of mail Mrs. Carter was getting, and the interview resulted in many good stories on the wide range of subjects people were writing to her about. As the crews left, a pleasantly shocked Mrs. Carter whispered in Rick's ear, "Don't you dare let those two women get away." Carolyn was hoping for a job with the Carter staff, so she stayed with me and we continued to help for several weeks. (Carolyn spent many years as an unpaid volunteer in campaigns. Later, she went to work in government and eventually became an administrator for senior citizen programs in Wayne County.)

As the inauguration drew near, the Carters decided they wanted to have private receptions during inaugural week to honor all the volunteers who had helped them. Working with their staffs, Jimmy and Rosalynn planned four separate events. Carolyn and I were asked to begin working on guest lists. Among the ones I worked on were the Georgia list and the labor list. The Carters and their staff members never knew, although they may have guessed, how all the CWA executive officers got invitations.

The Georgia list was another story. It had been hastily submitted by a Carter staff person who had been given a top appointment. She was now spending all her time learning about her new job. Her list was a disaster. Late one evening, when I was trying to make sense of four different spellings and addresses for one person, the telephone rang. Although I didn't know it, my rescuer had arrived.

A lovely, gentle lady, Maxine Reece, was calling from Plains, Georgia. She wanted me to check if a certain name was on the guest list. To her dismay, it was not. She asked me to check a couple more names. They weren't on the list either. We ended up spending a couple of hours a night for two or three evenings on the WATS line when everyone else was gone. She checked with the Georgia party officers and several of the volunteers, compiling a good list of names, with correct spellings and addresses. Except for the kindness of Maxine Reece, many of the Carters' close friends and hardest workers in Georgia would not have been invited to the receptions.

As the responses came in, we needed more and more volunteers. Again, I was able to call on my friends to help out. Linda Cook, who often had volunteered to help on my many projects, came into the public cafeteria in the old HEW building with her skates over her arm, on her way to the outdoor rink. She didn't get there until after the inaugural receptions, but she never regretted it.

Our work was not simply a matter of getting out invitations. Guests received forms in the mail and were asked to fill them out and provide Social Security numbers before returning them. Each list of names, alphabetized by state, had to be checked and photocopied several times before being submitted to the Secret Service. When people arrived at the receptions, there was an attractive, engraved invitation in a personally addressed envelope for each guest. All the engraved invitations had to be filed in alphabetical order for each of the four receptions. On inauguration day, I spent all afternoon and late into the evening in the White House, filing all the late entries—and then some. Whoever had done the filing didn't have an impressive knowledge of the alphabet.

We were not allowed to enter the White House until the stroke of twelve noon on inauguration day, when it became the Carters' White House. The receptions were held a few days after the inauguration, but there was so much work to do that I couldn't afford to waste any time. Rosalynn Carter's assistant also asked me to take charge of distributing the invitations during the four receptions, one in the morning and one in the afternoon, two days in a row. That meant I needed some helpers, so the eight friends who had worked with me on the lists also got to come and see the fun.

The guests arrived at the White House diplomatic entrance. They received their engraved invitations and went upstairs, where they were greeted by the Carters and the Mondales. Every guest went through the receiving line, so the meeting and greeting took hours at a time.

It was my happy duty to greet the guests at the diplomatic entrance, show them where to get their invitations, and direct them upstairs. All the people who had hosted a member of the Carter family in their homes overnight during the campaign were to get a bronze plaque engraved with the words: "A member of the Carter family stayed in this house during the 1976 campaign." If people didn't mention this connection, it was quite a trick to remember which were the ones with whom the Carters had stayed. About thirty plaques had to be mailed out after the receptions.

It was fun greeting so many people I knew at the door. They were all greatly surprised to see me and wanted to know what I was doing there. "Helping," I answered. Naturally, you couldn't have that many people and not have problems, but the military guards were cooperative and had a good sense of humor. It was hard for us to keep from laughing when one elderly lady arrived with what seemed to be all her clothes in a couple of shopping bags. Rosalynn Carter personally thanked my eight friends for their help. When the crowds thinned out, they were invited upstairs to go through the receiving line and have refreshments.

Poor Carolyn didn't have such a glamorous job. She was stationed at the gate with the guards to handle problems with people who didn't have proper identification. A whole group from India arrived and said they had been invited by Miss Lillian, Jimmy Carter's mother, although they were not on the lists. Carolyn knew Miss Lillian had been in India in the Peace Corps, but she also knew that a group of people from India was entertaining at one of the theaters. With a couple of judicious telephone calls, Carolyn was able to confirm that they had been invited by Miss Lillian, who came right out to greet them. Later we learned they were extremely prominent, so it was especially good Carolyn had been able to take care of them.

Carolyn's biggest problem with the receptions was that she hadn't worn boots the first day and nearly froze to death. She was later hired to work on Rosalynn Carter's staff—not a very lucrative position, but an interesting one. They asked me to volunteer for a little longer to clear up all of the problems left over and make sure all the bronze plaques were mailed to the people who had earned them.

Rosalynn Carter was in the office every day and always greeted me pleasantly. One day she came into my office and sat down. "I am so embarrassed," she said. "Do you have any plaques left over?" "Yes, there are a few," I replied, after I had checked. "I forgot both my best friend and my brother," she admitted.

The first guests Mrs. Carter invited to the White House after the volunteer receptions were the people who had worked on those receptions. We got formal invitations to have coffee with her in the Diplomatic Room. It was a rather small gathering, and she was very friendly. She told us she had hunted high and low to get shoes to match each of her costumes for the various inaugural parties and was pleased that she managed to find them. "Then, my husband got the idea of walking from the Capitol to the White House in the inaugural parade. You can't imagine what that did to my feet. I could not get on a single pair of my new shoes," she said. "I looked through all the shoes I had and found a new pair I had had a long time. They were a size too large, and I had forgotten to return them. They saved my life. I don't know if anyone noticed, but I wore them to every single event."

It was so typical of Mrs. Carter's down-to-earth approach during her years as first lady. Women everywhere could sympathize with the president's wife.

40

HONORS
FOR MENNEN AND NANCY,
A REUNION FOR SID,
AND A
GOLDEN ANNIVERSARY
FOR MENNEN

DURING MENNEN'S CAMPAIGN for his final term on the supreme court in 1978, he was the same old trouper. He even teased that he might run again for the office he had held for so long. "There's nothing in the Constitution that says I can't run again for governor!" he would say.[1]

After the election, it was decided that the next Jefferson-Jackson Day dinner would be a testimonial for Mennen and Nancy. It was an unprecedented honor, and party people responded enthusiastically. First Lady Rosalynn Carter was the main speaker. Several others took the podium to describe Mennen and Nancy's contributions over the years. The program book was full of accolades from Democrats around the state.

One of the most touching came from the Tuscola County Democratic party. Democrats generally were few and far between in Michigan's Thumb. "He restored the dignity and meaning to citizens' sovereign power—and gave us heart," the Tuscola Democrats said in their message near the back of the book.

Irving Bluestone, chairman of the UAW's political arm, the Community Action Program, wrote this message for the program book: "You once told us, 'There is no finer response than the smile on the face and the light in the eye of a person with whom you are shaking hands.' Wherever you go in Michigan, you will always get that response."

Nancy Williams was honored for her own distinct contributions. Libby Maynard, vice chairman of the Democratic State Central Committee, asked Nancy's friends to write a letter to Nancy in care of Libby. She assembled the letters in a book of reminiscences and tributes for Nancy.

300

As ably as Nancy had assisted Mennen in his campaigns and duties as governor, she also worked side by side with him in his assignments as assistant secretary of state for African affairs and ambassador to the Philippines. Both jobs required diplomacy, stamina, and the ability to develop warm relationships with people of various countries and cultures.

Those posts had taken them out of the country a great deal. With Mennen's election to the supreme court, they were able to settle back into their Michigan home. It had been so long since Mennen had been governor that people had gone their separate ways, and it wasn't often that we got together. Mennen and Nancy chose the occasion of Sid Woolner's retirement to host a reunion of the old group of Mennen's original supporters. They made it a farewell party for Sid. He and Doris were planning to move to California to be near their son, Tom.

Since Phil Hart's death in 1976, Sid had been involved in a number of projects, mostly in Washington. As many times as he had left Michigan to take on those jobs, everyone always expected him to be right back for the next Michigan Democratic emergency. We never had given him a farewell party. Perhaps everyone remembered they had given me one in 1960 and I was right back in 1962.

Mennen and Nancy wanted everyone who had worked with Sid to be invited to the reunion. They asked Adelaide Hart and me to put together the list. It had been nearly twenty years since Mennen had left the governor's office, so Adelaide and I spent a weekend together, jotting down names as they came to us. It was no easy task, but between us, and with Mennen and Nancy's help, we assembled a good list. The buffet luncheon at the Williamses' Grosse Pointe Farms home was a delightful reunion and garden party, with Mennen acting informally as toastmaster.

The afternoon was tinged with sadness, though, for we all feared this might be our last get-together. Janey Hart, Phil's widow, saved us by telling a slightly risqué joke, which I promptly forgot and cannot now remember. All I recall is that we laughed very hard. Janey went on to give a beautiful tribute to Sid, describing how much Sid's friendship had meant to Phil in his last days.

Thanks to Governor Jim Blanchard, the Williamses' garden party wasn't the last reunion of the old group. The summer of 1986 saw the start of Michigan's sesquicentennial celebration, and Governor Blanchard decided it would be an ideal time to honor Mennen Williams's fiftieth anniversary of public service. It was in 1936 that Mennen, not long out of law school, had taken a job as a staff attorney with the relatively new Social Security Board in Washington. The New Deal had captured Mennen's fancy because of its creative solutions to human problems. He chose the Social Security post over one in the Securities and Exchange Commission for reasons that were typical of Mennen: "I wanted to be out with

people, working with them and for them. I chose the more active job."[2]
Since 1986 was Mennen's last year on the supreme court, Governor
Blanchard's decision to honor him was most timely.

That party got me started writing this book, but I almost missed it.
A few days before the event, Mennen asked Jean Campbell, his and
Nancy's personal secretary, if she had heard from me. Jean replied that I
hadn't answered the invitation.

The problem was that it hadn't caught up with me. As I had done
for years, I was spending the summer at the home where I was born. My
nephew and niece, Kent and Pat Gagnon, are the owners now, but they
insist that the big front bedroom upstairs is mine. It was early in June.
This particular morning was beautiful and I had just come back from an
early swim. It was so quiet and peaceful that I didn't want to move. Pat
called me to the phone. It was Jean, telling me of Governor Blanchard's
plans for the party for Mennen at the executive residence in Lansing. Jean
had sent an invitation to Florida, where I had a mobile home. She finally
realized I must be in Massachusetts. Could I come?

Of course. It was like old times: pack like lightning, make arrangements, get to the airport. The party was Friday afternoon, only a day or
so away. By Friday morning, I was sleeping peacefully at Carolyn Burns's
home in Detroit. Carolyn had to work in the morning, so we were planning to drive to Lansing that afternoon.

Again, the phone rang for me in somebody else's home. "Governor
Williams is on the phone," Carolyn's sister, Jo Sinelli, said. "Buffy,"
Mennen asked, "did you hear about the celebration on the capitol steps
this morning?" "No," I answered. "All I've heard about is the reception
this afternoon. I'm coming up with Carolyn Burns." "We're having a big
anniversary celebration on the capitol steps at ten o'clock this morning,"
he went on, "and I want all the people who were with me in 1948 to be
there. Do you have a way of getting to Lansing?" he asked.

When he learned that Carolyn wouldn't be back until afternoon, he
said he would call me right back and asked me to stay by the phone.
Within minutes, he was on the line again to tell me that Barbara Patter-
son, who had succeeded Julie Lawler as Mennen's longtime office secretary, would pick me up in an hour. "Meet us in my office," Mennen said.

Wendy Williams Burns and her family and George and Peg Edwards were there when we arrived. Pictures were being taken, and Mennen insisted on having me included. He introduced me to a key member
of his staff, Marilyn Hall, and said she would look after me. It was a new
experience—someone watching over me—but Marilyn was a delightful
companion, and she took good care of me for the next two days. A bright
young lawyer with strong administrative skills, Marilyn later became the
state court administrator with responsibility for all state courts. Mennen

had recognized her potential early on and had given her a great deal of responsibility in helping him oversee the courts in his role as chief justice.

A white banner with a huge green-and-white polka-dot bow tie had been draped across the front of the capitol. "Thank you, Soapy, for 50 years" was lettered on the banner. Former Governors John Swainson and George Romney were both there, as well as many of Mennen's former staff and Ad Board members. It was sad to think of the members of our group who were no longer alive: Sandy Brown, Jim Hare, Billie Farnum, and Phil Hart. We also missed Helen and Adelaide Hart, who were recuperating from a terrible auto accident.

Otis Smith, the former supreme court justice and auditor general, was a witty master of ceremonies. When all the other members of the original group had been introduced, Otis turned to me and told the crowd that I had been "Mennen's lucky charm all through his campaigns."

There were many speeches about Mennen's significance to the state before Governor Blanchard introduced him. The applause was heartwarming, and Mennen glowed. "Now that I'm not running for office I can talk two hours if I want to," Mennen said, drawing laughter and groans. He singled out those of us who had been with him on the same platform when he was first inaugurated January 1, 1949. He thanked us publicly, as he had done so often in the past. Then he gave a short speech, straight from the heart.

When it was over, Secretary of State Richard Austin graciously offered his arm to escort me up the steps and into the capitol. His gesture was much appreciated; my mind was overwhelmed with all the memories. Marilyn Hall was waiting for me. We had lunch with Mennen, Nancy, Wendy and her family, and George and Peg Edwards. Carolyn Burns had two tickets for Saturday morning's opening ceremony for Michigan's 150th anniversary celebration, so we had a hotel room to retreat to before the reception.

That afternoon, the garden of the executive residence was filled with old friends, people I hadn't seen for as long as thirty years. Mennen and Nancy had fun, and so did I. One of Governor Blanchard's staff got a big kick out of watching people come in and say, "Why, there's Helen Berthelot." Several former capitol secretaries were in a group. When I introduced them to Marilyn, they all thought it was a big joke that anyone should have to take care of me. They proceeded to tell a series of stories about my adventures. Mary Margetts, who had worked for Mennen's press secretary, Paul Weber, asked me why I hadn't sent her any more tapes to transcribe for this book. She probably wishes she hadn't said that; I kept her very busy after that.

Mennen had such a long list of people to invite that Governor Blanchard scheduled two receptions for him. Carolyn and I were invited to stay for the second one, too, and saw many more old friends. Before we left, Mennen asked Governor Blanchard to have his picture taken with Mennen, Nancy, and me. Ron Thayer, one of Governor Blanchard's top aides, sent me a copy. It was an excellent picture of the three of them— but my eyes were closed. My problems with photographs hadn't changed a bit.

The next morning, Mennen was the speaker at the official opening of Michigan's 150th birthday celebration in the senate chambers. Mennen gave a thoughtful speech on the history of his beloved state. After he spoke, Mennen introduced several people he said had helped to build a better Michigan. Carolyn and I were included, which pleased us both very much.

When I got back to Massachusetts, my family wanted to know what had happened to me. They told me I looked twenty years younger, and that's exactly how I felt. With the joy that comes with fresh memories of beloved names and faces, I resumed the work that led to this book. In a letter written a few weeks later, Mennen encouraged me: "I am delighted to know that you're beginning to put some of the history you have lived on tape. I need to get to it, but somehow or other, it always gets put off. That is one of the things I hope to do after I leave the court."

If only he had done so.

NOTES

1. This is taken from a short political biography of G. Mennen Williams by Jack Casey published in the program book for the 1979 Jefferson-Jackson Day dinner. That year the Michigan Democratic party's annual fund-raising event honored Mennen and Nancy Williams. The program is among Helen Berthelot's papers in the Michigan Historical Collections, Bentley Historical Library, University of Michigan, Ann Arbor.

2. McNaughton, *Mennen Williams of Michigan*, p. 71.

41

THE SAD ENDING
OF A WONDERFUL ERA

I T WAS MY FIRM INTENTION to end this book on the happy story of the celebration of Mennen Williams's fifty years in government. As is so often true in life, there wasn't to be a happy ending. However, over that next year, Mennen received award after award for his contributions in every phase of Michigan life. As Helen Hart put it, "He'll have to put an addition on his house if he receives any more plaques." How wonderful that the love and admiration of the people were shown to him in so many ways while he was alive to enjoy them.

His sudden death on February 2, 1988, a little less than three weeks before his seventy-seventh birthday, was a shock to everyone. He had a massive cerebral hemorrhage at home the day before, and died in the hospital without regaining consciousness. As Nancy told it, he said, "'I have a terrible pain in my head,'" and then he collapsed. She rushed him to the hospital, but there was nothing that could be done. He was kept alive on life-support systems until their son Gery could arrive from his home in Pennsylvania.

Word reached me in Florida, where I was living at the time. It stunned me so that I could only say, "Yes, of course, I will be there." Another frantic call for plane reservations—this time, with a heavy heart. Carolyn Sinelli Burns phoned and told me to plan to stay with her. She said we would go together to Mennen's home, where the family was greeting people, and to the funeral. Personally, I still can't picture the world without him.

305

It was a long three-hour plane ride from Tampa to Detroit. There was no one sitting beside me to distract me, so my thoughts wandered back along the long road we had traveled during those wonderful years when Mennen was governor. First, there was his unbelievable election in 1948. Then, the realization of the enormous burden he had to face almost alone. The true condition of the state's financial situation was incredible. The Republican legislature had ignored the terms of the constitution for years. Even Governor Sigler had warned his Republican colleagues that they were inevitably facing financial disaster.

After Mennen surprised the Republicans by winning that first election, they firmly believed he could not be reelected. They had it all planned. After he was defeated in 1950, they would go back to running the state in cahoots with big business. The people decided otherwise. Mennen knew they trusted him and believed he would make Michigan a better place. With great determination, he was able to perform minor miracles, but Michigan's financial problems were too deep for him to solve without cooperation. As the years went on and the situation was becoming desperate, Mennen took his program directly to the people. He told them of his plan to have business pay its fair share of taxes while establishing a firm foundation for the state to provide for the education, health, safety, and welfare of the people.

The elections in 1950 and 1952 were nightmares, but the people were beginning to believe in his sincerity. Both were cliff-hangers that were eventually decided by recounts. Nothing could have brought the Democrats closer together than those recounts. Volunteers to count ballots showed up by the hundreds, and they fought doggedly for every vote. The knowledge that they had been able to elect a governor twice had given them confidence. By the time the 1954 election was approaching, these volunteers had told and retold their stories of the recounts and their victories. Campaign workers popped up like mushrooms across the state.

As I looked out the plane window, I thought what a wonderful victory that had been. Surrounded by the able and willing Democratic Ad Board, Mennen was able to make many of his dreams for Michigan come true. Some business leaders, with help from the newspapers, claimed that his programs were driving business out of Michigan. But the people knew better. They kept supporting him because his programs made their lives better.

They were right. While he was governor, Michigan had some of its most prosperous times. Business and industry made record profits and enjoyed tremendous growth. Workers gained a bigger share of the pie. The state moved toward the forefront of the nation in opportunity and economic expansion. This didn't happen by accident. Against the odds, and despite Republican majorities in both houses, Mennen successfully pushed to make long overdue changes. Education, civil rights, jobs and the workplace, the needs of the cities and the farms, the road system that ties everything together—these were his chief concerns. Because of Mennen Williams, the state began taking better care of the jobless, the mentally and physically disabled, and the elderly. Michigan established its first commission on the arts. Schools and hospitals were built and given the resources they needed. Community colleges and state universities were expanded and improved. Mennen's initiative helped Wayne University become a full-fledged state university and greatly enhanced the research and teaching at other state institutions of higher learning. Conservation and environmental protection were advanced. The list could go on and on.

Long after Mennen's funeral, I came across the statement he made in March of 1960 when he told the people of Michigan that he would not run again. In his own words, it summarizes his accomplishments:

> When I took office as your governor in 1949, the great challenge was to realize the social and economic gains a new technology made possible, and past neglect made imperative. . . .

> We have achieved great progress in many important fields. . . . We have improved all of our social services. The administration of justice has been tempered with mercy and understanding. We have made the language of the Declaration of Independence a living thing in Michigan as we approach closer, year by year, to the idea of equal dignity for all our citizens, regardless of race, creed or color.[1]

Mennen's use of the word "we" was deliberate. As I rode that plane back to Michigan, I closed my eyes and saw hundreds of faces, as if they were all in a dream. There were so many people who had served on boards and commissions and in the departments of state government at great personal sacrifice because they shared Mennen's vision. Seldom, if ever, had there been a group so united in the belief that government should serve every citizen of Michigan, not just the rich and powerful.

Mennen Williams was proud to be a Democrat. He was unashamed of his reputation as one of America's staunchest liberals. Because of him, Michigan became a two-party state. Before he came along, the Democratic party was weak and disorganized, easy prey for political opportunists. Mennen saw that it could be big enough for everyone if it became open and honest, truly the party of the people. He did more than his share of the work, more than most men or women could or would do. Mennen's example inspired the rest of us to do our best to build a strong Democratic party.

For most of the century before Mennen, Republicans had dominated state politics and government. And before Mennen, in more than half the counties in Michigan, Democrats were afraid to be publicly known as Democrats. They could lose their jobs, or be denied credit at the bank, or worse.

After years of hard work, the party began to grow. People saw that the Democratic party really did belong to everyone, and that it stood for something. In the twelve years he was governor, the people showed their belief in him and his programs by electing more and more Democratic candidates to Congress, the state legislature, the State Administrative Board, and statewide education boards.[2]

Mennen was always proud of the fact that he earned the trust of the people every two years. Under the constitution which took effect in 1963, Michigan governors now have to run for reelection only every four years. In fact, Mennen's six elections as governor broke a record for any governor of any political party in Michigan. Before Mennen, the last time a Democratic governor had been reelected was 1914. Only one other Democrat in Michigan had ever been elected governor three times, and that was years before the Civil War. At the time he left the governor's office, Mennen's record of six consecutive terms was unsurpassed in the country.[3] Mennen kept getting reelected because he believed in the people and they believed in him.

On that plane ride that seemed to last a lifetime, pictures of Mennen in every sort of circumstance flashed through my mind. They all had to do with his contact with the people. Nothing made him happier than to know that the people trusted him, unless it was the sheer enjoyment he got from being out with them.

Three scenes stood out most vividly in my mind. The first was a picture printed in the newspapers after a tornado struck the vicinity of Flint in June of 1953. Mennen had heard the news on the radio and gone immediately to the area. He stayed all night, working with the rescue people and the local authorities to assess the damage and protect the survivors from any further harm. In the picture, Mennen stands beside a woman and her small child; behind them is their home, utterly destroyed. The look of sadness and compassion on his face is indescribable. It says that he will do everything in his power to help. The fact that he was there, and had been there all night long, proved it. The people were comforted by his mere presence. He continued to help through the aftermath of that deadly storm.

The second image was not so much Mennen's face, but the faces of the people who were listening to him one evening. Years earlier, when Beirut was a beautiful city, Mennen had visited there and brought back a flag of Lebanon for his friends in Detroit. At a dinner upstairs at the Sheik restaurant in downtown Detroit, he presented that flag to the leader of the most prominent Arab-American group in the area. With his remarkable ability to convey what he saw and what he felt at the same time, Mennen described how that gorgeous city looked to him as the plane had circled before landing. His words brought tears to the eyes of the many elderly people in the audience who would never see their country again. They listened, heartbroken and yet grateful for Mennen's appreciation of the beauty of their homeland.

Even more powerful was my memory of Mennen at the Ford factory gates. He frequently visited plants to greet workers in the early morning. A campaign stop at "the Rouge"—the big complex which had a busy foundry at one end and a finished car coming off the line every few minutes on the other—was a tradition on election day.

It's difficult to describe how the workers look as they swarm out of an auto plant at the end of a hot, hard shift, no matter what time of day or night. They come out in droves, running as hard as they can to get to the parking lot. They are stoop-shouldered and grimy from the work they've just finished. On their faces, every one, is the look of grim determination that it takes to survive in the factory. There is not a smile or a word spoken.

Then, all of a sudden, they see that big, smiling man waiting to shake their hands. It's like a sunburst. The workers break into broad smiles themselves and quickly form two long lines. Mennen's hands work like pump handles as he greets each one. Everyone has a word of encouragement. "Hi, Soapy, we knew you'd be here." "Good luck, Soapy." "We'll vote for you, Soapy." In all the times I watched this scene I never saw more than half a dozen workers go by without stopping to shake hands.

Mennen was loved by those people as surely as he was loved by his family and friends. His dream was really their dream. He wanted to become governor so he could make the state a better place for the people— all the people. When it was all over, he had gone a long way toward making that vision a reality. His achievements moved Michigan forward when it desperately needed leadership. His greatness has stood the test of time.

My last vision before the plane landed was of the beautiful Mackinac Bridge outlined in green lights in honor of Mennen. That magnificent span will be a lasting memorial to the governor who made it possible and who was so greatly loved.

Mennen's death ended a lifetime of service to the people, but not his concern for them. It had been Mennen's express wish that his body be laid out at their home and that all his friends be welcome there. Nancy agreed with him completely.

They came from far and near, new friends and old ones, people who had known him well and those who knew him only in their hearts. For two days, from two in the afternoon until ten o'clock in the evening, a solid line of people came through the house. Mennen would have been so proud of Nancy and his children and grandchildren. Nancy and Gery Williams spoke with everyone, containing their own grief to comfort others. The only indication of Nancy's pain was when she quietly told me, "I can't stand it to see grown men cry."

The two girls, Nancy Williams Ketterer and Wendy Williams Burns, with their husbands and all eight grandchildren, took turns lining up at the door. They introduced themselves, welcomed the people as they came in, and thanked them for coming.

Gery, the oldest of the Williams children, ably assumed the role of family leader during this difficult time. Gery had never been inclined toward political life. However, he continued his parents' tradition of service to the public by becoming an executive in an important phase of the nation's transportation system. Gery always had a quiet but pleasantly outgoing nature. It was with great dignity and warmth that he escorted people to the casket.

When he came to me, I was so thankful that he held my hand tightly. We talked a little, and then with a half sob I said: "Gery, there's only one thing wrong. His tie is on straight." Gery smiled because he could remember how many times I had tried to straighten it before a television appearance. It always seemed to be on crooked.

The day of the funeral was bitterly cold, with a strong north wind. Despite the terrible weather, crowds gathered outside the Cathedral Church of St. Paul on Woodward Avenue in Detroit hours before the doors were opened. That huge church was packed to overflowing for the funeral. A television set and loudspeaker were placed in a room adjacent to the sanctuary so that many more people could see and hear the services.

The first three tributes were given by Governor James Blanchard, Supreme Court Justice Dennis Archer, and U. S. District Judge Horace Gilmore. Gery Williams gave the last one. He spoke about his father from the heart, as only a son could do. His words were simple but very moving.

Among the mourners were the leaders of the many ethnic groups Mennen had befriended. They applauded when Gery finished speaking. It was the only way they could show the depth of their feeling. They knew they would never again have a leader who would love and honor them as he did.

At the end of the service, Bishop H. Coleman McGehee, Jr., gave his blessing and dismissed the people. Then the huge pipe organ, with all stops pulled out, pealed forth with the beloved anthem, "The Battle Hymn of the Republic."

310

Sad Ending

As Mennen had intended, the people left that cathedral with hope in their hearts. You could see them stand straighter and pull back their shoulders as they literally marched out to carry on their beloved friend's dreams.

The years ahead hold great promise for the people of Michigan and the United States. It is up to us—you and me, whether as private citizens or public officials—to make that promise come true. A new decade is beginning. Let us strike forward, boldly remembering the words of the Psalmist—"I will lift up my eyes unto the hills, from whence cometh my strength."

—G. Mennen Williams

NOTES

1. A report detailing the accomplishments of the Mennen Williams administration, "*A Tentative First Accounting of the Achievements of Michigan State Government During the Six Terms of Governor G. Mennen Williams,*" written by Sidney Woolner in July 1960, is among Helen Berthelot's papers in the Michigan Historical Collections, Bentley Historical Library, University of Michigan, Ann Arbor.

2. An analysis of vote totals, using information from the Michigan Manuals, was done by the Michigan Democratic party and Sidney Woolner in 1959 to show the growth of Democratic party strength under Mennen Williams. The congressional vote shows dramatic changes, even in Republican districts. In 1947, there were three Michigan Democrats in the U. S. House of Representatives. By 1959, there were seven. This was before the Supreme Court gave heavily populated areas their fair share of representation, which raised the number of Democrats elected to Congress. In the years Mennen Williams was governor, there were increased Democratic percentages even in solidly Republican congressional districts. When he became governor, Michigan had no Democratic senators in the U. S. Congress. By 1959, both senators were Democrats. In 1947, there were four Democrats in the state senate and eight in the state house of representatives. Twelve years later, there were twelve Democratic state senators and fifty-five Democratic state representatives. In the same period, Democrats went from having few, if any, members on the elected education boards to having a majority, or at least a substantial representation. The year before Mennen Williams first ran for governor, the Democratic party had no members on the State Administrative Board, which consisted of the top elected officials of state government. In 1959, Democrats held all the seats.

3. Each edition of the Michigan Manual, published by the Legislative Council of the State of Michigan, contains a summary of the votes for governor—with candidates' names, political affiliations, and vote totals—from 1835, when Michigan was still a territory, to the present. In the 1993–94 edition, the summary is on pp. 926–29 and shows Mennen Williams was elected more times than any other Michigan governor. Mention of Mennen Williams's national record of six elections to the governorship is in Bald, *Michigan in Four Centuries*, p. 484. The National Governors Association does not keep statistics that would show whether his record stands.

APPENDIX

(A) State Dems' 'Hidden Punch':
She's Co-ordinator of Candidates' Activities
by Elizabeth Conway

Republicans of Michigan, beware!

Beware of the Democratic Party's "hidden punch."

She's Mrs. Helen Berthelot, newly appointed director of the statewide Democratic campaign.

Devotion to her job, to her party and its cause and to Gov. G. Mennen Williams are responsible for making her the whiz-bang person she is.

In her new post, Helen Berthelot is scoring a first for Michigan. And perhaps the country.

She is the first woman in the state to hold this position in the party and as far as she knows, the first and only one in the United States.

In her job she is co-ordinating the activities of Democratic candidates for governor, senator, lieutenant governor, congressmen, the administrative board and the Legislature.

Dynamic—yet calm, quiet and efficient—Helen Berthelot is dedicated to the cause of scoring another Democratic victory in Michigan.

She's an excellent example of the role women can play in politics.

However, she has a word of caution for milady who suddenly is stricken with political fever.

"There's a very definite place for women in politics. If they'll work hard wherever they're needed. At any level. If they'll do useful jobs instead of trying to start at policy level.

"Women must first become interested in the issues in their own area. Attend local meetings."

Helen Berthelot has warm praise for Gov. Williams. "He early recognized the importance of help from women. He made it easy on us."

From the *Detroit Times*, September 14, 1960, p. 17.

313

Active in Democratic campaigns since 1948 (she was Gov. Williams' campaign manager in his last three elections), she has until now, by her own choosing, stayed in the background—going about her chores with such proficiency the results speak for themselves.

A widow with two youngsters, Mrs. Berthelot never had an interest in or time for politics. "I was busy rearing my family, earning a living and working on special projects with the children.

"Working for the party was a solace to me after they had grown up and left home."

She broke into politics "back in 1946 when politics had a bad name. I can remember people saying to me, 'What does a nice girl like you want to get into politics for?'

"It's different now. There's a better tone to politics—it has become a family affair."

In 1946, Helen began working in her seventeenth congressional district, helping organize it for the Democratic party—canvassing neighborhoods, ringing doorbells, signing up party members, hunting for precinct delegates.

"I had had no previous experience and was so dumb I even had to ask 'what is a precinct delegate?'"

Hicks Griffiths was elected district chairman; Helen was named vice chairman (a job she held until 1953) and since then she's been a mainspring of the party, climbing to her present top post at a rapid pace. But not without a lot of hard work and long hours.

In 1948, Helen ran for the state Legislature of her district in a city-wide election. "I lost in the primaries but did pretty well considering I was completely unknown."

In 1952, she opened the party's first large campaign headquarters in Detroit ("before that we worked out of a cubby hole") and was named assistant to Sidney Woolner, statewide campaign manager—a job which prepared her for the one she recently assumed.

In 1955 she became a volunteer member on the staff of Neil Staebler, who had just been appointed head of the Democratic advisory committee on political organization. In 1957 she was appointed a permanent member of the committee.

Between campaigns, Helen has no official role in the party. She makes her headquarters in Washington where she's a staff member of the Communications Workers of America, AFL-CIO. She's now on leave of absence and will return to Washington Dec. 1.

(B) Key Staebler Aide Likes Winning—Behind Scenes
by George L. Walker

Democrats have rolled out their "secret weapon" for the quickening battle over Michigan's first congressman-at-large seat in 50 years.

The "secret weapon" is Mrs. Helen Berthelot, who will be campaign manager for Neil Staebler, former Democratic state chairman and the party's candidate for congressman-at-large.

Mrs. Berthelot is to begin the job officially on Saturday, but characteristically has already arrived at Democratic headquarters in the Book Building—eager to get things under way.

What makes Mrs. Berthelot more secret than other weapons is simply her preference for winning political battles from a strategic position behind the scenes.

Aside from the professional politicians, there aren't many people in the state who could identify former Gov. G. Mennen Williams' campaign manager of 1954, 1956 and 1958. It was Mrs. Berthelot.

From the *Detroit News*, August 29, 1962, p. 10-A.

Mrs. Berthelot has her work cut out for her in the little more than two months that remain before voters choose between Staebler and his Republican opponent, Alvin M. Bentley, Owosso industrialist.

Not Cheering

Staebler's showing against Bentley in the Aug. 7 primary turnout gave Democrats little to cheer about.

Nonetheless, Democrats say Mrs. Berthelot's arrival is not an emergency measure, but something that has been planned for months.

Mrs. Berthelot has been a legislative representative for the Communications Workers of America (CWA) in Washington. She is on leave for the balance of the Michigan campaign.

Started in 17th

A widow, she supported two small children as a telephone operator, and got into politics in the 17th District Democratic organization when Williams was unheard of.

Mrs. Berthelot was named state campaign manager for the Democratic Party in 1953, the first woman to hold the job.

At that time, Staebler said she was chosen because of her organizing ability, record of hard work and the respect in which she was held by party leaders.

What kind of campaign will she help Staebler devise? Mrs. Berthelot isn't revealing any strategy beyond a lot of hard work.

"It will be a team operation," she says. "We're going to dig down and work like we've never worked before."

Beyond this, she has one major goal for the 10 weeks ahead: That is to stay as anonymous as she can.

(C) Resolution by Hon. Blair Moody, Senator from Michigan, on Temporary Rule of Order

THE TEMPORARY CHAIRMAN: The Chair recognizes the delegate from Michigan, Senator Blair Moody, for the purpose of offering a resolution with regard to the temporary roll of the Convention.

HON. BLAIR MOODY: (U.S. Senator from Michigan): Mr. Chairman, ladies and gentlemen of the Convention: I move the adoption of the following resolution as the temporary rule of order of this Convention:

BE IT RESOLVED: That the temporary rules of this Convention shall be the rules of the 1948 Democratic National Convention, including the rules of the House of Representatives of the 82nd Congress as far as applicable.

BE IT FURTHER RESOLVED: That this Convention believes in the great American principle of majority rule. No delegate shall be seated unless he shall give assurance to the Credentials Committee that he will exert every honorable means available to him in any official capacity he may have, to provide that the nominees of this Convention for President and Vice President, through their names or those of electors pledged to them, appear on the election ballot under the heading, name or designation of the Democratic Party.

Such assurance shall be given by the Chairman of each delegation, and shall not be

From the *Official Report of the Proceedings of the Democratic National Convention, Chicago, Illinois, July 21–26, inclusive, 1952*, p. 55.

binding upon those delegates who shall so signify to the Credentials Committee prior to its report to this Convention.

Ladies and gentlemen, that is the text of the proposed resolution. I have been asked a question regarding it. The question is whether, if in the exercise of individual rights, an individual delegate refuses to make such certification, whether he would be seated in this Convention. The answer to that question is, no.

(D) Resolution on the late Blair Moody—Democratic State Convention, August 14, 1954, Grand Rapids, Michigan

The Democratic Party of Michigan in formal Convention assembled extends its deepest sympathy to Mrs. Blair Moody on her great and recent loss.

The death of Blair Moody means a great voice has been stilled in the land. He spoke out fearlessly as a reporter, as a Senator and as an American on the great and grave issues of the day.

Few men in recent times have won the hearts of the people of the Democratic Party of Michigan as did Blair Moody.

This was no accident. Not only was he a leader of the State and the Nation, he was a friend of all the people. He sought out the people for advice, and inspired them with his understanding of their problems. He fought for their rights as a reporter, as a United States Senator, and as a great American. He died still in their service.

Prior to his appointment to the Senate by Governor Williams in 1951, he had for 18 years accurately and impartially reported the Washington scene to the people of Michigan. He was the first working reporter to step from a seat in the press gallery to a seat on the Senate floor.

As a Senator, he labored tirelessly to strengthen American Democracy at home and abroad. He hated exploitation and poverty. He put integrity above victory. He fought for all the people, and brought to the Senate such leadership that after only seven months there, he was rated by the American Political Science Association in the top fifth of the Senate on the basis of character and integrity, legislative effectiveness, and understanding of the day's great problems.

He believed in the brotherhood of all men, and devoted himself to its realization.

Speaking of Blair Moody, Adlai Stevenson said, "I have known Blair Moody for many years. Young, intelligent, clean, honest, he is prepared to dedicate his best years to public service. When there are more men like him giving their time and talents to our service, our political life will be better."

Blair Moody did so dedicate his life. May he rest in peace.

We, the Democratic Party of Michigan, will now stand in one minute of silent tribute to the late Blair Moody.

(E) Looking Back on the Legacy of a Great Michigan Senator by Robert Perrin

Twenty years ago, the President of the United States suddenly put aside his schedule and flew to Detroit to attend a funeral. The spontaneous gesture was a salute to the son of Irish immigrants and a one-time pipefitter's apprentice in a New England shipyard.

From the *Muskegon Chronicle*, May 4, 1986.

Appendix

His name was Patrick Vincent McNamara, and at the time of his death at age 71, on April 30, 1966, he was the senior United States senator from Michigan.

Memories fade fast in politics, so on the 20th anniversary of his death this past week, it is appropriate to recall one of Michigan's most unusual political leaders and to reflect on a remarkable legacy of accomplishments. As McNamara's chief aide in Washington for more than 10 years, I had a privileged view of the senator and the man.

McNamara had come to Michigan from his native Massachusetts in 1921 to head a construction gang. He later entered management ranks and continued to earn his living in the construction business.

Even as an executive, McNamara was active in the labor movement. In 1934, he had helped found the first industrial union in the auto industry, a predecessor of the United Auto Workers. For 18 years, until his election to the Senate in 1955, he was the unsalaried president of Detroit Pipefitters Local 636.

This association often led McNamara to be described as a "labor" senator, but he shunned the title. "My vocation has been the construction industry, but my avocation has been the labor movement," he said. "I have never held a paid labor office."

Nevertheless, McNamara never forgot his roots. A small lapel pin he sometimes wore depicted a tiny section of railroad track, and McNamara said it was to remind him of on which side of the tracks he had been born.

A newspaper editorial at the time of his death put it another way. "He was elected by the vote of the humble and the trusting," it said "and the greatest possible accolade to his memory is that he never forgot it."

McNamara's entry into the Senate was typical of the unorthodoxy that marked his career. Although having held only two local elective offices (Detroit Common Council and Detroit Board of Education), he decided to challenge the anointed candidate of the Democratic Party in the 1954 senate primary.

As it turned out, his opponent, Blair Moody Sr., died during the campaign. How that scenario might have played out had Moody lived can only be speculative, but in the event, McNamara won not only the primary, but went on to a 40,000-vote upset victory over the Republican incumbent, Homer Ferguson.

After the stormy beginning, it took a while for the abraded relations between the Democratic regulars and the new senator to heal. But in time they did, and Govs. G. Mennen Williams and John Swainson never had reason to question the commitment and cooperation of their ally in Washington.

In the Senate, McNamara soon gravitated to the small but vocal bloc of northern Democrats that included Hubert Humphrey (Minn.), Joseph Clark (Pa.), Wayne Morse (Ore.), Paul Douglas (Ill.), and John F. Kennedy (Mass.) Together, they struggled to beat down the Senate rules that effectively strangled civil rights legislation, and they championed job training, health and education programs.

McNamara swiftly gained a reputation as a steadfast and outspoken advocate, and he could be as blunt about what he considered the shortcomings of his own Senate leaders as he could of the Eisenhower administration.

Because of his background, McNamara was assigned to the Senate Labor and Public Welfare Committee and the Public Works Committee. He focused his early efforts on education and fought through the first federal aid to education bill to pass the Senate in more than a decade.

In 1959, he also became a champion of the elderly when he was instrumental in creating the Senate Subcommittee on Problems of the Aged and Aging, the first formal congressional concentration on this growing segment of the population. As chairman, McNamara conducted hearings and studies that, over the years, would culminate in the adoption of Medicare, the Administration of Aging and other measures protecting the elderly.

Although McNamara was considered a strong candidate for re-election in 1960, the race almost ended prematurely when his health began to deteriorate rapidly as the result of a prostate condition. But in August, while his friend Jack Kennedy was winning the presidential nomination, McNamara entered a Detroit hospital for surgery. The operation was gratifyingly successful, and by the traditional Labor Day opening of the campaign his health was rebounding.

By November, the illness was forgotten as McNamara trounced Republican Congressman Alvin Bentley (Owosso) by 120,000 votes, heading a ticket that also saw Michigan victories for Swainson and Kennedy. (McNamara always looked back on that victory as the definitive answer to the charge that he had been an "accidental" senator.)

McNamara's seniority, influence and experience came to full flower in his second term, abetted now by a Democratic administration in the White House and his new Michigan partner in the Senate, Philip A. Hart, who had been elected in 1958.

McNamara was then chairman of the labor subcommittee and a member of the education panel, and his subcommittee on problems of the elderly had evolved into the Senate Special Committee on Aging, of which he remained chairman.

In 1963, he became chairman of the full Senate Public Works Committee, one of the most politically powerful bodies in the Senate for the billions of dollars in river and harbor projects, federal building construction, highways and other "porkbarrel" items it authorized. But it was not in McNamara's character to be a wheeler-dealer or a barterer in political favors, and he refused to use his position for personal aggrandizement.

He did use his position to support the budding environmental movement, creating the first subcommittee specifically to handle environmental matters and producing two documentary films on the threats of air and water pollution.

He also continued in the forefront of the fight for civil and voting rights, federal aid for education and Medicare, all of which came to fruition. He also was the Senate sponsor and manager of the bill that established the war on poverty program.

Time was running out, however. His second term would expire at the end of 1966. He then would be 72, along in years, but still a strong candidate should he choose to run.

In the fall of 1965, McNamara called me over to his small hideaway office tucked under the eaves of the Capitol to tell me that he would not seek re-election. "It's time for me to say thanks for the use of the hall," he said.

When the official announcement was made on Feb. 23, 1966, McNamara spoke of his gratification in serving Michigan and of his satisfaction that so many of the causes he espoused had become reality.

With his usual honesty, he added that "relatively minor ailments have served warning that I might not be able to do full justice to my Senate responsibilities for another full term," and he concluded that he should retire "rather than risk inability to meet my obligations."

The words were prophetic. Within weeks after the announcement, McNamara's health began to fail alarmingly, and he entered Bethesda Naval Hospital in Maryland for treatment.

In anticipation of his retirement, I had left the Senator's staff a few weeks before, but I spent as much time as I could at the hospital, visiting with him when possible, or with his wife, Mary.

On the evening of Saturday, April 30, we were sitting in a small room across the corridor from where McNamara labored for breath under an oxygen tent. Suddenly, I became conscious that the familiar background hum of the oxygen pump had stopped. I knew intuitively that Pat McNamara's heart had halted, too.

Mary McNamara asked me to come to Detroit to supervise the funeral arrangements, and we accompanied the senator's coffin in an Air Force jet on his final trip to Michigan.

And thus, it was on the evening before the services were to be held in the small, working-class Catholic church in Detroit, driving back to our hotel from the funeral home, two members of the senator's staff and I heard on the car radio that President Lyndon Johnson would fly to Detroit the following morning to pay his last respects.

That funeral, with the sudden, last-minute invasion of the secret service and the presidential party, is another story. For me, anyway, it made an already-emotional occasion sometimes bizarre and almost surrealistic. But, it showed the nation the depth of respect in which the senator was held.

Pat McNamara, I am sure, would have been uncomfortable at the attention. Sen. Phil Hart probably spoke for him when he said, "Millions of people will benefit from the programs he pushed without ever knowing who Pat McNamara was. That's nothing to be saddened by. That would suit Pat McNamara just fine."

Despite himself, though, the pipefitter's apprentice who wanted to thank others for granting him "the use of the hall" has gained his place in history.

INDEX

Index

Hart, 142, 191, 301; teamwork, 1954
election, 148, 150–53

Woolner, Tom, 301

World War II, 30, 41, 114–15, 142–43,
166, 189, 212, 233

Wottawa, Mary, 99–100

Wuthrich, Jack, 131

Yokich, Stephen, 130

Young, John, 111–12

Ypsilanti, Michigan, 43

Titles in
the Great Lakes Books Series

Hangdog Reef: Poems Sailing the Great Lakes, by Stephen Tudor, 1989

Detroit: City of Race and Class Violence, revised edition, by B. J. Widick, 1989

Deep Woods Frontier: A History of Logging in Northern Michigan, by Theodore J. Karamanski, 1989

Orvie, The Dictator of Dearborn, by David L. Good, 1989

Seasons of Grace: A History of the Catholic Archdiocese of Detroit, by Leslie Woodcock Tentler, 1990

The Pottery of John Foster: Form and Meaning, by Gordon and Elizabeth Orear, 1990

The Diary of Bishop Frederic Baraga: First Bishop of Marquette, Michigan, edited by Regis M. Walling and Rev. N. Daniel Rupp, 1990

Walnut Pickles and Watermelon Cake: A Century of Michigan Cooking, by Larry B. Massie and Priscilla Massie, 1990

The Making of Michigan, 1820–1860: A Pioneer Anthology, edited by Justin L. Kestenbaum, 1990

America's Favorite Homes: A Guide to Popular Early Twentieth-Century Homes, by Robert Schweitzer and Michael W. R. Davis, 1990

Beyond the Model T: The Other Ventures of Henry Ford, by Ford R. Bryan, 1990

Life after the Line, by Josie Kearns, 1990

Michigan Lumbertowns: Lumbermen and Laborers in Saginaw, Bay City, and Muskegon, 1870–1905, by Jeremy W. Kilar, 1990

Detroit Kids Catalog: The Hometown Tourist, by Ellyce Field, 1990

Waiting for the News, by Leo Litwak, 1990 (reprint)

Detroit Perspectives, edited by Wilma Wood Henrickson, 1991

Life on the Great Lakes: A Wheelsman's Story, by Fred W. Dutton, edited by William Donohue Ellis, 1991

Copper Country Journal: The Diary of Schoolmaster Henry Hobart, 1863–1864, by Henry Hobart, edited by Philip P. Mason, 1991

John Jacob Astor: Business and Finance in the Early Republic, by John Denis Haeger, 1991

Survival and Regeneration: Detroit's American Indian Community, by Edmund J. Danziger, Jr., 1991

Steamboats and Sailors of the Great Lakes, by Mark L. Thompson, 1991

Cobb Would Have Caught It: The Golden Years of Baseball in Detroit, by Richard Bak, 1991

Michigan in Literature, by Clarence A. Andrews, 1992

Under the Influence of Water: Poems, Essays, and Stories, by Michael Delp, 1992

The Country Kitchen, by Della T. Lutes, 1992 (reprint)

The Making of a Mining District: Keweenaw Native Copper 1500–1870, by David J. Krause, 1992

Kids Catalog of Michigan Adventures, by Ellyce Field, 1993

Henry's Lieutenants, by Ford R. Bryan, 1993

Historic Highway Bridges of Michigan, by Charles K. Hyde, 1993

Lake Erie and Lake St. Clair Handbook, by Stanley J. Bolsenga and Charles E. Herdendorf, 1993

Queen of the Lakes, by Mark L. Thompson, 1994

Iron Fleet: The Great Lakes in World War II, by George J. Joachim, 1994

Turkey Stearnes and the Detroit Stars: The Negro Leagues in Detroit, 1919–1933, by Richard Bak, 1994

Pontiac and the Indian Uprising, by Howard H. Peckham, 1994 (reprint)

Charting the Inland Seas: A History of the U.S. Lake Survey, by Arthur M. Woodford, 1994 (reprint)

Ojibwa Narratives of Charles and Charlotte Kawbawgam and Jacques LePique, 1893–1895. Recorded with Notes by Homer H. Kidder, edited by Arthur P. Bourgeois, 1994, co-published with the Marquette County Historical Society

Strangers and Sojourners: A History of Michigan's Keweenaw Peninsula, by Arthur W. Thurner, 1994

Sarkis, by Gordon and Elizabeth Orear, 1995

Win Some, Lose Some: G. Mennen Williams and the New Democrats, by Helen Washburn Berthelot, 1995